GMAT® FOR DUMMIES®

PREMIER 6TH EDITION

by Lisa Zimmer Hatch, MA and Scott A. Hatch, JD

WILEY

John Wiley & Sons, Inc.

GMAT® For Dummies®, Premier 6th Edition

Published by
John Wiley & Sons, Inc.
111 River St.
Hoboken, NJ 07030-5774
www.wiley.com

Library of Congress Control Number: 2012952202

ISBN 978-1-118-27383-8 (pbk); ISBN 978-1-118-41947-2 (ebk); ISBN 978-1-118-42126-0 (ebk); ISBN 978-1-118-50373-7 (ebk)

Manufactured in the United States of America

10 9 8 7 6 5 4 3 2 1

WILEY

About the Authors

Lisa Zimmer Hatch, M.A. and Scott A. Hatch, J.D. have prepared teens and adults since 1987 to excel on standardized tests, gain admission to colleges of their choice, and secure challenging and lucrative professional careers. For virtually 30 years, they have created and administered award-winning standardized test preparation and professional career courses worldwide for live lecture, online, and other formats through more than 500 universities worldwide.

Scott and Lisa have written the curriculum for all formats, and their books have been translated for international markets. Additionally, they wrote, produced, and appeared in the landmark weekly PBS "Law for Life" series. They continue to develop new courses for a variety of careers and extend their college admissions expertise to assist those seeking advanced degrees in law, business, and other professions. Together they have authored numerous law and standardized test prep texts, including *ACT For Dummies,* 5th Edition, *SAT II U.S. History For Dummies, SAT II Biology For Dummies, SAT II Math For Dummies, Catholic High School Entrance Exams For Dummies,* and *Paralegal Career For Dummies* (Wiley).

Lisa is currently an independent educational consultant and the president of College Primers, where she applies her expertise to guiding high school and college students through the undergraduate and graduate admissions and financial aid processes and prepares students for entrance exams through individualized coaching and small group courses. She prides herself in maximizing her students' financial aid packages and dedicates herself to helping them gain admission to the universities or programs that best fit their goals, personalities, and financial resources. She graduated with honors in English from the University of Puget Sound and received a master's degree in humanities with a literature emphasis from California State University. She is currently completing the UCLA College Counseling Certificate Program and is the editor of the newsletter for the Higher Education Consultants Association (HECA) and a member of the Rocky Mountain Association of College Admissions Counselors (RMACAC).

Scott received his undergraduate degree from the University of Colorado and his Juris Doctorate from Southwestern University School of Law. He is listed in *Who's Who in California* and *Who's Who Among Students in American Colleges and Universities* and is one of the Outstanding Young Men of America as determined by the United States Jaycees. He was also a contributing editor to McGraw-Hill's *Judicial Profiler* series and *The Colorado Law Annotated* series published *by Lawyers Cooperative Publishing.* He also served as editor of the *Freedom of Information Committee Newsletter* and functioned as editor of several national award winning periodicals. His current law books include *A Legal Guide to Probate and Estate Planning* and *A Legal Guide to Family Law* in B & B Legal Publication's Learn the Law series.

In addition to writing law books, periodical articles, television scripts, and college curricula, Scott was editor of his law school's nationally award-winning legal periodical, winner of two first place awards from the Columbia University School of Journalism, and another first-place award from the American Bar Association. He also contributed to Los Angeles's daily newspaper, *The Metropolitan News,* was an editorial assistant during the formation of the Los Angeles Press Club's Education Foundation, and served on the Faculty of Law at the City University of Los Angeles.

Dedication

We dedicate *GMAT For Dummies* to our children, Alison, Andrew, Zachary, and Zoe and to Dan, Paige, and Ryan. Our family demonstrated patience, understanding, and editorial assistance while we wrote this book, and we're very blessed to have them in our lives.

Authors' Acknowledgments

This book would not be possible without the contributions of Julia Brabant, Jackson Sutherland, Zachary Hatch, and Zoe Hatch, who provided practice test material and helpful input. We also acknowledge the input of thousands of our students who have completed our test preparation courses over the last 30 years. The classroom and online contributions offered by these dedicated and motivated learners have provided us with a significant amount of information about those subject areas that require the greatest amount of preparation for success on the GMAT.

Our project organization and attempts at wit were greatly facilitated by the editing professionals at Wiley. Our thanks go out to Chrissy Guthrie for her patience and guidance throughout the editing process and to copy editors Megan Knoll and Jennette ELNaggar. Thanks also to the technical editors, Bill Kenworthy and Frank Cavanaugh, for their attention to detail and helpful suggestions during the editing process.

Finally, we wish to thank our literary agent, Margo Maley Hutchinson, at Waterside Productions in Cardiff for her support and assistance and for introducing us to the innovative *For Dummies* series.

We thrive on feedback from our students and encourage our readers to provide comments and critiques at info@hatchedu.com.

Publisher's Acknowledgments

We're proud of this book; please send us your comments at `http://dummies.custhelp.com`. For other comments, please contact our Customer Care Department within the U.S. at 877-762-2974, outside the U.S. at 317-572-3993, or fax 317-572-4002.

Some of the people who helped bring this book to market include the following:

Acquisitions, Editorial, and Vertical Websites

Senior Project Editor: Christina Guthrie

    (Previous Edition: Tim Gallan, Natalie Faye Harris)

Executive Editor: Lindsay Lefevere

Copy Editors: Jennette ElNaggar, Megan Knoll

Assistant Editor: David Lutton

Editorial Program Coordinator: Joe Niesen

Technical Editors: Frank Cavanaugh, Bill Kenworthy

Vertical Websites: Laura Moss-Hollister

Media Developer: Spearhead Global, Inc.

Editorial Manager: Christine Meloy Beck

Editorial Assistants: Rachelle Amick, Alexa Koschier

Cover Photos: © blackred / iStockphoto.com,
    © vasavil / iStockphoto.com

Cartoons: Rich Tennant (`www.the5thwave.com`)

Composition Services

Project Coordinator: Sheree Montgomery

Layout and Graphics: Carrie A. Cesavice

Proofreaders: Betty Kish, Lauren Mandelbaum

Indexer: BIM Indexing & Proofreading Services

Publishing and Editorial for Consumer Dummies

    Kathleen Nebenhaus, Vice President and Executive Publisher

    David Palmer, Associate Publisher

    Kristin Ferguson-Wagstaffe, Product Development Director

Publishing for Technology Dummies

    Andy Cummings, Vice President and Publisher

Composition Services

    Debbie Stailey, Director of Composition Services

Contents at a Glance

Table of Contents

Introduction

You're merrily skimming through the admissions requirements for your favorite MBA programs when all of a sudden you're dealt a shocking blow. Your absolute top choice program — you'll die if you don't get in — requires that you take the Graduate Management Admission Test (GMAT). And you thought your days of speed reading passages and solving for *x* were over.

Many MBA programs include the GMAT as an admissions requirement, so you'll be in good company. But how do you prepare for such a comprehensive test? What are you going to do? Get out your spiral notebooks from undergraduate courses and sift through years' worth of doodles? Many years may have gone by since you encountered a geometry problem, and we bet your grammar skills have gotten a little rusty since English 101.

Clearly, you need a readable, concisely structured resource. Well, you've come to the right place. *GMAT For Dummies,* Premier 6th Edition, puts at your fingertips everything you need to know to conquer the GMAT. We give you complete math and grammar reviews and provide insights into how to avoid the pitfalls that the GMAT creators want you to fall into. We also try to make this book as enjoyable as a book that devotes itself to setting up equations and critiquing arguments can be.

About This Book

We suspect that you aren't eagerly anticipating sitting through the GMAT, and you're probably not looking forward to studying for it, either. Therefore, we've attempted to make the study process as painless as possible by giving you clearly written advice in a casual tone. We realize you have a bunch of things you'd rather be doing, so we've broken down the information into easily digested bites. If you have an extra hour before work or Pilates class, you can devour a chapter or even a particular section within a chapter. (If these eating metaphors are making you hungry, feel free to take a snack break.)

In this book, you can find

- ✔ Plenty of sample questions so you can see just how the GMAT tests a particular concept. Our sample questions read like the actual test questions, so you can get comfortable with the way the GMAT phrases questions and expresses answer choices.

- ✔ Detailed explanations of the strategies for mastering all four sections of the GMAT. Enjoy a grammar review for the verbal reasoning section, an extensive math lesson to help you with the quantitative reasoning section, a summary of good writing practices for the analytical writing assessment, and a how-to on reading all kinds of charts and graphs for the integrated reasoning section.

✔ Five practice tests. One appears in this book in Chapter 19, and you'll find that one plus four others on the accompanying CD. Ultimately, the best way to prepare for any standardized test is to practice on lots of test questions, and this book, along with the accompanying CD, has more than 500 of them.

✔ Time-tested techniques for improving your score. We show you how to quickly eliminate incorrect answer choices and make educated guesses.

✔ Tips on how to manage your time wisely.

✔ Suggestions for creating a relaxation routine to employ if you start to panic during the test.

We've included all kinds of information to help you do your best on the GMAT!

Conventions Used in This Book

You should find this book easily accessible, but a few things may require explanation. A few of the chapters may contain sidebars (a paragraph or two in a shaded box) with quirky bits of information that we think may interest you but aren't essential to your performance on the GMAT. If you're trying to save time, you can skip the sidebars.

The book highlights information you should remember in several ways. Lists are bulleted and marked with a solid bar to the left of the list. Icons appear in the margins to emphasize particularly significant information in the text. You can use these highlighting tools to focus on the most important elements of each chapter.

Foolish Assumptions

Although we guess it's possible that you picked up this book just because you have an insatiable love for math, grammar, and argument analysis, we're betting it's more likely that you're reading this book particularly because you've been told you have to take the GMAT. (We have been praised for our startling ability to recognize the obvious!) And because we're pretty astute, we've figured that this means that you intend to apply to MBA programs and probably are considering working toward a master's of business administration.

Generally, MBA programs are pretty selective, so we're thinking that you're a pretty motivated student. Some of you are fresh out of college and may have more recent experience with math and grammar. Others of you probably haven't stepped into a classroom in over a decade but possess work skills and life experience that will help you maximize your GMAT score despite the time that's passed since college.

If math and grammar are fresh in your mind and you just need to know what to expect when you arrive at the test site, this book has that information for you. If you've been out of school for a while, this book provides you with all the basics as well as advanced concepts to give you everything you need to know to excel on the GMAT.

How This Book Is Organized

The first part of this book introduces you to the nature of the GMAT beast and advises you on how to tame it. An in-depth discussion of how to approach and answer the questions in the verbal section of the test follows. We give you tips on how to succeed on the sentence correction, reading comprehension, and critical reasoning questions you'll encounter there. Then we tell you how to write the analytical essay. Even if you haven't written anything more than a grocery list in a while, you'll be ready to expound come test day. We follow the analytical writing portion with a comprehensive math review, covering everything from number types to standard deviation. To prepare you for the newest section of the GMAT, we include an extensive examination of the integrated reasoning section. This section essentially tests analytical and math skills in a different way.

Our discussion of each section ends with a mini practice test to prepare you for the full-length practice test that follows the math review and the four additional tests on the CD. Test your knowledge on these five tests and then see how you've done.

Part I: Putting the GMAT into Perspective

Read this part if you want to know more about what kinds of information the GMAT tests and how you can best handle it.

Part II: Vanquishing the Verbal Section

The verbal section of the GMAT includes three kinds of questions: sentence correction, reading comprehension, and critical reasoning. We show you what to look for in the sentence correction questions, how to read through a passage quickly and effectively for the reading questions, and how to break apart and analyze arguments for the critical reasoning questions. We end the part with a mini practice test of randomly organized questions of all three types.

Part III: Acing the Analytical Writing Section

The GMAT requires you to write an essay that analyzes an argument. We tell you what the GMAT is looking for and give you pointers on writing a well-organized and compelling essay.

Part IV: Conquering the Quantitative Section

This part is for you if you haven't solved equations in a while and if you work with math concepts every day. We cover basic arithmetic and algebra (things you may have forgotten after all these years) and explain more complex concepts like coordinate geometry and standard deviation. You find out how to tackle the data sufficiency question type that appears only on the GMAT. We tie up the part by giving you a mini practice test that covers all areas of math and both types of GMAT math questions.

Part V: Excelling on the Integrated Reasoning Section

The GMAT integrated reasoning section is like no other section on a standardized test. This part exposes you to the unique way that the GMAT tests how well you use your analysis skills in real-life scenarios. We provide strategies for approaching the section and review how to pull data from tables, charts, and graphs. You can practice your newfound skills on a computerized mini practice test on the accompanying CD.

Part VI: Practice Makes Perfect

After you feel comfortable with your GMAT prowess, you can practice on the full-length test found in this part and the four others on the CD. Each test comes complete with a scoring guide and explanatory answers to help you figure out which areas of the GMAT you have down pat and which ones you need to study more for.

Part VII: The Part of Tens

This part finishes up the fun with a summary of questions you can't miss, writing errors you should avoid, and ways to maximize your chances of getting into an MBA program.

Appendix and CD

The Appendix explains computer system requirements and how to use the CD that comes with this book.

The CD offers five full-length practice tests (including the one in Part VI), along with answers and explanations. Verbal and math flashcards help you memorize key concepts and formulas. And finally, bonus integrated reasoning information and practice questions help you sharpen your skills for this tricky section of the GMAT. *Note:* If you're using a digital version of this book, go to `http://booksupport.wiley.com` for access to the additional content.

Icons Used in This Book

One exciting feature of this book is the icons that highlight especially significant portions of the text. These little pictures in the margins alert you to areas where you should pay particularly close attention.

This icon highlights really important information that you should remember even after you close the book.

Throughout the book, we give you insights into how you can enhance your performance on the GMAT. The tips give you juicy timesavers and point out especially relevant concepts to keep in mind for the test.

Your world won't fall apart if you ignore our warnings, but your score may suffer. Heed these cautionary pointers to avoid making careless mistakes that can cost you points.

Whenever you see this icon in the text, you know you're going to get to practice the particular area of instruction covered in that section with a question like one you may see on the test. Our examples include detailed explanations of how to most efficiently answer GMAT questions and avoid common pitfalls.

Beyond the Book

This book comes with a companion CD-ROM that contains five full-length practice exams, as well as 100 flashcards and extra integrated reasoning practice questions. If you don't have access to a CD drive, or if you're reading this as an e-book, you can go to http:// booksupport.wiley.com and download the CD-ROM files.

Where to Go from Here

We know that everyone who uses this book has different strengths and weaknesses, so this book is designed for you to read in the way that best suits you. If you're a math whiz and need to brush up only on your verbal skills, you can skim Part IV and focus on Parts I, II, and III. If you've been writing proposals every day for the last ten years, you can probably scan Part III and focus your attention on the math review in Part IV. Because the integrated reasoning section differs so significantly from other standardized test questions, you'll benefit from reading Part V regardless of your math prowess or verbal genius.

We suggest that you take a more thorough approach, however. Familiarize yourself with the general test-taking process in the first two chapters and then go through the complete GMAT review, starting with the verbal section and working your way through the analytical writing, math, and integrated reasoning sections. You can skim through information that you know more about by just reading the Tips and Warnings and working through the examples in those sections.

Some of our students like to take a diagnostic test before they study. This is a fancy way of saying that they take one of the full-length practice tests before they read the rest of the book. Taking a preview test shows you which questions you seem to cruise through and which areas need more work. After you've taken a practice exam, you can focus your study time on the question types that gave you the most trouble during the exam. Then, when you've finished reading through the rest of the book (Parts I, II, III, IV, and V), you can take another practice test and compare your score to the one you got on the first test. This way, you can see just how much you improve with practice.

This book provides you with a bunch of practice tests, but you can never get enough practice. So you may want to visit the official GMAT website at www.mba.com and download the free GMATPrep software there. This software mimics the computerized format of the test and gives you practice on the types of mouse-clicking and eye-straining skills you need to succeed on the exam. That way, you can experience using the same software you'll see on the exam.

We're confident that if you devote a few hours a week to practicing the skills and tips we provide for you in this book, you'll do the best you can when you sit in front of that computer on GMAT test day. We wish you our best for your ultimate GMAT score!

Part I
Putting the GMAT into Perspective

The 5th Wave   By Rich Tennant

"I guessed my way to a perfect score on the GMAT, then I guessed my way through grad school and several middle management jobs. So — would you like me to guess your weight?"

In this part . . .

The first part of this book initiates you to the marvels of the GMAT. The chapters here introduce the format of the test and explain how to take the test seriously (but not too seriously). You may be tempted to skip this part and jump headlong into the reviews. If you do so, we strongly suggest that you come back to this part later. We include information in here that you may not get elsewhere.

Among other things, you find out what to expect on the test, how the test is scored, how the CAT (which stands for computer-adaptive format) works for the verbal and quantitative reasoning sections, and what stuff is tested on each of the test sections (analytical writing, integrated reasoning, verbal, and math). You also discover some helpful tips for organizing your time and relaxing if you get nervous.

Chapter 1

Getting the Lowdown on the GMAT

Congratulations on deciding to take a significant step in your business career! More than one hundred countries offer the Graduate Management Admission Test (GMAT), and according to the Graduate Management Admission Council, it's used by more than 5,000 graduate programs in admissions decisions. That said, you're probably not taking the GMAT because you want to. In fact, you may not be looking forward to the experience at all!

The GMAT need not be a daunting ordeal. A little knowledge can help calm your nerves, so this chapter shows you how admissions programs use your test score and addresses the concerns you may have about the GMAT's format and testing and scoring procedures.

Knowing Why the GMAT Is Important

If you're reading this book, you're probably thinking about applying to an MBA program. And if you're applying to an MBA program, you probably need to take the GMAT. Almost all MBA programs require that you submit a GMAT score for the admissions process. (Some may require other tests or no test at all, so make sure you check each program's admissions checklist.)

Your GMAT score gives the admissions committee another tool to use to assess your skills and compare you with other applicants. But if you're seeking a career in business, you're probably resigned to being continually assessed and compared. The GMAT doesn't attempt to evaluate any particular subject area that you may have studied, but instead it gives admissions officers a reliable idea of how you'll likely perform in the classes that make up a graduate business curriculum. Although the GMAT doesn't rate your experience or motivation, it does provide an estimate of your academic preparation for graduate business studies.

Not every MBA applicant has the same undergraduate experience, but every applicant takes the same standardized test. Other admissions factors, like college grades, work experience, the admissions essay or essays, and a personal interview are important, but the GMAT is the one admissions tool that admissions committees can use to directly compare you with other applicants.

The most selective schools primarily admit candidates with solid GMAT scores, and good scores will certainly strengthen your application to any program, but you shouldn't feel discouraged if your practice tests don't put you in the 90th percentile. Very few students achieve anything near a perfect score on the GMAT. Even if you don't score as high as you want to, you undoubtedly have other strengths in your admissions profile, such as work experience, leadership ability, good college grades, motivation, and people skills. You may want to contact the admissions offices of the schools you're interested in to see how much they emphasize the GMAT. That said, the GMAT is a very important factor in admissions, and because you're required to take the test anyway, you should do everything you can to perform your best!

Timing It Perfectly: When to Take the GMAT (And What to Bring)

Which MBA programs to apply to isn't the only decision you have to make. After you've figured out where you want to go, you have to make plans for the GMAT. You need to determine the best time to take the test and what to bring with you when you do. The following sections can help you out.

When to register for and take the GMAT

When is the best time to take the GMAT? With the computerized testing procedures, this question has become more interesting than it was in the days of paper-based tests. When the exam was a paper-and-pencil format with a test booklet and an answer sheet full of bubbles, you had a limited choice of possible test dates — about one every two months. Now you've got much more flexibility when choosing the date and time for taking the test. You can pick just about any time to sit down and click answer choices with your mouse.

Registering when you're ready

The first step in the GMAT registration process is scheduling an appointment, but don't put off making this appointment the way you'd put off calling the dentist (even though you'd probably like to avoid both!). Depending on the time of year, appointment times can go quickly. Usually, you have to wait at least a month for an open time. To determine what's available, you can go to the official GMAT website at www.mba.com. From there, you can choose a testing location and find out what dates and times are available at that location. When you find a date and time you like, you can register online, over the phone, or by mail or fax.

The best time to take the GMAT is after you've had about four to six weeks of quality study time and during a period when you don't have a lot of other things going on to distract you. Of course, if your MBA program application is due in four weeks, put this book down and schedule an appointment right away! Be sure to come right back, though. You need to start studying — and now! If you have more flexibility, you should still plan to take the GMAT as soon as you think you've studied sufficiently. All the following circumstances warrant taking the GMAT as soon as you can:

   ✔ **You want to start your MBA program right away.** If you're confident that you'd like to begin business school within the next few semesters, you should consider taking the GMAT in the near future. After you know your score, you'll be better able to narrow down the business schools you want to apply to. Then you can focus on the other parts of your application, and you won't have to worry about having an application due in four weeks and no GMAT score.

✔ **You're considering attending business school.** Maybe you don't know whether you want to pursue an MBA. Even so, now's a good time to take the GMAT. Your GMAT score may help you decide that you've got the skills to succeed academically in graduate business school. You may think that you don't have what it takes, but your performance on the GMAT may surprise you! When you do decide to apply to an MBA program, you'll already have one key component of the application under wraps.

✔ **You're about to earn (or have just earned) your bachelor's degree.** If you're nearing graduation or have just graduated from college and you think you may want to get an MBA, it's better to take the GMAT now than wait until later. You're used to studying. You're used to tests. And math and grammar concepts are probably as fresh on your mind as they'll ever be.

You don't have to start an MBA program right away. Your GMAT scores are generally valid for up to five years, so you can take the test now and take advantage of your current skills as a student to get you into a great graduate program later.

Giving yourself about four to six weeks to study provides you with enough time to master the GMAT concepts but not so much time that you forget what you've studied by the time you sit for the test.

Scheduling for success

Whenever you register, you want to consider your own schedule when picking a test date and time. Take advantage of the flexibility allowed by the computer format. The GMAT is no longer just an 8 a.m. Saturday morning option. You can take the test every day of the week except Sunday, and, depending on the test center, you may be able to start at a variety of times. Many centers offer 8 a.m. testing times, but some have other options, even 6:30 at night — great for those night-owls who consider 8 a.m. a good bedtime rather than a good exam time. You have a little bit of control over making the test fit into your life instead of having to make your life fit the test!

If you're not a morning person, don't schedule an early test if you can help it. If you're better able to handle a nonstop, two-and-a-half-hour barrage of questions — not to mention the analytical essay — when the sun hits its highest point in the sky, schedule your test for the afternoon or evening. By choosing the time that works for you, you'll be able to comfortably approach the test instead of worrying whether you set your alarm. We're guessing that you have enough to worry about in life as it is without the added stress of an inconvenient test time.

Check the GMAT website for the available testing times at the test centers near you. Then study for the test at the different available times of the day to see when you're at your best. Schedule your test session for that time. Even if you have to take a few hours away from work or classes, being able to take the test at a time that's best for you is worth it. And you may end up picking a test center based on its available times rather than its proximity to you.

While you're thinking about the time that's best for the test, you should think about days of the week as well. For some people, Saturday may be a good day for a test. For others, the weekend is the wrong time for that type of concentrated academic activity. If you're used to taking the weekends off, scheduling the test during the week may make more sense for you.

Choosing the time and day to take the GMAT is primarily up to you. Be honest with yourself about your habits, preferences, and schedule, and pick a time and day when you'll excel.

Things to take to the GMAT (and things to leave at home)

The most important thing you can bring to the GMAT is a positive attitude and a willingness to succeed. However, if you forget your admission voucher or your photo ID, you won't get the chance to apply those qualities! In addition to the voucher and ID, you may bring a list of five schools where you'd like to have your scores sent. You can send your scores to up to five schools for free if you select those schools when entering your pretest information at the test site. (You can skip this step at the testing center if you provide your school information when you register online.) You can, of course, list fewer than five schools, but if you decide to send your scores to additional schools later, you'll have to pay. If you can come up with five schools you'd like to apply to, you may as well send your scores for free.

Because you can take two optional eight-minute breaks, we recommend you bring along a quick snack, like a granola bar, and perhaps a bottle of water. You can't take food or drink with you to the testing area, but you're given a little locker that you can access during a break.

That's really all you need to bring. You can't use a calculator, and the test center provides a booklet of five noteboards, which you're required to use instead of pencil and paper. You can ask for another booklet if you fill yours up.

Forming First Impressions: The Format of the GMAT

The GMAT is a standardized test, and by now in your academic career, you're probably familiar with what that means: lots of questions to answer in a short period of time, no way to cram for or memorize answers, and very little chance of scoring 100 percent. The skills tested on the GMAT are those that leading business schools have decided are important for MBA students: verbal reasoning, quantitative reasoning, analytical writing, and integrated reasoning.

Getting familiar with what the GMAT tests

Standardized tests are supposed to test your academic potential, not your knowledge of specific subjects. The GMAT focuses on the areas that admissions committees have found to be relevant to MBA programs. The sections that follow are an introduction to the four GMAT sections. We devote the majority of the rest of this book to telling you exactly how to approach each one.

Demonstrating your writing ability

You type an original analytical writing sample during the GMAT. The test gives you 30 minutes to compose and type an essay that analyzes an argument. You're expected to write this essay in standard written English. Although you won't know exactly the nature of the argument you'll get on test day, examining previous essay prompts gives you adequate preparation for the type of task you're bound to see.

The readers of your GMAT essay score you based on the overall quality of your ideas and your ability to organize, develop, express, and support those ideas.

Integrating your reasoning skills

The second GMAT section is a 30-minute integrated reasoning test that examines your ability to read and evaluate charts, graphs, and other forms of presenting data. You'll examine a variety of data representation and answer 12 questions based on the information.

The GMAT categorizes the four basic question types in this section as graphics interpretation, two-part analysis, table analysis, and multi-source reasoning. Graphics interpretation and table analysis questions are self-explanatory: You interpret graphs and analyze tables — simple enough, right? The two-part analysis questions present a problem and related data provided in two columns. You choose a piece of information from each column to solve the problem. Multi-source reasoning questions provide you with a bunch of information from which you have to decide what piece or pieces of data actually gives you what you need to know to solve the problem.

Quizzing your quantitative skills

The quantitative section is pretty similar to most standardized math sections except that it presents you with a different question format and tests your knowledge of statistics and probability. In the 37-question section, the GMAT tests your knowledge of arithmetic, algebra, geometry, and data interpretation with standard problem-solving questions. You'll have to solve problems and choose the correct answer from five possible choices.

Additionally, GMAT data sufficiency questions present you with two statements and ask you to decide whether the problem can be solved by using the information provided by the first statement only, the second statement only, both statements, or neither statement. We show you exactly how to tackle these unusual math questions in Chapter 15.

Validating your verbal skills

The GMAT verbal section consists of 41 questions of three general types: the ubiquitous reading comprehension problems, sentence correction questions, and critical reasoning questions. Reading comprehension requires you to answer questions about written passages on a number of different subjects. Sentence correction questions test your ability to spot and correct writing errors. Critical reasoning questions require you to analyze logical arguments and understand how to strengthen or weaken those arguments.

Understanding the computerized format

The quantitative reasoning and verbal reasoning sections on the computerized GMAT can be taken only in *computer-adaptive test* (CAT) format. The CAT adapts to your ability level by presenting you with questions of various difficulty, depending on how you answer previous questions. If you're answering many questions correctly, the computer gives you harder questions as it seeks to find the limits of your impressive intellect. If you're having a tough day and many of your answers are wrong, the computer will present you with easier questions as it seeks to find the correct level of difficulty for you.

With the CAT format, your score isn't based solely on how many questions you get right and wrong but rather on the average difficulty of the questions you answer correctly. Theoretically, you could miss several questions and still get a very high score, so long as the questions you missed were among the most difficult available in the bank of questions. At the end of each section, the computer scores you based on your level of ability.

Answering in an orderly fashion

With the CAT format, the question order in the verbal and quantitative sections is different from the order on paper exams that have a test booklet and answer sheet. On the CAT, the first ten questions of the test are preselected for you, and the order of subsequent questions depends on how well you've answered the previous questions. So if you do well on the first ten questions, question 11 will reflect your success by being more challenging. If you do poorly on the initial questions, you'll get an easier question 11. The program continues to take all previous questions into account as it feeds you question after question.

Perhaps the most important difference of the CAT format is that because each question is based on your answers to previous questions, you can't go back to any question. You must answer each question as it comes. After you confirm your answer, it's final. If you realize three questions later that you made a mistake, try not to worry about it. After all, your score is based on not only your number of right and wrong answers but also the difficulty of the questions.

We're guessing you've figured out that the analytical writing assessment isn't in CAT format because it's not a multiple-choice test. But you may not know that the integrated reasoning section also isn't a CAT section. You receive questions in a pre-ordained order and that order doesn't change based on your answer selections. Like the CAT sections, though, after you've submitted an answer to a question, you can't change your answer.

Observing time limits

Both the verbal and quantitative sections have a 75-minute time limit. Because the quantitative section has 37 questions, you have about two minutes to master each question. The verbal section has 41 questions, so you have a little less time to ponder those, about a minute and three-quarters per question. The integrated reasoning section is shorter; you have 30 minutes to answer 12 questions, or about two and a half minutes per question. You don't have unlimited time in the analytical writing section, either; you have to write the essay within 30 minutes.

These time limits have important implications for your test strategy on the quantitative and verbal sections. As we discuss later in this chapter, your GMAT score for these two sections depends on the number of questions you're able to answer. If you run out of time and leave questions unanswered at the end of a section, you'll essentially reduce your score by the number of questions you don't answer. In Chapter 2, we present you with an efficient, workable strategy for managing your time and maximizing your score.

Honing your computer skills for the GMAT

Technically challenged, take heart! You need to have only minimal computer skills to take the computerized GMAT. In fact, the skills you need for the test are far less than those you'll need while pursuing an MBA! Because you have to type your essays, you need basic word-processing skills. For the multiple-choice sections, you need to know how to select answers by using either the mouse or the keyboard.

Knowing Where You Stand: Scoring Considerations

Okay, you know the GMAT's format and how many questions it has and so on. But what about what's really important to you, the crucial final score? Probably very few people take standardized tests for fun, so we give you the lowdown on scoring in the following sections.

How the GMAT testers figure your score

Because the GMAT is a computer-adaptive test, your verbal and quantitative scores aren't based just on the number of questions you get right. The scores you earn are based on three factors:

- ✔ **The difficulty of the questions you answer:** The questions become more difficult as you continue to answer correctly, so getting tough questions means you're doing well on the test.

- ✔ **The number of questions you answer:** If you don't get to all the questions in the verbal and quantitative sections, your score is reduced by the proportion of questions you didn't answer. So if you fail to answer 5 of the 37 quantitative questions, for example, your raw score would be reduced by 13 percent and your percentile rank may go from the 90th percentile to the 75th percentile.

- ✔ **The number of questions you answer correctly:** In addition to scoring based on how difficult the questions are, the GMAT score also reflects your ability to answer those questions correctly.

GMAT essay readers determine your analytical writing assessment (AWA) score. College and university faculty members from different disciplines read your response to the essay prompt. Two independent readers separately score your writing assignment on a scale from 0 to 6, with 6 being the top score. Your final score is the average of the scores from each of the readers.

If the two readers assigned to your writing task give you scores that differ by more than one point, a third reader is assigned to adjudicate. For example, if one reader gives you a 6 and the other gives you a 4, a third reader will also review your essay.

Your integrated reasoning score ranges in whole numbers from 1 to 8, with 8 being the highest. Scores of 1 and 2 are rare and unusually low, and very few GMAT-takers score as high as 7 or 8. Generally, if you receive a score of 4, 5, or 6, you've done a respectable job answering the integrated reasoning questions.

How the GMAT testers report your score

Your final GMAT score consists of separate verbal reasoning, quantitative reasoning, integrated reasoning, and analytical writing assessment scores and a combined verbal and quantitative score. When you're finished with the test — or when your time is up — the computer immediately calculates your verbal and quantitative scores and provides them to you in an unofficial score report. You'll have a separate scaled score from 0 to 60 for the verbal and quantitative sections. The two scores are added together and converted to a scaled score ranging between 200 and 800. The mean total score falls slightly above 500.

You won't see your integrated reasoning and analytical writing assessment scores immediately after the test. These scores are included in the official score report that's either mailed to you or made available online about 20 days after you take the exam. So although you'll be able to view your verbal, quantitative, and total scores immediately after the test, you'll need to wait three weeks to see how well you did on the AWA and integrated reasoning section.

When you do get your official score, the AWA score appears as a number between 0 and 6. This number is a scaled score that's the average of the scores for all the readings of your response. The final score is rounded to the nearest half point, so a 4.8 average is reported as 5. The integrated reasoning scaled score ranges between 1 and 8. Neither the AWA nor the integrated reasoning score affect your total GMAT score in any way. Both scores are reported separately, and each MBA program decides how to use them in their admissions decisions.

Official scores, including the verbal reasoning, quantitative reasoning, total, integrated reasoning, and AWA scores, are sent to the schools that you've requested receive them. The score reports they receive include all your scores, as well as a table showing the percentage of test-takers who scored below you. (For example, if your total score is 670, then about 89 percent of test-takers have a score lower than yours.) You don't have to pay for the five schools you select before you take the test to receive your scores, and for a fee, you can request your scores be sent to any other school at any time up to five years after the test.

Why you should (almost) never cancel your GMAT score

Immediately after you conclude the GMAT and before the computer displays your scores, you're given the option of canceling your scores. You may see this as a blessing if you've had a rough day at the computer. You may jump at the chance to get rid of all evidence of your verbal, quantitative, and writing struggles.

Canceling your scores is almost always a bad idea for several reasons:

- ✔ **People routinely overestimate or underestimate their performance on standardized tests.** The GMAT isn't a test on state capitals or chemical symbols, so knowing how well you did isn't always easy. So long as you answer most of the questions and are able to focus reasonably well during the test, you'll probably earn scores that aren't too different from the average scores you'd get if you took the test repeatedly. People who retake the GMAT and other standardized tests rarely see their scores change significantly unless they're initially unprepared to take the exam and later attempt it with significant preparation. You're reading this book, so you don't fall into that category of test-taker.

- ✔ **You may not have time to reschedule.** It may take a while to reschedule the test. If your applications are due right away, you could miss an application deadline because you don't have GMAT scores to submit.

- ✔ **You'll never know how you did.** If you cancel your scores, you'll never know how you did or what areas you need to work on to improve your score if you decide to retake the test later.

- ✔ **Your score cancellation will be added to your GMAT record.** Canceled scores are noted on all official GMAT score reports. Some schools may look on your canceled score unfavorably.

A few circumstances exist in which you should consider canceling your scores. These situations aren't based on your estimation of how you did, which may be inaccurate, but on extenuating factors:

- ✔ **You're pretty darn ill during the test.** Waking up on test day with a fever of 101 degrees or getting sick during the test may warrant canceling a GMAT score.

- ✔ **You were unable to concentrate during the test.** Unusual personal difficulties, like a death in the family or the demise of a close relationship, could distract you to the point where you freeze up in the middle of the exam.

- ✔ **You left many questions unanswered.** If you forget the time management techniques we discuss in Chapter 2 and you leave quite a few questions unanswered in the verbal and quantitative sections, you may consider canceling your scores.

Repeating the Process: Retaking the GMAT

Because most programs consider only your top scores, retaking the GMAT may be in your best interest if you aren't happy with your first score. The GMAT administrators let you take the test quite a few times if you want (that's pretty big of them, considering you have to pay for it every time). If you do retake the GMAT, make sure you take the process and test seriously. You should show score improvement. A college will be much more impressed with a rising score than a falling one.

Many colleges may be turned off if they see that you've taken the GMAT more than two or three times. The key is to prepare to do your best on the first try. Obviously, that's your goal if you've chosen to read this book.

Official GMAT reports contain scores for every time you take the test. So if you take the GMAT twice, both scores appear on your report. It's up to the business program to decide how to use those scores. Some may take the higher score and some may take the average. Keep in mind that your new scores won't automatically be sent to the recipients of previous scores, so you'll need to reselect those programs when you retake the test.

Chapter 2

Maximizing Your Score on the GMAT

· ·

In This Chapter

▶ Checking out guessing strategies

▶ Managing your time like a pro

▶ Knowing how to recognize a wrong answer

▶ Avoiding worthless activities that minimize your score

▶ Quieting your nerves with tried-and-true relaxation techniques

· ·

You enter the test center and stare down the computer. For the next three and a half hours, that machine is your adversary. The GMAT loaded on it is your nemesis. All you have to aid you in this showdown is a booklet of noteboards and your intellect. The questions come quickly, and your reward for answering a question correctly is another, usually more difficult question! Why did you give up your precious free time for this torture?

By the time you actually take the GMAT, you'll have already given up hours and hours of your free time studying for the test, researching business schools, and planning for the future. Those three and a half hours alone with a computer represent a rite of passage that you must complete to accomplish the goals you've set for yourself. And because the test is a necessary evil, you may as well get the highest score you're capable of achieving!

This chapter contains the techniques you need to apply to pull together a winning strategy for the GMAT. You already have the brains, and the test center provides the materials. In this chapter, we share with you the other tools you need to maximize your score.

Discovering Strategies for Successful Guessing

You may be surprised that we start this chapter by discussing guessing strategies. Your ideal GMAT test day scenario probably involves knowing the answers to most of the questions right away rather than randomly guessing! The reality is that almost no one is absolutely sure of every answer to every question on the GMAT. Think back; did you have to guess at any questions on the ACT or SAT? We bet you did! We provide a few guessing strategies in the following sections to improve your chances of answering more questions correctly, even if you otherwise have no clue of the correct answer.

Forcing yourself to guess so you can move on

Remember that standardized tests aren't like tests in your undergraduate college courses. If you studied hard in college, you may not have had to do much guessing on your midterms and finals. On the GMAT, however, the computer won't allow you to skip questions. So if you stumble upon some really difficult questions that you're not sure how to answer, you have to guess and move on. Don't fall into thinking that you must know the correct answer for each question to do well on the GMAT. The GMAT is designed to test the potential of a wide range of future MBA students, so some of the questions have to be ridiculously difficult to challenge that one-in-a-million Einstein who takes the GMAT. Almost everyone incorrectly answers a few questions in each section, and almost everyone has to guess on those really difficult questions. Don't worry if you have to guess; just figure out how to guess effectively!

With the computer-adaptive test (CAT) format, developing a strategy for successful guessing in the quantitative reasoning and verbal reasoning sections is actually more important than ever. In these sections, as you answer questions correctly, the level of difficulty continues to increase. Although the integrated reasoning section isn't in the CAT format, you can't skip the questions in this section, either, so be sure to apply the guessing strategies we discuss in this chapter to that section as well. Even if you do really, really well on the test, you'll probably find yourself guessing on some questions. On the GMAT, *everyone* guesses!

Understanding the importance of completing each section

To get the optimum score for the questions you answer correctly, you must respond to *all* the questions in each section. If you don't have time to complete the questions at the end of each section, your score is reduced in proportion to the number of questions you didn't answer. Therefore, it's important to move at a pace that allows you to get to all the questions.

One of the ways you can get into real trouble with the CAT format is by spending too much time early on trying to correctly answer questions that are more difficult. If you're reluctant to guess and, therefore, spend more than a minute or two on several difficult questions, you may not have time to answer the relatively easy questions at the end.

Answer every question in each section! If you notice that you have only three or four minutes remaining in a section and more than five questions left, spend the remaining minutes marking an answer for every question, even if you don't have time to read them. You always have a 20 percent chance of randomly guessing the correct answer to a verbal reasoning or quantitative reasoning question, which is better than not answering the question at all. If you have to guess randomly at the end of the section, mark the same bubble for each answer. For example, you may choose to mark the second bubble from the bottom. Chances are that at least one in five questions will have a correct answer placed second to the end. Marking the same bubble also saves time because you don't have to choose which answer to mark for each question; you already have your guessing strategy in mind, so you don't have to think about it.

Even the GMAT folks warn of a severe penalty for not completing the test. They claim that if you fail to answer just 5 questions out of the 41 in the verbal section, your score could go from the 91st percentile to the 77th percentile. That's the kind of score reduction that could make a huge difference to your admissions chances!

Winning the Race against the Clock

Random guessing as the clock runs out serves you better than leaving the remaining questions in a section unanswered, but it's not a good way to approach the test in general. Instead, adopt a strategy of good time management that combines proper pacing, an active approach to answering questions, and appropriate guessing. We discuss all these time-management strategies in the following sections.

Giving each question equal treatment

You may have heard that you should spend a lot of time on the first ten questions because your performance on them determines your ultimate score. Although your performance on the first ten questions *does* give the computer an initial estimate of your ability, in the end, these first questions don't carry greater significance than any other questions. You'll still encounter all the questions in the section eventually, so you really have no reason to spend an unreasonable length of time on the first ten.

If you spend too much time on the first ten questions and answer them all correctly, you'll have a limited amount of time in which to answer the 27 remaining quantitative or 31 remaining verbal questions. The computer program would give you a high estimated score after those first ten questions, but that initial estimate would then most likely fall steadily throughout the session as you hurry through questions and guess at those you didn't have time to answer at the end. The worst outcome of all would be if you were unable to finish the section and had your score reduced in proportion to the questions you couldn't answer. You can't cheat the system by focusing on the first few questions. If you could, the very intelligent, highly paid test designers would find a way to adjust the format to thwart you.

Making time for the last ten questions

A much better approach than lavishing time on the *first* ten questions is to allow ample time to answer the *last* ten questions in both the verbal and quantitative sections. Because the best way to score well is to give adequate time to each question, guess when necessary, and complete the entire test, you shouldn't spend a disproportionate amount of time answering the early questions.

Here are the steps to follow for this approach:

1. **Work through the first 55 minutes of the quantitative and verbal sections at a good pace (around two minutes per question for quantitative and a little more than a minute and a half per question for verbal).**

2. **Don't spend more than three minutes on any question during the first 75 percent of the quantitative and verbal sections.**

3. **When you have ten questions remaining in the section (when you're on Question 27 of the quantitative section or Question 31 of the verbal section), check the time remaining and adjust your pace accordingly.**

   For example, if you've answered the first 27 quantitative questions in only 50 minutes, you have a total of 25 minutes to work on the last ten questions. That means you can spend about two and a half minutes on each of the last ten questions. That extra 30 seconds per question may be what you need to answer a high percentage of those final ten questions correctly. Avoid random guesses on the last unanswered questions of either section.

We're not suggesting that you rush through the first 55 minutes of each section so you can spend lots of time on the last ten questions. Instead, you should stick to a pace that allows you to give equal time to all the questions in a section. You can't spend five or six minutes on a single question without sacrificing your performance on the rest of the test, so stick to your pace.

If you happen to have additional time when you get to the last ten questions, by all means, use it. There's a severe penalty for not finishing a section but no prize for getting done early.

When you work steadily and carefully through the first 75 percent of each section, you're rewarded with a score that stabilizes toward the higher end of the percentile and that may rise to an even higher level at the end of the section as you spend any extra time you have getting the last questions right. Talk about ending on a high note!

Keeping track of your pace

You may think that keeping an even pace throughout the test means a lot of clock watching, but this isn't the case if you go into the test site with a plan. You can conceal the clock on the computer to keep from becoming obsessed with time, but you should periodically reveal the clock to check your progress. For example, you may plan to check your computer clock after every eight questions you answer. This means revealing the feature about five or six times during the verbal and quantitative sections. You'll spend a second or two clicking on the clock and glancing at it, but knowing that you're on pace will be worth it.

If you time yourself during practice tests you take at home, you'll probably begin to know intuitively whether you're falling behind. During the actual exam, you may not have to look at your clock as frequently. However, if you suspect that you're using too much time on a question (more than three minutes), you should check the clock. If you've spent more than three minutes, mark your best guess from the choices you haven't already eliminated and move on.

Getting Rid of Wrong Answers

We've stressed that the key to success is to move through the test steadily so you can answer every question and maximize your score. Keeping this steady pace will probably require you to make some intelligent guesses, and intelligent guesses hang on your ability to eliminate incorrect answers.

Eliminating answer choices is crucial on the verbal and quantitative sections of the GMAT. Most questions come with five answer choices, and usually one or two of the options are obviously wrong (especially in the verbal section). As soon as you know an answer choice is wrong, eliminate it. After you've eliminated that answer, don't waste time reading it again. By quickly getting rid of choices that you know are *wrong,* you'll be well on your way to finding the *right* answer! In the following sections, we show you a few elimination strategies that help you cross off wrong answers so you can narrow in on the right ones.

Keeping track of eliminated answer choices for the computer test format

You may be thinking that eliminating answer choices on a computerized test won't work. In truth, doing so is more difficult than on a paper test where you can actually cross off the entire answer in your test booklet. However, you can achieve the same results on the computerized test with a little practice. You must train your mind to look only at the remaining choices and not read every word that your eyes fall upon. You can't afford to waste time rereading a choice after you've eliminated it. That's why you need a system.

You can use the booklet of noteboards you're given at the test site to help you eliminate answers. The test administrators will replenish your noteboard supply if you fill them up, so don't be afraid to write all over your noteboards.

Here are some simple steps to help you keep track of which answers you've eliminated:

1. **At the beginning of the section (especially the verbal one, where eliminating answer choices is easier), quickly write down "A, B, C, D, and E" in a vertical row on your noteboard.**

   A stands for the first answer choice, *B* for the second, *C* for the third, and so on, even though these letters don't appear on your computer screen.

2. **When you eliminate an answer choice, cross out the corresponding letter on your noteboard.**

   For example, if you're sure that the second and fifth answers are wrong, mark a line through *B* and *E* on your noteboard.

3. **If you look at your noteboard and see only one remaining answer letter, you've zeroed in on the right answer.**

   You don't need to reread the answer choices to remember which one was correct. It's listed right there on the noteboard.

4. **If you can't narrow down your choices to just one answer, eliminating three incorrect choices gives you a good chance of guessing correctly between the two options that remain.**

5. **Quickly rewrite the five letters for the next question and repeat the process.**

Practice this technique when you're taking your practice tests. The hard part isn't crossing out the letters on your noteboard; it's training your eyes to skip the wrong answers on the computer screen. Your brain will want to read through each choice every time you look at the answers. With the paper test booklet, you'd simply cross out the entire answer choice and then skip that choice every time you came to it. With the computerized test, you have to mentally cross out wrong answers. Developing this skill takes time. Mastering it is especially important for the verbal section, which has some long answer choices.

Recognizing wrong answers

So maybe you've mastered the art of the noteboard answer elimination system, but you may be wondering how you know which answers to eliminate. Most of the verbal questions are best answered by process of elimination because answers aren't as clearly right or wrong as they may be for the math questions. For many math questions, the correct answer is obvious after you've performed the necessary calculations, but you may be able to answer some math questions without performing complex calculations if you look through answers first and eliminate choices that don't make sense. So by using your common sense and analyzing all the information you have to work with (we show you how to do both in the next sections), you can reach a correct answer without knowing everything there is to know about a question.

Using common sense

Reading carefully reveals a surprising number of answer choices that are obviously wrong. In the quantitative and integrated reasoning sections, you may know before you even do a math calculation that one or two of the answers are simply illogical. In the verbal section, critical reasoning questions may have answer choices that don't deal with the topic of the argument, or some sentence correction answer choices may obviously display poor grammar or faulty sentence construction. You can immediately eliminate these eyesores from contention. If an answer is outside the realm of possibility, you don't ever have to read through it again. For example, consider the following sample critical reasoning question.

Most New Year's resolutions are quickly forgotten. Americans commonly make resolutions to exercise, lose weight, quit smoking, or spend less money. In January, many people take some action, such as joining a gym, but by February, they are back to their old habits again.

Which of the following, if true, most strengthens the preceding argument?

(A) Some Americans do not make New Year's resolutions.

(B) Americans who do not keep their resolutions feel guilty the rest of the year.

(C) Attempts to quit smoking begun at times other than the first of the year are less successful than those begun in January.

(D) Increased sports programming in January motivates people to exercise more.

(E) People who are serious about lifestyle changes usually make those changes immediately and do not wait for New Year's Day.

Chapter 5 gives you a whole slew of tips on how to answer critical reasoning questions, but without even looking closely at this one, you can eliminate at least two choices immediately. The argument states that people usually don't live up to New Year's resolutions and the question asks you to strengthen that argument. Two of the answer choices have nothing to do with keeping resolutions, so you can discard them right away: Choice (A) provides irrelevant information — the argument is about people who make resolutions, not those who don't — and Choice (D) brings up a completely different topic (sports programming) and doesn't mention resolutions.

Without even taxing your brain, you've gone from five choices down to three. Psychologically, dealing with three answer choices is much easier than dealing with all five. Plus, if you were short on time and had to quickly guess at this question, narrowing your choices to only three gives you a much better chance of answering it correctly.

Relying on what you know

Before you attempt to solve a quantitative problem or begin to answer a sentence correction question, you can use what you know to eliminate answer choices.

For example, if a quantitative question asks for a solution that's an absolute value, you can immediately eliminate any negative answer choices, because absolute value is always positive. (For more about absolute value, see Chapter 10.) Even if you don't remember how to solve the problem, you can at least narrow down the choices and increase your chances of guessing correctly. If you eliminate one or two choices and if you have the time, you may be able to plug the remaining answer choices back into the problem and find the correct answer that way. So if you approach questions with a stash of knowledge, you can correctly answer more questions than you realize.

Letting the question guide you

If you've ever watched a popular TV game show, you know that the clue to the answer can sometimes be found in the question. Although the answers to most GMAT questions aren't as obvious as the answer to "in 1959, the U.S. said 'aloha' to this 50th state," you can still use clues from the GMAT questions themselves to answer them.

In the critical reasoning example on New Year's resolutions, you were left with three answer choices. Paying attention to the wording of the question can help you eliminate two more.

The question asks you to *strengthen* the argument that Americans quickly forget their New Year's resolutions. Choice (B) seriously *weakens* the argument by indicating that instead of forgetting their resolutions, Americans are haunted by failed resolutions for the rest of the year. Likewise, Choice (C) indicates that a resolution to quit smoking at the beginning of the

New Year may be more successful than the same resolution at other times. Because these answers weaken the argument rather than strengthen it as the question asks, you can eliminate them, also. By process of elimination, you know that Choice (E) is the correct answer to the question, and you haven't yet seriously considered the logic of the argument!

Quickly recognizing and eliminating wrong answers after only a few seconds puts you on the path to choosing a right answer. This strategy works in the quantitative section as well. Consider this problem-solving question example.

If $\frac{1}{2}$ of the air in a balloon is removed every 10 seconds, what fraction of the air has been removed from the balloon after 30 seconds?

(A) $\frac{1}{8}$

(B) $\frac{1}{6}$

(C) $\frac{1}{4}$

(D) $\frac{5}{6}$

(E) $\frac{7}{8}$

You can immediately eliminate any choices with fractions smaller than one-half because the problem tells you that half the air departs within the first ten seconds. So you can discard Choices (A), (B), and (C). Without performing any calculations at all, you've narrowed down your choices to just two!

Another benefit of eliminating obviously wrong answer choices is that you save yourself from inadvertently making costly errors. The GMAT offers Choices (A), (B), and (C) to trap unsuspecting test-takers. If you mistakenly tried to solve the problem by multiplying $\frac{1}{2} \times \frac{1}{2} \times \frac{1}{2}$, you'd come up with $\frac{1}{8}$. But if you've already eliminated that answer, you'd know you've done something wrong. By immediately getting rid of the answer choices that can't be right, you may avoid choosing a clever distracter. By the way, $\frac{1}{8}$ is the amount of air remaining in the balloon after 30 seconds. After the first 10 seconds, $\frac{1}{2}$ of the air remains. After 20 seconds, $\frac{1}{2}$ of that, or $\frac{1}{4}$, remains. After 30 seconds, the balloon still has $\frac{1}{2}$ of $\frac{1}{4}$ of its air, which is $\frac{1}{8}$.

So the amount of air removed in 30 seconds is Choice (E), $\frac{7}{8}$, because $1 - \frac{1}{8} = \frac{7}{8}$.

Dealing with questions that contain Roman numerals

The GMAT presents a special type of question that pops up from time to time. This question gives you three statements marked with the Roman numerals I, II, and III and asks you to evaluate their validity. You'll find these questions in the quantitative and verbal reasoning sections. You're supposed to select the answer choice that presents the correct list of either valid or invalid statements, depending on what the question is looking for.

To approach questions that contain statements with Roman numerals, follow these steps:

1. **Evaluate the validity of the first statement or the statement that seems easiest to evaluate.**

2. **If the first statement meets the qualifications stated by the question, eliminate any answer choices that don't contain Roman numeral I; if it doesn't, eliminate any choices that have Roman numeral I in them.**

3. **Examine the remaining answer choices to see which of the two remaining statements are best to evaluate next.**

4. **Evaluate another statement and eliminate answer choices based on your findings.**

   You may find that you don't have to spend time evaluating the third statement.

Here's an example to show how the approach works.

If x and y are different integers, each greater than 1, which of the following must be true?

   I. $x + y > 4$

   II. $x - y = 0$

   III. $x - y$ results in an integer

   (A) II only

   (B) I and II

   (C) I, II, and III

   (D) I and III

   (E) III only

Consider the statements one by one. Start with Statement I and determine whether the expression $x + y > 4$ is true. Because x and y are greater than 1, they must be positive. The smaller of the two integers must be at least 2, and the other number can't be less than 3. So because $2 + 3 = 5$, $x + y$ must be at least 5, meaning the statement is correct.

Don't read Statement II yet. Instead, run through the answer choices and eliminate any that don't include Statement I. Choice (A) and Choice (E) don't include Statement I, so cross out those letters on your noteboard. The remaining choices don't give you any indication which statement is best to evaluate next, so proceed with your evaluation of Statement II, which states that $x - y = 0$. This statement can't be correct because x and y have different values. The only way one number subtracted from another number can result in 0 is when the two numbers are the same. The difference of two different integers will always be at least 1.

Because Statement II isn't correct, eliminate choices that include Statement II. You can cross out Choice (B) and Choice (C), which leaves you with Choice (D). By process of elimination, Choice (D) has to be right. You don't even need to read Statement III, because you know the correct answer. Not all Roman numeral questions are so helpful, but many are, and in those cases, the strategy is a real timesaver!

Playing It Smart: A Few Things You Shouldn't Do When Taking the Test

Most of this chapter focuses on what you *should* do to maximize your score on the GMAT. However, there are also a few things you *shouldn't* do, which we discuss in the following sections. Avoid these mistakes, and you'll have an advantage over many other test-takers!

Don't lose your focus

You may be used to the fast-paced world of business or the cooperative world of group presentations that are popular in many business classes. Don't be surprised if 180 minutes of multiple-choice questions peppered with 30 minutes of essay writing gets a little boring. We know the prospect is shocking!

Don't allow yourself to lose focus. Keep your brain on a tight leash, and don't let your mind wander. This test is too important. Just remind yourself how important these three and a half hours are to your future. Teach yourself to concentrate and rely on the relaxation tips we give you at the end of the chapter to avoid incessant mind wandering. You'll need those powers of concentration in that MBA program you'll soon be starting!

Don't read questions at lightning speed

We hate to break it to you, but you probably aren't a superhero named "Speedy Reader." You'll be anxious when the test begins, and you may want to blow through the questions at record speed. Big mistake! You don't get bonus points for finishing early, and you have plenty of time to answer every question if you read at a reasonable pace. You may take pride in your ability to speed-read novels, and that skill may help you with the reading comprehension passages, but don't use it to read the questions. You need to read questions carefully to capture the nuances the GMAT offers and understand exactly what it asks of you.

Many people who get bogged down on a few questions and fail to complete a section do so because of poor test-taking techniques, not because of slow reading. Do yourself a favor: Relax, read at a reasonable pace, and maximize your score!

Don't waste all your time on the hardest questions

Although you shouldn't try to work at lightning speed, remember not to get held back by a few hard questions, either. The difficulty of a question depends on the person taking the test. For everyone, even the high scorers, a few questions on a test are just harder than others. When you confront a difficult question on the GMAT, do your best, eliminate as many wrong answers as you can, and then make an intelligent guess. Even if you had all day, you may not be able to answer that particular question. If you allow yourself to guess and move on, you can work on plenty of other questions that you'll answer correctly.

Don't cheat

We aren't sure how you'd cheat on the computerized GMAT, and we won't be wasting our time thinking of ways! Spend your time practicing for the test and do your best. Cheating is futile.

Tackling a Case of Nerves with Relaxation Techniques

All this talk about time management, distracting answer choices, blind guessing, and losing focus may be making you nervous. Relax. After you've read this book, you'll have plenty of techniques for turning your quick intellect and that packet of noteboards into a high GMAT score. You may feel a little nervous on the day of the test, but don't worry about it, because a little nervous adrenaline can actually keep you alert. Just don't let anxiety ruin your performance.

You may be working along steadily when suddenly, from out of the blue, a question appears that you don't understand at all. Instead of trying to eliminate answer choices and solve the problem, you may stare at the question as if it were written in a foreign language. You may start to second-guess your performance on the test as a whole. You panic and think that maybe you're just not cut out for a graduate business degree. You're on the verge of freaking out — help!

Because much of the GMAT is in CAT format, encountering a super-hard quantitative or verbal question probably means you're doing pretty well. Besides, if you do miss a question, you'll just get an easier question next — unless you're on the last question, in which case you needn't freak out at all. Heck, you're nearly done!

If you do find yourself seizing up with anxiety partway through the test, and if these facts about the CAT format don't ease your tension, try these techniques to get back on track:

- ✔ **Inhale deeply.** When you stress out, you take shallow breaths and don't get the oxygen you need to think straight. Breathing deeply can calm you and supply the air you need to get back to doing your best.

- ✔ **Stretch a little.** Anxiety causes tension, and so does working at a computer. Do a few simple stretches to relax and get the blood flowing. Try shrugging your shoulders toward your ears and rolling your head from side to side. You can put your hands together and stretch your arms above your head or stretch your legs out and move your ankles up and down (or both!). Last, shake your hands as though you've just washed them and don't have a towel.

- ✔ **Give yourself a mini massage.** If you're really tense, give yourself a little rubdown. The shoulders and neck usually hold the most tension in your body, so rub your right shoulder with your left hand and vice versa. Rub the back of your neck. It's not as great as getting a full rubdown from a professional, but you can book that appointment for after the test!

- ✔ **Think positive thoughts.** Give yourself a quick break. The GMAT is tough, but don't get discouraged. Focus on the positive; think about the questions you've done well on. If you're facing a tough question, realize that it will get better.

- ✔ **Take a little vacation.** If nothing else is working and you're still anxious, picture a place in your mind that makes you feel comfortable and confident. Visit that place for a few moments and come back ready to take charge!

Part II
Vanquishing the Verbal Section

In this part . . .

The GMAT verbal section tests a variety of skills using three different question types. This part shows you how to excel on all three of them.

Sentence correction questions challenge your knowledge of the rules of standard written English. Because the questions don't test your knowledge of common *spoken* English, you won't always be able to correct sentence errors based on what sounds right. Don't worry: We provide you with the means to catch and correct the errors the GMAT writers are most fond of throwing at you.

Also included in the verbal section is the customary reading comprehension question. You've seen it before on almost every standardized test you've ever taken. It's not particularly hard to read a passage and answer questions about it, except when you have only a few minutes to do so! That's why this part provides you with techniques to help you move through the passages quickly and focus on only the most important information when you answer questions.

The critical reasoning exercises are like miniature reading comprehension questions, requiring you to read information and answer questions. But these beauties are usually limited to one paragraph and only one question. You can get really good at evaluating the arguments and answering the questions because we show you how to apply our time-tested strategy for approaching critical reasoning arguments.

This part covers a lot of information. We make sure you remember it all by ending it with a short version of a GMAT verbal section so that you can see how all three question types come together.

Chapter 3

Applying What You Learned (We Hope) in Grammar Class: Sentence Correction

. . . .

In This Chapter

▶ Grasping grammar basics

▶ Recognizing commonly tested errors

▶ Mastering the approach to sentence correction questions

. . . .

*B*usiness success depends on a number of diverse skills, and one of the most important of these skills is the ability to communicate effectively. The GMAT can't test your speaking ability (not yet, anyway), so it focuses on your reading and writing skills. In fact, about half of the GMAT is devoted to reading and writing. And, of course, knowing the rules of standard written English is essential to good writing. The GMAT test-makers have developed diabolically effective ways to use multiple-choice questions to test your knowledge of written English. They present you with a sentence and underline a portion of it. Your job is to figure out whether the underlined part is okay the way it is. If it needs to be changed, you have to pick the answer choice that offers the proper correction.

Sentence correction questions appear in the verbal reasoning section along with reading comprehension and critical reasoning questions. You have 75 minutes to answer the 41 questions that appear in the entire section. So you have a little less than two minutes to answer each question. You'll likely need more time to ponder reading questions, so plan to spend no more than one minute answering each sentence correction question.

Punctuation, subject-verb agreement, parallel construction, and other keys to good grammar may have you lying awake at night. Take heart. We won't let your dream of attending the business school of your choice die on the sentence correction portion of the GMAT. Fortunately, the kinds of sentence errors that crop up on the GMAT don't change much, so you can focus your study on the common ones.

In this chapter, we review the grammar basics you should have down before test day. We also show you what sentence correction questions look like, which common errors the GMAT likes to test, and what's the best way to approach the questions.

Building a Solid Foundation: Grammar Basics

Luckily, the rules of grammar are really pretty logical. After you understand the basic rules regarding the parts of speech and the elements of a sentence, you've got it made. The following sections provide what you need to know to do well on sentence correction questions. As an added bonus, this refresher can help you write the GMAT analytical writing essay.

Getting wordy: The parts of speech

Sentence correction questions consist of, well, sentences. Sentences are made up of words, and each word in a sentence has a function. The parts of speech in the English language that are important to know for GMAT grammar are verbs, nouns, pronouns, adjectives, adverbs, conjunctions, and prepositions.

Acting out: Verbs

Every sentence has a verb, which means that a sentence isn't complete without one. You should be familiar with three types of verbs:

- **Action verbs:** These verbs state what the subject of the sentence is doing. *Run, jump, compile,* and *learn* are examples of action verbs.

- **To be:** The verb *to be* (conjugated as *am, is, are, was, were, been,* and *being*) functions sort of like an equal sign. It equates the subject with a noun or adjective. For example: *Ben is successful* means *Ben = successful. She is a CEO* means *she = CEO.*

- **Linking verbs:** These words join (or link) the subject to an adjective that describes the condition of the subject. Like the verb *to be,* they express a state of the subject, but they provide more information about the subject than *to be* verbs do. Common linking verbs are *feel, seem, appear, remain, look, taste,* and *smell.*

Telling it like it is: Nouns

You've undoubtedly heard nouns defined as persons, places, or things. They provide the "what" of the sentence. A noun can function in a sentence in different ways:

1. The *subject* plays the principal role in the sentence. It's what the sentence is about or who is doing the action.

2. A *direct object* receives the action of an action verb.

3. An *indirect object* receives the direct object. Sentences with direct objects don't need indirect objects, but you need a direct object before you can have an indirect object.

4. The *object of a preposition* receives a preposition. (See the "Joining forces: Conjunctions and prepositions" section, later in this chapter.)

5. The *object in a verbal phrase* serves as the receiver of the *gerund* (which is a verb form that functions as a noun, like *singing*).

6. *Appositives* clarify or rename other nouns.

7. *Predicate nouns* follow the verb *to be* and regard the subject.

So you can see how these different types of nouns function, we've marked their appearances in these two sentences with numbers that correspond to the list:

Being a *businesswoman (5)* with great leadership *abilities (4), Anna Arnold (1),* an *MBA (6),* gave her *employees (3)* the *opportunity (2)* to succeed. *Anna (1)* was a supportive *supervisor (7).*

The GMAT won't ask you to define the various noun functions, but being familiar with them helps when we talk about the different types of sentence errors you may encounter.

One of the most important things to remember about nouns and verbs on the GMAT is that the subject and verb of a sentence have to agree in number. See the later section "Pointing Out Mistakes: Common Sentence Correction Errors" for details.

Standing in: Pronouns

Pronouns figure prominently in the sentence correction portion of the GMAT. Pronouns rename nouns and provide a means of avoiding the needless repetition of names and other nouns in a sentence or paragraph. On the GMAT, pronoun errors are common. To correct these errors, you need to be familiar with the three types of pronouns: personal, indefinite, and relative:

- **Personal pronouns:** These words rename specific nouns. They take two forms: subjective and objective.

  - The subjective personal pronouns are *I, you, he, she, it, we,* and *they. Subjective personal pronouns* are used when the pronoun functions as a subject or predicate noun (see the preceding section for info on noun functions).

  - The *objective* personal pronouns are *me, you, him, her, it, us,* and *them. Objective personal pronouns* are properly used when they function as an object in the sentence.

- **Indefinite pronouns:** These pronouns refer to general nouns rather than specific ones. Some common examples are *everyone, somebody, anything, each, one, none,* and *no one.* It's important to remember that most indefinite pronouns are singular, which means they require singular verbs: ***One** of the employees is being laid off.*

- **Relative pronouns:** These words, like *that, which,* and *who,* introduce adjective clauses that describe nouns. *Who* refers to persons; *which* and *that* refer primarily to animals and things: *He is a manager **who** is comfortable leading. The consulting work **that** she does usually saves companies money, **which** makes her a very popular consultant.*

Filling in the details: Adjectives

Adjectives describe and clarify nouns and pronouns. For example: *The secretive culture of the corporation created discontented employees. Secretive* defines the kind of culture and *discontented* describes the feeling of the employees. Without the adjectives, the sentence is virtually meaningless: *The culture of the corporation created employees.*

With sentence correction questions, make sure adjectives are positioned correctly in the sentence so each adjective modifies the word it's supposed to. For example, *I brought the slides to the meeting **that I created** makes it seem that the author of the sentence created the meeting rather than the slides. The descriptive clause *that I created* is in the wrong place. The better composition is *I brought the slides **that I created** to the meeting.*

Describing the action: Adverbs

Adverbs are like adjectives because they add extra information to the sentence, but adjectives usually modify nouns, and adverbs primarily define verbs. Adverbs include all words and groups of words (called *adverb phrases*) that answer the questions *where, when, how,* and *why: The stock market **gradually** recovered from the 1999 crash. Gradually* defines how the stock market recovered.

Some adverbs modify adjectives or other adverbs: *The **extremely** unfortunate plumber yodeled **very well.** See Chapter 6 for more examples of how adverbs are used in this way.

You'll recognize many adverbs by the *-ly* ending. But not all adverbs end in *-ly.* For example, in *The company's manufacturing moved **overseas,** the adverb *overseas* reveals where the manufacturing is located. In *The Human Resources director resigned **today,** today* explains when the director resigned.

Positioning adverbs correctly is important on the GMAT. Separating adverbs from the words they modify makes sentences imprecise.

Joining forces: Conjunctions and prepositions

Conjunctions and prepositions link the main elements of the sentence.

- **Conjunctions:** This part of speech joins words, phrases, and clauses. The three types of conjunctions are *coordinating, correlative,* and *subordinating*. Don't worry about memorizing these terms; just remember that the three types exist.

  - The seven coordinating conjunctions — *and, but, for, nor, or, so,* and *yet* — are the ones most people think of when they consider conjunctions.

  - Correlative conjunctions always appear in pairs: *either/or, neither/nor, not only/ but also*. These conjunctions correlate two similar clauses in one sentence. Therefore, if you use *either* as a conjunction, you have to include *or*.

  - Subordinating conjunctions introduce dependent clauses and connect them to independent clauses. *Although, because, if, when,* and *while* are common examples of subordinating conjunctions. We talk more about clauses in the section "In so many words: Phrases and clauses."

- **Prepositions:** These words join nouns to the rest of a sentence. We'd need several pages to list all the prepositions, but common examples are *about, above, at, for, in, over, to,* and *with*. A preposition can't function within a sentence unless the preposition is connected to a noun, so prepositions always appear in prepositional phrases. These phrases consist of a preposition and noun, which is called the *object of the preposition: The woman* **in the suit** *went* **to the office** *to sit down*. The preposition *in* relates its object, *suit*, to another noun, *woman*, so *in the suit* is a prepositional phrase that works as an adjective to describe *woman; to the office* is an adverbial prepositional phrase that describes where the woman went. Note that the word *to* in *to sit down* isn't a preposition; rather, it's part of the infinitive form of the verb *to sit* — the phrase doesn't have an object, so you don't have a prepositional phrase.

Prepositions often play a part in sentence correction questions. The GMAT may provide you with a sentence that contains an improper preposition construction. Here's a simple example: *He watched the flood while sitting in the roof*. The correct preposition is *on*, not *in*. Other types of preposition questions may not be so easy, but we highlight these for you in the section "Pointing Out Mistakes: Common Sentence Correction Errors."

Pulling together: The parts of a sentence

The parts of speech work together to form sentences. And the thrust of the sentence's information is conveyed by three main elements: the subject, the verb, and the element that the verb links to the subject. To locate the main idea of a sentence, you focus on these three elements. Other information within the sentence is secondary.

Trouble comes in threes: Subject, verb, and third element

The subject is the main character of the sentence; it's the noun that carries out the action of the sentence or whose condition the sentence describes. The verb describes the action or links the subject and predicate. Depending on the verb used, the third important part of the sentence could be a direct object, an adverb, an adjective, or a predicate noun. The third element for a sentence with a *transitive verb* (an action verb that must be followed by a direct object) is always a direct object. *Intransitive verbs* (action verbs that can't be followed by direct objects) may be completed by adverbs. You can follow the verb *to be* with either an adjective or a predicate noun. Recognizing the three main elements of the sentence helps you spot errors in the sentence correction questions.

In so many words: Phrases and clauses

In addition to the main elements, a sentence may contain single words, phrases, or clauses that convey more information about the sentence's main message. Phrases and clauses are groups of words that work together to form a single part of speech, like an adverb or adjective. The difference between phrases and clauses is that clauses contain their own subjects and verbs, and phrases don't. A good understanding of both clauses and phrases can help you greatly on the sentence correction portion of the GMAT.

Phrases

Phrases are groups of words that function together as a part of speech. Many tested errors on the GMAT concern phrases, and we discuss them in more depth in the section "Pointing Out Mistakes: Common Sentence Correction Errors."

Independent and dependent clauses

The distinguishing characteristic of clauses is that they contain subjects and verbs. The two types of clauses are independent and dependent. Recognizing the difference between independent and dependent clauses can help you with many of the sentence correction problems on the GMAT.

TIP

✔ **Independent clauses:** These clauses express complete thoughts and could stand as sentences by themselves. Here's an example of a sentence that contains two independent clauses: *The firm will go public, and investors will rush to buy stock.* Each clause is a complete sentence: *The firm will go public. Investors will rush to buy stock.*

Punctuate two independent clauses in a sentence by joining them either with a semicolon or with a comma and a coordinating conjunction.

✔ **Dependent clauses:** These clauses express incomplete thoughts and are, therefore, sentence fragments. Even though they contain a subject and verb, they can't stand alone as sentences without other information. For example, in the sentence *After the two companies merge, they'll need only one board of directors,* the dependent clause in the sentence is *after the two companies merge.* The clause has a subject, *companies,* and a verb, *merge,* but it still leaves the reader needing more information. So the clause is dependent. To form a complete sentence, a dependent clause must be paired with an independent clause.

TIP

Punctuate a beginning dependent clause by placing a comma between it and the independent clause that comes after it. If the dependent clause follows the independent clause, you don't need any punctuation: *They'll need only one board of directors after the two companies merge.*

When you understand the difference between independent and dependent clauses, you'll be better able to recognize sentence fragments and faulty modification errors (more about those appears in the section "Pointing Out Mistakes: Common Sentence Correction Errors").

Not so needy: The functions of dependent clauses

Dependent clauses that function as adverbs begin with subordinating conjunctions and answer the questions *how, when, where,* or *why.* For example, *The woman got the job **because she was more qualified.*** The bolded portion is a dependent clause explaining *why* the woman got the job. On the other hand, an adjectival clause usually begins with a relative pronoun to provide more information about the noun it modifies, like in this sentence: *The judge is a man **who requires a silent courtroom.*** The bolded clause describes what type of man the judge is. Dependent clauses may also function as nouns: *The insurance company was focusing on **how much money the hurricane would cost.*** The dependent clause in this sentence is the object of the preposition *on.*

Before we talk about the most commonly tested errors in the sentence correction questions, we need to share one more thing about dependent clauses. Dependent clauses can be classified as either restrictive or nonrestrictive. Distinguishing between the two can be tricky.

- ✔ **Restrictive clauses are vital to the meaning of the sentence.** Without them, the sentence's original meaning is lost. For example, in *She never wins her cases that involve the IRS,* the restrictive clause *that involve the IRS* provides essential information about the particular type of cases she never wins. The point of the sentence is that she never wins IRS cases.

- ✔ **Nonrestrictive clauses provide clarifying information, but they aren't mandatory for the sentence to make sense.** In the sentence *She never wins her cases, which involve the IRS,* the nonrestrictive clause, *which involve the IRS,* makes a "by the way" statement. It provides additional information about what type of cases she handles. The main point of the sentence is that she never wins a case.

Note that in the preceding examples, the restrictive clause begins with *that* and the nonrestrictive clause begins with *which.* You don't use commas before clauses that begin with *that* because they're restrictive clauses and integral parts of the sentence. You should use commas to set nonrestrictive clauses apart from the rest of the sentence.

Pointing Out Mistakes: Common Sentence Correction Errors

Sentence correction questions test your ability to edit written material so it follows the rules of standard written English. The questions provide you with sentences that contain underlined parts. From the five provided answer choices, you have to choose the answer that expresses the underlined portion of the sentence in the way that conforms to the dictates of standard written English.

The first answer choice is always the same as the underlined portion of the sentence. So if you think the sentence is fine as is, select the first answer. The other four choices present alternative ways of expressing the idea in the underlined part. Your task is to determine whether the underlined portion of the statement contains an error and, if so, which of the four alternatives best corrects the error.

You correct errors in sentence correction sentences by applying the basic rules of English grammar. The good news is that you won't be asked to define or spell words or diagram sentences! And no question expects you to correct specific punctuation errors, though knowing the rules for placing commas helps you eliminate answer choices in some cases.

The GMAT is a test for admission to business school. Therefore, sentence correction questions center on errors that adversely affect the quality of business writing, such as improper word choices, incomplete or run-on sentences, and verb tense and agreement issues. The kind of errors you'll be asked to correct on the GMAT are the kind you should avoid if you want to write successfully in business.

Can't we all just get along? Errors in subject-verb and noun-pronoun agreement

One of the most fundamental skills in writing is the ability to make the elements of a sentence agree. If your subject is singular but your verb is plural, you've got a problem! Even in less formal kinds of communication, like quick e-mails, errors in subject-verb or noun-pronoun agreement can obscure the message you hope to communicate. You can be sure that the GMAT sentence correction problems will contain some agreement errors.

Subject-verb agreement

When we say the subjects and verbs agree, we don't mean they're having a meeting of minds. We mean that plural subjects pair with plural verbs and singular subjects require singular verbs. Errors in simple constructions are pretty easy to spot. It just doesn't sound right to say *He attend classes at the University of Michigan.*

It's when the subject isn't simple or obvious that determining subject-verb agreement gets a little more difficult. For example, take a look at this sentence: *His fixation with commodities markets have grown into several prosperous ventures, including a consulting business.* The subject is *fixation,* but the prepositional phrase *with commodities markets* may confuse you into thinking that *markets* is the subject. *Markets* is a plural noun, so it would take a plural verb if it were the subject. But you know that *markets* can't be the subject of the sentence because *markets* is part of a prepositional phrase. It's the object of the preposition *with,* and a noun can't be an object and a subject at the same time. The subject has to be *fixation,* so the singular verb *has,* rather than the plural *have,* is proper.

Focus on the three main elements of any complex sentence by mentally eliminating words and phrases that aren't essential to the sentence's point. Then you can check the subjects and verbs to make sure they agree. For example, when you remove the prepositional phrase *with commodities markets* from the sample sentence we just discussed, you get *His fixation have grown,* which reveals an obvious disagreement in number between the subject and verb.

Noun-pronoun agreement

Another relationship you need to keep on track is the one between nouns and the pronouns that refer to them. A pronoun must agree in number with the noun (or other pronoun) it refers to. Plural nouns take plural pronouns, and singular nouns take singular pronouns. For example, this sentence has improper noun-pronoun agreement: *You can determine the ripeness of citrus by handling them and noting their color.* *Citrus* is a singular noun, so using plural pronouns to refer to it is incorrect. It would be correct to say *You can determine the ripeness of citrus by handling it and noting its color.*

Another problem with pronouns is unclear references. To know whether a pronoun agrees with its subject, you have to be clear about just what the pronoun refers to. For example, it's not clear which noun the pronoun in this sentence refers to: *Bobby and Tom went to the store, and he purchased a candy bar.* Because the subject of the first clause is plural, the pronoun *he* could refer to either Bobby or Tom or even to a third person. To improve clarity in this case, you'd use the name of the person who bought the candy bar rather than the ambiguous pronoun.

If a GMAT sentence correction question contains a pronoun in the underlined portion, make sure the pronoun clearly refers to a particular noun in the sentence and that it matches that noun in number. Otherwise, you need to find an answer choice that clarifies the reference or corrects the number.

Here's a sample question that contains both types of agreement errors:

Much work performed by small business owners, like managing human relations, keeping track of accounts, and paying taxes, <u>which are essential to its successful operation, have gone virtually unnoticed by their employees</u>.

(A) which are essential to its successful operation, have gone virtually unnoticed by their employees

(B) which are essential to successful operations, have gone virtually unnoticed by their employees

(C) which is essential to its successful operation, have gone virtually unnoticed by its employees

(D) which are essential to successful operation, has gone virtually unnoticed by their employees

(E) which are essential to successful operation, has gone virtually unnoticed by its employees

The underlined portion contains several agreement errors, and your job is to locate and fix all of them. To accomplish this task, isolate the three main elements of this sentence:

- The subject is *work*. None of the other nouns or pronouns or noun phrases in the sentence can be the main subject because they're all either objects *(owners, managing, keeping, paying, relations, accounts, taxes, operation, employees)* or subjects of dependent clauses *(which)*.

- The main verb is *have gone*. The other verb *(are)* belongs to the dependent clause, so it can't be the main verb.

- The third element is *unnoticed*.

So the essential sentence states that *work have gone unnoticed*. Well, that doesn't sound right! You know you have to change the verb to the singular *has* to make it agree with the singular subject *work*. Eliminate any answer choices that don't change *have* to *has*, which leaves you with Choices (D) and (E).

You'll notice that both Choice (D) and Choice (E) contain the verb *are*. So the pronoun *which* must refer back to *managing, keeping,* and *paying* (which, together, are plural), so the verb that corresponds to *which* has to be plural, too. Also, both choices eliminate *its* before *successful operation* because it's unclear what *its* refers to.

The difference between the two choices is that Choice (E) changes *their* to *its*. Ask yourself which noun the pronoun before *employees* refers to. Who or what has the employees? The only possibility is *business owners,* which is a plural noun. So the pronoun that refers to it must also be plural. *Their* is plural; *its* is singular. Therefore, Choice (D) is the best answer: *Much work performed by small business owners, like managing human relations, keeping track of accounts, and paying taxes, which are essential to successful operation, has gone virtually unnoticed by their employees.*

Building code violations: Faulty construction

Errors in construction threaten the stability, readability, and even existence of a sentence! You have, no doubt, been told to avoid incomplete and run-on sentences. It's equally important to avoid sentences that confuse your reader. Some sentences may not contain grammatical errors, but they can be constructed so poorly that they obscure the point. Both grammatical and rhetorical constructions rely on correct punctuation, proper ordering of clauses, and parallel sentence structure.

The most commonly tested errors in grammatical construction are sentence fragments, run-on sentences, and sentences that lack parallel structure. After you get used to them, these errors are pretty easy to spot.

Sentence fragments

Sentence fragments on the GMAT usually show up as dependent clauses pretending to convey complete thoughts or as a bunch of words with something that looks like a verb but doesn't act like one (technically, a *verbal*).

✔ **Dependent clauses standing alone are fragments because they don't present complete thoughts.** For example, this clause comes complete with a subject and verb: *Although many companies have failed to maintain consistent profits with downsizing.* However, it begins with a subordinating conjunction, *although,* so it leaves you hanging.

✔ **Phrases with a verbal instead of a verb can appear to be complete if you don't read them carefully.** The verbal phrases in this sentence look like verbs but don't function as verbs: *The peacefulness of a morning warmed by the summer sun and the verdant pastures humming with the sound of busy bees.* *Warmed* and *humming* can function as verbs in other instances, but in this sentence, they're part of phrases that provide description but don't tell what the subjects (peacefulness and pastures) are like or what they're doing.

You get the hang of recognizing sentence fragments with practice. If you read the sentence under your breath, you should be able to tell whether it expresses a complete thought.

Correcting fragments is usually pretty simple. You just add the information that completes the thought or change the verbal phrase to an actual verb. For example, you can make *although many companies have failed to maintain consistent profits with downsizing* into a complete sentence by adding a comma and *some still try,* like so: *Although many companies have failed to maintain consistent profits with downsizing, some still try.* To complete *the peacefulness of a morning warmed by the summer sun and the verdant pastures humming with the sound of busy bees,* you can change the verbal phrases: *The peacefulness of a morning is warmed by the summer sun, and the verdant pastures hum with the sound of busy bees.*

Run-on sentences

Run-on sentences occur when a sentence with multiple independent clauses is improperly punctuated. Here's an example: *I had a job interview that morning so I wore my best suit.* Both *I had a job interview* and *I wore my best suit* are independent clauses. You can't just stick a coordinating conjunction between them to make a sentence. Here are the two rules for punctuating multiple independent clauses in a sentence:

✔ **Independent clauses may be joined with a comma and a coordinating conjunction.** You can correct the problem by adding a comma, like this: *I had a job interview that morning, so I wore my best suit.*

✔ **Independent clauses may be joined by a semicolon.** The sentence can look like this: *I had a job interview that morning; I wore my best suit.*

Of course, you can change one of the independent clauses to a dependent clause, like this: *Because I had a job interview that morning, I wore my best suit.* If you do that, remember to separate the clauses with a comma when the dependent clause precedes the independent one.

The GMAT probably won't give you a run-on sentence to correct, but it may give you an answer choice that looks pretty good except that it makes the original sentence a run-on. Make sure the answer you choose doesn't create a run-on sentence.

Verb tense issues

In addition to checking for subject-verb agreement, make sure the verbs in the underlined portion of the sentence correction question are in the proper tense. The other verbs in the sentence give you clues to what tense the underlined verbs should be in.

Lack of parallelism

You can count on several sentence correction questions that test your ability to recognize a lack of parallel structure. The basic rule of parallel structure is that all phrases joined by conjunctions should be constructed in the same manner. For example, this sentence has a problem with parallelism: *Ann spent the morning e-mailing clients, responding to voice mails, and she wrote an article for the newsletter.*

The problem with the sentence is that the three phrases joined by the coordinating conjunction *(and)* in this sentence are constructed in different ways. *E-mailing* and *responding* both take the gerund (or *-ing*) form, but *she wrote* initiates a clause. Changing *wrote* to its gerund form and eliminating *she* gets rid of the clause and solves the problem: *Ann spent the morning e-mailing clients, responding to voice mails, and writing an article for the newsletter.*

Parallel structure is also a factor when you make comparisons. The following sentence lacks parallel structure: *To be physically healthy is as important as being prosperous in your work.* The sentence compares a phrase in the infinitive form, *to be physically healthy,* with a phrase in the gerund form, *being prosperous in your work.* Changing one of the constructions to match the other does the trick: *Being physically healthy is as important as being prosperous in your work.*

When you see a sentence correction question with an underlined list, check for lack of parallelism. Look for phrases joined by coordinating conjunctions. If the phrases or sentence parts exhibit dissimilar constructions, you have to correct the parallelism error.

Here's how the GMAT may question you about parallel structure:

The consultant recommended that the company <u>eliminate unneeded positions, existing departments should be consolidated, and use outsourcing when possible.</u>

- (A) eliminate unneeded positions, existing departments should be consolidated, and use outsourcing when possible

- (B) eliminate unneeded positions, consolidate existing departments, and outsource when possible

- (C) eliminate unneeded positions, existing departments should be consolidated, and when possible outsourcing used

- (D) eliminate unneeded positions and departments and use outsourcing when possible

- (E) eliminate unneeded positions, existing departments are consolidated, and outsourcing used when possible

The underlined portion of this sentence contains a list joined by *and,* which is a pretty good clue that you should be vigilant for any lack of parallelism. Because the three phrases joined by *and* are not all constructed the same way, you know there's an error, so eliminate Choice (A).

Next, eliminate the answers that don't solve the problem. Choice (C) keeps the same faulty construction as the original statement in the first two recommendations, and it introduces even more awkwardness by changing *use* to *used* and adding it to the end of the third recommendation. You can clearly eliminate Choice (C). Get rid of Choice (E) because it's also worse than the original. Each of the three elements in Choice (E) has a completely different construction.

Both Choice (B) and Choice (D) seem to correct the error by introducing each recommendation with a similar construction, but Choice (D) creates a new error because it changes the meaning of the sentence. If you select Choice (D), you're stating that some departments are also unneeded and should be eliminated. The original, however, stated that departments should be consolidated. An answer can't be correct if it changes the meaning of the original sentence, so Choice (D) is wrong.

Choice (B) solves the problem without changing the original meaning, so it's the one to choose: *The consultant recommended that the company eliminate unneeded positions, consolidate existing departments, and outsource when possible.*

Is that a rhetorical question? Other construction errors

It may surprise you to know that a GMAT sentence can be grammatically accurate and still need correction. Sentences that exhibit awkward, wordy, imprecise, redundant, or unclear constructions require fixing. The GMAT calls these *errors in rhetorical construction.* The good news is that you can often use your ear to correct these problems. The right answer will often simply sound better to you.

✔ **Using passive instead of active voice makes a sentence seem weak and wordy.** Passive voice beats around the bush to make a point, so it lacks clarity. For example, this passive voice sentence masks the doer of an action: *The speech was heard by most members of the corporation.* The sentence isn't technically incorrect, but it's better to say it this way: *Most members of the corporation heard the speech.* Notice also that the active voice sentence uses fewer words. So if all else is equal, choose active voice over passive voice.

✔ **Using repetitive language adds unnecessary words and seems silly.** A sentence shouldn't use more words than it needs to. For example, it's a bit ridiculous to say the following: *The speaker added an additional row of chairs to accommodate the large crowd.* The construction of *added an additional* isn't grammatically incorrect, but it's needlessly repetitive. It's more precise and less wordy to say *The speaker added a row of chairs to accommodate the large crowd.*

The bottom line is that any sentence that uses an excessive number of words to convey its message probably has construction problems. Often, wordiness accompanies another type of error in the underlined part. Look for the answer that uses the fewest words to correct the main error. Try it out with this sample question.

Recently, the price of crude oil <u>have been seeing fluctuations with</u> the demand for gasoline in China.

(A) have been seeing fluctuations with

(B) have fluctuated with

(C) fluctuate with

(D) has fluctuated with

(E) has changed itself along with

The main error in the sentence concerns subject-verb agreement. The singular subject, *price,* requires a singular verb. Additionally, the underlined portion is needlessly wordy. First, eliminate answer choices that don't correct the agreement problem. Then, focus on choices that clarify the language.

Both Choices (B) and (C) perpetuate the agreement problem by providing plural verbs for the singular subject. Eliminate those along with Choice (A), and you're left with Choices (D) and (E).

Choice (E) is constructed even more awkwardly than the original sentence, so Choice (D) is the best answer: *Recently, the price of crude oil has fluctuated with the demand for gasoline in China.*

Follow the idiom: Correct use of standard expressions

Idiomatic expressions are constructions English speakers use because, well, those are the expressions they use. In other words, we use certain words in certain ways for no particular reason other than because that's the way we do it. However, even native English speakers often fail to use idiomatic expressions correctly. It's common to hear people use *further* instead of *farther* when they mean distance or *less* instead of *fewer* when they're talking about the number of countable items.

The GMAT tests you on your knowledge of idiomatic expressions because sentences that are idiomatically incorrect can damage your credibility and interfere with the clarity of your message. The only way to know idiomatic constructions is to memorize them. Luckily, you probably know most of them already. To help you along, Table 3-1 lists some commonly tested idioms and how to use them correctly.

Table 3-1	**Idiomatically Correct Constructions for the GMAT**	
Expression	**Rule**	**Correct Use**
among/ between	Use *among* for comparing three or more things or persons, *between* for two things or persons.	*Between* the two of us there are few problems, but *among* the four of us there is much discord.
as . . . as	When you use *as* in a comparison, use the construction of *as . . . as.*	The dog is *as* wide *as* he is tall.
being	Don't use *being* after *regard as.*	She is *regarded as* the best salesperson on the team. (Not: She is *regarded as being* the best salesperson.)
better/best and worse/worst	Use *better* and *worse* to compare two things, *best* and *worst* to compare more than two things.	Of the two products, the first is *better* known, but this product is the *best* known of all 20 on the market.
but	Don't use *but* after *doubt* or *help.*	He could not *help* liking the chartreuse curtains with the mauve carpet. (Not: He could not *help but* like the curtains.)
different from	Use *different from* rather than *different than.*	This plan is *different from* the one we implemented last year. (Not: This plan is *different than* last year's.)
effect/affect	Generally, use *effect* as a noun and *affect* as a verb.	No one could know how the *effect* of the presentation would *affect* the client's choice.

Expression	Rule	Correct Use
farther/further	Use *farther* to refer to distance and *further* to refer to time or quantity.	Carol walked *farther* today than she did yesterday, and she vows to *further* study the benefits of walking.
hopefully	*Hopefully* is an adverb meaning *with hope* and should never be used to mean *I hope* or *it is hoped*.	*I hope* they offer me the managerial position. (Not: *Hopefully,* they'll offer me the managerial position.)
however	*However* used at the beginning of a sentence (without a comma) means *to whatever extent.*	*However* they try to discourage his antics, he continues to engage in office pranks.
imply/infer	Use *imply* to mean to suggest or indicate, *infer* to mean deduce.	From his *implication* that the car was packed, I *inferred* that it was time to leave.
in regard to	Use *in regard to* rather than *in regards to.*	The memo was *in regard to* the meeting we had yesterday. (Not: The memo was *in regards to* the meeting.)
less/fewer	Use *less* to refer to unmeasured quantity, *fewer* to refer to number.	That office building is *less* noticeable because it has *fewer* floors.
less/least	Use *less* to compare two things and *least* to compare more than two things.	He is *less* educated than his brother is, but he is not the *least* educated of his entire family.
like/as	Use *like* before simple nouns and pronouns, *as* before phrases and clauses.	*Like* Ruth, Steve wanted the office policy to be just *as* it had always been.
loan/lend	Use *loan* as a noun, *lend* as a verb.	Betty asked Julia to *lend* her a car until she received her *loan.*
many/much	Use *many* to refer to number, *much* to refer to unmeasured quantity.	For *many* days I woke up feeling *much* anxiety, but I'm better now that I'm reading *GMAT For Dummies.*
more/most	Use *more* to compare two things, *most* to compare more than two things.	Of the two girls, the older is *more* educated, and she is the *most* educated person in her family.
try/come	*Try* and *come* take the infinitive form of a subsequent verb.	*Try to* file it by tomorrow. (Not: *Try and* file it by tomorrow.)

In addition to the expressions listed in Table 3-1, you should also memorize the correlative expressions in Table 3-2, which shows you words that must appear together in the same sentence. To maintain parallel structure, the elements that follow each component of the correlative should be similar. Thus, if *not only* precedes a verb and direct object, the *but also* that follows it should also precede a verb and direct object.

Table 3-2	Correlative Expressions
Expression	Example
not only . . . but also	He *not only* had his cake *but also* ate it.
either . . . or	*Either* do it my way *or* take the highway.
neither . . . nor	*Neither* steaming locomotives *nor* wild horses can persuade me to change my mind.

Here's how you may see idioms tested on the GMAT:

Never before had American businesses confronted <u>so many challenges as they did during</u> <u>the Great Depression.</u>

(A) so many challenges as they did during the Great Depression

(B) so many challenges at one time as they confronted during the Great Depression

(C) at once so many challenges as they confronted during the Great Depression

(D) as many challenges as it did during the Great Depression

(E) as many challenges as they did during the Great Depression

You've memorized that the proper comparison construction is *as . . . as,* so you know that the sentence contains an idiomatically improper construction (it also probably sounds strange to you!). Start by eliminating all answers that don't correct *so many . . . as* to *as . . . as.* Choices (A), (B), and (C) retain the improper construction, so cross them out.

Now consider Choices (D) and (E). Both maintain the original verb, which is fine. The sentence compares two different periods of time. The first portion of the sentence refers to the period before the Great Depression, which requires the past perfect verb *had . . . confronted.* The underlined part of the sentence simply requires the past tense verb *did* to maintain the proper tense. Choice (D) creates a new error in pronoun agreement by using the singular pronoun *it* to refer to the plural noun *businesses.* Choice (E) is the correct answer: *Never before had American businesses confronted as many challenges as they did during the Great Depression.*

Implementing an Approach to Sentence Correction Questions

The key to performing well on sentence correction questions is to approach them systematically:

1. **Determine the nature of the original sentence's error (if one exists).**

   If a sentence has more than one error, focus on one error at a time. If you can, come up with a quick idea of how to fix the error before you look at the answers.

2. **Skim through the answer choices and eliminate any choices that don't correct the error.**

3. **Eliminate answer choices that correct the original error but add a new error or errors.**

   You should be left with only one answer that fixes the original problem without creating new errors.

4. **Reread the sentence with the new answer choice inserted just to make sure that you haven't missed something and that the answer you've chosen makes sense.**

To show you how this process works, we'll refer to this example question throughout the next few sections.

Because the company is disorganized, <u>they will never reach their goal</u>.

(A) they will never reach their goal

(B) it will never reach their goal

(C) it will never reach its goal

(D) their goal will never be reached

(E) its goal will never be reached

Spotting the error

When you read the sentence correction question, pay particular attention to the underlined portion and look for at least one error.

- ✔ If the underlined section contains verbs, make sure they agree with their subjects and are in the proper tense.

- ✔ Check any pronouns to determine whether they agree in number with the nouns they refer to.

- ✔ Look at lists to confirm that their construction is parallel.

- ✔ Note any tricky idiomatic phrases to verify that they're used correctly.

- ✔ Look for repetitive and otherwise wordy language.

If you don't see any obvious errors, read through the answer choices just to make sure they don't reveal something you may have missed. If you still don't see a problem, choose the first answer choice. About 20 percent of the sentence correction sentences contain no errors.

Don't look for errors in the portion of the sentence that isn't underlined. Even if you find something, you can't correct it!

The underlined portion of the sample question contains a verb *(will reach),* but it agrees with its subject and is in the proper tense. There's also a pronoun, *they. They* refers to company, but *company* is a singular noun and *they* is a plural pronoun. You can't have a plural pronoun refer to a singular noun. Therefore, the underlined section definitely has a pronoun agreement error.

Eliminating answers that don't correct errors

If you spot an error in the underlined portion, read through the answer choices and eliminate those that don't correct it. If you see more than one error in the underlined portion of the statement, begin with the error that has the more obvious correction. For example, if the underlined portion has both a rhetorical error and an error in subject-verb agreement, begin with the error in subject-verb agreement. Eliminating answer choices that don't address the agreement problem is quick and easy. After you've eliminated the choices that don't fix the obvious error, move on to the other error or errors. Comparing rhetorical constructions in answer choices can take a while, so eliminating choices before this step saves you time.

After you've eliminated an answer choice, don't reread it! Chapter 2 gives you tips on how to "erase" wrong answer choices. Follow the guidelines in Chapter 2 to avoid wasting time on answers you've already determined are wrong.

You know the example problem has an error, so you can eliminate Choice (A). Now eliminate any choices that don't correct the incorrect pronoun reference. Choice (D) doesn't; it still uses a plural pronoun *(their)* to refer to a singular subject. Eliminate Choice (D), and don't look at it again. The other three choices, Choices (B), (C), and (E), seem to fix that particular pronoun error.

The underlined portion contains another problem with noun-pronoun agreement, though. *Their* in the original sentence is also plural but refers to the singular noun *company.* Although Choice (B) makes the first plural pronoun singular, it retains the second problem pronoun, so you can eliminate Choice (B). Only Choices (C) and (E) remain.

Eliminating choices that create new errors

The next step is to eliminate answers that create new errors.

A new error in an answer choice usually isn't the same type of error as the original one. GMAT writers know you'll look for pronoun errors if a pronoun error occurs in the original sentence, so the new error in an answer choice may be an improper expression or a verb tense problem.

Check the remaining answer choices for new errors. Choice (E) doesn't contain an agreement error, but it changes the underlined portion of the sentence to a passive construction. On sentence corrections, active voice is always better than passive voice. Choice (C) is the answer that corrects the pronoun problem without creating new errors.

You should end up with only one answer choice that corrects the existing errors without creating new ones. If you end up with two seemingly correct answer choices, read them both within the context of the original sentence. One will have an error that you've overlooked.

Rereading the sentence

Don't skip this step! Check your answer by replacing the underlined portion with your answer choice and reading the new sentence in its entirety. Don't just check to see whether the answer sounds good in the sentence; also check for errors that you may not have noticed as you worked through the question.

Missing errors is easy when you focus only on the underlined portion of the statement. After you integrate your answer choice with the rest of the sentence, errors you've missed may suddenly become obvious. Reading the statement with your answer choice inserted is the best way to check your answer.

When you reread the sentence with Choice (C), you get this: *Because the company is disorganized, it will never reach its goal.* The corrected sentence contains the proper noun-pronoun agreement.

Reviewing the process and guessing on sentence corrections

The approach outlined in this section works well as long as you have time to determine the error in the sentence or recognize that no error exists. If you're running short on time or can't tell whether the statement is correct as written, you may need to guess. Eliminate the choices you know are wrong because they contain their own errors. Then read each of the possible choices in the context of the entire statement. You may find errors that you didn't notice before. If you still can't narrow down your choices to one answer, pick one from the remaining answers and move on.

Sentence Correction Practice Problems with Answer Explanations

After you master the approach to sentence correction questions, they'll seem a lot less daunting. To help you solidify your plan of attack, answer the following eight practice questions. Try to answer them in eight minutes or less. When you're finished, check your answers with the explanations that follow.

Practice problems

1. Most state governors now have the power of line item veto, <u>while the U.S. President does not</u>.

   (A) while the U.S. President does not

   (B) a power which is not yet available to the U.S. President

   (C) which the U.S. President has no such power

   (D) the U.S. President does not

   (E) they do not share that with the U.S. President

2. Although all state governments faced budget problems after the economic downturn of 2007, the problems were <u>worse</u> in states with high-tech industries.

   (A) worse

   (B) worst

   (C) more

   (D) great

   (E) worsening

3. The PTA held monthly meetings to discuss matters concerning the schoolchildren, determine what fundraisers to implement, <u>and for coming up with ways to balance the budget</u>.

   (A) and for coming up with ways to balance the budget

   (B) and to balance the budget in creative ways

   (C) and discovering ways to balance the budget

   (D) and to determine how to come up with ways the budget should be balanced

   (E) and come up with ways to balance the budget

4. Many tourists <u>seem to be avoiding the Tijuana/Rosarito Beach area because they are experiencing an upsurge in the occurrence of border violence</u>.

   (A) seem to be avoiding the Tijuana/Rosarito Beach area because they are experiencing an upsurge in the occurrence of border violence

   (B) seem to avoid the Tijuana/Rosarito Beach area because they are experiencing an upsurge of violence on the border

   (C) avoid the Tijuana/Rosarito Beach area because they are experiencing an upsurge of border violence occurrence

   (D) seem to be avoiding the Tijuana/Rosarito Beach area because it is experiencing an upsurge in the occurrence of border violence

   (E) seem to be avoiding the Tijuana/Rosarito Beach area because it experiences an upsurge in the occurrence of border violence

5. Historians believe that roughly 600 deaths have occurred at the Grand Canyon since the 1870s; <u>many resulted from drowning, plane crashes into canyon walls</u>, and the actions of overzealous hikers.

   (A) many resulted from drowning, plane crashes into canyon walls

   (B) many of these resulting from drowning deaths, planes crashing into canyon walls

   (C) many of these deaths being the results of drowning, plane crashes into canyon walls

   (D) many of these were drowning deaths, plane crash deaths

   (E) with many as a result from drowning, planes crashing into canyon walls

6. After Great America Bank incited public outrage with its announcement of new debit card fees, many customers withdrew their funds and joined credit unions instead, which seems <u>as if to indicate that</u> America's mistrust of big banks is still widespread.

   (A) as if to indicate that

   (B) indicative of

   (C) like an indication of

   (D) like it is indicative that

   (E) to indicate that

7. Despite arguments made by parent watch-dog groups, <u>neither violent behavior or disruptiveness have been directly linked to violent video games</u>.

   (A) neither violent behavior or disruptiveness have been directly linked to violent video games

   (B) neither violent behavior nor disruptiveness has been directly linked to violent video games

   (C) neither violent behavior or disruptiveness have been directly linked to violent video games

   (D) neither violent behavior nor disruptiveness have been directly linked to violent video games

   (E) neither violent behavior nor disruptiveness were directly linked to violent video games

8. Russell & Carmody, LLC, and Rutledge, Inc., merged in 2012 to create Russell, Carmody and Rutledge, Inc., <u>and they are now the most successful public relations firm in the metro area</u>.

   (A) and they are now the most successful public relations firm in the metro area

   (B) it is now the most successful public relations firm in the metro area

   (C) and they are now the most successful public relations firms in the metro area

   (D) which is now the most successful public relations firm in the metro area

   (E) and it is now the most successful public relations firms in the metro area

Answer explanations

1. **A.** Always begin by trying to identify the error in the underlined portion of the statement. The underlined words don't contain any pronouns and the subject and verb agree, so you don't have any agreement errors. Parallel construction doesn't seem to be an issue. The use of *while* to mean *although* may have alerted you. However, while the primary purpose of *while* is to indicate an event that happens at the same time as another, you may also use *while* to mean *although*. In fact, we just used it that way in the previous sentence!

   This question doesn't seem to have an error. But just to be sure, read each answer choice to make sure you haven't missed something. Choice (B) is wrong because it uses *which* instead of *that* to introduce a restrictive clause, and the pronoun *which* in Choice (C) has no clear reference. You can't use Choice (D) or Choice (E) because they're independent clauses. Plugging in either of these choices creates a comma splice. None of the answer choices offer a better construction for the sentence.

   Remember that about 20 percent of the time, the underlined part contains no error. Don't assume that the sentences always contain errors.

2. **B.** This example has only one underlined word, which is nice because you know just what to focus on. If you were to simply go by what sounds right, you may think this example is fine the way it is. You probably hear English speakers use *worse* like this in everyday conversations. But the GMAT doesn't test common spoken English; it tests *standard written English*.

   You use *worse* to compare two entities and *worst* to compare three or more.

   The sentence talks about a situation among *all state governments*. *Worse* would be appropriate for a comparison between two states or two groups of states. But this sentence compares budget problems in *all* the states, so use the superlative form *worst* instead. That's the answer you find in Choice (B).

   You can double-check your answer by reading through the other choices. You've found an error, so Choice (A) can't be right. Choices (C) and (D) aren't superlatives, and Choice (E) uses the progressive form *were worsening*, which changes the meaning of the sentence.

3. **E.** The underlined words are part of a series, so adjust your error antennae to feel out a parallelism problem. Check the grammatical construction of each element. The underlined portion contains the gerund form *coming*, but the other two PTA purposes are expressed in the infinitive form. All three reasons should be in the same form. Both Choices (A) and (C) use the *-ing* form, so they can't be right. Choice (D) is unnecessarily wordy, so now you know the correct answer must be either Choice (B) or Choice (E). Both choices properly use the infinitive form, but Choice (B) unnecessarily repeats *to* and it adds information to the original sentence.

4. **D.** The underlined portion is lengthy, so use your powers of concentration to home in on the potential errors. You see a couple verbs and the pronoun *they*. Check the pronoun first.

Whenever you see an underlined pronoun, check its reference to make sure it's clear and that it agrees in number with the noun.

The pronoun *they* is plural, but the only plural noun in the sentence is *tourists*. It doesn't make sense that tourists would be experiencing an upsurge in the occurrence of border violence. It's more likely that *they* refers to the beach area, which is experiencing increased violence. Only one area is mentioned, so the pronoun should be singular, *it*. That narrows your choices considerably. The only two answers that change *they* to *it* are Choices (D) and (E). The difference between the two is that Choice (E) changes the verb tense to the simple present. The upsurge is ongoing, so the original progressive tense in Choice (D) is better.

5. **A.** The first thing you likely notice about the underlined part is that it contains a series of causes of Grand Canyon deaths. An underlined series means check for parallel structure. Each cause is presented as a noun, so there isn't a blatant problem with parallelism. Some of the answer choices change *plane crashes* to *planes crashing* to match *drowning,* but they introduce new errors. Choices (B), (C), and (E) create sentence fragments, which don't work with the semicolon. The semicolon has to be followed by an independent clause. Choice (D) unnecessarily repeats *deaths*. It doesn't make sense to say the deaths result from drowning deaths. The best answer is to leave this one exactly as it is.

6. **E.** To say that something *seems as if to* is improper, so Choice (A) is out. You can eliminate Choices (B) and (C) as well, because their use of *of* doesn't fit with the rest of the sentence. You use *like* to compare simple nouns, and Choice (D) improperly uses *like* to compare *which* to the clause *it is indicative*. The best answer has to be Choice (E). It gets rid of *as if* without creating another error.

7. **B.** The original sentence contains both a conjunction error and a subject-verb agreement error.

Whenever you see *neither,* you must also see *nor.* Neither Choice (A) nor Choice (C) pairs *nor* with *neither*. Eliminate them.

You're left with Choices (B), (D), and (E). The verbs in these three choices are different. Choice (B) contains a singular verb, and the other two have plural verbs. The subject of the clause is *neither,* and *neither* is singular. Therefore, Choice (B) has to be correct because it contains the singular verb.

8. **D.** This sentence correction question involves a commonly tested pronoun reference problem. Although the sentence initially refers to two separate companies, it then states that they merged into one firm, so the correct pronoun to use when referring to only one company is *it*. Therefore, you can eliminate Choices (A) and (C). Choice (E) contains the proper pronoun, *it,* but refers to the new company in the plural, *firms,* so you can cross that one out as well. You're left with Choices (B) and (D), but Choice (B) creates a comma splice because it's an independent clause.

Chapter 4

Not as Enticing as a Bestseller: Reading Comprehension

In This Chapter

▶ Getting familiar with the format of reading comprehension questions

▶ Reading through passages efficiently

▶ Taking a look at the kinds of passages that appear on the GMAT

▶ Checking out the types of reading questions

*I*f you find yourself reading approximately 350 words about white dwarfs in space, you're not encountering a sci-fi fable about the seven companions of an astronomical Snow White. You're more likely tackling a reading comprehension problem on the GMAT. The GMAT test-makers present yet another way to poke and prod your intellect with several paragraphs of fascinating reading material and a few questions to test your comprehension of it. The questions may be specific and focus on highlighted portions of the passage, or they may concern general themes, like the author's main idea.

Reading comprehension questions are designed to test how well you understand unfamiliar reading material. But you're probably less concerned with the reason these passages are included on the GMAT than you are with getting through all that reading and question-answering with enough time left over to confront those pesky sentence correction and critical reasoning problems. What you need is a proven strategy. And in this chapter, we deliver by introducing you to the types of passages and questions you'll encounter and telling you how to deal with them.

Judging by Appearances: What Reading Comprehension Questions Look Like

The verbal section of the GMAT mixes reading comprehension questions with critical reasoning questions and sentence correction questions. So you may correct grammatical errors in a few sentences and then come across a set of reading comprehension questions. About one-third of the 41 questions in the verbal section are reading questions. You'll see a split screen with an article passage on the left and a question with five answer choices on the right.

Although every passage has more than one question (usually, passages have about 5 to 8 questions), only one question pops up at a time. You read the passage (which contains about 350 words), click on the choice that best answers the question, and confirm your answer. As soon as you confirm your answer, another question pops up on the right side of the screen. The passage remains on the left. Sometimes a question refers to a particular part of the passage. For these questions, the GMAT highlights the portion of the passage you need to focus on to answer the question.

Approaching Reading Passages

Reading comprehension questions don't ask you to do anything particularly unfamiliar. You've probably been reading passages and answering multiple-choice questions about them since you were in elementary school. If you're having difficulty answering reading comprehension questions correctly, don't worry: Your reading skills are likely fine. You're probably just not familiar with the specific way you have to read for the GMAT.

You have less than two minutes to answer each reading comprehension question, and that includes reading the passage. Generally, you shouldn't spend more than five minutes reading a passage before you answer its questions, so you have to read as efficiently as you can. You need a plan for getting through the passage in a way that allows you to answer questions correctly and quickly. When you read a passage, focus on the following elements:

✔ The passage's general theme

✔ The author's tone

✔ The way the author organizes the passage

Unless you have a photographic memory, you won't be able to remember all a passage's details long enough to answer the questions. Don't try to figure out the passage's minutiae while you're reading it. If you encounter a question about a little detail, you can go back and reread the relevant section. Instead of sweating the small stuff, make sure you understand the author's main point, the author's tone, and the overall way the author presents the information.

Mastering the message: The main point

Generally, people write passages to inform or persuade. Most of the passages on the GMAT are informative rather than argumentative, and even the argumentative ones are pretty tame.

The main point of GMAT passages is often *to discuss a topic, to inform the reader about a phenomenon,* or *to compare one idea to another.* Rarely does a GMAT passage seek to condemn, criticize, or enthusiastically advocate a particular idea or position.

Because most authors present the main theme in the first paragraph or two, you'll probably figure it out in the first few seconds of your reading. If it's not clear in the first paragraphs, it probably appears in the last paragraph, when the author sums up the ideas. After you've figured out what the author's overall theme is, quickly jot down on your noteboard a word or two to help you remember the theme. For a passage that describes the differences between the flight patterns of houseflies and horseflies, you can write *compare flight — house/horse.* Your notation gives you something to refer to when you're asked the inevitable main theme synthesis question (which we discuss in greater detail in the later section "Getting to the point: Main theme questions").

Absorbing the ambiance: Author's tone

In addition to understanding the author's main point, you need to know how the author feels about the issue. You get clues to the author's tone or mood by the words he or she uses. GMAT passages either inform the reader about something or try to persuade the reader to adopt the author's viewpoint. Informative passages are often more objective than persuasive ones, so the author's tone is usually neutral. Authors of persuasive passages may exhibit more emotion. You may sense that an author is critical, sarcastic, pessimistic, optimistic, or supportive. When you figure out how the author feels about the topic, write a short description on your noteboard, like *objective, hopeful,* or *mildly critical.* Knowing the tone of a passage helps you choose answers that exhibit the same tone or level of bias.

Regardless of the author's mood, don't let your personal opinions about a passage's subject matter influence your answer. Getting emotionally involved with the content of the passage can cloud your judgment. You may subconsciously rely on your opinions as you answer questions. To avoid doing so, you may find it helpful to remind yourself that correct answers are true *according to the passage* or *according to the author.*

Finding the framework: The passage's outline

Knowing the structure of a passage is much more important than understanding its details. Instead of trying to comprehend everything the author says, focus on how the author lays out the information.

Standard essay format includes an introduction with a thesis, two or three supporting paragraphs, and a conclusion. Many GMAT passages are excerpts from larger works, so they may not exhibit exact standard essay form, but they'll contain evidence of all three elements. As you read, determine the passage's overall point and the main points of each paragraph.

You may find it helpful to construct a mini-outline of the passage as you read it. Underneath the main theme, jot down a word or two on your noteboard that describes the type of information contained in each paragraph. So under *compare flight — house/horse,* you may list a synopsis of each supporting paragraph: *difference in wingspan, size difference — horse 3x bigger, ways flight helps house.* This outline tells you that in the first supporting paragraph, you find info about how the two flies differ in wingspan. The second supporting paragraph is where you find out how the greater size of horseflies affects their flight. And from the third supporting paragraph, you find out how the housefly's flight helps it in everyday life. Although you may not understand all the fascinating details of the author's account, you know where to go in the passage if you have to answer a detail question.

Building an outline in your head or on your noteboard helps you know where in the passage you can find answers to questions about particular details. Doing so also helps you answer any questions that ask you *how* an author develops his or her point.

Even though you don't need to read and understand every detail of a passage before you answer its questions, we highly recommend that you scan the entire passage before you attempt the questions. You need an idea of what a passage is about and how it's organized before you look at the questions. Any minutes you save by not reading the passage first will be wasted when you have to read and reread paragraphs because you don't know where information is located or what the passage is about.

Sticking to the Subject: Types of Passages

You may think that because the GMAT measures your aptitude for MBA programs, its reading passages deal with subjects like marketing and economics. You're wrong. Although some of the passages do concern business matters, you'll also read about topics from the natural and social sciences. The GMAT wants to see how well you analyze a variety of topics, unfamiliar and familiar, so it presents you with articles about everything from the steel-making process to the quality of artifacts from the Bronze Age.

In the following sections, we explore the types of reading passages found on the GMAT.

Experimenting with natural science passages

Physical and biological sciences mean big business. Some of the areas of commerce that depend on science include pharmaceuticals, computers, agriculture, the defense industry, household products, and materials manufacturing (such as plastics and polymers). These industries, taken together, exert a huge influence on American quality of life and the nation's bottom line. Just think of this country without computers and pharmaceuticals, not to mention modern agriculture!

Although you may concede that the natural sciences are important, you may not be eager to confront a chemistry passage halfway through the GMAT verbal section. The good news is that the reading comprehension questions don't assume that you have any previous knowledge in the subject. If you do come across a reading passage on chemistry and it's been 20 years since you've studied the periodic table, relax. The answer to every question is located somewhere in the passage.

You really don't need to know a lot about a passage topic to answer the questions correctly. Although it's true that a chemistry major may read a passage about polymers more quickly than someone who never took a college chemistry course, that doesn't necessarily mean the chemistry expert will answer more questions correctly. The chemistry major may actually be at a disadvantage because he or she may try to answer questions based on outside knowledge instead of using only the information stated in the passage.

Reading comprehension questions test your reading skills, not the plethora of details you keep tucked away in your long-term memory. When you come across a passage on a subject that you're familiar with, don't rely on your outside knowledge to answer the question! Make sure the answers you choose can be justified by information contained in the passage.

Natural science passages tend to be more objective and neutral than persuasive in tone. So usually the main theme of a natural science topic is *to explain, describe,* or *inform* about a scientific event.

Gathering in social circles: Social science passages

In addition to natural science passages, the GMAT presents passages about a different kind of science: social science, which includes topics like law, philosophy, history, political science, archeology, sociology, and psychology. The good news about social science passages is that their topics tend to crop up more in the news and in daily conversation than does, for example, physics! So you're more likely to be comfortable, if not necessarily familiar, with them.

Although passages about the social sciences are still mostly descriptive and informative, they're more likely to be persuasive than natural science passages, so you may see more variety in the kinds of tones these passages display.

Getting down to business passages

Business passages may be objective or persuasive and are generated from fields like economics, marketing, resource management, and accounting, among others. Finally, topics you're familiar with! You can forgo the archeology of New Zealand or an anatomy lesson on the long-horned beetle. This is business, your chosen field of study. At least it's a topic you're clearly interested in. You'll probably breeze right through most of these passages. But don't let familiarity with the topic serve as an excuse to slack off. You need your powers of concentration for every passage topic.

If the passage is on a familiar subject, don't fall into the trap of using your own information to answer questions. Being familiar with a passage topic is an advantage, but only if you approach each question reminding yourself that the correct answer is based on information in the passage and not on what you studied last semester in your marketing courses or discussed last week in your sales meeting.

Approaching Reading Comprehension Questions

The GMAT verbal section has 41 questions, and you're allotted 75 minutes to answer them. That comes out to less than two minutes per question. If you spend too much time answering reading comprehension questions, you'll have less time to consider the sentence correction and critical reasoning questions that also comprise the verbal section. So having a system for tackling reading comprehension questions is just as important as knowing how to read through the passages. Your approach should include

- Recognizing the type of question
- Quickly eliminating incorrect answer choices
- Managing questions that ask for the answer that *isn't* supported by the passage

We show you how to do all three of these things in the following sections and provide a few examples of what to look for so you know how to answer the questions correctly.

Identifying the question type

The first step in answering a reading comprehension question correctly is identifying the type of question. Most reading comprehension questions fall into one of these four categories:

- Summarizing the main theme
- Finding specific information
- Making inferences
- Assessing the author's tone

Each of the four question types requires a slightly different approach. Main theme and tone questions ask you to make determinations about the passage as a whole, and specific information and inference questions usually ask you to home in on particular parts of the passage. For example, when you know that a question is about specific details in the passage, you can focus your attention on the portion of the passage that's relevant to the information in the question.

We share all the details about each of the four categories of reading comprehension questions in the following sections.

Getting to the point: Main theme questions

Main theme questions ask you to identify the primary purpose of the whole passage. Almost every passage has at least one question that asks you to identify the thesis of the passage, and often it's the first question you answer for a particular reading passage.

You can identify main theme questions by the language they contain. Here are some examples of the ways main theme questions may be worded:

> ✔ The author of the passage is primarily concerned with which of the following?
>
> ✔ The author's primary goal (or purpose) in the passage is to do which of the following?
>
> ✔ An appropriate title that best summarizes this passage is

While you read the passage, look for its main theme because you know you'll probably be asked about it. You may even want to write a sentence that briefly states the passage's primary purpose. Then, if you're asked a question about the passage's main theme, you'll look for an answer that conveys an idea similar to your statement of the author's purpose.

The best answer to a main theme question is general rather than specific. If an answer choice concerns information that's discussed in only one part of the passage, it probably isn't the correct answer to a main theme question. Here are some other ways to narrow in on the correct answer for main theme questions:

> ✔ Eliminate answer choices that contain information that comes only from the middle paragraphs of the passage. These paragraphs probably deal with specific points rather than the main theme.
>
> ✔ Eliminate any answer choices that contain information that you can't find in the passage. These choices are irrelevant.
>
> ✔ Look at the first words of the answer choices to see whether you can eliminate any answer choices based on the first words only. For example, if you're trying to find the best answer to the author's purpose in an objectively written natural science passage, you can eliminate answers that begin with less objective terms, such as *to argue that . . ., to criticize . . .,* and *to refute the opposition's position that. . . .*

Finding the details: Specific information questions

Some GMAT reading comprehension questions ask you about specific statements in the passage. These questions are potentially the easiest type of reading comprehension question because the information you need to answer them is stated in the passage. You just need to find it. This information may be quantitative, such as years, figures, or numbers, or it may be qualitative, like ideas, emotions, or thoughts.

Specific information questions are worded in many different ways, but they almost always contain some reference to the passage. For example:

> ✔ The passage states that . . .
>
> ✔ According to the passage, . . .
>
> ✔ In the passage, the author indicates that . . .

Sometimes, the GMAT highlights in yellow the portion of the passage that discusses the material in question. If the test highlights information for you, you know that you'll be doing more than just finding an answer that duplicates the wording in the passage.

To succeed on specific information questions, read the question carefully and refer to the outline of the passage you've written on your noteboard to remind you where the passage addresses certain types of information. And keep in mind that the correct answer may paraphrase the passage rather than provide a word-for-word repeat.

Reading between the lines: Inference questions

Inference questions ask you about information that's *implied* by the passage rather than directly stated. These questions test your ability to draw conclusions, using evidence that appears in the passage. For inference questions, you're normally required to do one of these three things:

✔ Identify a different interpretation of an author's statement.

✔ Infer the intended meaning of a word that's used figuratively in the passage.

✔ Interpret the author's statements one step beyond what is actually written.

For example, suppose you read a passage that compares the rapidity of wing beats between houseflies and horseflies. Information in the second paragraph may state that the wings of horseflies beat at 96 bps (beats per second). Information in the fourth paragraph may say that a Purple Winger is a type of horsefly. From this information, you can infer that the wings of the Purple Winger beat at a rate of 96 bps. This is an example of the third bullet: taking the author's statements one step beyond what is actually written. Note that the horsefly conclusion doesn't require that you make great leaps of logic.

When you're answering an inference question, look for the choice that slightly extends the meaning of the passage. Choices that go beyond the scope of the passage are usually incorrect. Don't choose an answer that requires you to come up with information that isn't somehow addressed by the passage.

Sometimes knowing a great deal about a passage's topic can be a detriment, because you may be tempted to answer questions based on your own knowledge rather than the passage itself. Simply answer the questions as they're asked, and make inferences that can be justified by information in the passage.

The GMAT loves inference questions, so expect to see a lot of them. They're easily recognizable because they usually contain either *infer* or *imply* in the question, like these examples:

✔ It can be inferred from the passage that . . .

✔ The passage implies (or suggests) that . . .

✔ The author brings up . . . to imply which of the following?

Feeling moody: Questions about the author's tone and style

As you read the passage, be sure to look for clues to the author's tone as well as his or her purpose. You're bound to see questions that ask you to gauge how the author feels about the topic. Tone and style questions commonly ask you to figure out the author's attitude or complete the logical flow of the author's ideas. The author may be neutral, negative, or positive and may have different attitudes about different types of information within the same passage. It's up to you to determine the nature and degree of the author's feeling from the language used in the passage. With practice, you'll figure out how to distinguish between an enthusiastic author and one who's faking enthusiasm to mock the subject of the passage.

You can recognize questions about tone and style by the way they're worded. Here are some examples of how tone and style questions may appear on the GMAT:

- ✔ The author's attitude appears to be one of . . .
- ✔ With which of the following statements would the author most likely agree?
- ✔ The tone of the passage suggests that the author is most skeptical about which of the following?

When making determinations about the author's style and tone, consider the passage as a whole. You may find one or two examples of praise in an article that is otherwise over-whelmingly critical of a subject. Don't make the mistake of quickly categorizing the passage from a few words that happen to catch your attention. Instead, determine the main idea of the passage and the author's purpose (you need to do this to answer other questions, anyway) and use that information to help you discern the author's style and tone. For example, if an author's purpose is to argue against a particular point of view, critical words regarding the proponents of that viewpoint reveal an overall critical attitude. However, you wouldn't say the same about an author of a passage that supports a viewpoint overall but includes one or two criticisms about some supporters of the viewpoint.

Style and tone questions may point you to a specific portion of a passage, or they may be about the entire passage. Even if a question does reference a specific part of the text, it'll do so in relation to the passage as a whole. For example, you can usually answer a question that asks you why an author chose to use certain words in a particular sentence only within the context of the entire passage. So if you know the main idea, author's purpose, and tone of the entire passage, you should be able to effectively deal with questions about the use of a particular word or phrase in one part of the passage.

Eliminating answer choices

One of the most effective ways of moving through reading comprehension questions is to eliminate incorrect answer choices. That's because you're looking for the best answer choice, not necessarily the perfect answer choice. Sometimes, you'll have to choose the best choice out of five pretty great choices, and other times you'll choose from five really crummy ones. Because the definitive answer usually won't pop right out at you, you have to know how to eliminate obviously wrong choices. Chapter 2 gives you general tips for eliminating answer choices. In this section, we show you how to apply those techniques specifically to reading comprehension questions.

Much of the time, you can eliminate wrong choices without having to refer back to the passage. As long as you carefully read the passage and have a good idea of the main theme, the author's purpose in writing the selection, and the author's style or tone, you should be able to recognize some wrong answers immediately.

Some common wrong answers include the following:

- ✔ **Choices that concern information that isn't found in the passage:** Some answer choices contain information that's beyond the scope of the passage. Even if the information in these choices is true, you can't choose them. You have to choose answers based on what's stated or implied in the passage. Eliminate these choices, no matter how tempting they may be.

- ✔ **Choices that contradict the main theme, author's tone, or specific information in the passage:** After you've read through the passage, you should be able to quickly eliminate most of the choices that contradict what you know about the passage.

✔ **Choices that counter the wording of the question:** You can also eliminate some answer choices by paying careful attention to the wording of the question. For example, a question may ask about a *disadvantage* of something discussed in the passage. If one of the answer choices lists an advantage instead of a disadvantage, you can eliminate that choice without thinking too much about it. Or a question may ask you to choose which answer the author is most optimistic about. If one of the things listed is something the author is negative about, you can eliminate that choice.

The GMAT may try to entice you with answer choices that deal with information directly stated in the passage but don't relate to the actual question at hand. Don't choose an answer just because it looks familiar. Make sure it actually answers the question.

✔ **Choices that contain *debatable* words:** Question any answer choice that uses absolutes. Examples are *all, always, complete, never, every,* and *none*. An answer choice that contains a word that leaves no room for exception is probably wrong. The GMAT makers don't want you calling them up complaining that you know of a circumstance where, say, not all fire engines are red. Beware: Usually the rest of an answer choice that includes a debatable word sounds pretty good, so you may be tempted to choose it.

Don't automatically eliminate an answer choice that contains a debatable word. If information in the passage justifies the presence of *all* or *none* in an answer choice, it may be right. For example, if a passage tells you that all horseflies beat their wings at a rate of 96 bps, the choice with *all* in it may be accurate.

Dealing with exception questions

Most questions ask you to choose the one correct answer, but some questions are cleverly disguised to ask for the *one* false answer. We call these gems *exception questions*. You'll recognize these questions by the presence of a negative word, usually *except* or *not*. When you see these words capitalized in a question, you know you're looking for the one answer choice that *doesn't* satisfy the requirements of the question.

You won't see many exception questions on the GMAT, but when you do see that negative word, take a moment to make sure you know exactly what the question is asking. Don't get confused or rush and automatically choose the first choice that looks good. ***Remember:*** The question is asking for the *one* answer out of five that's false or not part of the information stated or implied in the passage.

Exception questions aren't that difficult if you approach them systematically. Determining that an answer definitely isn't discussed in the passage takes time. You have to carefully look through the passage for the choice and *not* find it — then check again just to be sure. But a better way does exist: Instead of determining that an answer isn't discussed, eliminate the four true answers, which leaves you with the one false (and, therefore, correct) answer.

Identifying those choices that *do* appear in the passage is much easier than determining the one choice that isn't in the passage. After you've identified the four correct answers (remember to use your erasable noteboard to keep track), you can click on the one false answer as the choice for that question.

Take a look at two exception questions based on a fairly difficult natural science passage.

This passage is excerpted from *The Earth Through Time*, 7th Edition, by Harold L. Levin (Wiley).

Geologists have proposed the term *eon* for the largest divisions of the geologic time scale. In chronologic succession, the eons of geologic time are the Hadean, Archean, Proterozoic, and Phanerozoic. The beginning of the Archean corresponds approximately to the ages of the oldest known rocks on Earth. Although not universally used, the term

Hadean refers to that period of time for which we have no rock record, which began with the origin of the planet 4.6 billion years ago. The Proterozoic Eon refers to the time interval from 2,500 to 544 million years ago.

The rocks of the Archean and Proterozoic are informally referred to as Precambrian. The antiquity of Precambrian rocks was recognized in the mid-1700s by Johann G. Lehman, a professor of mineralogy in Berlin, who referred to them as the "Primary Series." One frequently finds this term in the writing of French and Italian geologists who were contemporaries of Lehman. In 1833, the term appeared again when Lyell used it in his formation of a surprisingly modern geologic time scale. Lyell and his predecessors recognized these "primary" rocks by their crystalline character and took their uppermost boundary to be an unconformity that separated them from the overlying — and therefore younger — fossiliferous strata.

The remainder of geologic time is included in the Phanerozoic Eon. As a result of careful study of the superposition of rock bodies accompanied by correlations based on the abundant fossil record of the Phanerozoic, geologists have divided it into three major subdivisions, termed eras. The oldest is the Paleozoic Era, which we now know lasted about 300 million years. Following the Paleozoic is the Mesozoic Era, which continued for about 179 million years. The Cenozoic Era, in which we are now living, began about 65 million years ago.

The passage uses all the following terms to describe *eons* or *eras,* except

(A) Archean

(B) Paleozoic

(C) Holocene

(D) Phanerozoic

(E) Cenozoic

The terms in this passage may be unfamiliar to you, but if you read the passage carefully, you should be able to get a general sense of what it's talking about. For this exception question, which tests you on unfamiliar terms, the best way to approach the question is to consult the text and eliminate the four terms that it uses to describe eons or eras.

First, scan the answer choices so you have an idea of the words you're looking for. Then begin at the top of the passage and look for words that resemble the answer choices. You should be especially aware of any lists that occur in the text, because exception questions often focus on lists. It's very difficult for test-makers to come up with a good exception question without a list.

The passage contains three lists. The first one appears in the first paragraph. It names eons of geologic time. The question refers to eons, and uses four terms that certainly resemble the answer choices. Consult this first list and eliminate any choices that appear on it. The terms *Archean* and *Phanerozoic* appear, so you can eliminate Choices (A) and (D). In the second paragraph, you see the term *Precambrian* (which isn't an answer choice) and a list of geologists who have mentioned Precambrian rocks. The second paragraph doesn't help with this question, so move quickly to the third paragraph.

The third paragraph also provides a list of eras that are part of the Phanerozoic eon. In this list, you see the terms *Paleozoic, Mesozoic,* and *Cenozoic. Paleozoic* is Choice (B), and *Cenozoic* is Choice (E), so you can eliminate both of these terms. Therefore, the correct answer to this exception question is Choice (C), *Holocene,* which isn't mentioned in the passage and, in fact, is neither an eon nor an era but the epoch in which you're living!

Here's another exception question based on the same passage.

Which of the following terms is *not* used in the passage to describe rocks that are more than 544 million years old?

(A) Precambrian

(B) Cenozoic

(C) Primary Series

(D) Archean

(E) Proterozoic

This question is more difficult because all the terms appear in the passage, but one of them doesn't apply to rocks that are more than 544 million years old. Begin in the same way you did for the previous question, by scanning the answer choices so you know the kinds of words you're looking for.

When you find a term, don't automatically eliminate it. In this example, you must confirm that it refers to rocks more than 544 million years old before you can cross it off.

The list in the second sentence of the first paragraph doesn't help because it has no corresponding dates for the eons. The next sentence, however, says that *Archean* rocks are the "oldest known rocks on Earth." You can probably eliminate Choice (D), but keep reading to be sure. The last sentence of the paragraph says that Proterozoic rocks are 544 million to 2,500 million (2.5 billion) years old. And because Archean rocks are older than that, you can eliminate both Choices (D) and (E).

At the beginning of the second paragraph, you discover that both Archean and Proterozoic rocks are referred to as *Precambrian.* Because both types of rock are older than 544 million years, you can also eliminate Choice (A). Finally, in the very next sentence, you find out that Precambrian rocks are also called *Primary Series* rocks, so you can eliminate Choice (C). Choice (B) is the correct answer.

You'd also know that Choice (B) is the correct answer if you happen to look at the last sentence of the passage. That sentence tells you that the Cenozoic era started just 65 million years ago. The question asks for the rocks that are *not* older than 544 million years. Clearly, Cenozoic rocks are, at most, 65 million years old. So Choice (B) must be the one.

You can definitely skip the elimination process if you happen to stumble onto the right information, but that haphazard method won't work for all elimination questions. You're better off approaching the question by eliminating the four answers that you find in the passage or that satisfy the criteria and locating the exception by process of elimination.

Exception questions can take some time, but they're among the easier reading comprehension questions because often the answers are right there in the text! So don't get in a hurry and make a mistake. Relax and use the proper approach, and you'll do exceptionally well.

Reading Comprehension Practice Questions with Answer Explanations

To practice the approach to answering reading comprehension questions, try your hand at these practice questions. Read the passages and answer the questions, using the techniques we've discussed in this chapter. When you're finished, read through the answer explanations that follow.

Reading comprehension practice questions

In this practice section, we provide you with three passages, one of each of the subject types you'll see in the GMAT verbal reasoning section. Try to answer the following ten questions in about ten minutes. For each question, choose the best answer from the five options.

The GMAT won't label answer choices with letters as we have here to make our explanations easier to follow. To choose an answer on the computerized test, you'll simply click on the oval next to the choice.

Answer Questions 1–3 based on the following passage.

For most Americans and Europeans, this should be the best time in all of human history to live. Survival — the very purpose of all life — is nearly guaranteed for large parts of the world, especially in the "West." This should allow people a sense of security and contentment. If life is no longer as Thomas Hobbes famously wrote, "nasty, brutish and short," then should it not be pleasant, dignified, and long? To know that tomorrow is nearly guaranteed, along with thousands of additional tomorrows, should be enough to render hundreds of millions of people awe-struck with happiness. And modern humans, especially in the West, have every opportunity to be free, even as they enjoy ever-longer lives. Why is it, then, that so many people feel unhappy and trapped? The answer lies in the constant pressure of trying to meet needs that don't actually exist.

The term "need" has been used with less and less precision in modern life. Today, many things are described as needs, including fashion items, SUVs, vacations, and other luxuries. People say, "I need a new car," when their current vehicle continues to function. People with many pairs of shoes may still say they "need" a new pair. Clearly, this careless usage is inaccurate; neither the new car nor the additional shoes are truly "needed."

What is a need then? The Oxford English Dictionary defines the condition of "need" as "lack of means of subsistence." This definition points the way toward an understanding of what a need truly is: A need is something required for survival. Therefore, the true needs of life are air, food, water, and, in cold climates, shelter. Taken together, this is the stuff of survival. Because the purpose of life is to survive — or more broadly, to live — then these few modest requirements are all that a modern human truly needs. Other things make life exciting or enjoyable, and these are often referred to as "the purpose of life"— but this is surely an exaggeration. These additional trappings are mere wants and not true needs.

1. Which of the following most accurately states the main idea of the passage?

   (A) Modern Americans and Europeans feel unhappy and trapped because they don't distinguish true needs from mere wants.

   (B) There are no human needs, and all so-called needs are merely wants.

   (C) Human needs can never be satisfied in this life and, therefore, people will always be unhappy.

   (D) The satisfaction of human needs has resulted in nearly universal happiness for people in the United States and Europe.

   (E) There is no difference between needs and wants; the desire for wealth and power are just as real as the need for food and shelter.

2. According to the author, which of the following is an example of a fulfillment of a need?

   (A) Adding a roof to block moonlight from shining on a rudimentary sleeping structure built on a tropical island

   (B) Creating a pair of slippers from deer hide to protect one's bare feet from being cut by sharp rocks and stones

   (C) Traveling several miles through dense foliage to obtain a particular berry, known for its sweetness and antioxidant properties, to accompany one's regular bland diet of rice and beans

   (D) Climbing a steep rock face for the exhilaration and sense of accomplishment

   (E) Digging a hole to locate a new water supply after one's prior single source of refreshment has run out

3. Which of the following best defines the way the first paragraph of the passage is organized?

   (A) The author poses a question and provides context and then suggests an answer to the question.

   (B) The author presents an argument and develops that argument by referencing a famous quote that reiterates the point that precedes it.

   (C) The author presents an argument and then supports that argument by defining an essential term.

   (D) The author compares life in one area of the world to life in another area of the world and shows how one way of thinking about life is better than the other.

   (E) The author poses a rhetorical question and explains why modern humans are incapable of answering that question.

Answer Questions 4–6 based on the following passage.

A logarithmic unit known as the decibel (dB) is used to represent the intensity of sound. The decibel scale is similar to the Richter scale used to measure earthquakes. On the Richter scale, a 7.0 earthquake is ten times stronger than a 6.0 earthquake. On the decibel scale, an increase of 10 dB is equivalent to a 10-fold increase in intensity or power. Thus, a sound registering 80 dB is ten times louder than a 70 dB sound. In the range of sounds audible to humans, a whisper has an intensity of 20 dB; 140 dB (a jet aircraft taking off nearby) is the threshold of immediate pain.

The perceived intensity of sound is not simply a function of volume; certain frequencies of sound appear louder to the human ear than do other frequencies, even at the same volume. Decibel measurements of noise are, therefore, often "A-weighted" to take into account the fact that some sound wavelengths are perceived as being particularly loud. A soft whisper is 20 dB, but on the A-weighted scale, the whisper is 30 dBA. This is because human ears are particularly attuned to human speech. Quiet conversation has a sound level of about 60 dBA.

Continuous exposure to sounds over 80 dBA can eventually result in mild hearing loss, while exposure to louder sounds can cause much greater damage in a very short period of time. Emergency sirens, motorcycles, chainsaws, construction activities, and other mechanical or amplified noises are often in the 80 to 120 dBA range. Sound levels above 120 dBA begin to be felt inside the human ear as discomfort and eventually as pain.

Unfortunately, the greatest damage to hearing is done voluntarily. Music, especially when played through headphones, can grow to be deceptively loud. The ear becomes numbed by the loud noise, and the listener often turns up the volume until the music approaches 120 dBA. This level of noise can cause permanent hearing loss in a short period of time, and in fact, many young Americans now have a degree of hearing loss once seen only in much older persons.

4. The primary purpose of the passage is to

   (A) argue for government mandates that decibel levels produced by headphones be reduced

   (B) compare the scale used to measure intensity of sound to the scale used to measure the strength of earthquakes

   (C) describe the way that sound intensity is measured and explain its effect on human hearing

   (D) define which volume levels and sound exposure times are safe for humans and which are harmful

   (E) warn readers about the harmful effects of continuous exposure to sounds over 80 dBA

5. The author mentions that "emergency sirens, motorcycles, chainsaws, construction activities, and other mechanical or amplified noises" fall in the 80 to 120 dBA range. It can be inferred from this statement that these noises

   (A) are unwanted, outside intrusions common in urban life

   (B) can cause hearing loss with constant exposure

   (C) are more dangerous to hearing than sounds of the same dBA level from headphones

   (D) are loud enough to cause immediate pain

   (E) have no negative impacts

6. The second paragraph of the passage states "Decibel measurements of noise are therefore often 'A-weighted' to take into account the fact that some sound wavelengths are perceived as being particularly loud. A soft whisper is 20 dB, but on the A-weighted scale the whisper is 30 dBA." Therefore, for any particular sound, the A-weighted decibel level differs from the unweighted decibel level in that

   (A) the A-weighted number is 10 points higher than the unweighted number

   (B) the A-weighted number is based on the way the noise is perceived in the human ear

   (C) the unweighted number is always higher than the A-weighted number

   (D) the A-weighted number is measured by more accurate instruments

   (E) only on the unweighted scale does a 10 dB increase in sound equal a ten-fold increase in intensity

Answer Questions 7–10 based on the following passage.

This passage is an excerpt from *Microeconomics Theory and Applications,* 9th Edition, by Edgar K. Browning and Mark A. Zupan (Wiley):

In 1980, Washington, D.C., city officials, hard-pressed for tax revenues, levied a 6 percent tax on the sale of gasoline. As a first approximation (and a reasonable one, it turns out), this tax could be expected to increase the price of gasoline by 6 percent. The elasticity of demand is a key factor in the consequences of this action, because the more sharply the sales of gasoline fall, the less tax revenue the city will raise. Presumably, city officials hoped that gasoline sales would be largely unaffected by the higher price. Within a few months, however, the amount of gasoline sold had fallen by 33 percent.[1] A 6 percent price increase producing a 33 percent quantity reduction means the price elasticity was about 5.5.

The sharp sales drop meant that tax revenue was not increased. Further indications were that when consumers had fully adjusted to the tax, tax revenues would actually decrease. (There had been a 10 cent per gallon tax before the 6 percent tax was added, so although the 6 percent levy was raising revenue, the gain was largely offset by the loss in revenue from the initial 10 cent tax following the reduction in sales.) This was not a general increase in gasoline prices but a rise only within the D.C. city limits. Gasoline sold in the District of Columbia is a narrowly defined product that has good substitutes — gasoline sold in nearby Virginia and Maryland. Higher gasoline prices in the District of Columbia, when the prices charged in Virginia and Maryland are unchanged, indicate high elasticity in the market.

No economist would be surprised at the results of this tax, but apparently city officials were. Observed one city councilman: "We think of ourselves here in the District as an island to ourselves. But we've got to realize that we're not. We've got to realize that Maryland and Virginia are right out there, and there's nothing to stop people from crossing over the line." The 6 percent gasoline tax was repealed five months after it was levied.

[1]"Barry Asks Gasoline Tax Repeal," *Washington Post,* November 2, 1980, p. A1.

7. The author is primarily concerned with doing which of the following?

(A) Arguing for increased gas taxes

(B) Arguing against increased gas taxes

(C) Ridiculing all local government officials

(D) Advancing a particular ideology

(E) Explaining certain principles of supply and demand

8. It can be inferred from the passage that *elasticity* in the last sentence of the second paragraph refers to

(A) fluctuations in the price of gasoline in Washington, D.C.

(B) fluctuations in the price of gasoline in Virginia and Maryland

(C) changes in the amount of tax collected at 6 percent

(D) changes in the number of vehicles in the region

(E) fluctuations in the demand for gasoline sold in Washington, D.C.

9. For which of the following reasons does the second paragraph of the passage mention the original gas tax of 10 cents per gallon?

(A) To show that Washington, D.C., residents were already overtaxed

(B) To distinguish between a straight 10 cent per gallon tax and a percent tax

(C) To explain why residents should not be subjected to different kinds of taxes

(D) To contrast the 10 cent tax that was included in the pump price and the 6 percent sales tax that was added after the sale

(E) To show that with a sufficient decrease in gasoline sales, the city would actually lose money despite the higher tax

10. The passage suggests that a reason the tax increase failed to raise tax revenues in the District of Columbia is that

    (A) District of Columbia consumers decreased the amount of fuel they purchased and limited their overall vehicle usage

    (B) the amount of gas consumed by District of Columbia residents in their commute to nearby states was sufficiently negligible to justify purchasing fuel outside the city limits

    (C) consumers in the District of Columbia were upset that city council members would decrease fuel taxes to increase tax revenues

    (D) as a result of the tax increase, residents of Virginia and Maryland discontinued making gas purchases in the District of Columbia

    (E) District of Columbia city council members failed to convince legislators in nearby states to increase their fuel taxes

Answer explanations

1. **A.** First, identify the question type. This one's pretty easy because it contains the phrase *main idea* right in the question. You're dealing with a main theme question, so the answer concerns the general idea and purpose of the passage and is probably found in the first or last paragraphs of the passage.

   Eliminate any choices that go beyond the scope of the information discussed in the passage. You recall that the passage distinguished *true needs* from *mere wants*. Choice (C) says, "Human needs can never be satisfied in this life. . . ." The reading passage never mentions anything about needs not being satisfied in this life. You may or may not agree with the statement in Choice (C), but you can eliminate it because it discusses ideas that aren't covered in the passage.

   Next, look for choices that contradict what you remember from reading through the passage. Choice (B) states that "there are no human needs." The passage specifically lists human needs of food, water, shelter, and so on. So Choice (B) has to be wrong. You may also recall that this list of needs is included in a section in which the author distinguishes between needs and wants. Choice (E) says that there's "no difference between needs and wants"; you know that the passage says otherwise, so you can eliminate that option.

   You're left with Choices (A) and (D). If you have trouble choosing between them, consult the passage. Concentrate on the first paragraph, which says that although Americans and Europeans should be happy, many are "unhappy and trapped." You can, therefore, eliminate Choice (D).

   Choice (A) should be the correct answer. But take a moment to reread Choice (A) to make sure it makes sense as the main idea of the passage. Choice (A) says, "Modern Americans and Europeans feel unhappy and trapped because they don't distinguish true needs from mere wants." This statement agrees with the author's questioning of the reasons behind modern unhappiness found in the first paragraph and the author's distinguishing of needs from wants in the last paragraph.

2. **E.** The author describes a need as "something required for survival" and lists the true needs as "air, food, water, and, in cold climates, shelter." Eliminate answers choices that don't have something to do with air, food, water and shelter. Climbing a rock face for the fun of it likely falls within the author's definition of a want because it makes life "exciting or enjoyable." So you can eliminate Choice (D). As nice as it would be to maintain your pedicure with a nice pair of soft deer-hide slippers, foot apparel doesn't fall within the author's criteria for survival. (Apparently, in the author's world, clothing is optional!) Cross off Choice (B).

You're left with Choice (A), which concerns shelter; Choice (C), which deals with food; and Choice (E), which regards water. Each of the remaining answer choices addresses one of the author's categories of needs, so it's up to you to determine which is required for survival. Although it would be nice to sleep peacefully without the interruption of pesky moonlight, the roof in Choice (A) is more likely a want than a need. The author clarifies that shelter is a need in cold climates, not tropical islands. Because Choice (C) tells you that the berry seekers already have a regular diet of rice and beans, you know they're not searching for the berry for survival purposes. The berry isn't necessary for survival, so it's unlikely that it fits the author's idea of a need.

By process of elimination, you settle on Choice (E) as the best answer. The purpose of the hole excavation is to find one of the author's required elements for survival: water. And you know that the exercise is urgent because the hole-digger has no other source for water.

Don't be fooled by the reference to *refreshment* in Choice (E). You may think that refreshment pertains to a want rather than a need, but the author tells you that water is necessary. Therefore, you can conclude that refreshment that refers to water is also necessary.

3. **A.** Examine the way the author introduces the point in the first paragraph of the passage. The first several sentences explain that modern humans should be happy because their daily survival is virtually guaranteed. The author inserts the Hobbes quote about how rough life used to be to show that modern life has improved considerably. The author then wonders, given how good we've got it, why modern humans are unhappy. The paragraph's ending statement is the author's answer to this question. Find the answer that best describes this organization.

Choice (D) and Choice (E) are pretty easy to eliminate. The author provides an answer to the question, so modern humans aren't incapable of answering it, and Choice (E) can't be right. The author references the "West" but doesn't compare western thinking to the way people think about life in other parts of the world. Choice (D) is wrong.

You may be tempted by Choice (B). The first paragraph has a famous quote, but that quote about the nastiness of life doesn't restate the prior point that people should feel secure and content. Choice (C) may also sound good at first, but it describes the organization of the entire passage rather than just the first paragraph. The author doesn't define a need until the last paragraph.

When you're asked to evaluate the organization of reading content, make sure you know the parameters of the portion you're supposed to consider.

The best answer has to be Choice (A). The first several sentences provide background for the author's question about why modern humans aren't happy. Then the author answers the question by stating that humans aren't happy because they don't know what a need is.

4. **C.** This passage is almost exactly 350 words, so it's as long as any passage on the GMAT is going to get. Don't let the unfamiliar scientific concepts worry you. You're probably familiar with the term *decibel,* but you may have never encountered the *A-weighted decibel* or *dBA,* as it's abbreviated. Focus on the main point of the passage, which is to describe dBAs and how human ears perceive them, and what type of information appears in each paragraph so that you can approach this main theme question systematically:

  ✔ First, check out the first word of each answer choice to find obvious incorrect answers. The tone of the passage is primarily objective and descriptive, so an answer that begins with *argue* is likely wrong. If you read Choice (A) further, you know you can eliminate it. The author doesn't mention anything about government mandates.

  Natural science passages are usually objective and informative. Their primary purpose is rarely to argue in favor of or against a particular position.

✔ Next, eliminate answer choices that deal with information found in only one area of the passage. The scales mentioned in Choice (B) appear only in the first paragraph, so a comparison of them can't be the purpose of the passage. The author discusses the harmful effects of exposure to sound only in the last two paragraphs, so Choice (E) isn't the primary purpose. For the same reason, you can likely eliminate Choice (D). While the author does indeed define the sound exposure levels and times that are safe for humans and does warn readers about the harmful effects of sound exposure, neither Choice (E) nor Choice (D) provides the overall reason for the passage.

✔ Finally, choose the answer that incorporates information from the passage as a whole. Choice (C) brings together the information in the first two paragraphs (how sound intensity is measured) and the information in the last two (how sound intensity affects humans). Therefore, it's the best answer.

5. **B.** The word *infer* in the question gives you a fairly obvious clue to the type of question you're dealing with. Again, you can rely on the process of elimination to answer it.

Begin by eliminating those choices that rely on outside information. This passage focuses on noise levels and health effects. The passage doesn't mention societal concerns, such as the intrusive impacts of a plethora of noise in urban life. Therefore, you can cross out Choice (A). All the other choices have something to do with noise levels and health, so don't eliminate them yet.

Next, look for choices that contradict what you know about the passage. One of the author's purposes in writing the passage is to warn young people of the hearing loss associated with headphone use (or abuse). To say that the noises mentioned in the question are *more* dangerous than noises at the same decibel level from headphones would be contradictory. Because Choice (C) is inconsistent with what you find out from the passage, you can eliminate it.

You can use the information in the question to narrow down your choices. The question indicates that the noises mentioned are in the 80 to 120 dBA range. Even if you don't remember all the specifics of the passage, you probably remember that noises over 100 dBA are very loud. You may even remember that 120 dBA is the threshold for feeling discomfort in the ear. It's, therefore, not logical to say, as Choice (E) does, that noises in this range would have *no* health effects. Noises that loud have some impact on the ear!

You can also eliminate Choice (E) because it contains an implicit debatable word. *No impacts* in this answer choice suggests *none,* and answer choices that contain the word *none* are almost always wrong because *none* doesn't allow for any exceptions. If the answer were worded a little differently to say "may have no negative impacts," it could be correct. Short exposure to noise may, in fact, have no impact.

You're left with just two answer choices. If you happen to remember that 140 dB is the threshold for immediate pain, you can answer the question without having to refer back to the text. However, if you have any doubt, take a few seconds to be sure. Remember, with the computerized test, you can't go back to check your answers. After you confirm an answer, it can't be changed.

The last sentence of the first paragraph indicates that 140 dB is the threshold of immediate pain, and in the third paragraph, you read that 120 dBA can "eventually lead to pain." Therefore, you can eliminate Choice (D), so Choice (B) is probably the answer. Glancing at the passage confirms that it indicates that constant exposure to sounds over 80 dBA can result in hearing loss.

6. **B.** On the computerized test, the question would refer to a highlighted part of the passage on the screen instead of quoting it, but for our purposes, we use the quotation. This problem is probably a specific information question because it refers to details of the passage without using *infer* or *imply.*

You can eliminate Choice (E) because the passage doesn't mention a difference between a 10 dB increase and a 10 dBA increase. Choice (D) also refers to information not covered in the passage. Nowhere does the reading suggest that instruments used to measure A-weighted decibels are more accurate; it just indicates that sounds are measured differently with the A-weighted scale. Cross out Choice (D). Likewise, Choice (C) is incorrect because it directly contradicts prominent information from the reading. A whisper registers a higher number on the A-weighted scale, as does quiet conversation, so Choice (C) can't be correct.

The two choices that are left, Choices (A) and (B), both provide correct information, but only one answers the question. A whisper does register 30 dBA on the A-weighted scale, as opposed to 20 dB on the normal decibel scale, so Choice (A) provides good information. But if you refer back to the passage, you find that some wavelengths are heard more clearly than others. The passage specifically states that the reason for the A-weighted scale is to take into account those noises that are perceived better by the human ear, which is how the A-weighted scale differs from the unweighted scale. Because sounds other than a whisper may have more or less than 10 points difference between their A-weighted and unweighted numbers, Choice (B) is a better answer than Choice (A).

7. **E.** When you're answering a question about an author's purpose, looking at the beginning words of each answer choice can be helpful. The author doesn't appear to be particularly argumentative or condescending in this piece, so you can probably eliminate Choices (A), (B), and (C) right off the bat. Additionally, Choice (C) contains the debatable word *all*. The author doesn't talk about *all* local officials in D.C., much less *all* local officials in general.

This leaves Choices (D) and (E). You can eliminate Choice (D) because the author doesn't advance "a particular ideology." Instead, the author is stunned that the city council didn't know the basic theory of supply and demand. Choice (E) is the best answer of the five.

To double-check your answer, read through the answers you eliminated based solely on first words. Choice (A) is clearly wrong because the author shows that increased taxes actually resulted in decreased revenues. Choice (B) seems more logical because the author is showing the problems with the gas tax increase in Washington, D.C. But if you check the passage, you'll notice that the author never advocates for lower taxes in the passage. The author explains why the gas tax failed in the unique case of Washington, D.C., but that isn't enough to make Choice (B) the primary purpose for writing the passage. The author is primarily concerned with explaining the principles of supply and demand, using the Washington, D.C., gas tax as a case study.

8. **E.** That this question is an inference question is pretty obvious. Be careful not to make an inference that goes beyond the scope of what's stated in the passage.

Eliminate incorrect answer choices. Because this is an inference question, it may be hard to recognize answer choices that use outside knowledge. The point of inferring is, after all, to extend the reasoning beyond what's actually written. But one of the choices strays too far from the information in the passage. Choice (D) mentions changes in the number of vehicles in the region, but the passage says nothing about people getting rid of their cars or not driving through D.C. in reaction to the increase in the price of gas. Eliminate Choice (D).

Choice (B) is inconsistent with the passage as a whole, so you can also cross it off. The passage is about price increases in Washington, D.C., and specifically not about price increases in Maryland and Virginia. This leaves you with three possible answers, each of which could fit with the term *elasticity* in this passage. You need to go back and reread the sentence that's referenced in the question and also reread the surrounding sentences to understand the sentence's context.

The sentence clearly doesn't apply to "the amount of tax collected at 6 percent," so you can cross out Choice (C). The sentence does mention changes in price in D.C., yet if you read the entire second paragraph carefully, especially the last two sentences, you'll see that the author discusses lower demand in D.C. because of good substitutes: gas in Maryland and Virginia. The paragraph states outright that prices have gone up in D.C. — but this is an inference question, which means you're looking for an implication. It's not the prices that are elastic, which means Choice (A) is wrong. *Elasticity* must refer to the demand for gas, because low price and demand are positively related. So Choice (E) is the best answer to this difficult question.

9. **E.** This question is also an inference one, even though it doesn't contain words that suggest inference. You know it's an inference question because you're asked about the reason the author mentions something, and the passage doesn't directly state the reason.

As usual, start by eliminating obviously incorrect answer choices that don't deal with the subject matter of the passage. The author doesn't mention residents being overtaxed or undertaxed; the article just mentions gas prices and shifting demand. So you can eliminate Choice (A). Choice (D) is incorrect because the passage doesn't mention collecting the taxes differently or at different times. The article makes no effort to distinguish between the straight 10 cent tax and the percentage tax, so you can also cross out Choice (B).

This leaves you with just two possible answers, Choices (C) and (E). Quickly referring to the second paragraph of the passage reveals that before the authors mention the 10 cent tax, they indicate that lower demand may actually result in lower tax revenue. To show how this could be true, the authors mention that the city was previously collecting 10 cents on each gallon. When less gasoline was sold, the city lost this revenue. Choice (E) is a better answer than Choice (C) because it pinpoints the authors' reasons for mentioning the earlier tax.

10. **B.** To answer this inference question, note that the tax increase was implemented with the intent to increase tax revenue. The passage states that tax revenues didn't increase essentially because city officials didn't account for the elasticity in the market. Consumers found equal, less expensive substitutes in nearby gas stations outside the D.C. city limits.

Eliminate answer choices that are blatantly wrong. Choice (C) presents information that's contrary to the details of the passage. City officials didn't *decrease* fuel taxes; they increased them. You can easily narrow your choices to four.

Choice (A) provides an explanation for the decreased revenues. If consumers limited their overall gas consumption, tax revenues would fall. This isn't the reason the author suggests, however. The passage doesn't say that D.C. residents stopped buying fuel altogether. It suggests that they stopped buying fuel in D.C. and started buying it in Virginia and Maryland. Eliminate Choice (A).

Just because an answer choice makes logical sense doesn't mean it's correct. The answer has to make sense given the information in the passage.

You can also cross off Choices (D) and (E) from the list. Both answers require you to infer information that's beyond the scope of the passage. You don't know anything about the fuel-buying habits of Virginia and Maryland residents, nor can you imagine that D.C. officials tried to work with officials in neighboring states. In fact, the passage states that D.C. officials were surprised that their constituents bought gas elsewhere, so it's unlikely that they had the forethought to negotiate with other governments.

The remaining answer is Choice (B). If D.C. residents went outside of the city limits to purchase fuel, the overall cost of the trip must have been more cost effective than buying gas within the city. Otherwise, they would have continued to purchase fuel in D.C.

Chapter 5

Let's Think This Through Logically: Critical Reasoning

ou're taking the GMAT to go to business school, not to get a PhD in philosophy, so you're probably wondering why you need to be tested in logic and critical reasoning. Don't worry — answering the critical reasoning questions on the GMAT doesn't require any knowledge of formal logic. You won't be constructing syllogisms or using fancy Latin words, like *ad hominem,* for logical fallacies. The GMAT verbal section contains questions that test you on informal logic, which is a lot like the kind of reasoning you use to decide between a chocolate frosted doughnut and a bran muffin when the office pastry cart passes by. We fill you in on this logic (for the GMAT, not the pastry cart) in this chapter. The people who run the admissions offices at business schools want to make sure their future students can think through situations clearly and carefully. That's where the critical reasoning question comes in.

About a third of the questions in the GMAT verbal section are critical reasoning questions. This question type tests your ability to analyze an argument. The good news is that you analyze arguments all the time even though you may not know you're doing so. When you see a commercial advertising a new product that claims it'll make your life better, you probably question that claim. If a weight-loss drug helped someone lose 50 pounds, you ask, "Is that a typical result?" If four out of five dentists recommend a chewing gum, you say, "Did they ask only five dentists?" When a mutual fund boasts of its performance, you ask, "Is that better than the market average?" You'll use this same kind of thinking to ace the critical reasoning questions on the GMAT.

Focusing on "Critical" Concepts: An Overview

Critical reasoning questions consist of an argument, a question, and five answer choices. You'll encounter short passages from a variety of sources, such as speeches, advertisements, newspapers, and scholarly articles. You may see an argument like this: "The local sales tax must be raised to fund city services. Admittedly, this increased sales tax will impose a greater hardship on the poorest citizens. But if the sales tax is not increased, all city services for the poor will have to be cut." The paragraph reflects the type of arguments you encounter in the news every day.

In the following sections, we clue you in on what to expect when you approach a critical reasoning question on the GMAT — from the length and format of the argument, to the type of questions you'll be asked, to how to figure out the correct answer.

Understanding the structure of the questions

Each critical reasoning question has essentially the same structure. The question usually begins with a two- to five-sentence paragraph that contains the argument. The question contains all the information you need to answer the question. Don't rely on any outside information! Even if you happen to be an expert in the area a question covers, don't rely on your expertise to answer the question.

The short argument paragraph is followed by a question (or possibly two questions, although the computer displays only one at a time). The questions usually fall conveniently into one of a few types. The question may ask that you weaken or strengthen an argument, draw a conclusion, analyze the structure of an argument, or identify an unstated assumption the author makes. We examine each of these question types in the section "Getting from point A to point B: Types of reasoning," later in this chapter.

Each question has five possible answer choices, which are often long, sometimes even longer than the argument or question. For this reason, you'll spend most of your time for each question examining the answer choices.

As with most GMAT questions, you can quickly eliminate one or two of the answers that are obviously wrong. The remaining answers will be more difficult to eliminate, so spend your time analyzing these better answer choices.

Figuring out how to answer the questions

To break down a critical reasoning question, follow these three steps:

1. **Read the question.**
2. **Read the argument paragraph, focusing on the specific information you need to know to answer the question.**
3. **As you read the argument, look for inconsistencies and/or assumptions in the logic.**

The best way to tackle a critical reasoning question is to read the question first to determine its type. The later section "Thinking Inside the Box: Question Types" shows you how to distinguish critical reasoning question types. When you first read the question, don't read all the answer choices; doing so takes way too much time and clutters your thinking. You need to concentrate on only the information you need to find to answer the question.

After you figure out what kind of question you're dealing with, you can read the paragraph very carefully. Be sure to locate the conclusion of the argument. The conclusion may come at the beginning, middle, or end of the paragraph. When you've identified the conclusion, you can better understand the rest of the paragraph. As you read the paragraph, look for inconsistencies or gaps in the argument that may help you answer the question. Isolating the argument's premises, assumptions, and conclusion helps you determine the method of reasoning.

The argument paragraph usually isn't too complicated, and therefore you may be tempted to read it too quickly. Force yourself to read slowly and carefully so you don't skim over the word or words that provide the keys to the argument. If you read thoroughly enough, you'll be able to eliminate some — or even most — of the answer choices. When you're down to two possible answers, you can then easily refer back to the text to make sure you choose the correct answer.

Making a Case: Essentials of Informal Logic

You can score well on the GMAT critical reasoning questions without knowing the elements of informal logic, but if you understand a few terms and concepts, you can score even higher. You really just need to know the two basic components of a logical argument and a few methods of coming up with a conclusion, which we outline in the following sections.

Fighting fair: The elements of an argument

A logical argument consists of premises and a conclusion, and when you're analyzing arguments, identifying what parts are premises and what makes up the conclusion can help. The *premises* give the supporting evidence that you can draw a conclusion from. You can usually find the *conclusion* in the argument because it's the statement that you can preface with *therefore*. The conclusion is often but not always the last sentence of the argument. For example, take a look at this simple argument:

> All runners are fast. John is a runner. Therefore, John is fast.

The premises in the argument are "All runners are fast" and "John is a runner." They provide the supporting evidence for the conclusion that John is fast, which is the sentence that begins with *therefore*. Not all conclusions in the GMAT critical reasoning arguments will begin with *therefore* or other words like it (such as *thus* and *so*), but you can try adding *therefore* to any statement you believe is the conclusion to see whether the argument makes sense. We give you plenty of sample arguments in this chapter so you can use them to practice identifying premises and conclusions.

Getting from point A to point B: Types of reasoning

Each logical argument has premises and a conclusion, but not every argument comes to a conclusion in the same way. For the purposes of the GMAT, you should be familiar with two basic types of logical reasoning: deductive and inductive (which we explain further in the next sections). You use both types of reasoning all the time, but now you can apply definitions to your logical genius.

Sure sounds Greek to me: Origins of logical thought

Legend has it that a Greek philosopher named Parmenides in the 5th century BC had plenty of time on his hands while living in a Greek colony off the west coast of Italy. So he whiled away the hours contemplating logical thought and became one of the first Westerners to record his findings. He penned a philosophical poem in which an unnamed goddess instructs him in the ways of determining truth about the universe. His poem explored the contrast between truth and appearance and portrayed truth to be firm and steadfast, whereas appearance (the way mortal men usually think) was unstable and wavering. Parmenides's work influenced other great Greek thinkers, like Plato, Aristotle, and Plotinus.

Unfortunately, you won't have a goddess to guide you through the critical reasoning questions of the GMAT, but you can rely on Aristotle's method of developing syllogisms to examine GMAT arguments. He's the one who came up with this famous syllogism: "All humans are mortal; Socrates is human; therefore, Socrates is mortal."

Elementary, my dear Watson: Deductive reasoning

In *deductive reasoning*, you come up with a specific conclusion from more general premises. The great thing about deductive reasoning is that if the premises are true, the conclusion must be true! The following is an example of a deductive reasoning argument:

> All horses have hooves. (General premise)
>
> Bella is a horse. (More specific premise)
>
> Therefore, Bella has hooves. (Very specific conclusion)

If the premise that all horses have hooves is true, and if Bella is, in fact, a horse, then it must be true that Bella has hooves. The same holds true for all examples of deductive reasoning. Here's another example:

> All who take the GMAT must complete an analytical essay. (General premise)
>
> You're taking the GMAT. (More specific premise)
>
> Therefore, you have to complete an analytical essay. (Very specific conclusion)

This example shows the relationship between the truth of the premises and that of the conclusion. The first premise is categorically true: The GMAT requires you to write an essay. The second premise, however, may not be true. Certainly, you're thinking of taking the GMAT or you wouldn't be reading this book, but you may still decide not to take the test. This possibility doesn't affect the logic of the argument. Remember, in deductive reasoning, the conclusion must be true *if* the premises are true. If you take the test, you have to write an essay, so this argument is valid.

When you analyze deductive reasoning arguments for the GMAT, the only way you can prove that a conclusion is true is by showing that all premises are true. The only way to prove that a deductive reasoning conclusion is false is to show that at least one of the premises is false.

Perhaps I'm just generalizing: Inductive reasoning

In deductive reasoning, you draw a specific conclusion from general premises. With *inductive reasoning,* you do just the opposite; you develop a general conclusion from specific premises. Inductive reasoning differs from deductive reasoning in that the conclusion in an inductive reasoning argument could be false even if all the premises are true. With inductive reasoning, the conclusion is essentially your best guess. That's because an inductive reasoning argument relies on less complete information than deductive reasoning does. Consider this example of an inductive argument:

> Bella is a horse and has hooves. (Specific premise)
>
> Smoky is a horse and has hooves. (Specific premise)
>
> Nutmeg is a horse and has hooves. (Specific premise)
>
> Shadow is a horse and has hooves. (Specific premise)
>
> Therefore, it is likely that all horses have hooves. (General conclusion)

Because inductive reasoning derives general conclusions from specific examples, you can't come up with a statement that "must be true." The best you can say, even if all the premises are true, is that the conclusion can be or is likely to be true.

Inductive reasoning arguments come in all sorts of flavors, but the folks who create the GMAT tend to favor three types: analogy, cause and effect, and statistical. To excel on the GMAT, you want to get very familiar with these three methods of inductive reasoning:

✔ **Analogy arguments:** An analogy argument tries to show that two or more concepts are similar so that what holds true for one is true for the other. The strength of the argument depends on the degree of similarity between the persons, objects, or ideas being compared. For example, in drawing a conclusion about Beth's likes, you may compare her to Alex: "Alex is a student, and he likes rap music. Beth is also a student, so she probably likes rap music, too." Your argument would be stronger if you could show that Alex and Beth have other similar interests that apply to rap music, like hip-hop dancing or wearing bling. If, on the other hand, you show that Alex likes to go to dance clubs while Beth prefers practicing her violin at home, your original conclusion may be less likely.

✔ **Cause-and-effect arguments:** A cause-and-effect argument concludes that one event is the result of another. These types of arguments are strongest when the premises prove that the alleged cause of an event is the most likely one and that no other probable causes exist. For example, after years of football watching, you may conclude the following: "Every time I wear my lucky shirt, my favorite team wins; therefore, wearing my lucky shirt causes the team to win." The above example is weak because it doesn't take into consideration other, more probable reasons (like the team's talent) for the wins.

✔ **Statistical arguments:** Arguments based on statistical evidence rely on numbers to reach a conclusion. These types of arguments claim that what's true for the statistical majority is also true for the individual. But because these are inductive reasoning arguments, you can't prove that the conclusions are absolutely true. When you analyze statistical arguments on the GMAT, focus on how well the given statistics apply to the circumstances of the conclusion. For example, if you wanted people to buy clothing through your website, you may make this argument: "In a recent study of the preferences of consumers, 80 percent of shoppers surveyed spent more than six hours a day on the Internet; therefore, you'll probably prefer to buy clothes online." You'd support your conclusion if you could show that a positive correlation occurs between the amount of time people spend on the Internet and a preference for buying clothing online. If you can't demonstrate that correlation, the statistics regarding time spent on the Internet have little to do with predicting one's preference for online shopping.

To do well on the critical reasoning questions, you need to recognize premises and conclusions in arguments, determine whether the argument applies deductive or inductive reasoning (most will be inductive), and, if the argument is inductive, figure out the method the author uses to reach the conclusion. As you can induce, knowing a little about logical reasoning is essential to scoring well on the GMAT!

Thinking Inside the Box: Question Types

When you were growing up, you probably experienced clichés. You had your jocks, your stoners, the smart kids (that was you!), and various other categories. Labels were important because they gave you clues on how to deal with someone who was a member of a particular group. You knew better than to pick a fight with a jock, and it was a good bet that you could get a match from a stoner. Well, we categorize GMAT questions for the same reason. After you figure out a critical reasoning question's type, you know just how to deal with it. Most of the critical reasoning questions you'll encounter on the GMAT fit into one of the following five categories:

✔ **Strengthening or weakening arguments:** The argument presents premises and a conclusion and asks you to evaluate the answer choices to determine which one would best strengthen or weaken the author's conclusion.

✔ **Drawing conclusions from premises:** The argument paragraph consists of a bunch of premises but doesn't provide a conclusion. Your job is to choose the best conclusion for the argument.

✔ **Seeking assumptions:** This more subtle type of question requires you to discover an essential premise of the argument that the author doesn't state directly.

✔ **Making inferences:** For these less common question types, you have to surmise information that isn't directly stated, usually about one of the premises rather than the conclusion.

✔ **Finding the method of reasoning:** In these questions, you'll be asked to find an argument in the answer choices that uses the same method of reasoning as the original given argument.

Because each question type has a best way to handle it, recognizing what type of question you're dealing with before you try to answer it is important. That's why you read the question before you tackle the argument. You'll immediately know what you need to look for when you read the argument from the wording of the question.

Stalking Your Prey: How to Approach Each Question Type

Knowing the types of questions you'll face is valuable only if you know the specialized strategies for dealing with each one. The following sections give you the tips you need to make approaching each of the question types second nature. You get some practice questions, too, so you'll know just what to expect when you take the actual GMAT.

Strengthening or weakening arguments

Critical reasoning questions that ask you how to best support or damage an argument are some of the easiest to answer, which is a good thing because they appear the most frequently. You probably analyze ideas every day and think of evidence to attack or defend those ideas. Because you already have the skill to evaluate arguments, it doesn't take much work for you to modify that skill to fit this specific GMAT question format. This question category has two subtypes: One asks you to strengthen an argument, and the other asks you to weaken it. You'll recognize these questions because they include words that mean to strengthen or weaken (like *support, bolster,* or *impair*), and they almost always contain an "if true" qualifier.

Here are a couple samples of the ways the questions could be worded:

✔ Which of the following statements, if true, would most seriously weaken the conclusion reached by the business owners?

✔ Which of the following, if true, provides the most support for the conclusion?

Nearly all these questions contain the words *if true,* but not all questions that have *if true* in them are strengthening- or weakening-the-argument types. To make sure an "if true" question is really a strengthening or weakening question, look for the identifying language that asks you to either strengthen or weaken the argument.

Here are three simple steps to follow when approaching strengthening- or weakening-the-argument questions:

1. **Read the question carefully so you know exactly what you'll be strengthening or weakening.**

   In most cases, you'll be asked to strengthen or weaken the conclusion of the main argument. But in less frequent cases, you may be asked to support or impair a different conclusion, like the view of the author's opponent.

2. **Examine the argument to find the premises and conclusion and to determine what method of reasoning the author uses to reach the conclusion.**

   Usually the author uses inductive reasoning, so you'll need to figure out whether the argument relies on analogy, statistics, or cause and effect to arrive at the conclusion. In the following sections, we tell you what to look for in each type of reasoning.

3. **Evaluate the answer choices to determine which choice best fits with the author's conclusion and method of reasoning.**

   Assume all the answer choices are true and then determine which one best either supports or undermines the specific conclusion addressed in the question.

Always assume that all the answers to strengthening- or weakening-the-argument questions are true. Almost all these questions include the words *if true* in them to remind you that you're supposed to assume that each answer choice presents a true statement. Don't fall into the trap of trying to evaluate whether answer choices are true or false! Your only job is to determine whether the choices help or hurt the argument. This means that a statement like "humans do not breathe air" could be a correct answer choice even though you know it's not true. Perhaps you're supposed to weaken the conclusion that a company must pump air into an underwater habitat for humans. If humans don't breathe air, pumping in air may not be necessary. Make sure you don't dismiss any answer choices simply because you know they aren't usually true.

Analyzing analogy arguments

Analogy arguments rely on the similarity of the two persons, things, or ideas being compared. Therefore, if the author uses an analogy to reach a conclusion, answer choices that show similarities between the compared elements will support the conclusion, and choices that emphasize the differences between the elements will weaken the conclusion. Take a look at this example of an analogy argument.

Hundo is a Japanese car company, and Hundos run for many miles on a gallon of gas. Toyo is also a Japanese car company; therefore, Toyos should get good gas mileage, too.

The author's conclusion would be best supported by which of the following?

(A) All Japanese car manufacturers use the same types of engines in their cars.

(B) British cars run for as many miles on a tank of gas as Hundos do.

(C) The Toyo manufacturer focuses on producing large utility vehicles.

(D) Toyo has been manufacturing cars for more than 20 years.

(E) All Japanese cars have excellent service records.

Recognizing the premises and conclusion in this argument is simple. The author states directly that Hundo cars are Japanese and get good gas mileage and that Toyo cars are Japanese; therefore, Toyos also get good gas mileage. Your job is to find the answer that perpetuates the similarity between Hundos and Toyos.

You can generally eliminate answer choices that introduce irrelevant information, such as Choices (B), (D), and (E). The author compares Japanese cars, so what British cars do has nothing to do with the argument. The length of time that Toyo has been in business tells you nothing about how similar its cars are to Hundo's. And the question is talking about gas mileage, not service records, so don't spend too much time considering Choice (E).

Choice (C) tells you the focus of Toyo producers, but it doesn't give you any information about how that compares to Hundo, so the best answer is Choice (A). If all Japanese manufacturers supply their cars with the same engines and Hundo and Toyo are both Japanese manufacturers, it's more likely that Toyos will achieve a gas mileage similar to that experienced by Hundos.

Considering cause-and-effect arguments

Questions that ask you to evaluate arguments often apply cause-and-effect reasoning. If the argument uses cause and effect to make its point, focus on the causes. Almost always, the correct answer to a question that asks you to strengthen the conclusion is an answer choice that shows the cause mentioned is the most likely source of the effect. The best answer for a question for which you have to weaken the argument points to another probable cause of the effect. Here's how you'd apply this reasoning to a sample question.

Average hours of television viewing per American have rapidly increased for more than three decades. To fight the rise in obesity, Americans must limit their hours of television viewing.

Which of the following, if true, would most weaken the author's conclusion?

(A) A person burns more calories while watching television than while sleeping.

(B) Over the last 30 years, the number of fast food restaurants in America has increased.

(C) Americans spend most of their television time watching sporting events rather than cooking shows.

(D) Television viewing in Japan has also increased over the past three decades.

(E) Studies show that the number of television commercials that promote junk food has risen over the past ten years.

To tackle this question, first identify the conclusion you're supposed to weaken and the premises the author states or implies to reach that conclusion. The conclusion is pretty easy to spot. The last thought of the argument is that Americans must limit their hours of television viewing to curb the rise in obesity. The author makes this judgment, using the following evidence:

> ✔ The author directly states that the number of television viewing hours has increased over the last 30 years.
>
> ✔ According to the author, the number of obese Americans has also increased.
>
> ✔ The author implies that television viewing causes obesity.

To weaken the argument that Americans have to reduce their television watching, you have to find the answer choice that shows that there's another cause for the rise in obesity.

You may have been tempted to select Choice (A) because it shows that television watching may be less fat-producing than another activity, sleeping. But it doesn't give you another reason for the rise in obesity. Choice (A) could be correct only if it showed that Americans were sleeping more than they were 30 years ago. It doesn't, so move on.

On the other hand, stating that during the same time period, the number of fast food restaurants also increased introduces another possible cause of obesity and weakens the conclusion that Americans have to stop watching so much TV to get slimmer. Maybe it's the popularity of fast food that's the culprit! Choice (B) is a better answer than Choice (A), but read through all the possibilities before you commit. Choice (C) is wrong because there's nothing in the argument that suggests that the type of television Americans watch affects their obesity; nor does Choice (C) show that viewing patterns have changed over the last three decades. Choice (D) is also out because it doesn't correlate what's happening in Japan with what's happening in America. You don't know whether Japanese citizens weigh more now than they did 30 years ago, so the information in Choice (D) is useless.

If the question had asked you to strengthen the conclusion, Choice (E) would be a good option. It shows a reason that increased television watching could cause obesity. But the question asks you to weaken the conclusion, so Choice (B) is the best answer. It's the only one that shows that another cause could be to blame for the rise in obesity.

Taking a stab at statistical arguments

If you see statistics used to promote an argument, you're looking for an answer that shows whether the statistics actually relate to the topic of the conclusion. If they do, you'll strengthen the conclusion. On the other hand, an answer choice that shows the statistics are unrelated to the conclusion significantly weakens that conclusion. The following is an example of a statistical argument critical reasoning question you could find on the GMAT.

In a survey of 100 pet owners, 80 percent said that they would buy a more expensive pet food if it contained vitamin supplements. Consequently, CatCo's new premium cat food should be a top-seller.

Which of the following best demonstrates a weakness in the author's conclusion?

(A) Some brands of cat food contain more vitamin supplements than CatCo's does.

(B) CatCo sells more cat food than any of its competitors.

(C) Some of the cat owners surveyed stated that they never buy expensive brands of cat food.

(D) Ninety-five of those pet owners surveyed did not own cats.

(E) Many veterinarians have stated that vitamin supplements in cat food do not greatly increase health benefits.

Because the argument hinges on statistics, eliminate answers that don't directly address the statistical evidence. Those surveyed stated that they'd pay more for pet food with vitamin supplements, but they didn't provide information on whether the amount of vitamin supplements was important. So even though Choice (A) may entice you, it isn't the best answer because it doesn't address the statistics used in the argument. Choice (B) doesn't regard the survey results, either, and it supports the conclusion rather than weakens it. The argument has nothing at all to do with veterinarians, so Choice (E) can't be right. Only Choices (C) and (D) deal with the survey the author uses to reach the conclusion that CatCo's premium cat food will be a big seller.

You can eliminate answer choices that show an exception to the statistical evidence. Exceptions don't significantly weaken a statistical argument.

Therefore, Choice (C) is wrong and Choice (D) is the best answer because it demonstrates a weakness in the statistics the author uses to support the conclusion. The preferences of dog or bird owners isn't a good indicator of the habits of cat owners.

Dabbling in deductive reasoning arguments

Rarely will you see a strengthen or weaken the argument question that uses deductive reasoning to reach a conclusion. It's just too hard to come up with challenging answer choices for weakening deductive arguments, because the only way to weaken them is to question the accuracy of the evidence, and correct answers are pretty easy to spot. The only way to strengthen a deductive argument is to reinforce the validity of the premises, which seems sort of silly. Even though GMAT creators don't want to make things too easy for you, one or two deductive arguments may crop up. To weaken an argument with a conclusion that must be true, look for an answer choice that shows that one of the premises is untrue. For example, you may see a question with the following argument:

> All horses have tails. Nutmeg is a horse. Therefore, Nutmeg must have a tail.

The only way to weaken this argument is to question one of the two premises. Answer choices like "Scientists have recently developed a breed of horses that has no tail" or "Although Nutmeg looks like a horse, she's really a donkey" would weaken the conclusion.

Delving into drawing conclusions

Another common critical reasoning question type tests your ability to draw logical conclusions (or hypotheses). The GMAT gives you a series of premises (the evidence), and you choose an answer that best concludes the information. Questions that ask you to draw conclusions from premises may be worded like this:

- ✔ Which of the following conclusions is best supported by the preceding information?
- ✔ Assuming the preceding statements are true, which of the following must also be true?
- ✔ The experimental results support which of the following hypotheses?

As you read through the premises, think of a logical conclusion of your own. Then look through the answer choices to see whether one listed comes close to what you've thought up.

The key to correctly answering drawing-conclusions questions is to look for an answer choice that addresses all the information contained in the premises. Eliminate any choices that are off topic or incomplete. A conclusion that addresses only part of the information may be plausible, but it probably isn't the best answer. For example, consider the following premises:

> Five hundred healthy adults were allowed to sleep no more than five hours a night for one month. Half of the group members were allowed 90-minute naps in the afternoon each day; the remaining subjects were allowed no naps. Throughout the month, the subjects of the experiment were tested to determine the impact of sleep deprivation on their performance of standard tasks. By the end of the month, the group that was not allowed to nap suffered significant declines in their performance, while the napping group suffered more moderate declines.

The best conclusion for these premises would have to address all the following:

- ✔ The nightly sleep deprivation of healthy adults
- ✔ The allowance for naps for half of the study group
- ✔ The smaller decline in performance of standard tasks for the group who took naps

Any conclusion that fails to address all three points isn't the best conclusion. For example, the statement "Sleep deprivation causes accumulating declines in performance among healthy adults" wouldn't be the best conclusion because it fails to address the effect of naps. A better conclusion would be "Napping helps reduce the declines in performance caused by nightly sleep deprivation among healthy adults."

You'll often see more than one plausible conclusion among the answer choices. Your task is to identify the best choice. Don't fall for the trap of choosing an answer that just restates one of the premises. Answer choices that restate a premise may entice you because they echo part of the information in the argument, but the best choice must contain an element of each of the pieces of information presented in the question.

The process is pretty simple, really. Try this sample question to see for yourself.

Over the last eight years, the Federal Reserve Bank has raised the prime interest rate by a quarter-point more than ten times. The Bank raises rates when its Board of Governors fears inflation and lowers rates when the economy is slowing down.

Which of the following is the most logical conclusion for the preceding paragraph?

(A) The Federal Reserve should be replaced with regional banks that can respond more quickly to changing economic conditions.

(B) The Federal Reserve has raised the prime rate in recent years to try to control inflation.

(C) The economy has entered a prolonged recession caused by Federal Reserve policies.

(D) The monetary policy of the United States is no longer controlled by the Federal Reserve.

(E) The Federal Reserve has consistently raised the prime rate over the last several years.

You know from the language that this is a drawing-conclusions question, so you don't have to look for a conclusion in the argument. Just read through the premises and formulate a quick conclusion, something like "Because the Federal Reserve has raised interest rates many times over the last eight years, it must fear inflation."

Eliminate answer choices that aren't relevant or that contain information not presented by the premises. The argument says nothing about regional banks or the termination of the Federal Reserve's control over U.S. monetary policy, so you can disregard Choices (A) and (D). Then get rid of any choices that don't take all premises into consideration. Choice (E) just reiterates the first premise, so it's wrong. You're left with Choices (B) and (C), but Choice (C) contradicts the information in the premises. The problem says the Federal Reserve responds to the economy, not the other way around, so it'd be wrong to say the Federal Reserve causes a recession. Choice (B) is clearly the best answer. It takes into consideration the information that the Federal Reserve has raised rates and that raising rates is its response to inflation.

Be careful to avoid relying on outside knowledge or opinions when answering drawing-conclusions questions. You may have studied the Federal Reserve Bank and have opinions about monetary policy. Choices (A), (C), and (D) reflect some possible opinions about the Federal Reserve. Don't get trapped into choosing an answer because it supports your opinion.

Spotting those sneaky assumptions

Some GMAT critical reasoning questions ask you to identify a premise that isn't there. For these types of questions, the author directly states a series of premises and provides a clear conclusion, but in getting to that conclusion, the author assumes information. Your job is to figure out what the author assumes to be true but doesn't state directly in drawing the conclusion to the argument. Seeking-assumptions questions may look like these:

✔ The argument in the preceding passage depends on which of the following assumptions?

✔ The conclusion reached by the author of the preceding passage is a questionable one. On which of the following assumptions did the author rely?

✔ The preceding paragraph presupposes which of the following?

Words like *assume, rely, presuppose, depend on,* and their derivatives usually indicate seeking-assumptions questions. Remember, these questions ask you to look for the ideas the author relies on but doesn't state.

As you read seeking-assumptions questions, look for information that's necessary to the argument but isn't stated by the author. In these questions, the author always takes for granted something on which the entire argument depends. You just need to identify what that is. To do so effectively, choose an answer that links the existing premises to the conclusion. The assumption you're seeking always bears directly on the conclusion and ties in with one or more premises, often with the last premise. Therefore, the best answer often contains information from both the last premise and the conclusion.

Women receive fewer speeding tickets than men do. Women also have lower car insurance rates. It is clear that women are better drivers than men.

The preceding conclusion is based on which of the following assumptions?

I. Men and women drive cars equal distances and with equal frequency.

II. Having lower car insurance rates indicates that one is a better driver than those who have higher rates.

III. Speeding tickets are equally awarded for violations without any gender bias on the part of police officers.

(A) I only

(B) III only

(C) I and III only

(D) II and III only

(E) I, II, and III

As always, read the question first. Because it references assumptions, we bet you figured out pretty quickly that it's a seeking-assumptions question.

Next, read through the argument and try to figure out the assumption or assumptions the author makes in reaching the conclusion that women are better drivers. The author moves from the premises to the conclusion pretty quickly and assumes that fewer speeding tickets and lower car insurance rates indicate better driving skills. The author also assumes that men and women have equal driving experiences. Use this information to examine each of your options.

Look at Statement I first. It fits with your second observation that men and women experience equal driving situations, so eliminate any answer choices that *don't* include Statement I. This means that you can get rid of Choices (B) and (D), which leaves you with Choices (A), (C), and (E).

Before you continue reading through your options, examine the remaining answer choices. You'll see that it's best to examine Statement II next, because if it's true, you won't even have to read Statement III; you'll know the answer is Choice (E). You have to read Statement III only if you determine that Statement II isn't an assumption. (For more about strategies for answering Roman numeral questions, see Chapter 2.)

The information in Statement II links the author's last premise, that women have lower insurance rates, to the conclusion that women are better drivers. Thus, Statement II is also correct. You can eliminate Choices (A) and (C), and by process of elimination, the answer must be Choice (E). If you read through Statement III, you'll confirm that it, too, is an assumption the author makes about men and women having an equal playing field in the driving game.

If you find seeking-assumption questions to be tricky, try arguing the opposite position. For example, in the sample question, you could've taken the opposing view, that men are better drivers. This means you'll be looking for ways to undermine the conclusion. If you assume the premises to be true, the best way to attack the conclusion is to show that the author assumes things that aren't true. For example, you may argue that men have more accidents because they drive more, they get more tickets because police are less forgiving with male speeders, and they have higher car insurance rates because they drive more expensive cars. Those counterarguments expose the author's assumptions!

Using your noggin to make inferences

Critical reasoning inference questions ask you to make an inference (using inductive reasoning) based on the argument in the passage. Making-inferences questions are pretty easy to recognize because they usually include the word *infer*, such as the following examples:

- ✔ Which of the following statements can be correctly inferred from the preceding passage?
- ✔ Which of the following can be inferred from the preceding statements?

The key to answering these questions correctly is to know that they usually ask you to make an inference about one of the premises in the argument rather than about the entire argument or the conclusion. Because these questions usually deal with the premises and not the conclusion, you should choose an answer that makes a plausible inference about one or more of the premises. Like the correct answer choices for the drawing-conclusions questions, the best answers to this type of question don't go beyond the scope of the information provided in the paragraph. Here's what one looks like.

The highest rated television shows do not always command the most advertising dollars. Ads that run during shows with lower overall ratings are often more expensive because the audience for those shows includes a high proportion of males between the ages of 19 and 34. Therefore, ads that run during sporting events are often more expensive than ads running during other types of programs.

Which of the following can properly be inferred from the preceding passage?

(A) Advertisers have done little research into the typical consumer and are not using their advertising dollars wisely.

(B) Sports programs have higher overall ratings than prime time network programs.

(C) Advertisers believe males between the ages of 19 and 34 are more likely to be influenced by advertisers than are other categories of viewers.

(D) Advertising executives prefer sports programs and assume that other Americans do as well.

(E) Ads that run during the biggest sporting events are the most expensive of all ads.

You know you're dealing with an inference question before you read through the argument because you've read the question first and it contains the word *inferred*. Focus on the premises of the argument as you read it. Then look through the answer choices and eliminate any that don't address one of the premises or that present inferences that require additional information.

The argument says nothing about advertising research or whether the particular advertising practice is wise, so you can eliminate Choice (A) immediately. You're stretching beyond the scope of the information if you infer that advertisers are unwise. Likewise, Choice (D) mentions the preferences and assumptions of advertisers, but none of the premises discuss advertisers, so you can get rid of Choice (D). The inference in Choice (E) relates to the conclusion rather than any of the premises, so you can probably eliminate it right away. Furthermore, just because sporting events ads are "often more expensive" than other ads doesn't necessarily mean that they're always the most expensive. This leaves you with Choices (B) and (C).

Choice (B) contradicts information in the argument. The author implies that some sporting events have lower overall ratings even though they have higher advertising rates. You're left with Choice (C). You need an explanation for the information in the second sentence that states that advertising is often more expensive for lower rated shows viewed by males who are between 19 and 34 years old. This practice would be logical only if males of these ages were more susceptible to advertising than other groups. It makes sense that Choice (C) is the correct answer.

Remember to check your outside knowledge about the critical reasoning subjects at the door! You may know that Super Bowl ads are the most expensive ads, which may tempt you to pick Choice (E). Using your own knowledge rather than what's expressly stated in the test questions will cause you to miss questions that someone with less knowledge may answer correctly.

Making your way through method-of-reasoning questions

Method-of-reasoning questions are the rarest form of GMAT critical reasoning question types. This type of question either directly asks you what type of reasoning the author uses to make an argument or, more often, asks you to choose an answer that uses the same method of reasoning as the argument. You may see method-of-reasoning questions phrased like these:

- ✔ Which of the following employs the same method of reasoning as the preceding argument?
- ✔ The author's point is made by which method of reasoning?
- ✔ David's argument is similar to Katy's in which of the following ways?

The two types of method-of-reasoning questions may seem different, but each of them asks you to do the same thing: to recognize the type of reasoning used in the argument.

For the purposes of the GMAT, the methods of reasoning are as follows:

- ✔ Deductive, which is reaching a specific conclusion from general premises
- ✔ Inductive, which is drawing a general conclusion from specific premises and includes the following methods:
  - • Analogy, which shows that one thing is sufficiently similar to another thing such that what holds true for one is true for the other
  - • Cause and effect, which shows that one event resulted from another
  - • Statistics, which uses population samples (surveys) to reach conclusions about the population as a whole

Questions that ask you to specifically choose what kind of reasoning the author uses are straightforward, so we focus on the other type of question, which asks you to choose an answer that mimics the reasoning method of the given argument. When you know you're dealing with this type of question, you just need to focus on the way the author makes the argument to make sure you choose an answer that follows the logic most exactly.

Don't choose an answer just because it deals with the same subject matter as the given argument. These choices are often traps to lure you away from the answer that more exactly duplicates the author's logic but addresses another topic.

It doesn't matter whether the argument makes sense. If the given argument isn't logical, pick an answer choice that isn't logical in the same way.

You may focus on the method of reasoning better if you substitute letters for ideas in the argument. For example, say you're presented with this argument: "Balloons that contain helium float. Jerry's balloon doesn't float, so it contains oxygen rather than helium." You could state this logic with letters like this: "All A (helium balloons) are B (floaters). C (Jerry's balloon) isn't B (a floater), so C isn't A." Then you can apply that formula to your answer choices to see which one matches best.

Some of the reasoning methods may be as obscure as the one in this sample question.

A teacher told the students in her class, "The information that you read in your history book is correct because I chose the history book and I will be creating the test and assigning your grades."

The reasoning in which of the following statements most closely resembles that of the preceding argument?

(A) The decisions made by the Supreme Court are just because the Court has the authority to administer justice.

(B) The people who have fame are famous because they deserve to be famous.

(C) Those who play sports get better grades because of the link between the health of the body and the health of the mind.

(D) Because my favorite teacher chooses to drive this kind of car, I should as well.

(E) Of 100 professors surveyed, 99 agree with the conclusions reached by the scientist in his paper on global warming.

Reading the question first tells you that you'll have to analyze the way the author reaches the conclusion in the argument. As you read, you find that this illogical cause-and-effect argument states that information is correct because someone in a position of authority (the teacher) says so, so you need to find an equally illogical argument based on power and authority.

Because this is a cause-and-effect argument, you can eliminate any choices that don't use cause and effect to reach a conclusion. All choices contain an element of cause and effect except Choice (D), which presumes an analogy between a favorite teacher and the writer, and Choice (E), which uses statistical evidence. (Note that just because Choice [D] also concerns a teacher doesn't automatically make it the correct answer.) Disregard Choices (D) and (E) and examine the other three choices.

Among Choices (A), (B), and (C), the only choice that uses power to justify a cause-and-effect relationship is Choice (A). Choice (B) is faulty because it uses circular reasoning, which means it uses its conclusion as a premise, instead of using power to advance its position. Choice (C) doesn't work because its logic isn't necessarily faulty. Instead, it relies on a logical correlation between physical health and intellectual prowess. Therefore, Choice (A) is the answer that most nearly matches the kind of reasoning in the original argument.

Critical Reasoning Practice Questions and Answer Explanations

With practice, you'll probably find that critical reasoning questions become some of the easiest question types to master in the GMAT verbal section. To master your approach, work through these practice questions and read through the answer explanations.

Critical reasoning practice questions

This set of seven critical reasoning practice questions gives you a taste of what to expect from this verbal question, which tests your ability to analyze arguments. To mimic the approximate amount of time you'll have to answer critical reasoning questions on the actual exam, try to answer these seven questions in about 12 minutes. Answer each question based on the passage that precedes it, and choose the best answer from the five answer choices provided.

Don't expect to see letters before the answer choices on the computerized GMAT. Each answer will have an oval next to it that you select by clicking on it. We've put letters next to the answers in this practice section to make it easier to discuss the answer in the explanations that follow the questions.

1. It seems that Americans are smarter than they were 50 years ago. Many more Americans are attending college now than in the past, and the typical entry-level job in business now requires a college degree.

   Which of the following statements, if true, would most seriously weaken the argument in the preceding paragraph?

   (A) High-school courses are more rigorous now than they were in the past.

   (B) Tuition at colleges and universities has more than tripled in the past 25 years.

   (C) High-school class sizes have gotten smaller, and computers have introduced a more individualized curriculum.

   (D) Businesses are not requiring as high a level of writing or math skills as they did in past decades.

   (E) Many of the skills and concepts taught in high school 50 years ago are now taught in college.

Questions 2 and 3 are based on the following argument.

Rachel: The legal drinking age in America should remain at 21, because teens have not yet reached an age where they are able to consume alcohol responsibly. Additionally, the actions of 18-year-olds are more likely to be imitated by teens aged 15 to 17 than are the actions of those who are significantly older, so lowering the drinking age to 18 would also result in increased alcohol consumption by younger teens trying to emulate the actions of their older peers.

Mackenzie: The drinking age in America should be lowered to 18, because keeping it at 21 has not only failed to curb teen drinking but has encouraged those teens who *do* drink to do so in private, uncontrolled environments where they are more prone to life-endangering behavior. Many youths in European countries drink from an early age, and those countries have substantially fewer alcohol-related problems than we do in America.

2. Which of the following, if true, would most significantly weaken Mackenzie's argument?

   (A) The idea that Europeans and other nations with low or no minimum drinking ages do not have alcohol-related problems is a myth.

   (B) If Americans are allowed to give their lives for this country at age 18, then they should be considered old enough to make the proper decision as to what to put in their bodies.

   (C) More American high-school students drink now than they did decades ago, when the drinking age was lower.

   (D) In European culture, youths are taught at an early age that it is acceptable to either abstain from alcohol entirely or drink in moderation and that it is never acceptable for them to abuse alcohol, regardless of their age.

   (E) European youths are just as likely as American youths to drink in private, uncontrolled environments.

3. Rachel's argument is based on which of the following assumptions?

   (A) Those who have reached the age of 21 are able to consume alcohol more responsibly than those who are 18.

   (B) When European teenagers consume alcohol, they do so in public, controlled environments.

   (C) Teens who are 15 to 17 years old are more impressionable than those who are aged 18 or older.

   (D) The impressionability of one's actions on others should not be a consideration when deciding the legal age to consume alcohol.

   (E) Consuming alcohol in private, uncontrolled environments is not more dangerous than consuming alcohol in more public environments, such as bars or restaurants.

4. A recent census of all American females revealed that the current average age that females in America marry is 27. The average age that females have their first child is also 27. According to a census taken 20 years ago, the average ages that females married and had their first child were 23 and 25 years, respectively.

   If the information recorded in the two censuses is true, which of the following must also be true about American females?

   (A) Currently, more females are having their first child before they marry than they did 20 years ago.

   (B) On average, females are currently waiting longer to have their first child than they did 20 years ago.

   (C) Females today are more likely to complete their education before getting married and having children than they were 20 years ago.

   (D) On average, females had larger families 20 years ago than they have today.

   (E) Twenty years ago, most females waited at least two years after they were married to have their first child.

5. Continuous technological advances are critical to many types of business, because they allow machines to do the work previously done by humans — and they don't have to be compensated. Banking executives are always looking for ways to cut costs, so they support a heavy emphasis on automated technology in the workplace. Yet what customers look for most in their banks is to be recognized by their teller and feel a sense of familiarity and friendliness upon entering, so the reliance of banks on machines should be minimized, rather than exacerbated.

   Which of the following best outlines the main idea of the argument?

   (A) Banks should reduce their dependence on technology.

   (B) Bank patrons desire personal attention.

   (C) Machines can work faster than humans.

   (D) Bank executives are a greedy bunch.

   (E) Bank automation is inevitable.

6. A school board candidate has indicated that cheating through the use of cellphones in the classroom is on the rise this year and has proposed a ban on cellphones in schools altogether. School officials cite only a marginal increase in the number of students who cheat this year in comparison to the last two years, so this is just a ploy to make voters think a quality education is his top priority.

   Which of the following, if true, best strengthens the conclusion of the preceding argument?

   (A) The school board candidate has continuously voted down proposals to increase the budget for area schools.

   (B) The school board candidate has continuously voted in favor of budget increases for area schools.

   (C) This year, schools in the district have smaller class sizes and better student/teacher ratios than they have had in past years.

   (D) The ratio of teachers to number of students has decreased significantly over the past several years because of a growth in number of students district-wide without a concomitant rise in the number of teachers to accommodate the increase.

   (E) The school board candidate has a daughter who attends a school in the district, and he does not want her to own a cellphone.

7. Springfield is the first city to ban fast-food advertisements marketed specifically toward children. Although eating fast food has been linked to weight gain, banning these advertisements will do little to curb childhood obesity, and it should be the job of the parent, not the government, to tell children what to eat.

   The argument would be most weakened if which of the following were true?

   (A) Families are increasingly relying on the fast-food industry for financial reasons and will continue to frequent these establishments on their own terms, regardless of their children's preferences.

   (B) Studies indicate that, generally speaking, adults tend to be more influenced by advertising than children.

   (C) If children learn that adults are trying to limit their fast-food intake, they will want to consume fast food even more.

   (D) Those opposed to fast-food marketing geared toward children are welcome to buy airtime for their cause, too.

   (E) Watching an advertisement has been shown to increase one's desires for a product, particularly when the product is a food item.

Answer explanations

1. **E.** Read the question first so you know what to focus on in the passage. Because this question asks you to weaken the argument, you know you need to figure out what the conclusion is and what kind of reasoning the author uses in moving from the premises to the conclusion.

   When you examine the argument, you may notice that the conclusion actually comes first. The author concludes that Americans are smarter than they were 50 years ago and does so by contrasting current college participation and entry-level job requirements with those of the past. The method of reasoning is similar to analogy, except instead of showing similarities between Americans now and 50 years ago, the author shows the differences. To weaken the conclusion that Americans are smarter today, you need to find the answer choice that shows that things really aren't all that different today than they were 50 years ago.

   First, eliminate answer choices with irrelevant information. Neither college tuition rates nor class size and curriculum have anything to do with levels of intelligence, so Choices (B) and (C) are wrong. Plus, you're looking for an answer that shows that things aren't much different between now and yesterday, and Choices (B) and (C) accentuate the difference.

   Then, get rid of any answer that tends to strengthen rather than weaken the conclusion that Americans are smarter. More difficult high-school courses seem to indicate that Americans may indeed be smarter, so disregard Choice (A). This leaves you with Choices (D) and (E), and your job is to choose the one that shows that now and then aren't all that different. Not only does Choice (D) demonstrate a difference between the eras, but it also refutes the premise that businesses are looking for the higher skill levels of a college education.

   The correct answer must be Choice (E). If skills that were part of the high-school curriculum 50 years ago are now offered in college, actual education hasn't changed all that much from then to now. Americans must now attend college to acquire the high-school skills of earlier times, and businesses need to require college degrees to make sure their employees have the same skills that high-school students had in the past. If the skill levels are the same, Americans aren't really any smarter than they were 50 years ago.

    You must know precisely what point a paragraph is arguing before you can strengthen or weaken that argument. Take the time to understand the premises, conclusion, and method of reasoning so you can quickly eliminate answer choices and accurately select the best answer. When you really understand the argument, attacking or defending it is fairly easy.

2. **E.** First, a quick review of Mackenzie's argument indicates that she is in *favor* of lowering the drinking age, not opposed, so you can quickly eliminate any answer choices that include support for doing so, such as Choices (B) and (C), because those choices actually strengthen Mackenzie's argument.

   Now, determine which of the remaining options *best* weakens Mackenzie's argument that the legal drinking age should be lowered. The remaining answers focus on Mackenzie's premise that because European countries have lower drinking ages and fewer problems with alcohol, lowering the drinking age in America would likewise lead to fewer alcohol-related problems. She makes her argument based on an analogy between Europe and America, so weaken her contention by showing that Europe and America are substantially similar in their approach to teenage drinking. It may sound surprising to weaken an analogy with a similarity, but in this case Mackenzie's analogy seeks to liken the alleged present state of affairs in Europe to the supposed future state of affairs in America if the American drinking age is lowered. Showing a similarity between present day Europe and present day America can therefore weaken the argument that a change in the drinking age will reduce alcohol-related problems in America.

Mackenzie doesn't say that European countries have *no* alcohol-related problems, just that there are fewer, so Choice (A) is irrelevant to her argument. Choice (D) provides a concrete difference between European and American culture that reveals why European teens tend to be more responsible than American teens when it comes to alcohol consumption, so this is an answer choice that seems to lend support to Mackenzie's argument that a lower drinking age won't result in less responsible drinking among American teens. On the other hand, Choice (E) reveals a similarity between European and American youth, which best serves to weaken Mackenzie's analogy between the lower drinking age in Europe and the proposed lower drinking age in America. If both European and American youths drink in private, uncontrolled environments despite the difference in the drinking ages of the two cultures, it's unlikely that changing the drinking age in American will affect the behavior that Mackenzie claims is dangerous (drinking in private).

3. **A.** Rachel argues for retaining the current legal drinking age of 21. She bases her conclusion on the premises that younger drinkers are more likely to influence the behavior of 15- to 17-year-olds and that teens haven't reached an age where they can drink alcohol responsibly.

To find the correct answer to questions that ask for an assumption, look for the answer choice that links one or more of the premises to the conclusion. Eliminate answer choices that don't relate to at least one of the premises of the argument.

Choices (B) and (E) relate to one of Mackenzie's premises, so it's unlikely that they would reveal one of Rachel's assumptions. Cross out those two answers on your noteboard.

You can also check off Choice (D) because it contradicts Rachel's premise that the effect an 18-year-old's alcohol consumption can have on younger peers is an important consideration in determining the legal drinking age. It's also unlikely that Choice (C) is correct because Rachel doesn't make comparisons regarding the impressionability of teens based on their ages. Her premise is that younger teens are more likely to be influenced by 18-year-olds than 21-year-olds. Furthermore, Choice (C) doesn't link one of Rachel's premises to her conclusion in the way that Choice (A) does.

If Rachel concludes that the legal drinking age must remain at 21 because younger drinkers don't consume alcohol responsibly, she must think that 21-year-olds have achieved some level of responsibility that's greater than those who are younger. Choice (A) links the relevance of one of Rachel's premises (a lower level of responsible drinking) to her conclusion that people who are younger than 21 shouldn't be able to legally consume alcohol. So the correct answer is Choice (A).

4. **B.** This question asks you to come up with a conclusion based on the information in the paragraph.

Notice that the question asks you for what *must* be true rather than what *could* be true. So you can cross out any answers that aren't absolutely true given the data in the paragraph.

All you know from the paragraph is the average marrying age for females today and 20 years ago and the average age that females have their first child today compared to 20 years ago. The paragraph says nothing about the *number* of children females have or had, so you can easily wipe Choice (D) out of contention. Furthermore, the paragraph provides no explanation for why the data has changed over the years, so you can't know the reason that the average age has increased. So Choice (C) can't be right.

Don't choose an answer based on an assumption or your own experience. The paragraph merely reports data instead of commenting on it, and it treats the age of marrying and having one's first child as two separate statistics. You can't make assumptions about how the two sets of data are related.

That means that Choice (A) doesn't have to be true. Just because the average age for marrying and having a first child are currently the same doesn't mean that more American females are having their first child before they marry. For example, the increased marrying age could be the result of females who marry when they're older and have no children. Eliminate Choice (E) for the same reason. You can't assume from these limited statistics that the females who are 23 when they marry are the ones who are having their first child at 25. There are too many other variables in the population.

The only thing you know for sure is that, because the average age for having a first child has risen over the last 20 years, on average, females are having their first child at a later age than they did 20 years ago. Choice (B) is the only answer that must be true.

5. **A.** Asking for the main point of an argument is another sneaky way of getting you to pick out the conclusion. This paragraph makes it easy for you because the conclusion follows the *so* in the last sentence: Banks should rely less on machines. The first sentence of the argument equates machines with technological advances, which means that you can say that the main point is that banks should rely less on technology, Choice (A).

Choices (C), (D), and (E) require you to make assumptions that aren't supported by the argument. Because you read newspaper headlines, you may think that Choice (D)'s assertion about the avarice of bank executives is a foregone conclusion, but, alas, it isn't mentioned in the argument. (You should also have been alerted by the debatable word *inevitable* in Choice [E]). The paragraph does suggest that bank patrons want personal attention (Choice [B]), but this statement is a premise rather than the conclusion. So the correct answer is Choice (A).

6. **D.** The first step to answering any question that asks you to strengthen a conclusion is to figure out exactly what that conclusion is. In this case, the paragraph argues that the candidate's proposal to ban cellphones in schools is a campaign strategy to make voters think he cares about the quality of education. The argument is based on the statistic that the increase in the number of students who cheat has been insignificant. To support the author's argument, find the answer that best supports the contention that cheating really hasn't increased all that much.

Eliminate choices that don't pertain to the author's argument. You can disregard Choices (A) and (B). The argument is concerned with the implications surrounding a cellphone ban, not the candidate's position on a budget increase. You're assuming too much (or relying on your own opinion) to make a determination of whether the candidate's vote for or against a budget increase has anything to do with education quality.

Choice (E) indicates that a reason other than cheating may be the reason the candidate wishes to impose the cellphone ban, but that absurd personal reason doesn't support the author's argument that the candidate is proposing the ban for political reasons.

The answer must be either Choice (C) or Choice (D). Both deal with number of actual students in the district, so they may reflect on the validity of the candidate's claim that cheating has increased and the author's claim that it hasn't. Having smaller class sizes tells you nothing about the overall number of students. The district could have hired more teachers to accommodate the same number of students. The only answer that relates to the cheating statistic is Choice (D). The marginal increase in cheating could be due to an increase in number of students rather than an increase in cellphone cheating, which supports the author's argument that the candidate's reason for banning cellphone use is unfounded.

7. **E.** The implication is that the advertising ban is designed to curb childhood obesity. The author states that this ban won't work, which suggests that the author thinks that the fast-food advertisements don't cause childhood obesity. To weaken this argument, show that the advertisements do indeed lead to obesity. If it's been proven that watching an ad increases one's desire for something, then banning the ads *would* reduce the desire for fast food that produces weight gain in children. Choice (E) weakens the author's argument by showing that the advertisement ban will indeed curb childhood obesity. Choice (A) seems to strengthen the author's argument, and Choices (B), (C), and (D) deal with tangents that don't relate to whether the advertisement would be effective in curbing childhood obesity. The correct answer is Choice (E).

Chapter 6

Bringing It Together: A Mini Practice Verbal Section

· ·

In This Chapter

▶ Practicing sentence correction, reading comprehension, and critical reasoning questions

▶ Finding out why right answers are right and wrong answers are wrong

· ·

*L*ike the real GMAT verbal section, the mini practice test in this chapter has an equal distribution of each of the three types of verbal questions. It contains seven reading comprehension questions, seven sentence correction questions, and seven critical reasoning questions. The total of 21 questions makes this mini verbal test just about half the size of the 41-question GMAT verbal section. To get more practice, take the full-length practice exams included with this book.

Although we can't simulate a computer in this book, don't let that deter you. Just mark the answers right in the book, and try not to look at the answers until *after* you've answered the questions. We designate each answer choice with a letter to make it easier to reference it in the answer explanations, but on the actual computerized exam, you'll simply click the oval that precedes each answer choice to mark your answer.

To best mimic the computer experience during this mini practice test, answer each question in sequence and don't go back and change any of your answers after you've moved on to the next question. At the actual exam, you won't have a test booklet to write in, so try not to write anything except your answers on the pages of this book. To keep your notes and record eliminated answers, use scratch paper to simulate the noteboard you'll use on test day.

Take the time to read through the answer explanations at the end of the chapter, even for the questions you get right. The explanations apply the techniques covered in the other chapters of this book and show you why a certain answer is a better choice than the others.

Working Through Verbal Reasoning Practice Questions

If you're the competitive type and want to subject yourself to a timed test, give yourself just a little more than 30 minutes to complete the 21 questions in this section.

Here's a quick review of the directions for the three types of verbal questions that appear in this mini practice test (and on the real GMAT):

✔ **Sentence correction questions:** Choose the answer choice that best phrases the underlined portion of the given sentence according to the rules of standard English. The first answer choice duplicates the phrasing of the underlined portion; the other four choices provide alternative phrasings. Choose the one that rephrases the sentence in the clearest, most grammatically correct manner.

✔ **Reading comprehension questions:** Choose the best answer to every question based on what the passage states directly or indirectly.

✔ **Critical reasoning questions:** Pick the answer choice that best answers the question about the argument provided.

1. A study of energy consumption revealed that homeowners living within 100 miles of the Gulf of Mexico used less energy from November 1 to April 30 than did homeowners in any other region of the United States. The same study found that from May 1 to October 31, those same homeowners used more energy than any other homeowners.

   Which of the following, if true, would most contribute to an explanation of the facts above?

   (A) People who own homes near the Gulf of Mexico often own second homes in cooler locations, where they spend the summers.

   (B) Air conditioning a home is a more energy-efficient process than heating a similarly sized home.

   (C) Homes near the Gulf of Mexico require very little heating during the warm winters, but air conditioners must run longer in the summer to cool the warm, humid air.

   (D) The average daily temperature is lower year-round near the Gulf of Mexico than in other areas of the United States.

   (E) Because of the large number of refineries located in the Gulf region, the price of energy there is less than in any other area of the country.

2. A conservation group is trying to convince Americans that the return of gray wolves to the northern United States is a positive development. Introduction of the wolf faces significant opposition because of the wolf's reputation as a killer of people and livestock. So that the wolf will be more acceptable to average Americans, the conservation group wants to dispel the myth that the wolf is a vicious killer.

   Which of the following, if true, would most weaken the opposition's claim?

   (A) Wolves are necessary for a healthy population of white-tailed deer because wolves kill the weaker animals and limit the population to sustainable numbers.

   (B) In a confrontation, black bears are much more dangerous to humans than wolves are.

   (C) Wolves are superb hunters, operating in packs to track down their prey and kill it.

   (D) There has never been a documented case of a wolf killing a human in the 500-year recorded history of North America.

   (E) Wolves occasionally take livestock because domestic animals are not equipped to protect themselves the way wild animals are.

Questions 3–5 refer to the following passage.

This passage is excerpted from *The Big Splat, or How Our Moon Came to Be,* by Dana Mackenzie, PhD (Wiley).

It is hard for us to imagine today how utterly different the world of night used to be from the daylight world. Of course, we can still re-create something of that lost mystique. When we sit around a campfire and tell ghost stories, our goose bumps (and our children's) remind us of the terrors that night used to hold. But it is all too easy for us to pile in the car at the end of our camping trip and return to the comfort of our incandescent, fluorescent, floodlit modern word. Two thousand, or even two hundred, years ago there was no such escape from the darkness. It was a physical presence that gripped the world from sunset until the cock's crow.

"As different as night and day," we say today. But in centuries past, night and day really were different. In a time when every scrap of light after sunset was desperately appreciated, when travelers would mark the road by piling up light stones or by stripping the bark off of trees to expose the lighter wood underneath, the Moon was the traveler's greatest friend. It was known in folklore as "the parish lantern." It was steady, portable, and—unlike a torch—entailed no risk of fire. It would never blow out, although it could, of course, hide behind a cloud.

Nowadays we don't need the moon to divide the light from the darkness because electric lights do it for us. Many of us have never even see a truly dark sky. According to a recent survey on light pollution, 97 percent of the U.S. population lives under a night sky at least as bright as it was on a half-moon night in ancient times. Many city-dwellers live their entire lives under the equivalent of a full moon.

3. The primary purpose of this passage is to

   (A) compare and contrast nighttime in the modern world with the dark nights of centuries past

   (B) explain why the invention of the electric light was essential to increasing worker productivity

   (C) lament the loss of the dark nights and the danger and excitement that moonless nights would bring

   (D) describe the diminishing brightness of the moon and the subsequent need for more electric lights

   (E) argue for an end to the excessive light pollution that plagues 97 percent of the U.S. population

4. The passage mentions all the following as possible ways for travelers to find the path at night *except*

   (A) piles of light-colored stones

   (B) the moon

   (C) a torch

   (D) railings made of light wood

   (E) trees with the bark stripped off

5. The author includes the statistic "97 percent of the U.S. population lives under a night sky at least as bright as it was on a half-moon night in ancient times" to primarily emphasize which of the following points?

   (A) Modern humans have the luxury of being able to see well at night despite cloud cover or a moonless night.

   (B) Most modern people cannot really understand how important the moon was to people in centuries past.

   (C) Americans are unique among the people of the world in having so much artificial light at night.

   (D) A full moon in ancient times was brighter than modern electric lights, which are only as bright as a half-moon.

   (E) Light pollution is one of the most important problems facing the United States in the 21st century.

6. The sugar maples give us syrup in March, a display of beautiful flowers in spring, and <u>their foliage is spectacular in October</u>.

   (A) their foliage is spectacular in October

   (B) spectacularly, their foliage changes color in October

   (C) has spectacular foliage in October

   (D) spectacular foliage in October

   (E) October foliage that is spectacular in orange and red

7. The Industrial Revolution required levels of financing <u>which were previously unknown</u>; for instance, Florence had 80 banking houses that took deposits, made loans, and performed many of the other functions of a modern bank.

   (A) which were previously unknown

   (B) that were previously unknown

   (C) unknown before that time

   (D) which had been unknown in earlier times

   (E) that was previously unknown

8. His efforts to learn scuba diving, a major goal Bob had set for himself for the coming year, <u>has not significantly begun, seeing as how</u> his fear of claustrophobia is triggered anytime he is underwater.

   (A) has not successfully begun, seeing as how

   (B) have not successfully begun, seeing as how

   (C) have not been successful because

   (D) has not been successful because

   (E) have not yet met with success, on account of

Questions 9 and 10 are based on the following information.

Tom: The unemployment rate has dropped below 5 percent, and that is good news for America. A lower unemployment rate is better for almost everyone.

Shelly: Actually, a low unemployment rate is good for most workers but not for everyone. Workers are certainly happy to have jobs, but many businesses are negatively affected by a low unemployment rate because they have fewer applicants for jobs, and to expand their workforce, they have to hire workers they would not usually hire. The wealthiest Americans also privately complain about the inability to get good gardeners, housecleaners, and nannies when most Americans are already employed. So a low unemployment rate is not, in fact, good for America.

9. Which of the following, if true, would most weaken the argument that a low unemployment rate is bad for business?

(A) Businesses must pay skilled or experienced workers higher salaries when the unemployment rate is low.

(B) The states don't have to pay unemployment compensation to as many workers when unemployment is low.

(C) Higher unemployment generally means higher enrollment levels in college and graduate school.

(D) Inflation can increase with low unemployment, making capital more expensive for any business seeking to expand.

(E) Low unemployment rates generally mean that Americans have more money to spend on the goods and services created by American businesses.

10. Shelly's conclusion that "a low unemployment rate is not, in fact, good for America" relies on the assumption that

(A) What is bad for businesses owners and the wealthy is bad for America.

(B) Fluctuations in the unemployment rate affect the number of applicants for job openings.

(C) Wealthy Americans rarely employ other Americans to clean their houses or as nannies for their children.

(D) Business owners always want what is best for their workers even when it negatively impacts the bottom line.

(E) Low unemployment hurts some workers because they would prefer to stay at home and collect unemployment checks.

11. A particular company makes a system that is installed in the engine block of a car and, if that car is stolen, relays the car's location to police via satellite. The recovery rate of stolen cars with this device is 90 percent. This system helps everyone because it is impossible for a thief to tell which cars it is installed on. For these reasons, insurance companies try to encourage customers to get this system by offering lower rates to those who have the system. Competing systems include brightly colored steel bars that attach to the steering wheel and loud alarms that go off when the car is tampered with. These systems simply encourage thieves to steal different cars, and when cars with these devices are stolen, the police rarely recover them.

Which of the following is the most logical conclusion to the author's premises?

(A) Insurance companies should give the same discount to car owners who have any protective system because their cars are less likely to be stolen.

(B) The police shouldn't allow car owners to install the loud sirens on their cars because everyone simply ignores the sirens anyway.

(C) Car owners with the system that relays location to the police should prominently advertise the fact on the side window of their cars.

(D) Thieves should simply steal the cars with loud alarms or bright steel bars because those cars probably wouldn't also have the more effective system installed.

(E) Insurance companies should give less of a discount, or no discount at all, to the siren and steering wheel systems because they aren't as effective as the relay system.

12. The managers were asked to rate <u>their depth of knowledge having been increased</u> as a result of the emergency simulation, and in each area, they reported large gains.

(A) their depth of knowledge having been increased

(B) how much their depth of knowledge had increased

(C) if they had more knowledge

(D) how deep their knowledge is

(E) their knowledge depth

13. Keeping the nose of her kayak directly into the wind, she paddled fiercely toward the safety of the harbor <u>through the seeming endless waves, each of those larger than the last</u>.

(A) through the seeming endless waves, each of those larger than the last

(B) through the seeming endless waves, each larger than the last

(C) through the seemingly endless waves, each of those larger than the last

(D) through the seemingly endless waves, each larger than the last

(E) through waves that seemingly have no end, each larger than the last

14. Companies X and Y have the same number of employees working the same number of hours per week. According to the records kept by the human resources department of each company, the employees of company X took nearly twice as many sick days as the employees of company Y. Therefore, the employees of company Y are healthier than the employees of company X.

Which of the following, if true, most seriously weakens the conclusion?

(A) Company X allows employees to use sick days to take care of sick family members.

(B) Company Y offers its employees dental insurance and company X doesn't.

(C) Company X offers its employees a free membership to the local gym.

(D) Company Y uses a newer system for keeping records of sick days.

(E) Both companies offer two weeks of sick days per year.

Questions 15–18 refer to the following passage.

This passage is excerpted from *Brand Name Bullies: The Quest to Own and Control Culture,* by David Bollier (Wiley).

For millennia, the circulation of music in human societies has been as free as the circulation of air and water; it just comes naturally. Indeed, one of the ways that a society constitutes itself as a society is by freely sharing its words, music, and art. Only in the past century or so has music been placed in a tight envelope of property rights and strictly monitored for unauthorized flows. In the past decade, the proliferation of personal computers, Internet access, and digital technologies has fueled two conflicting forces: the democratization of creativity and the demand for stronger copyright protections.

While the public continues to have nominal fair use rights to copyrighted music, in practice the legal and technological controls over music have grown tighter. At the same time, creators at the fringes of mass culture, especially some hip-hop and remix artists, remain contemptuous of such controls and routinely appropriate whatever sounds they want to create interesting music.

Copyright protection is a critically important tool for artists in earning a livelihood from their creativity. But as many singers, composers, and musicians have discovered, the benefits of copyright law in the contemporary marketplace tend to accrue to the recording industry, not to the struggling garage band. As alternative distribution and marketing outlets have arisen, the recording industry has sought to ban, delay, or control as many of them as possible. After all, technological innovations that provide faster, cheaper distribution of music are likely to disrupt the industry's fixed investments and entrenched ways of doing business. New technologies allow newcomers to enter the market and compete, sometimes on superior terms. New technologies enable new types of audiences to emerge that may or may not be compatible with existing marketing strategies.

No wonder the recording industry has scrambled to develop new technological locks and broader copyright protections; they strengthen its control of music distribution. If metering devices could turn barroom singalongs into a market, the music industry would likely declare this form of unauthorized musical performance to be copyright infringement.

15. Which of the following most accurately states the main idea of the passage?

  (A) Only with the development of technology in the past century has music begun to freely circulate in society.

  (B) The recording industry is trying to develop an ever-tighter hold on the distribution of music, which used to circulate freely.

  (C) Copyright protection is an important tool for composers and musicians who earn their living from their music.

  (D) Technology allows new distribution methods that threaten to undermine the marketing strategies of music companies.

  (E) If music is no longer allowed to flow freely through the society, then the identity of the society itself will be lost.

16. Given the author's overall opinion of increased copyright protections, what is his attitude toward "hip-hop and remix artists" mentioned in paragraph 2?

  (A) wonder that they aren't sued more for their theft of copyright-protected music

  (B) disappointment that they don't understand the damage they are doing to society

  (C) envy of their extravagant lifestyle and increasing popularity

  (D) approval of their continued borrowing of music despite tighter copyright controls

  (E) shock at their blatant sampling of the music of other artists

17. According to the passage, new technology has resulted (or will result) in each of the following *except*

    (A) new locks on music distribution

    (B) newcomers' competing in the music market

    (C) better music

    (D) democratization of creativity

    (E) faster, cheaper distribution of music

18. The final sentence of the passage seems to imply what about the executives of the record industry?

    (A) They have found ways to make money from any performance of any music at any time.

    (B) They are boldly leading the music industry into a new technological era of vastly increased profits.

    (C) They want their music to be performed as often as possible by the maximum number of people to create greater exposure for artists.

    (D) They don't actually like music or know anything about music and are attempting to limit the society's exposure to music.

    (E) No performance of music anywhere is safe from their attempts to control the distribution of all music.

19. Five new loon pairs successfully raised chicks this year, <u>bringing</u> to 24 the number of pairs actively breeding in the lakes of Massachusetts.

    (A) bringing

    (B) and brings

    (C) and it brings

    (D) and it brought

    (E) and brought

20. New laws make it easier to patent just about anything, from parts of the human genome to a peanut butter and jelly sandwich. Commentators are concerned about the implications of allowing patents for things that can hardly be described as "inventions." However, the U.S. Patent and Trademark Office believes that allowing for strong copyright and patent protections fosters the kind of investment in research and development needed to spur innovation.

    Which of the following can be properly inferred from the preceding statements?

    (A) It was not possible in the past to patent something as common as a peanut butter and jelly sandwich.

    (B) The U.S. Patent and Trademark Office is more interested in business profits than in true innovation.

    (C) Investment in research and development is often needed to spur innovation.

    (D) The human genome is part of nature and shouldn't be patented.

    (E) Commentators who are concerned about too many patents aren't very well informed.

21. Despite the fact that they were colonists, <u>more Americans thought of themselves as British citizens</u>, and throughout the early years of the American Revolution, more than half of all Americans were loyal to Britain.

    (A) more Americans thought of themselves as British citizens

    (B) fewer Americans felt that they were British citizens

    (C) most Americans thought of themselves as British citizens

    (D) many of them felt like British citizens

    (E) most Americans believed we were British citizens

Understanding What's Right with Answer Explanations

You can check your answers to the practice questions by reading through the following explanations. To get the most benefit, read through every explanation, even the ones for the questions you answered correctly.

1. **C.** This critical reasoning question asks you to strengthen the argument by providing a piece to the cause-and-effect pattern. With cause-and-effect questions, you select the answer choice that could logically cause the effects noted in the premises. So for this problem, you have to decide which of the five choices helps explain why Gulf Coast homes use little energy in the winter *and* a great deal of energy in the summer. Without even looking at the answer choices, you may conclude that the Gulf Coast climate is milder than other parts of the nation in the winter and perhaps hotter in the summer. The correct answer probably addresses that issue.

   You can eliminate Choice (A) because if most Gulf Coast residents spend the summer elsewhere, their vacant homes would use less energy during summer months rather than more. This answer would produce the opposite effect of that explained in the argument. Choice (B) would also produce the opposite effect of that found in the argument. Another important reason for eliminating Choice (B) is that it doesn't provide a way of comparing energy use in the Gulf region to energy use in the rest of the country, which is the real issue in this argument.

   Choice (C) sounds like the answer we imagined before reading through the choices. It explains why the Gulf region would have lower energy use in winter and higher use in summer, which may explain why it's different from the rest of the country as a whole. Although Choice (C) is probably the correct answer, read through the remaining two choices just to be sure.

   Choice (D) doesn't work because a region that's cool year-round would have high energy consumption in the winter for heat and low consumption in the summer. And you can eliminate Choice (E) because the argument is about energy consumption, not energy price. So the correct answer is Choice (C).

2. **D.** This critical reasoning question asks you to weaken the opposition's statement that the wolf is vicious, so look for a statement that shows that the wolf isn't a danger to people or livestock. Begin by eliminating answers that don't address the appropriate conclusion. Choice (A) deals with the beneficial impact of wolves on the ecosystem but doesn't talk about their propensity toward viciousness, so eliminate it. You can also eliminate Choice (C) because the hunting prowess of the wolf isn't the issue, and this choice may actually strengthen the contention that wolves are dangerous. Choice (E) also doesn't weaken the

conclusion in question; it argues that wolves may threaten livestock. This leaves you with Choices (B) and (D). Choice (B) compares the danger posed by wolves with the danger posed by black bears. Even if a wolf is less dangerous than a bear, that doesn't mean a wolf isn't dangerous. The best answer is Choice (D), because it provides a statistic that weakens the opposition's argument that wolves are dangerous to humans.

3. **A.** For a primary purpose reading comprehension question, you're looking for the reason the author wrote the passage.

Focus on the passage as a whole and not on any particular portion. You usually can find clues to the main theme and the author's purpose in the first and last paragraphs.

The main idea of this passage is that night was very different in centuries past than it is in current times, and the author's purpose is to show how this is true. So look for an answer that reflects this purpose.

You can start by eliminating answers based on their first words. The words *compare and contrast, explain,* and *describe* reflect the author's purpose, but *lament* and *argue* imply more emotion on the part of the author than is displayed in the passage, so eliminate Choices (C) and (E). Worker productivity has nothing to do with showing how our ancestors perceived night differently, so you can eliminate Choice (B). Choice (D) is simply wrong; the author doesn't maintain that the moon is actually getting darker, just that it's become overshadowed by electric lights. So that leaves Choice (A) as the correct answer.

4. **D.** This specific information exception question asks you to refer to the text to eliminate answers that *are* ways in the passage that travelers can find a path at night. The second paragraph specifically mentions Choice (A), light-colored stones; Choice (B), the moon; Choice (C), torches; and Choice (E), trees with the bark stripped off. Railings, Choice (D), aren't mentioned anywhere in the passage so it's the correct answer.

5. **B.** This question asks you about the use of a specific statistic. To answer this question correctly, keep in mind the author's purpose for writing the passage, which you've already considered in the third question. Find the choice that links the statistic to the author's purpose of comparing nighttime now and nighttime in centuries past. Eliminate Choice (C) because the author compares time periods, not modern countries. Because the passage doesn't indicate that the moon is brighter than electric lights, you can eliminate Choice (D). Although the 97 percent statistic may lead you to conclude that light pollution is a big problem, that's not the author's reason for using the statistic, so eliminate Choice (E). Choice (A) is a little more plausible, but Choice (B) is better because the author is more concerned with showing how night skies are different now than with showing that the modern well-lit sky is a luxury.

6. **D.** This sentence correction question has a parallelism problem. You know this because the underlined portion is a part of a list of elements joined by a conjunction and not all the elements in the list exhibit the same construction. The third element is expressed as a clause, and the other elements are noun phrases. Because the sentence contains an error, you know Choice (A) is wrong. Choices (B) and (C) don't change the clause to a phrase. Although Choice (E) is a noun phrase, its construction is unnecessarily wordy: *foliage that is spectacular* versus *spectacular foliage.* Choice (E) also introduces new information (the colors orange and red), which alters the original sentence. Choice (D) maintains parallel construction without adding unnecessary words, so it's the correct answer.

7. **B.** This sentence correction question has an improperly used pronoun. You use *which* to introduce nonessential clauses. Because the information after the *which* is essential to the meaning of the sentence, you have to use *that* instead. You can eliminate Choices (A) and (D) because both keep the *which* construction. Choice (C) uses too many words to mean previously unknown, and Choice (E) changes *which* to *that* but presents a new problem because *that* refers to *levels,* which is plural, so it requires the plural verb *have.* So Choice (B) is the only answer that corrects the problem without creating new ones.

8. **C.** The underlined portion of this sentence correction question has problems with agreement and rhetorical construction. The plural subject *efforts* doesn't work with the singular verb *has*. Because you find an error, you automatically eliminate Choice (A). Choice (D) doesn't correct the agreement error. This leaves you with Choices (B), (C), and (E), all of which correct the agreement problem, but *because* is a better, clearer construction than *seeing as how* and *on account of,* so Choice (C) is the best answer.

9. **E.** This critical reasoning question requires you to weaken Shelly's argument that a low unemployment rate is bad for business. Choices (A) and (D) give two examples of how low unemployment hurts businesses, so they actually strengthen the argument instead of weaken it. Eliminate them along with Choices (B) and (C), because these statements are basically off topic; they deal with government and universities, not businesses. Choice (E) is the correct answer, because employed American workers' buying more American products provides a significant advantage for businesses.

10. **A.** This critical reasoning question asks you to identify an assumption that Shelly relied on in making her conclusion that a low unemployment rate isn't "good for America."

When you're asked to find an assumption, look for a statement that supports the conclusion but isn't actually stated in the argument.

Eliminate choices that don't support the conclusion. Whether businesses favor workers over the bottom line may affect the unemployment rate, but it doesn't show how low unemployment isn't good for America, so Choice (D) is incorrect. Choice (E) doesn't support the conclusion, either. The conclusion is about what's good for America in general, not a select few disinclined workers.

A person's assumption wouldn't contradict a stated premise, so Choice (C) can't be right. Choice (B) may support the conclusion, but it's actually stated in the given premises and, therefore, can't be an unstated assumption. Choice (A) is the correct answer because it links Shelly's premises about businesses and wealthy Americans to her conclusion about America in general.

11. **E.** This critical reasoning question requires you to draw a conclusion from the premises included in the argument.

Look for an answer choice that addresses all the information in the premises. You can eliminate conclusions that are off topic or incomplete.

Eliminate choices that don't include all the elements of the argument. Choices (B), (C), and (D) don't mention the insurance companies that are the subject of one of the premises. This leaves you with Choice (A) and Choice (E), which offer nearly opposite conclusions. The premises indicate that one of the reasons insurance companies like the engine-block system is that thieves don't know which cars have it installed. Choice (A) concludes that cars with any protective system, including alarms and steering wheel bars, should get a discount because those cars are less likely to be stolen. This conclusion doesn't flow logically from the premises, however, because the reasons given for the insurance discounts are a high recovery rate of stolen vehicles and the general deterrent to all car thefts. Neither of these advantages comes from the alarms or steering wheel bars. Choice (E) addresses all the premises and logically concludes the argument, making it the correct answer.

12. **B.** The underlined portion in this sentence correction question is passive, so you can eliminate Choice (A). Choices (C), (D), and (E) don't address both the knowledge increase *and* the knowledge depth, so you can eliminate them, too. The best answer is Choice (B). It makes the construction active and includes both the increase and depth of knowledge.

13. **D.** You probably first noticed that the underlined portion of this sentence correction question contains a modification error. Adjectives like *seeming* modify nouns and pronouns. They can't modify other adjectives like *endless*. Adverbs must be used for that. Instead of *seeming,* you can use the adverb *seemingly*. Therefore, you know you can disregard Choice (A). You can also eliminate Choice (B) because it doesn't make the change to *seemingly*. Choices (C), (D), and (E) change *seeming* to *seemingly.*

This underlined portion also has a problem with redundancy. *Each* refers sufficiently to *waves; of those* isn't necessary. Choice (C) doesn't fix this error, so it's wrong. Choices (D) and (E) both fix each of the errors, but Choice (E) creates another. The sentence is past tense, so the verb *have* should be in past tense like this: *seemingly had no end.* Choice (D) corrects both original errors and doesn't introduce more, so it's the correct answer.

14. **A.** This critical reasoning question asks you to weaken the conclusion that the employees of company Y are healthier than the employees of company X. The author draws the conclusion that Y's employees are healthier than X's employees based on the cause-and-effect argument that more sick days mean sicker employees.

To weaken cause-and-effect arguments, look for an answer choice that shows another cause is possible for the effect.

Choice (E) doesn't distinguish between the two companies. It can't show another cause for the different number of sick days and, therefore, can't be right. Choice (D) differentiates between the two companies' record keeping, but it doesn't explain how company Y's new records system accounts for fewer sick days. Dental insurance shouldn't affect the number of sick days, so Choice (B) doesn't work. Choice (C) doesn't address the issue of company X's greater number of sick days, so free gym memberships don't matter. The best answer is Choice (A) because it provides a reason other than employee health for the greater number of sick days that company X's employees take.

15. **B.** This reading comprehension question asks for the main idea of the passage.

Answers to main theme questions are usually more general than specific in their wording.

Choices (C) and (D) each focus on sub-themes in the passage but not the main idea. Copyright protection and technology are specific subjects covered in the passage, but they don't make up the main idea, which is that the music industry is trying to control distribution of music. You can eliminate Choice (A) because it's not supported by any part of the passage. The passage clearly states that music has circulated freely in society for millennia. Choice (E) is wrong because it goes beyond what's stated in the passage. The author may well imply that without the free flow of music, society will lose its identity, but this isn't the passage's main idea. So that leaves Choice (B) as the best answer.

16. **D.** This reading comprehension question asks about the author's attitude toward *hip-hop* and *remix artists* as specifically mentioned in the second paragraph. The real GMAT would highlight this phrase in yellow. You've already answered a question about the main idea, so you know the author's concerned about the tightening grip the recording industry has on the distribution of music. Because the hip-hop and remix artists defy the music industry, they'll likely meet with the author's approval. Although Choice (A) may express a valid opinion, you can eliminate it because it isn't supported by the passage. The author probably approves of hip-hop and remix artists, so he or she doesn't think they're doing damage — Choice (B) is completely off base. Envy and shock are usually too strong emotions for GMAT passages, so rule out Choices (C) and (E). The correct answer is Choice (D).

17. **C.** Here's another specific information reading comprehension question looking for an exception. Examine the text and eliminate the answers you find there. The one that remains is your correct answer. In connection with technology, the passage mentions Choice (A), new locks on music distribution; Choice (B), newcomers' competing in the market; Choice (D), democratization of creativity; and Choice (E), faster, cheaper distribution of music. The author certainly doesn't mention better music. So Choice (C) is correct.

18. **E.** For this reading comprehension inference question, you need to determine what the final sentence implies about recording-industry executives. The final sentence mentions that if it were possible, executives would try to stop unauthorized singalongs. This shows that the author thinks that executives will go to any length to control the distribution of music. Choices (B) and (C) paint the executives in a positive light, which is certainly not warranted by the last sentence. You can also eliminate Choice (D) because the last

sentence has nothing to do with whether executives like or dislike music. Choice (A) is closer, but the sentence doesn't talk about making money from singalongs so much as stopping them altogether. That makes Choice (E) the correct answer.

19. **A.** This sentence correction question tests your knowledge of verb forms and grammatical construction. You're not dealing with word choice, because all the answer choices include a form of the verb *to bring.* Choices (C) and (D) introduce the pronoun *it,* which has no clear reference, so they're not right. Choice (B) applies a singular verb to a plural subject. Choice (E) includes *and,* which would make the comma in the non-underlined part of the sentence improper. The sentence is best as is.

20. **A.** This critical reasoning question asks you to draw an inference from the passage. Inference questions generally focus on a premise rather than on a conclusion. The passage implies that the patent office wants to promote invention, so Choice (B) doesn't work. Choices (D) and (E) express opinions that aren't presented in the passage. Although you may agree that the genome shouldn't be patented or that people who are concerned about patents aren't well informed, the question doesn't ask you for your opinion.

Don't choose answer choices to critical reasoning questions just because you agree with them. Base your answers on the opinions stated or implied by the paragraph.

Because Choice (C) is stated in the passage, it can't be an inference. The answer must be Choice (A), because it flows logically from the first premise and isn't stated in the passage.

21. **C.** The final sentence correction question contains an improper comparison. The term *more* requires a comparison between two things (more Americans thought of themselves as British citizens than what?). The sentence doesn't offer a comparison. Because there's an error, eliminate Choice (A). Choice (B) uses the term *fewer,* which also requires a comparison, and this answer choice changes the meaning of the sentence. Choice (D) gets rid of *more* but introduces the pronoun *them,* which doesn't have a clear reference and, therefore, can't be right. Choice (E) also contains a pronoun error: its inclusion of the first-person pronoun *we.* We weren't around during the American Revolution, so Choice (E) is incorrect. Choice (C) changes *more* to *most,* so it eliminates the comparison problem and is the correct answer.

Part III
Acing the Analytical Writing Section

The 5th Wave   By Rich Tennant

"It's a shame, really. Every time he gets close to finishing the GMAT, a truck drives by and he's out the window."

In this part . . .

The GMAT isn't all about clicking on answers to questions with your mouse. The first section expects you to type an essay. We guess MBA programs want to know that their potential students can communicate. For some folks, the analytical writing section is the most intimidating of the four sections. If you're one of them, this part can help put your mind at ease.

We give you a complete description of the topics you'll have to write about and let you know exactly what the GMAT readers look for when they score your essay. Then we tell you how to write what they're looking for by giving you tips on how to avoid grammar and mechanics errors and by providing techniques for organizing your thoughts.

Chapter 7

Analyze This: What to Expect from the Analytical Writing Assessment (AWA)

The analytical writing assessment (or AWA, as it's affectionately known) can be intimidating. You're required to write an analytical essay on a topic that the computer reveals to you just as your time begins to tick away. To earn the top score, you're expected to provide an excellent analysis and insightful examples and demonstrate a mastery of standard written English. Did we mention that you're supposed to do this in only 30 minutes? If it seems a little overwhelming, relax. You can do it; we show you how in this chapter.

First, you need to know what you're up against, so we walk you through the AWA and let you know what to expect. Then, we give you a sneak peak at the writing task required of you. Finally, we get to the part that interests you most — how the AWA is scored.

Fitting in the AWA with the Rest of the GMAT

The AWA is a stand-alone section of the GMAT. The GMAT reports your analytical writing score separately from your integrated reasoning score and your quantitative and verbal reasoning scores. In other words, your combined total GMAT score (with a maximum of 800 points) reflects how well you do on only the multiple-choice verbal and quantitative reasoning sections of the test. So you can write gibberish on the essay portion of the test and still earn an 800 for your GMAT score (but we certainly don't recommend that strategy!).

Each business program determines the importance of the analytical writing section differently. Some schools may give it the same weight as your combined quantitative and verbal score. Other schools may assign it less weight. Check with the specific schools you're interested in attending to see how they use the AWA score. The bottom line is that regardless of how a business program uses your essay score, it will be reported to them. So it's to your advantage to do as well on the AWA as you can.

Another reason to be well prepared for the AWA is that it's the first section of the GMAT. If you feel that you did well on the essay, this confidence may sustain you through the rest of the test. However, if you're unprepared for the AWA and have a difficult time completing the essay, your bad start can have a negative impact on your entire test session.

Calling 411: Your AWA Writing Tools

The analytical writing assessment consists of one essay prompt, which the GMAT refers to as a *task*. The task requires you to write an analytical essay within 30 minutes. You type your response, using the computer software provided at the testing center. At the end of the 30 minutes, your task is complete and only what you've actually typed into the computer contributes to your score, meaning any handwritten notes or great ideas in your head don't count!

You'll be able to use typical word-processing functions like cut, copy, paste, undo, and redo. You can access these word-processing functions with the mouse or by using special keystrokes that the GMAT specifies for you before you begin the test. You can also use your noteboard to take notes as you plan your response.

Some of the following word-processing features you may be accustomed to won't be available:

- **Automatic corrections:** If you regularly use a program like Word or WordPerfect, you probably don't even notice the automatic corrections anymore. You type in *comittment* and your computer displays *commitment* without your even realizing it. The GMAT won't automatically correct your mistakes.

- **Spelling and grammar check:** You know that spelling-and-grammar-check function that has saved you from turning in some truly hideous college papers? The function tells you, for example, that you have just written a passive sentence with subject-verb agreement problems and three misspelled words. You can't count on that because spelling and grammar check won't be available, either!

- **Synonym finder:** You won't have access to that groovy built-in thesaurus that helped you find synonyms for six of your seven uses of the word *cool* (one of which is *groovy*).

Analyzing an Argument

The analytical writing assessment task requires you to analyze an argument. The GMAT doesn't want your opinion on a topic. Instead, you're supposed to critique the way *someone else* reaches an opinion. To score well on this task, you need to analyze the reasoning behind the argument and write a critique of the argument. First, you need to briefly explain what kind of reasoning the author uses (for all about different kinds of reasoning, consult Chapter 5). Next, you point out the strengths and weaknesses of the argument. Finally, you consider the validity of the assumptions that the author makes and what effect alternative explanations would have on the author's conclusion.

Here's a paraphrase of the directions for the analysis of an argument task on the GMAT:

- Write a critique of the argument presented but don't provide your own opinion.

- Think for a few minutes about the argument and organize your response before you start writing. Leave time for revisions when you're finished.

You'll be scored based on your ability to accomplish these tasks:

- Organize, develop, and express your thoughts about the given argument.

- Provide pertinent supporting ideas with examples.

- Apply the rules of standard written English.

Now that you have the directions down, check out this example essay prompt:

The following is an excerpt written by the head of a governmental department:

"Stronger environmental regulations are not necessary in order to provide clean air and water. We already have lots of regulations on the books and these are not being adequately enforced. For example, the Clean Air Act amendments, adopted in 1990, have never been fully enforced and, as a result, hundreds of coal-burning power plants are systematically violating that law on a daily basis. The Clean Water Act is also not being enforced. In the state of Ohio alone there were more than 2,500 violations in just one year. Instead of passing new regulations that will also be ignored, this department should begin by vigorously enforcing the existing laws."

Examine this argument and present your judgment on how well reasoned it is. In your discussion, analyze the author's position and how well the author uses evidence to support the argument. For example, you may need to question the author's underlying assumptions or consider alternative explanations that may weaken the conclusion. You can also provide additional support for or arguments against the author's position, describe how stating the argument differently may make it more reasonable, and discuss what provisions may better equip you to evaluate its thesis.

Racking Up the Points: How the GMAT Scores Your Essay

According to the folks who make the GMAT, the AWA is designed to measure your ability to think and your ability to communicate your ideas. To assess how well you do in each of these areas, the GMAT employs the services of two separate readers (one of which may be a computer program called an automated essay-scoring engine). Based on their analysis of your written masterpiece, these readers individually assign you a score between 0 and 6, with 6 being the highest.

In the following sections, we give you the lowdown on who evaluates your AWA, what the different scores mean, and how to get a new score if the first one you receive is way off.

Getting to know your readers

Two independent readers judge your analytical writing task, and each of the readers assigns your essay a score from 0 to 6 in half-point increments. If the two readers who are scoring your essay differ by more than a single point, a third reader will adjudicate. This means that the third reader's score will be used in conjunction with the other scores.

For example, if one reader assigns your essay a 3 and the other reader gives it a 5, a third reader is brought in. If the third reader also gives your essay a 5, then the 3 would be discarded and your two scores for that essay would be 5 and 5. If, however, the third reader splits the difference and assigns you a 4, you'd have two 4s (the score from the third reader and the average of the first two scores).

The benefit of having more than one reader evaluate your essay is that if one reader happens to assign you an unfairly low score, he won't be able to sabotage your score.

College and university faculty members from a variety of academic disciplines score your essays. Some are from business management programs, but you can't expect that the particular readers who score your tasks will have any special knowledge of business. So avoid using jargon or assuming that your reader has had all the same business classes that you've had.

The automated scoring program that may grade your essay is designed to reflect the judgment of human readers, so it looks for the same elements that human readers do. Regardless of who (or what) reads your essay, your goal is to present quality analysis and sound reasoning with a minimum of grammatical errors. In Chapter 8, we tell you how to avoid common writing errors.

Readers look for two things when they take on your essays: clear analysis and good writing. For an essay to earn a score of 5 or 6, it must clearly analyze the argument, demonstrate good organization, and provide specific, relevant examples and insightful reasoning. The essay must demonstrate clear control of language and apply a variety of sentence structures. It can have some minor flaws in the way you use standard written English but not too many.

Keeping all these things in mind as you write your essay is a tough order for 30 short minutes. To help you through the process, consult Chapter 8, where we discuss strategies for analyzing arguments quickly and effectively and go over the most common errors test-takers make when they write under pressure.

Interpreting the scores

The GMAT reports your AWA score as a number from 0 to 6 in half-point increments. For one administration, a score of 6, the highest possible score, lands you in the 91st percentile, meaning that 91 people out of every 100 test-takers received a lower score. A score of 6 is obviously difficult to earn, and only about 8 percent of test-takers achieve that score! For the same test, a score of 5.5 puts you in the 75th percentile; a score of 5, in the 57th percentile; 4.5, the 36th percentile; and 4, the 20th percentile. You can find a full score and percentile chart on the GMAT website at www.mba.com.

The mean final score on the AWA is 4.4. The typical essay, therefore, falls somewhere between 4 (adequate) and 5 (strong). A number of papers fall into the 3 (limited) category or lower, and the cream of the crop is recognized with a 6 (outstanding). To make sure your score surfaces to the creamy top, practice using the techniques we provide in Chapter 8.

Requesting your essay be rescored

After receiving your essay score, you may think it's too low. If that's the case and you truly think you wrote a better essay than your score represents, you can take advantage of the GMAT's AWA rescoring service. Within six months of your exam, you can pay $45 to have an independent reader score your essay. The new score stands, whether it increases or decreases, so requesting a new score can be risky. But if you think a real discrepancy exists, you can take your chances by sending in a rescoring request form. The new score result is sent to you and the schools that have already received your original AWA score.

The rescoring service applies only to the AWA. The GMAT won't rescore the other three sections, which makes sense because you can't do much to change a multiple-choice test score!

Chapter 8

Present Perfect Paragraphs: How to Write a GMAT Essay

● ●

In This Chapter

▶ Writing the right way: Errors to avoid

▶ Boosting your score with writing strategies

● ●

*K*nowing what to expect from the analytical writing assessment (AWA) gives you an advantage on the GMAT, but if you want to earn a high score, you need to know what you're expected to do and how to do it. To perform well on the analytical writing task, you have to combine good analysis with a good writing style. If you lack either of these key components, your score will suffer. In this chapter, we start with common writing errors that you should avoid and then discuss the steps to writing your analysis.

Avoiding Grammar, Punctuation, and Mechanics Errors

One of the aspects of the analytical writing assessment that causes the most trouble for test-takers is the requirement that they demonstrate a good control of standard written English. Standard written English isn't so standard anymore, and it doesn't mirror the way most Americans speak (or text and e-mail, for that matter!). E-mailed messages are often sentence fragments, and you don't have to worry about things like spelling and punctuation when you text. Because you can't always rely on what sounds right to you, you have to know the writing rules.

In the following sections, we identify a few common mistakes that plague GMAT test-takers. Writers everywhere seem to repeat these same writing errors. The essay readers will notice these errors, and their presence in your essay will affect your score. If you identify the errors you make most often, you can begin to eliminate them now. Don't wait until test day to isolate your writing issues! In addition to the information we give you in this chapter, you can find more info on applying the rules of grammar and punctuation and on correcting writing problems in Chapter 3 and in *English Grammar For Dummies* by Geraldine Woods (Wiley).

Punctuation errors

The role of punctuation is to guide the reader through sentences and paragraphs. Without proper punctuation, your reader won't know where one thought ends and another begins. Punctuation errors are among the most common mistakes test-takers make on the essay portion of the GMAT, and we're not talking about simply ending a sentence with a period.

Many people confuse colons and semicolons. Semicolons join independent clauses when the thoughts they convey are related enough to keep them in the same sentence: *It's almost test day; I need to write a practice essay this weekend.* (Independent clauses can stand alone as complete sentences. For more information on the difference between independent and dependent clauses, see Chapter 3.) On the other hand, you primarily use colons to introduce lists or to precede an example.

The most common punctuation errors involve commas. You use commas to separate items in a series, to replace omitted words, and to set off clauses and parenthetical expressions. You also use them to separate parts of the sentence:

- Insert a comma before the coordinating conjunction *(for, and, nor, but, or, yet, or so)* that joins two independent clauses.

- Include a comma between a beginning dependent clause and an independent clause. (But don't put a comma between the clauses if the independent clause comes first.)

Two comma errors GMAT essay-writers often make are comma splices and run-on sentences:

- **Comma splices** occur when you join two independent clauses with just a comma and no coordinating conjunction, like this: *Harold made several errors in his GMAT essay, one was a comma splice.* To correct a comma splice, you make the independent clauses two separate sentences *(Harold made several errors in his GMAT essay. One was a comma splice.)*, substitute a semicolon for the comma *(Harold made several errors in his GMAT essay; one was a comma splice.)*, or add a coordinating conjunction after the comma *(Harold made several errors in his GMAT essay, and one was a comma splice.)*.

- You make a **run-on sentence** when you join together two independent clauses with a coordinating conjunction and no comma: *Harold made several punctuation errors in his GMAT essay and one was a run-on sentence that made his writing seem needlessly wordy.* To correct a run-on, you just add a comma before the conjunction: *Harold made several punctuation errors in his GMAT essay, and one was a run-on sentence that made his writing seem needlessly wordy.*

Sentence structure problems

GMAT essay-readers focus on more than how you punctuate your sentences. They also notice how you form your words. To avoid a negative critique, steer clear of these two problems with sentence structure:

- **Sentence fragments:** You may be able to blame your propensity for sentence fragments on technology, but you can't translate your e-mail and texting style to the GMAT essays. A sentence must have a subject and a verb and convey a complete thought. Watch out for dependent clauses masquerading as complete sentences. Even though they contain subjects and verbs, they can't stand alone as sentences without other information. Here are some examples:

  • **A sentence and a fragment:** I will return to the workforce. After I earn my MBA.

  • **Complete sentence:** I will return to the workforce after I earn my MBA.

- **Modifier errors:** Modifiers are words and phrases that describe other words. The rule of thumb is to place modifiers as close as possible to the words they modify:

  • **Sloppy:** The assistant found the minutes for the meeting held on Saturday on the desk.

  • **Better:** The assistant found Saturday's meeting minutes on the desk.

Faulty forming of possessives

One writing element that you may overlook when you're frantically composing a 30-minute essay is forming possessives. Although your training in putting together proper possessives likely began in elementary school, you may appreciate this refresher:

- **Standard issue nouns:** Use the possessive form of a noun when the noun is immediately followed by another noun that it possesses. Most possessives are formed by adding an apostrophe and *s* to the end of a singular noun: *Steve's boss.* This practice is usually true even if the singular noun ends in *s: Charles's test score.* If the possessive noun is plural and ends in *s,* you just add an apostrophe to the end of the word: *The brothers' dogs; many clients' finances.*

- **Pronouns:** The possessive forms of personal pronouns are *my, his, her, your, its, our,* and *their* for pronouns that come before the noun and *mine, his, hers, yours, its, ours,* and *theirs* for possessive pronouns that occur at the end of a clause or that function as a subject.

None of the possessive personal pronouns contains an apostrophe. *It's* is a contraction of *it is,* not the possessive form of *its.* As opposed to proper pronouns, possessive indefinite pronouns do contain apostrophes: *Somebody's dog has chewed my carpet.* For information on indefinite and personal pronouns, see Chapter 3.

Spelling issues

If you're like most people in America, you've come to rely on your word processing program to correct your errors in spelling. The spell-check feature is one of the most popular and useful tools because it allows you to take your mind off of spelling and concentrate on what you're writing. And if you use an autocorrect feature on your word processing program, you may not even realize how often your computer corrects your misspelled words.

The bad news is that you won't have a spell-check function available when you write your essay on the GMAT. This means that when you take the GMAT, you'll be responsible for correcting your own spelling, perhaps for the first time in years! One or two spelling errors may not be enough to lower your score, but in conjunction with any of the other errors we discuss in this chapter, a few spelling mistakes can make the significant difference between one score and the next half-point higher.

A good way to avoid potential spelling errors is to steer clear of unfamiliar words. If you've never used a word before and have any doubt about its meaning or how it's spelled, avoid using it. If you use unfamiliar words, you risk not only misspelling the word but also using it inappropriately. Stick to what you know when you write your analytical essay. If you have enough time before the test, you can always broaden your vocabulary. Developing an extensive vocabulary will pay off in your career as well as on the GMAT.

More dos and don'ts

Here are a few more things to keep in mind when preparing for your essay:

- **Use simple, active sentences.** To increase your score, keep your sentences simple and active. The more complex your sentences, the greater your chances of making mistakes in grammar. You may think that long sentences will impress your readers, but they won't. Furthermore, they may cause you to make writing errors more easily.

  Another important characteristic of strong persuasive sentences is the use of active voice. Active voice is clearer and more powerful than passive voice.

✔ **Provide clear transitions.** Use transitions to tell the reader where you're going with your argument. You need only a few seconds to provide your readers with words that signal whether the next paragraph is a continuation of the previous idea, whether it refutes the last paragraph, or whether you're moving in a new direction. Transitions are key to good organization.

✔ **Use precise descriptions.** Use descriptive words to keep your readers interested and informed. If you use specific, well-chosen words to clearly illustrate your points and examples, your writing will have more impact and you'll earn a higher score.

✔ **Avoid slang expressions.** Stick to formal English, and avoid contractions and slang. Your readers are professors and should be familiar with formal English, so they expect you to use it in your essays. Using sentence fragments and slang is okay when e-mailing a friend, but on the GMAT, employ a more professional style.

Practice makes perfect!

You can practice writing in GMAT style in creative ways. For example, if you write a lot of e-mails, practice writing them more formally. When your friends send you unpunctuated e-mails full of misspellings and grammatical errors, respond with proper punctuation, superior spelling, good grammar, and perfect paragraphs.

You can't prepare for the GMAT with e-mails alone, so here are some things to think about when writing practice essays:

✔ Write your essay under test conditions. Give yourself a 30-minute time limit and study in a quiet environment.

✔ Use only those items you'll have available on the test. Type on your word processor but disable your automatic spell correction, use an erasable board or a single sheet of paper for scratch, and don't use reference books.

✔ Take your practice essays seriously (practice the way you want to perform).

Building a Better Essay: Ten Steps to a Higher Score

If you're going to write well, you need something to write about. Remember that your analytical writing score is based on the quality of your argument as well as the quality of your writing. Even though you've been writing for years in college or in the workplace, you probably haven't had to produce very many analytical essays in just 30 minutes. We'll take you through a ten-step process to help you create better essays in less time.

With a plan in mind, you can use your essay time more efficiently and earn a better score. Using part of your 30 minutes to develop a plan means you'll be more organized than someone who just starts writing whatever comes to mind. In fact, you'll likely type for only about 20 minutes during the 30-minute task because you'll spend 5 minutes outlining your argument and 5 minutes proofreading what you've typed.

Work out your timing during your practice tests and note the amount of time you generally need for each part of the task. Remember that you have only 30 minutes, so you'll never have all the time you want for any of the three stages, but with practice you'll find the formula that fits your strengths. For example, you may be an excellent typist who can write very fast when you get started. In that case, you can afford a little more time for pre-writing and will need additional time for proofreading all that text you typed. If, on the other hand, you write or type fairly slowly, you'll need to spend at least 20 minutes to get your great ideas on the computer screen and saved for posterity. Here are the ten steps you should follow during your 30-minute analytical writing task:

1. **Read the analytical writing prompt carefully before you begin writing.**

   Although this step may seem obvious, you may hurry through reading the prompt in your rush to start the essay and may miss important elements of your assignment. Take enough time to truly understand the argument you're to analyze. Read the prompt more than once; read it quickly the first time to get an idea of the subject matter and then read it more slowly to catch all the details. Some of your best arguments and examples will come to you when you're reading the prompt carefully.

2. **Don't waste time reading the directions.**

   You can make up some of the time you spend carefully reading the prompt by skimming over the directions that follow. We've paraphrased the instructions for the essay in Chapter 7 and on the practice tests, so you know what you're supposed to do. The most you need to do is skim the directions to make sure nothing's changed and move on.

3. **Plan your essay format ahead of time.**

   Knowing how to structure your essay can help you plan it. Make sure you have an introduction that discusses and presents your position (or *thesis*), supporting paragraphs that use examples and arguments to persuade others to see your way of reasoning, and a conclusion that briefly summarizes what you've said in the previous paragraphs. The length of your essay isn't as important as the quality of your analysis. Use as many paragraphs as you need to make your point in the allotted time. Just be sure that you know what you're going to write about before you begin writing.

4. **Use the erasable noteboard.**

   Brainstorm and write down your thoughts so you don't forget them. Don't rely on your memory; that's what the noteboard is for. Jotting down a word or two can preserve your idea until you're ready to write about it.

5. **Write a brief thesis statement.**

   Write a brief thesis statement indicating the main points of your evaluation of the argument and why you think that way. We recommend that you actually type this statement on the computer because it's the key sentence of your introductory paragraph.

   For example, say you're asked to evaluate the strength of this argument: "Corporations exist to make a profit for shareholders; therefore, the primary duty of the corporation is not to employ workers or to provide goods and services but to make as much money as possible." Your thesis may be that the argument errs in simplifying the role of corporations and failing to provide adequate support for making the simplistic assertion that corporations exist primarily for shareholder profits.

6. **Create a quick outline based on your thesis.**

   After you've created your thesis and have typed it into the computer, return to your notepad and make a brief outline. Because your ideas are already on the noteboard, outlining is a very simple process. Select the best arguments and examples to support your thesis. Decide in what order you want to address these ideas and number them for use as the topic sentences for the supporting paragraphs of your essay. Under each topic, list several examples and anecdotes that you'll use to support your topic.

   For example, your main topics in the evaluation of the purpose of corporations argument may be that (1) the conclusion is too simplistic, and (2) the argument fails to provide adequate support for its position.

7. **Write your introduction.**

   Move from a general statement to more specific ones and end with your thesis. In fact, your introduction may consist of only two sentences: a general introduction to the topic and your thesis statement. A complete introduction for the shareholder duty argument could consist of an introductory sentence or two that restates the conclusion and premises of the original argument. Then you'd lead into the thesis statement with a statement of the problems with the argument.

8. **Write your supporting paragraphs.**

   After you've put together an outline and written the introduction, you've completed the hardest parts of the task. Then you just need to write your supporting paragraphs clearly with as few errors as possible. Begin with the idea you designated as *1*. Introduce the paragraph with a topic sentence, provide a few supporting examples, and conclude your point. The first supporting paragraph could point out other important considerations for corporations, such as "a duty to care for the consumer and an obligation to perform research, that supersede the dangerous desire to make as much money as possible."

   Repeat the process for your remaining points.

9. **Write a brief conclusion.**

   End your essay with a simple summary of the points you've already made. Provide a synopsis of the conclusions you reached in each of your supporting paragraphs and end with a restatement of your thesis. Move from specific statements to more general ones. Many people try to make too much out of their conclusions, but this paragraph isn't the place to introduce new ideas or argue your position. Instead, just remind the reader of your supporting points and thesis.

10. **Proofread.**

   When you've finished writing, make sure you have time left over to read through what you've written. Look for spelling and punctuation errors and other careless mistakes that you may have made in your rush to complete the assignment on time. Concentrate on errors that you can correct in a few seconds, and don't try to rewrite entire paragraphs.

If you follow these steps in your practice writings and on test day, you'll come away with an analytical writing assessment score to be proud of.

Chapter 9

Deconstructing Sample GMAT Essays

. . . .

. . . .

This chapter defines analytical writing assessment (AWA) scores for you and provides you with some sample GMAT AWA essays so you can see what these babies look like and apply some elements of the examples to your own writing. By deconstructing sample essays to figure out what makes for a great essay per GMAT standards, you'll have a much better chance of constructing great essays of your own.

Defining GMAT AWA scores

The difference between an essay that's simply adequate and one that's outstanding comes down to a few important factors. Here's how the GMAT differentiates among essays that score 4, 5, and 6, based on analysis and organization:

✔ An outstanding essay (score 6) thoroughly analyzes and evaluates an argument and addresses whether the case the author makes is logically sound. The analysis uses logical reasoning to identify any flaws in the argument and offers insight as to how to minimize or eliminate these flaws. The essay is thorough and organized.

✔ A strong essay (score 5) still offers a powerful, well-reasoned analysis, but it may not be as insightful as an outstanding (score 6) essay. The essay contains well-chosen examples for support and is also well organized, though it's likely not as tightly organized as an outstanding essay.

✔ An adequate essay (score 4) offers a competent analysis of an argument. This essay interprets the strength and validity of an argument made by another and supports its points with relevant examples. The analysis may not be particularly well developed, but the fact that the essay shows competence in at least attempting to validate or disprove the assertions of another distinguishes it from lower-scoring essays.

Here's how the GMAT distinguishes among the top three scores based on quality of writing:

✔ An outstanding essay (score 6) demonstrates superior control of the language and employs a variety of grammatically accurate and detailed sentences. This essay uses effective transitions. Although the essay may have a few minor errors, it generally reflects a superior ability in grammar, usage, and mechanics of standard written English.

✔ A strong essay (score 5) is similar to an outstanding essay, but the sentences may not have quite as much variety, and the choice of words may not convey as much detail. This essay employs transitions but not as effectively as an outstanding essay. This essay may have a few minor errors but reflects a facility for grammar, usage, and mechanics.

✔ An adequate essay (score 4) lacks sentence variety and, although the diction may be accurate, the word choice isn't particularly detailed or precise. This essay may employ transitions, but they're likely to be somewhat abrupt. The adequate essay reflects a familiarity with standard written English but may contain several minor errors or a few more-serious flaws.

In addition to the top three possible scores, four lower scores reflect flaws of differing magnitudes. We give less time to describing these categories, because after you've read Chapters 7 and 8 and practiced writing essays for the exam, you aren't likely to produce one of these lower scores on the GMAT:

✔ A limited essay (score 3) is like an adequate paper in most respects, but it's clearly flawed in one or more areas. This essay may make an ineffective interpretation of the argument, lack organization, fail to present relevant examples, have problems in sentence structure, or contain errors in grammar, usage, and mechanics numerous enough to interfere with conveying meaning.

✔ A seriously flawed essay (score 2) demonstrates more significant errors than a limited essay. It may fail to properly follow the directions stated in the prompt, lack any semblance of organization, neglect to provide any examples, have serious problems with language or sentence structure, and contain errors in grammar, usage, or mechanics that seriously interfere with meaning.

✔ A fundamentally deficient essay (score 1) provides little evidence of the ability to effectively interpret the strength of the argument in the prompt. This essay may also have grave and pervasive writing errors that seriously interfere with the meaning of the essay.

✔ A no-score essay (score 0) is blank, completely off topic, or not written in English.

Taking a Look at Sample Essays

The task for the analytical writing assessment is to analyze an argument. The prompt asks you to write an essay that uses logical reasoning to critique an argument made by another. Its focus is how well you evaluate an argument instead of what your own views and opinions may be on a particular topic. In the following sections, we provide sample essay prompts as well as sample essay responses and walk you through the elements of an effective, well-written response.

Sample essay #1

If you have an extra 30 minutes just lying around, you can take the time to analyze the essay prompt in this section and write a full essay before you read the sample response we provide. If not, at least take five minutes before you read the sample essay to create a quick outline, using steps 1 through 6 from Chapter 8. Read the instructions following the argument very carefully, and remember: The idea here is to analyze the given argument, not create your own. Here's the sample prompt:

The following appeared as part of an editorial in a business newsletter:

"Gasoline prices continue to hover at record levels, and increased demand from China and India assures that the days of one dollar per gallon gasoline are over. Continued threat of unrest in the oil-producing regions of the Middle East, Africa, and South America means a perpetual threat to the U.S. oil supply. American leaders have acknowledged the need for new sources of power to fuel the hundreds of millions of cars and trucks in America. Despite this acknowledgment, the U.S. government has yet to provide substantial funding for this important research. Officials are relying on private industry and university researchers to undertake this research that is vital to the economy and national security. Given the long interval before new technologies are likely to become profitable and the tremendous cost, research into new fuels will be successful only if funded by the U.S. government using taxpayer funds."

Examine this argument and present your judgment on how well reasoned it is. In your discussion, analyze the author's position and how well the author uses evidence to support the argument. For example, you may question the author's underlying assumptions or consider alternative explanations that may weaken the conclusion. You can also provide additional support for or arguments against the author's position, describe how stating the argument differently may make it more reasonable, and discuss what provisions may better equip you to evaluate its thesis.

After you've attempted your own response to the prompt, read through this sample:

The author of this editorial presents the idea that the development of new technology for fueling the automobiles of America is an absolutely necessary project and provides substantial evidence to support this claim, for example, the rising price of gasoline, the swelling demand for oil in overseas markets, and warning signs of turbulence and instability in oil-producing countries. However, the author has not provided much evidence or reasoning behind the statement that the U.S. government should fund this research.

The editorial states that it will take a long time and a lot of expense to develop these new technologies, but the argument fails to include evidence of this. The author is making the assumption that readers will know that private companies and universities have been working for decades on projects such as hydrogen fuel cells, bio-diesel, ethanol, and electric cars. The editorial would be much stronger if it included one or two sentences on the fact that each of these technologies is feasible and that with increased funding could be brought rapidly to market.

Furthermore, it is suggested that the development of new fuel technologies is "vital to the economy and national security" of the U.S., but this statement is neither explained nor substantiated. It seems to me that if a greater amount of government funding is dedicated to scientific research, the budgets of other programs and departments will have to be cut, which could have serious negative impacts on national security, and possibly also the economy. If the editorial were to compare the hundreds of millions needed to fund research into alternatives to oil with the hundreds of billions spent each year on national security, then the argument would be stronger.

Clearly, the author of this editorial has made several assumptions about his/her readers, the most important probably being that readers of this business newsletter are familiar with this issue and will be able to provide the details of government funding and alternative fuel research lacking in the editorial. The evidence that the author does provide is strong. The editorial's conclusions seem valid. However, the editorial lacks the necessary foundation of facts and reasoning that would demonstrate, for example, why funding alternative fuel research now will allow new fuel technologies to gradually replace dependence on oil before a crisis hits.

This editorial discusses a very important issue and raises the critical subject of government funding for research into alternative fuels. However, the author has not provided much evidence or reasoning behind the conclusion that the U.S. government should fund this research.

Discussion of sample essay #1

This response is well developed and clearly articulated. The essay begins with a very strong introductory paragraph that develops the position, credits the editorial's strong points, and then clearly states the thesis that the author has made too many assumptions and not provided the necessary evidence. From the start, this essay appears to merit at least a 5.

The middle three paragraphs provide specific examples of assumptions that the editorial makes and indicate how the author could strengthen the argument. The first example is the assumption that the reader will know that alternative fuel technologies take a long time to develop. This essay provides the specific examples that the editorial itself lacked. The next paragraph discusses the claim that the economy and national security depend on alternative fuels. This is probably the weakest paragraph in the essay. The essay sidesteps the editorial's point when the essay turns to the issue of reducing the budgets of other programs. Still, this is a well-written paragraph that does offer valid suggestions for strengthening the editorial. The fourth paragraph ties everything together by pointing out the specific assumptions that the editorial is making about its readers. This paragraph demonstrates the sophistication of the essay by pointing out the editorial's intended audience, the weaknesses of the assumptions it makes, its strengths, and finally, ways to make the editorial better.

This essay is strong because it's specific and well developed. The essay singles out particular points in the editorial and explains not only the weaknesses of those points but also ways to make them stronger. It provides a clear introduction and thesis statement. The conclusion is brief and fulfills its purpose of restating the thesis. The diction used in this essay is precise and descriptive. The sentences are simple but varied, and they mostly demonstrate active rather than passive voice. There are no obvious errors in grammar, usage, or mechanics. This essay overall would likely garner a 5 but definitely nothing lower than a 4.5.

Sample essay #2

Here's another prompt for you to try. Again, if possible, attempt your own essay before you read through the sample response; if you don't have time to write an entire essay, take at least five minutes to create a quick outline, using steps 1 through 6 from Chapter 8.

The following is an excerpt from an editorial that appeared in a periodical dedicated to education topics:

"The most important factor in choosing a career should be the potential salary. It all comes down to quality of life. A high salary ensures that you'll be able to pay your bills, live in a nice house, drive a nice car, and afford a comfortable, enjoyable lifestyle that's sure to be the envy of your friends. This is most easily achieved by securing a job with the highest salary possible. Well-paid positions like those of doctors, lawyers, and architects are important to society, well respected, and profitable, so these are the types of positions you should shoot for. While many believe it is important to find a job that you enjoy first and foremost, if that job doesn't pay well, you'll be faced with numerous stresses and hardships sure to affect your overall quality of life and you will ultimately come to regret not prioritizing financial stability above all else."

Examine this argument and present your judgment on how well reasoned it is. In your discussion, analyze the author's position and how well the author uses evidence to support the argument. For example, you may question the author's underlying assumptions or consider alternative explanations that may weaken the conclusion. You can also provide additional support for or arguments against the author's position, describe how stating the argument differently may make it more reasonable, and discuss what provisions may better equip you to evaluate its thesis.

Attempt your own response to the prompt, and then read through the following sample essay:

> The author of this essay clearly states his belief that, when choosing a career path, earning potential is paramount. While he offers a number of reasons as to why he feels this way, such as an improved overall quality of life, a comfortable home, and the ability to impress your friends, his arguments are based on generalizations and assumptions about what others value most in life and the overall strength of his stance suffers as a result.
>
> For example, the author "ensures" the reader that a high salary will enable them to live a lavish lifestyle and a life of little stress and strife. Yet he doesn't take into account the fact that high-paying jobs are also often high-demand, sometimes at the expense of a happy marriage, quality time with the kids, or simply time to kick back and relax.
>
> Furthermore, he is assuming that happiness is achieved through material comforts, such as a fancy house and car, but he fails to recognize that his idea of happiness is not necessarily shared by the rest of the population. Nor does he consider other ways of finding happiness, like, say, helping others or finding a way to make a difference in the world.
>
> Throughout the essay, a fundamental problem with the author's reasoning is his assumption that his readers share his feelings as to what is most valuable in life. Even when he acknowledges the fact that others feel that finding a career you enjoy should be top priority, he fails to devote any time or attention to the notion that one can feel "rich" even without a thick wallet and flashy car if they're able to engage in a career that they find fulfilling and gratifying.
>
> While the author of this essay is sure to make his personal stance known in regard to what's most important in choosing a career, he fails to offer concrete evidence or devote sufficient attention as to why what is true for him fails to be true for the masses.

Discussion of sample essay #2

How do you think this essay would likely score? The essay asserts early on that the author in the prompt fails to acknowledge the fundamental differences as to what constitutes happiness and backs this up with examples and reasoning, so it's unlikely to receive a score below 4.

The response refutes the author's assertions that happiness is achieved through finding a job with the highest possible salary and backs this up with examples, such as the fact that high-paying jobs are frequently also high-stress and that other areas of one's life are often neglected. The essay also argues against the claim that material goods are the key to quality of life by noting that one person's opinion of what constitutes a high quality of life isn't necessarily true for someone else. To improve the quality of the supporting examples, the author could have been more specific, and she could have provided more compelling evidence for her point by referring to individuals in the public spotlight. For example, the author could have talked about the recent nervous breakdown of a wealthy celebrity to show that wealth doesn't necessarily lead to a stress-free life. And the author could have supplemented her assertion that money doesn't buy happiness by expounding on the fulfilling life of Mother Theresa.

Generally, the essay makes its points, using strong, concise English with few grammatical errors, although the concluding paragraph is constructed as one long sentence that would read more clearly if it were broken down into two. And the author includes a couple of pronouns that don't agree in number with their references. For example, the author uses the plural pronoun *they* to refer to the singular noun *one* in ". . . one can feel 'rich' even without a thick wallet and flashy car if *they're* able to engage in a career that *they* find fulfilling and gratifying." The essay also paraphrases the same general idea several times when it discusses the idea that the author of the prompt's idea of happiness differs from that of others. This essay would likely score a solid 4 or, possibly, as high as a 5.

Compare what you've written in response to the prompt to the sample essay. Evaluate your masterpiece and ask yourself how it measures up to — and perhaps accomplishes more than! — the sample. Use your evaluation to perfect your writing achievement. You'll find more opportunities to turn your logical reasoning powers into outstanding essays in the practice tests included with this book.

Part IV
Conquering the Quantitative Section

The 5th Wave   By Rich Tennant

"Did any of you fall for that trap in question 7?"

In this part . . .

Here it is — the long-awaited math review! And we give you a thorough going-over of all the important and most commonly tested math concepts on the GMAT. We start with the basics, like fundamental operations, fractions, and exponents, because you don't want to miss the easy points. Then we take you on a trip down memory lane with good old algebra. Remember quadratic equations and functions? If not, don't despair. They're covered here.

The GMAT plane and coordinate geometry questions ask you to measure lines, angles, arcs, and the shapes they create, like rectangles and triangles. We remind you of the formulas for finding area and perimeter, and we give you timesaving tips for finding side lengths of triangles. Speaking of formulas, we also review the ones you need to find the distance between points on the coordinate plane and the slope of a line. After reading this part, you'll be in good shape for the geometry problems on the GMAT.

It is decidedly probable that a healthy percentage of your GMAT quantitative section will cover statistics and probability, so this part provides you with the highlights of data interpretation, probability, and sets, from the essential concepts of mean and mode to more complex calculations of standard deviation and probability.

And you may be surprised to see that the GMAT math questions come in two varieties: the standard five-answer, multiple-choice, problem-solving kind and something called data sufficiency. Data sufficiency questions can be a bit tricky if you've never seen them before, but this part tells you exactly how to handle them like a pro.

Our computations predict that you'll have a high degree of success on math questions after you study this part, and to prove it, we end with a mini test so you can see how much you've retained.

Chapter 10

Getting Back to Basics: Numbers and Operations

Those of you who majored in math in college probably look at the math section of the GMAT like an old friend. Those of you who haven't stepped into a math class since high school are more likely dreading it. You know who you are! Don't worry, this chapter takes you back to the beginning with a review of the concepts you've learned through the years but may have temporarily forgotten. In this chapter, you see problems that test your knowledge of the math building blocks, such as number types, basic operations, exponents and radicals, fractions, and ratios. These concepts form the foundation of more complicated math problems, so this stuff is important to know. For example, you could end up with a completely wrong answer if you solve for real numbers when the question asks for integers. Some GMAT-takers may end up kicking themselves (and that looks just plain odd) for missing relatively simple problems because they were unfamiliar with some basic terminology. To avoid this unfortunate (and awkward) position, make sure you're well heeled in math basics.

Just Your Type: Kinds of Numbers

Since the Stone Age, humans have found it necessary to rely on numbers to get through daily living. In hunter-gatherer cultures, the people made notches in bones to count, for example, the number of days in a lunar cycle or perhaps to indicate how long the nomadic tribe spent in a particular location until it found food. But through the millennia, humankind soon realized that numbers could become large and unwieldy. Hence, the advent of number classifications and operations!

Although understanding modern mathematical operations may have burst prehistoric man's cerebral cortex, it'll surely be easier for you after you complete this review. For the GMAT, you need to know the more common types of numbers, such as integers, rational numbers, real numbers, and prime numbers. And you should at least be aware of some of the less common types, such as irrational and imaginary numbers.

REMEMBER

- ✔ **Integers:** Numbers that belong to the set of all positive and negative whole numbers with 0 included. Integers can't be fractions or decimals or portions of a number. Integers include –5, –4, –3, –2, –1, 0, 1, 2, 3, 4, and 5 and continue infinitely on either side of 0. Integers greater than 0 are called *natural numbers* or *positive integers*. Integers less than 0 are called *negative integers*.

  Take care when working with 0. It's neither positive nor negative.

- ✔ **Rational numbers:** Numbers that are expressed as the *ratio* of one integer to another; that is, numbers that can be expressed as fractions. Rational numbers include all positive and negative integers, fractions, and decimal numbers that either end or repeat. For example, the fraction $\frac{1}{3}$ can be expressed as 0.33333. . . . Rational numbers don't include numbers like π or radicals like $\sqrt{2}$ because the decimal equivalents of these numbers don't end or repeat. They're called *irrational numbers*.

- ✔ **Real numbers:** All numbers that you normally think of as numbers. Real numbers belong to the set that includes all integers, rational numbers, and irrational numbers. Think of real numbers as those numbers represented by all the points on a number line, either positive or negative. Real numbers are also those numbers you use to measure length, volume, or weight. So when the GMAT asks you to give an answer expressed in terms of real numbers, just solve the problem as you normally would.

- ✔ **Imaginary numbers:** Any number that isn't a real number. So an imaginary number is a number like $\sqrt{-2}$. Think about it: You know that when you square any positive or negative real number, the result is a positive number. This means you can't find the square root of a negative number unless it's simply not a real number. So imaginary numbers include square roots of negative numbers or any number containing *i*, which represents the square root of –1. Won't you be a fascinating conversationalist at your next soiree!

- ✔ **Prime numbers:** All the positive integers that can be divided by only themselves and 1; 1 isn't a prime number. The smallest prime number is 2, and it's also the only even prime number. This doesn't mean that all odd numbers are prime numbers, though. Also, 0 can never be a prime number because you can divide 0 by every natural number there is. To determine prime numbers, consider this series: 2, 3, 5, 7, 11, 13, 17, 19, 23, 29, and so on. What makes these numbers unique is that the only two factors for these numbers are 1 and the number itself.

You probably won't encounter this term on the GMAT, but in case it comes up at cocktail parties, you should know that 0 and positive numbers other than 1 that aren't prime numbers are called *composite numbers*. A composite number has more than two factors, so it's the product of more than simply itself and the number 1. Questions regarding prime numbers appear fairly frequently in GMAT math sections. Here's a sample of one you may see.

An irrational feat with an irrational number

Recently, a team of computer engineers in Japan calculated π out to over 1.24 *trillion* decimal digits. It still didn't end, meaning that π is truly irrational. And it may be irrational to attempt to prove otherwise! Thankfully, the GMAT won't ask you to attempt this task or anything remotely like it.

Which of the following expresses 60 as a product of prime numbers?

(A) $2 \times 2 \times 3 \times 5$

(B) $2 \times 2 \times 15$

(C) $2 \times 3 \times 3 \times 5$

(D) $2 \times 3 \times 5$

(E) $1 \times 2 \times 5 \times 6$

This question tests your knowledge of prime numbers. Because the correct answer has to be a series of prime numbers, eliminate any choice that contains a composite (or non-prime) number. So Choices (B) and (E) are out (even though the product of both is 60) because 15, 1, and 6 aren't prime numbers. Then, eliminate any answers that don't equal 60 when you multiply them. Choice (C) is 90, and Choice (D) is 30, so the answer must be Choice (A). It's the correct answer because it contains only prime numbers whose product equals 60.

It's Not Brain Surgery: Basic Operations

Now that you're a bit more comfortable with some terms, it's time to take a stab at manipulating numbers. Figuring out how to do operations, which we discuss in the following sections, is pretty simple, almost as simple as 1-2-3. It doesn't take a brain surgeon to open your mind to endless possibilities.

Adding, subtracting, multiplying, and dividing

You're probably pretty familiar with the standard operations of addition, subtraction, multiplication, and division. But even these math basics have some tricky elements that you may need to refresh your memory on.

Putting two and two together: Addition

Adding is pretty simple. Addition is just the operation of combining two or more numbers to get an end result called the *sum*. For example, here's a simple addition problem:

$$3 + 4 + 5 = 12$$

Addition also has two important properties that you may remember from elementary school: the *associative property* and the *commutative property*. Understanding these simple concepts for the GMAT math questions is important:

- ✔ **The associative property states that the order in which you choose to add three or more numbers doesn't change the result.** It shows how numbers can group differently with one another and still produce the same answer. So regardless of whether you add 3 and 4 together first and then add 5 or add 4 and 5 together followed by 3, you still get an answer of 12.

  $$(3 + 4) + 5 = 12$$
  $$3 + (4 + 5) = 12$$

- ✔ **The commutative property states that it doesn't matter what order you use to add the same numbers.** Regardless of what number you list first in a set of numbers, they always produce the same sum. So $2 + 3 = 5$ is the same as $3 + 2 = 5$.

Depleting the supply: Subtraction

Subtraction, as you probably know, is the opposite of addition. You take away a value from another value and end up with the *difference*. So if 3 + 4 = 7, then 7 – 4 = 3.

In subtraction, order *does* matter, so neither the associative property nor the commutative property applies. You get completely different answers for 3 – 4 – 5, depending on what method you use to associate the values. Here's what we mean:

$$(3 – 4) – 5 = – 6$$

but

$$3 – (4 – 5) = 4$$

The order of the values counts in subtraction, too. For example, 3 – 4 isn't the same as 4 – 3 (3 – 4 is –1, but 4 – 3 is 1).

Increasing by leaps and bounds: Multiplication

Think of multiplication as repeated addition with an end result called the *product*: 3×5 is the same as 5 + 5 + 5. They both equal 15.

On the GMAT, you may see several signs that represent the multiplication operation. A multiplication sign can be designated by $\times$ or simply with a dot, like $\cdot$. And in many instances, especially when variables are involved (for more about variables, see Chapter 11), multiplication can be indicated by just putting the factors right next to each other. So *ab* means the same thing as $a \times b$, and *2a* is the same as $2 \times a$. One of these back-to-back factors may appear in parentheses: 2(3) means 2×3.

Multiplication is like addition, in that the order of the values doesn't matter. So it obeys the commutative property:

$$a \times b = b \times a$$

And the associative property:

$$(a \times b) \times c = a \times (b \times c)$$

Another property associated with multiplication is the *distributive property*. So you may encounter this multiplication problem:

$$a(b + c) =$$

You solve it by distributing the *a* to *b* and *c*, which means that you multiply *a* and *b* to get *ab* and then *a* and *c* to get *ac*, and then you add the results together like this: $a(b + c) = ab + ac$.

Sharing the wealth: Division

Finally, there's division, which you can consider to be the opposite of multiplication. With division, you split one value into smaller values. The end result is called the *quotient*. So whereas $3 \times 5 = 15$, $15 \div 5 = 3$, and $15 \div 3 = 5$.

As in subtraction, order matters, so division doesn't follow either the commutative or associative properties. Also, just so you're familiar with any terms you may encounter on the GMAT, the number at the beginning of any equation using division (15 in the last expression) is called the *dividend* and the number that goes into the dividend is the *divisor* (3 in the last expression).

The division sign may be represented by a fraction bar. For more info on fractions, see "Splitting Up: Fractions, Decimals, and Percentages," later in this chapter.

Checking out the real estate: Properties of real numbers

In addition to basic operations, the GMAT expects you to know the fundamental properties of the numbers you're working with. These include absolute values, evens and odds, and positives and negatives.

Absolutes do exist: Absolute value

To simplify things, just think of the absolute value of any real number as that same number without a negative sign. It's the value of the distance a particular number is from 0 on a number line. The symbol for absolute value is | |, so the absolute value of 3 is written mathematically as |3|. And because the number 3 sits three spaces from 0 on the number line |3| = 3. Likewise, because –3 sits three spaces from 0 on the number line, its absolute value is also 3: |–3| = 3.

The GMAT loves to trip you up when dealing with multiple numbers and absolute values. Remember that absolute value pertains only to the value contained within the absolute value bars. So if you see a negative sign outside the bars, the resulting value is negative. For example, –|–3| = –3 because although the absolute value of –3 is 3, the negative sign outside the bars makes the end result a negative.

A balancing act: Even and odd numbers

We're pretty sure you know that *even numbers* are integers divisible by 2: 2, 4, 6, 8, 10, and so on. And *odd numbers* are those integers that aren't divisible by 2: 1, 3, 5, 7, 9, 11, and so on.

You're probably with us so far, but what's important to remember for the GMAT is what happens to even or odd numbers when you add, subtract, or multiply them by one another.

Here are the rules regarding evens and odds for addition and subtraction:

- ✔ When you add or subtract two even integers, your result is an even integer.
- ✔ When you add or subtract two odd integers, your result is also even.
- ✔ If you add or subtract an even integer and an odd integer, your result is an odd integer.

Here's what you should know about multiplying even and odd integers:

- ✔ When you multiply an even number by an even number, you get an even number.
- ✔ When you multiply an odd number by an even number, you also get an even number.
- ✔ The only time you get an odd number is when you multiply an odd number by another odd number.

Division rules are a little more complex because the quotients aren't always integers; sometimes they're fractions. Here are a few rules to know:

- ✔ When you divide an even integer by an odd integer, you get an even integer or a fraction.
- ✔ An odd integer divided by another odd integer results in an odd integer or a fraction.

- ✔ An even integer divided by another even integer can result in either an odd or even quotient, so that's not very helpful.

- ✔ When you divide an odd integer by an even one, you always get a fraction; because fractions aren't integers, the quotient for this scenario is neither odd nor even.

You may be wondering why you need to know these rules. Here's why: Memorizing them can be a big timesaver when it comes to eliminating answer choices. For example, if you have a multiplication problem involving large even numbers, you know you can eliminate any odd-number answer choices without even doing the math! Here's a sample question that shows you just how valuable knowing the rules can be.

If a and b are different prime numbers, which of the following numbers must be odd?

(A) ab

(B) $4a + b$

(C) $a + b + 3$

(D) $ab - 3$

(E) $4a + 4b + 3$

To solve this number theory question, think of numbers for a and b that represent their possible values. Then substitute these values into the answer choices to eliminate all that can be even. When considering values for a and b, make sure to include 2 because it's the only even prime number. Neither 1 nor 0 is an option because neither is prime.

Substitute 2 for a or b in Choice (A), and you see that it can be even because the rules tell you that any time you multiply an even number by another number, you get an even number. You also know that Choice (B) can be even because 4 (an even number) times any number is an even number. If $b = 2$ and you added that to $4a$, you'd be adding two even numbers, which always gives you an even sum. Again, if $b = 2$ in Choice (C), then a would have to be an odd prime number. You add a (odd) to b (even) to get an odd sum. Then you add that odd number to the odd number 3, which results in an even number. Choice (D) can be even if both a and b are odd. An odd number times an odd number is an odd number. When you subtract an odd number, like 3, from another odd number, you get an even number.

By process of elimination, the answer must be Choice (E). It doesn't matter whether a or b in Choice (E) is even or odd; $4a$ and $4b$ will always be even, because anytime you multiply an even number by another number, you get an even number. When you add two evens, you get an even number, so $4a + 4b$ is an even number. And because an even number plus an odd number is always odd, when you add that even result to 3, you get an odd number, always. The correct answer is Choice (E).

Half empty or half full: Positive and negative numbers

Positive and negative numbers have their own set of rules regarding operations, and they're even more important to remember than those for even and odd integers. Here's what you need to know for multiplying and dividing:

- ✔ When you multiply or divide two positive numbers, the result is positive.

- ✔ When you multiply or divide two negative numbers, the result is also positive.

- ✔ Multiplying or dividing a negative number by a positive number gives you a negative result (as does dividing a positive number by a negative number).

As you may expect, you need to know some things about adding and subtracting positives and negatives:

- ✔ When you add two positive numbers, your result is a positive number.

- ✔ If you subtract a negative number from another number, you end up adding the positive version of the negative number to the other number. For example, $x - (-3)$ is the same thing as $x + 3$.

Using Little Numbers for Big Values: Bases and Exponents

Because multiplication can be thought of as repeated addition, you can think of exponents as repeated multiplication. This means that 4^3 is the same as $4 \times 4 \times 4$ or 64. In the example, you refer to 4 as the *base* and the superscript 3 as the *exponent*. If you add a variable into this mix, such as $4b^3$, the base becomes b and the 4 becomes what's known as the *coefficient*. In our example, the coefficient 4 is simply multiplied by b^3.

As a high-school algebra teacher used to scream (usually when he caught his students napping): "The power governs only the number immediately below it!" (that is, the base). So the exponent doesn't affect the coefficient. Only the base gets squared or cubed or whatever the exponent says to do.

This rule brings up some fascinating properties regarding positive and negative bases and even and odd exponents:

- ✔ A positive number taken to an even or odd power remains positive.
- ✔ A negative number taken to an odd power remains negative.
- ✔ A negative number taken to an even power becomes positive.

What all of this means is that any number taken to an even power either remains or becomes positive and any number taken to an odd power keeps the sign it began with. Another interesting tidbit to digest is that any term with an odd power that results in a negative number will have a negative root, and this is the only possible root for the expression. For example, if $a^3 = -125$, then $a = -5$. That is, the cube root of -125 is -5.

On the other hand, anytime you have an exponent of 2, you have two potential roots, one positive and one negative, for the expression. For example, if $a^2 = 64$, then $a = 8$ or -8. So 64 has two possible square roots: either 8 or -8.

In the following sections, we outline a few rules for adding, subtracting, multiplying, and dividing exponents. We also clue you in on how to figure out the powers of 0 and 1 and what to do with fractional and negative exponents.

Adding and subtracting exponents

The only catch to adding or subtracting exponents is that the base and exponent of each term must be the same. So you can add and subtract like terms such as $4a^2$ and a^2 like this: $4a^2 + a^2 = 5a^2$ and $4a^2 - a^2 = 3a^2$. Notice that the base and exponent remain the same and that the coefficient is the only number that changes in the equation.

Multiplying and dividing exponents

The rules regarding multiplying and dividing exponents are pretty numerous, so to keep them straight, we've set up Table 10-1 for you. The table describes each rule and gives you an example or two.

Table 10-1	Rules for Multiplying and Dividing Exponents
Rule	**Examples**
To multiply terms with exponents and the same bases, add the exponents.	$a^2 \times a^3 = a^5$
If the expression contains coefficients, multiply the coefficients as you normally would.	$4a^2 \times 2a^3 = 8a^5$
When you divide terms with exponents and the same bases, just subtract the exponents.	$a^5 \div a^3 = a^2$
Any coefficients are also divided as usual.	$9a^5 \div 3a^3 = 3a^2$
To multiply exponential terms with different bases, first make sure the exponents are the same. If they are, multiply the bases and maintain the same exponent.	$4^3 \times 5^3 = 20^3$; $a^5 \times b^5 = (ab)^5$
Follow the same procedure when you divide terms with different bases but the same exponents.	$20^3 \div 5^3 = 4^3$; $(ab)^5 \div b^5 = a^5$
When you raise a power to another power, multiply the exponents.	$(a^3)^5 = a^{15}$; $(5^4)^5 = 5^{20}$
If your expression includes a coefficient, take it to the same power.	$(3a^3)^5 = 243a^{15}$

Figuring out the powers of 0 and 1

Exponents of 0 and 1 have special properties that you'll have to commit to memory:

- The value of a base with an exponent of 0 (such as 7^0) is always 1.
- The value of a base with an exponent of 1 (such as 3^1) is the same value as the base ($3^1 = 3$).

Dealing with fractional exponents

If you see a problem with an exponent in fraction form, consider the top number of the fraction (the *numerator*) as your actual exponent and the bottom number (the *denominator*) as the root. So to solve $256^{\frac{1}{4}}$, simply take 256 to the first power (because the numerator of the fraction is 1), which is 256. Then take the fourth root of 256 (because the denominator of the fraction is 4), which is 4, and that's your answer. (Find out more about roots in the "Checking Out the Ancestry: Roots" section later in this chapter.) Here's what it looks like mathematically:

$$256^{\frac{1}{4}} = \sqrt[4]{256^1} = \sqrt[4]{256} = 4$$

The GMAT may also present you with a variable base and a fractional exponent. You handle those the same way, like this:

$$a^{\frac{2}{3}} = \sqrt[3]{a^2}$$

This is what you get when you take a to the second power and then find its cube root.

Working with negative exponents

A negative exponent works like a positive exponent with a twist. A negative exponent takes the positive exponent and then flips it around so the exponent becomes its reciprocal (see the section "Defining numerators, denominators, and other stuff you need to know about fractions," later in this chapter), like this:

$$3^{-3} = \frac{1}{3^3} = \frac{1}{27}$$

To see how this works, check out a sample problem that divides two exponential expressions. When you divide powers that have the same base, you subtract the exponents.

$$3^3 \div 3^6 = 3^{-3} = \frac{1}{27}$$

When you work with negative exponents, don't fall for the trick of assuming that the negative exponent somehow turns the original number into a negative number. It ain't gonna happen! For example, $3^{-5} \neq -243$ or $-\frac{1}{243}$ or $-\frac{1}{15}$ or anything like them.

Checking Out the Ancestry: Roots

If you like exponents, you'll *love* roots, which are also known as *radicals.* Roots are sort of the opposite of exponents. The square root of a number is the number that you square to get that number. So because you square 3 to get 9, the square root of 9 is 3. What could be simpler?

There are as many roots as there are powers. Most of the time, the GMAT has you work with square roots, but you may also see other roots. That won't intimidate you, though. If you come upon a cube root or fourth root, you'll recognize it by the radical sign, $\sqrt{\ }$.

For example, the cube root of 27 is expressed as $\sqrt[3]{27}$. This expression asks what number, when raised to the third power, equals 27. Of course, the answer is 3 because $3^3 = 27$.

Radicals, even the seemingly ugly ones, can often be simplified. For example, if you come up with an answer of $\sqrt{98}$, you're not done yet. Just think of the factors of 98 that are perfect squares. You know that $2 \times 49 = 98$, and 49 is a perfect square: $7^2 = 49$. Put these factors under the radical sign: $\sqrt{2 \times 49}$. Now you can extract the 49 from the square root sign because its square root is 7. The result is $7\sqrt{2}$. Here's how you may see this situation on the GMAT.

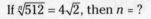

If $\sqrt[n]{512} = 4\sqrt{2}$, then $n = ?$

(A) 1

(B) 2

(C) 3

(D) 4

(E) 5

You can solve this equation most easily by simplifying the radical. The n root of 512 is equal to 4 times the n root of 2. Consider the factors of 512: 2×256, so $\sqrt[n]{2 \times 256}$, which also equals $4\sqrt{2}$. So you're looking for the value of n that completes this equation: $4^n = 256$. Because $4 \times 4 \times 4 \times 4 = 256$, $4^4 = 256$. So $n = 4$, and Choice (D) is the correct answer.

Roots obey the same rules as exponents when it comes to performing operations. You can add and subtract roots as long as the roots are of the same order (that is, square root, cube root, and so on) and the same number. Here are a couple examples:

$$5\sqrt{7} + 6\sqrt{7} = 11\sqrt{7}$$
$$11\sqrt{a} - 5\sqrt{a} = 6\sqrt{a}$$

When you need to multiply or divide radicals, make sure the roots are of the same order and you're good to go! For multiplication, just multiply what's under the radical signs, like this:

$$\sqrt{9} \times \sqrt{3} = \sqrt{9 \times 3} = \sqrt{27}$$

Divide what's under the radical signs like this:

$$\sqrt{9} \div \sqrt{3} = \sqrt{3}$$
$$\sqrt{8} \div \sqrt{5} = \sqrt{\frac{8}{5}}$$

And here's how a question about operations with radicals may appear on the GMAT.

$$\sqrt{16 + 9} = ?$$

(A) 5

(B) 7

(C) $12\frac{1}{2}$

(D) 25

(E) 625

Pay attention to the values underneath the radical. In this question, the line of the square root symbol extends over the entire expression, so you're supposed to find the square root of 16 + 9, not $\sqrt{16} + \sqrt{9}$. It's a subtle but major difference!

First, add the values under the radical sign: 16 + 9 = 25. The square root of 25 is 5, so Choice (A) is the correct answer. If you chose 7, you determined the square root of each of the values before you added them together. So $\sqrt{16}$ (or 4) plus $\sqrt{9}$ (or 3) is 7. For 7 to be the correct answer, your problem should have been written with two separate square root signs, $\sqrt{16} + \sqrt{9}$.

Order of Operations: Please Excuse My Dear Aunt Sally

Basic arithmetic requires that you perform the operations in a certain order from left to right. Okay, so maybe you don't have an aunt named Sally, but this section's title is a helpful mnemonic for the order you use when you have to perform several operations in one problem. What that means is that if you have an expression that contains addition, subtraction, multiplication, division, exponents (and roots), and parentheses to boot, it helps to know which operation you perform first, second, third, and so on.

The acronym *PEMDAS* (**P**lease **E**xcuse **M**y **D**ear **A**unt **S**ally) can help you remember to perform operations in the following order:

✔ **P**arentheses

✔ **E**xponents (and roots)

✔ **M**ultiplication and **D**ivision

✔ **A**ddition and **S**ubtraction

Here's an example:

$$20(4-7)^3 + 15\left(\frac{9}{3}\right)^1 = x$$

First, evaluate what's inside the parentheses:

$$20(-3)^3 + 15(3)^1 = x$$

Then evaluate the exponents:

$$20(-27) + 15(3) = x$$

Then multiply:

$$-540 + 45 = x$$

Finally, do the addition and subtraction from left to right:

$$-495 = x$$

Splitting Up: Fractions, Decimals, and Percentages

Fractions, decimals, and percentages are interrelated concepts; they all represent parts of a whole. You'll likely need to convert from one form to the other to solve several problems on the GMAT math.

Fractions are really division problems. If you divide the value of *a* by the value of *b*, you get the fraction $\frac{a}{b}$. So $1 \div 4 = \frac{1}{4}$.

To convert the fraction to a decimal, you simply perform the division indicated by the fraction bar: $\frac{1}{4} = 1 \div 4 = 0.25$.

To convert a decimal back to a fraction, you first count the digits to the right of the decimal point; then divide the original number over a 1 followed by the same number of zeroes as there were digits to the right of the decimal. Then you simplify. So $0.25 = \frac{25}{100}$, which simplifies to $\frac{1}{4}$; $0.356 = \frac{356}{1,000}$, which is $\frac{89}{250}$ in its simplest form.

Changing a decimal to a percent is really pretty easy. Percent simply means *per one hundred*, or ÷ 100. To perform the conversion, you move the decimal two places to the right. Then you write the resulting number as a percent. For example, $0.25 = 25\%$, and $0.925 = 92.5\%$.

To turn a percent back into a decimal, you follow the procedure in reverse. You move the decimal point two spaces to the left and lose the percent sign, like this: 1% = 0.01

The GMAT probably won't specifically ask you to express answers in all three formats (fractions, decimals, and percentages), but you need to know that answer choices can appear in any one of the three formats when you're dealing with percentage problems.

You may encounter a GMAT problem that asks you to find something like the portion of garbage that's paper when you know that out of 215 million tons of garbage, about 86 million tons of the total garbage are paper products. You should be able to express the answer as a fraction, decimal, and percent:

- As a fraction: $\frac{86}{215}$ or $\frac{2}{5}$
- As a decimal: $\frac{2}{5} = 2 \div 5 = 0.40$
- As a percent: 0.4 = 40%

Don't worry: We provide all the details you need to know about dealing with fractions and percentages in the following sections.

Defining numerators, denominators, and other stuff you need to know about fractions

GMAT questions may refer to the numerator or the denominator of a fraction. The *numerator* is the number on top and represents the part of the whole. The *denominator* is the number on the bottom and represents the whole.

To better understand these terms, picture a cherry pie sliced into eight equal pieces (see Figure 10-1) and a hungry family of seven, each of whom has a slice after dinner (or before dinner if they're sneaky).

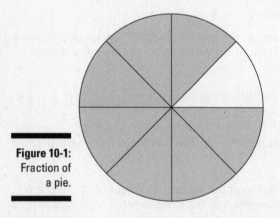

Figure 10-1:
Fraction of
a pie.

The shaded pieces of pie show how much of the dessert was gobbled up by the family; the unshaded piece shows what's left of the pie when the family is finished.

To put this pie into terms of a fraction, the total number of pieces in the pie to begin with (the whole) represents the denominator, and the number of pieces that were eaten (the part of the whole) is represented by the numerator. In this case, the number of pieces that were eaten made up $\frac{7}{8}$ of the total pie, so 7 is the numerator and 8 is the denominator. To look at the scenario another way, you can say that the fraction of pie that was left is $\frac{1}{8}$ of what you started with.

Here are a few other fraction definitions you should be familiar with:

- ✔ **Proper fractions:** Fractions where the numerator is less than the denominator. Examples of proper fractions are $\frac{3}{4}$, $\frac{7}{8}$ and $\frac{13}{15}$.

- ✔ **Improper fractions:** Fractions where the numerator is either greater than or equal to the denominator. Here are some examples: $\frac{15}{2}$, $\frac{5}{3}$, and $\frac{7}{7}$.

- ✔ **Mixed fractions:** Another way of formatting improper fractions with a whole number and a proper fraction, like these: $1\frac{1}{2}$, $7\frac{3}{4}$, and $2\frac{2}{3}$.

- ✔ **Reciprocal:** The flip-flop of a fraction. The numerator and denominator switch places. So the reciprocal of $\frac{3}{5}$ is $\frac{5}{3}$. To get the reciprocal of a whole number, you simply divide 1 by your number. So the reciprocal of 5 is $1 \div 5$ or simply $\frac{1}{5}$. The reciprocal of a variable, such as a, is $\frac{1}{a}$, just as long as $a \neq 0$.

When you work with fractions on the GMAT, you may have to substitute mixed fractions for improper fractions and vice versa. You'll find that changing a mixed fraction into an improper fraction before you perform operations is often easier. To change a mixed fraction to an improper fraction, you multiply the whole number by the denominator, add the numerator, and put that value over the original denominator, like this:

$$2\frac{2}{3} = \frac{8}{3}$$

You multiply the whole number (2) by the denominator (3) to get 6; add the numerator (2) to 6, which gives you 8; and place that value over the original denominator of 3.

To convert an improper fraction to a mixed number, you divide the numerator by the denominator and put the remainder over the denominator, like this:

$$\frac{31}{4} = 7\frac{3}{4}$$

First, you divide 31 by 4: 4 goes into 31 seven times with a remainder of 3 ($4 \times 7 = 28$ and $31 - 28 = 3$). Put the remainder over the original denominator, and place that fraction next to the whole number, 7.

Another thing you should know about fractions is how to simplify them. You may be thinking that fractions are simple enough, that it just can't get any easier. Simplifying a fraction means reducing it to its simplest terms. You make the larger terms smaller by dividing both the numerator and denominator by the same value. Here's an example of reducing or simplifying a fraction:

$$\frac{12}{36} \div \frac{12}{12} = \frac{1}{3}$$

The largest common factor of 12 and 36 is 12. When you divide the fraction by $\frac{12}{12}$, it's the same as dividing by 1. And any number divided by 1 equals the original number. You know that $\frac{1}{3}$ has the same value as $\frac{12}{36}$. It's just in simpler terms.

Adding and subtracting fractions

Because fractions are parts of whole numbers, they're not as easy to add together as $2 + 2$. To add or subtract fractions, you must give them the same denominator. Then all you do is either add or subtract the numerators and put that value over the original denominator, like this: $\frac{2}{7} + \frac{4}{7} = \frac{6}{7}; \frac{6}{5} - \frac{4}{5} = \frac{2}{5}$.

Be careful when you're asked to add and subtract fractions with different denominators. You can't just add or subtract the numerators and denominators. You have to change the fractions so they have the same denominator. So you have to find what's called the *least common denominator*. For example, if you see $\frac{2}{3} + \frac{1}{9}$, you know you have to change the denominators before you add.

To determine the least common denominator, consider values that are divisible by both 3 and 9. When you multiply 3 by 9, you get 27. So both 3 and 9 go into 27, but that's not the smallest number that both 3 and 9 go into evenly. Both 3 and 9 are factors of 9, so the least common denominator is 9 rather than 27.

Convert $\frac{2}{3}$ to $\frac{6}{9}$ by multiplying the numerator and denominator by 3. The second fraction already has a denominator of 9, so you're ready to add:

$$\frac{6}{9} + \frac{1}{9} = \frac{7}{9}$$

Multiplying and dividing fractions

Multiplying fractions is easy. Just multiply the numerators and the denominators. Reduce if you have to:

$$\frac{4}{5} \times \frac{5}{7} = \frac{4 \times 5}{5 \times 7} = \frac{20}{35} = \frac{4}{7}$$

An easier and faster (and faster is better on the GMAT) way to perform this task is to simply cancel out the fives that appear in the denominator of the first fraction and the numerator of the second one, like so:

$$\frac{4}{{}_1\cancel{5}} \times \frac{\cancel{5}^{1}}{7} = \frac{4}{1} \times \frac{1}{7} = \frac{4}{7}$$

Dividing fractions is pretty much the same as multiplying them except for one very important additional step. Here's what you do to divide two fractions:

1. Find the reciprocal of the second fraction in the equation (that is, turn the second fraction upside down).

2. Multiply (yes, multiply) the numerators and denominators of the resulting fractions.

Here's an example:

$$\frac{2}{7} \div \frac{3}{5} = x$$
$$\frac{2}{7} \times \frac{5}{3} = x$$
$$\frac{10}{21} = x$$

To test your knowledge of how to perform operations with fractions, the GMAT may present you with a straightforward equation, such as the following.

$$\frac{1}{2} + \left(\frac{3}{8} \div \frac{2}{5}\right) - \left(\frac{5}{6} \times \frac{7}{8}\right) =$$

(A) $\frac{1}{8}$

(B) $\frac{15}{16}$

(C) $\frac{17}{24}$

(D) $2\frac{1}{6}$

(E) $\frac{5}{6}$

To solve this problem, you need to know how to perform all four operations with fractions. Be sure to follow the order of operations. (See the earlier section "Order of Operations: Please Excuse My Dear Aunt Sally" for details.)

First, compute the operations inside the first set of parentheses:

$$\frac{3}{8} \div \frac{2}{5} = \frac{3}{8} \times \frac{5}{2} = \frac{15}{16}$$

Then, figure out the value of the second set of parentheses:

$$\frac{5}{6} \times \frac{7}{8} = \frac{35}{48}$$

Now the equation looks like this:

$$\frac{1}{2} + \frac{15}{16} - \frac{35}{48} =$$

The least common denominator of 2, 16, and 48 is 48. To convert the denominator in the first fraction to 48, you multiply the fraction by $\frac{24}{24}$. So $\frac{1}{2} \times \frac{24}{24} = \frac{24}{48}$.

To convert the denominator in the second fraction to 48, you need to multiply by $\frac{3}{3}$: $\frac{15}{16} \times \frac{3}{3} = \frac{45}{48}$.

Now you can compute the expression:

$$\frac{24}{48} + \frac{45}{48} - \frac{35}{48} = \frac{34}{48}$$

That's not one of your answer options, so you need to simplify the fraction. Divide the numerator and denominator by 2 to get $\frac{17}{24}$, which is Choice (C).

Knowing how to perform operations with fractions comes in handy for percent problems, too.

What is 75% of $7\frac{1}{4}$?

(A) $\frac{37}{130}$

(B) $5\frac{3}{4}$

(C) $5\frac{7}{16}$

(D) $7\frac{3}{4}$

(E) $21\frac{3}{16}$

This question asks you to determine a percent of a fraction. Note that the answers are in fraction form rather than decimal form, which means you need to work out the problem so it ends up as a fraction rather than a decimal.

Whenever you see the word *of* in a word problem, you know it means multiply. Therefore, you're multiplying 75 percent by $7\frac{1}{4}$. Converted to a fraction, 75 percent is $\frac{3}{4}$, so you're trying to find the answer to $\frac{3}{4} \times 7\frac{1}{4}$. Converting $7\frac{1}{4}$ from a mixed fraction gives you $\frac{29}{4}$, so the answer is $\frac{3}{4} \times \frac{29}{4}$ or $\frac{87}{16}$.

Convert to a mixed fraction: $\frac{87}{16} = 5\frac{7}{16}$. The answer is Choice (C).

You can easily eliminate Choices (D) and (E). Obviously, 75 percent of $7\frac{1}{4}$ has to be less than $7\frac{1}{4}$.

Calculating percent change

Percent change is the amount a number increases or decreases expressed as a percentage of the original number. For example, if a store normally sells tennis shoes for $72 and has them on sale for $60, what is the percent change of the markdown? To get the percent decrease, simply take the difference in price, which is $12, and divide that number by the original price:

$$12 \div 72 = 0.1667 \text{ or } 16\frac{2}{3}\%$$

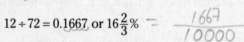

Pay careful attention when figuring percent change. For example, if the store then increases the marked down price by $16\frac{2}{3}$ percent, you may think the price returns to its original value. But that's not right. If you increase the lower price of $60 by 0.1667, you get just about a $10 increase. The price goes from $60 to just about $70: $60 \times 0.1667 = 10.002$; $60 + 10.002 = 70.002$.

How can that be? The reason the numbers don't seem to add up is because when you drop the price the first time, you take $16\frac{2}{3}$ percent of $72, which is a bigger number to take a percent from than the lower sale price.

So what percent of the marked down price of $60 must you increase the price by in order to get the original price of $72? To find out, take the difference in price, $12, and determine what percent that is of the sale price of $60:

$$12 \div 60 = \frac{12}{60} = \frac{2}{10} = 0.20 = 20\%$$

So it's a 20 percent increase from 60 to 72.

If you know what the percent increase or decrease of an original number is and want to find out how that increase or decrease changes the original number, keep these two important details in mind:

- ✔ To find the amount of increase, multiply the original number by 1 plus the rate.
- ✔ To find the amount of decrease, multiply the original number by 1 minus the rate.

So if you increase 100 by 5 percent, you multiply 100 by (1 + 0.05):

$$100 \times (1 + 0.05) = 100 \times 1.05 = 105$$

If you decrease 100 by 5 percent, you multiply 100 by (1 – 0.05).

$$100 \times (1 - 0.05) = 100 \times 0.95 = 95$$

Try a sample percent change problem.

A file cabinet that originally cost $52 is on sale for 15% off. If the sales tax on office furniture is 5% of the purchase price, how much is the total cost of the file cabinet at its sale price?

(A) $7.80

(B) $40.00

(C) $44.20

(D) $46.41

(E) $48.23

This word problem asks you how to deal with two percentages, the subtraction of the percentage discount and the addition of the percentage sales tax. First, calculate the discount.

You can figure 15 percent in your head by knowing that 10 percent of 52 is 5.20 and half of that (5 percent) is 2.60, so the discount is $7.80. Now subtract the discount from the original price: $52.00 – $7.80 = $44.20. The discount price for the cabinet is $44.20.

You still need to calculate the sales tax, so don't choose Choice (C)! You know that 5 percent of 44.20 is half of 4.42 (10 percent), or 2.21. You add $2.21 to $44.20. The only answer that ends in 1 is Choice (D). You can do the math to verify your guess, but Choice (D) is the correct answer: $44.20 + $2.21 = $46.41. Not a bad price for some much needed organization!

Taking it further: Repeated percent change

Now suppose you want to show a percent change repeated over a period of time, such as when you need to figure out how much interest accrues on a bank account after several years. To do so, you take the formula for percent change a step further.

Suppose you have $100 in a bank account at the end of 2012, and you want to know how much money will be in that same account at the end of 2022 at an annual interest rate of 5 percent. No fair pulling it out when the stock market is making a bull run! One way to figure this out is by using the percentage increase formula. The first step looks something like this:

$$100 \times (1 + 0.05) = 105$$

So you have $105 at the end of the first year.

Don't make the mistake of thinking that all you have to do is multiply by 10 and you have $1,050 after 10 years. You wish! This type of question will trap anyone who isn't paying attention every time.

To get the correct answer, tweak the formula a bit by adding an exponent. The exponent will be the number of times the original number changes. The formula looks like this, where n is the number of changes:

Final Amount = Original Number $\times$ $(1 + \text{Rate})^n$

Plug the numbers into the formula and solve:

$$100 \times (1 + 0.05)^{10} = x$$
$$100 \times 1.05^{10} = x$$
$$100 \times 1.6289 = x$$
$$162.89 = x$$

So after 10 years, you'd have $162.89 in the bank.

To show a repeated percent decrease over time, you'd use this similar formula:

Final Amount = Original Number $\times$ $(1 - \text{Rate})^n$

Making Comparisons: Ratios and Proportions

A ratio is the relation between two like numbers or two like values. A ratio may be written as a fraction ($\frac{3}{4}$), as a division expression (3 ÷ 4), or with a colon (3:4), or it can be stated as "3 to 4."

Because a ratio can be regarded as a fraction, multiplying or dividing both terms of a ratio by the same number doesn't change the value of the ratio. So 1:4 = 2:8 = 4:16. To reduce a ratio to its lowest terms, simplify the ratio as you would a fraction. (See the earlier section "Defining numerators, denominators, and other stuff you need to know about fractions.")

Ratios often crop up in word problems. Suppose an auto manufacturer ships a total of 160 cars to two dealerships at a ratio of 3 to 5. This means that for every three cars that go to Dealer 1, five cars ship to Dealer 2. To determine how many cars each dealership receives, add the terms of the ratio, or 3 + 5, to get the total number of fractional parts each dealership will get: 3 + 5 = 8. The first dealership will receive $\frac{3}{8}$ of 160 cars, or $\frac{3}{8} \times 160$, which equals 60. The second dealership receives $\frac{5}{8}$ of 160 cars, or 100.

As long as the total number of *items* in a ratio problem can be evenly divided by the total number of fractional parts, you can find the total number of items that are attributable to each part.

A *proportion* is a relationship between two equal ratios. It may be written as the proportion sign :: or with an equal sign. So you can read 1:4 :: 2:8 as "1 is to 4 as 2 is to 8."

The first and last terms in a proportion are called the *extremes,* and the second and third terms are called the *means.* If you multiply the means together and multiply the extremes together and then compare the products, you find that the products are the same:

$$1 \times 8 = 2 \times 4$$

Anytime you know three terms of a proportion, you can find the missing term first by multiplying either the two means or the two extremes (depending on which are known) and then dividing the product by the remaining term. This is also known as cross-multiplying. So if you know 7:8 :: x:104, you can solve for x by using cross-multiplication:

$$\frac{7}{8} = \frac{x}{104}$$
$$7(104) = 8x$$
$$728 = 8x$$
$$91 = x$$

Be sure to keep the elements of your ratios and proportions consistent. For example, if your proportion is "3 is to 4 as 5 is to x," you must set up the problem like this:

$$\frac{3}{4} = \frac{5}{x}$$

rather than this:

$$\frac{3}{4} = \frac{x}{5}$$

Here's what a GMAT ratio problem may look like.

If the ratio of $4a$ to $9b$ is 1 to 9, what is the ratio of $8a$ to $9b$?

(A) 1 to 18

(B) 1 to 39

(C) 2 to 9

(D) 2 to 36

(E) 3 to 9

At first, this problem may appear to be more difficult than it actually is. If $4a$ to $9b$ is a 1 to 9 ratio, then $8a$ to $9b$ must be a 2 to 9 ratio, because $8a$ is 2 times $4a$. If $4a$ equals 1, then $8a$ must equal 2. The answer, therefore, has to be Choice (C).

Playing the Numbers: Scientific Notation

Scientific notation is a simple way to write out humongous (technical term) or teensy weensy (another technical term) numbers so they're more manageable. You express a number in scientific notation by writing it as the product of a number and a power of 10. Simply move the decimal point so all digits except one are to the right of the decimal point; then multiply that decimal number times 10 raised to an exponent that equals the number of places you moved the decimal point. If you're working with a large number and you moved the decimal point to the left, the exponent is positive:

$$1{,}234{,}567 = 1.234567 \times 10^6$$
$$20 \text{ million } (20{,}000{,}000) = 2.0 \times 10^7$$

To display very small numbers in scientific notation, you move the decimal point to the right so one value is to the left of the decimal point. When you move the decimal point to the right, the exponent is negative. In this example, the decimal point moved six places to the right:

$$0.0000037 = 3.7 \times 10^{-6}$$

Here's how the GMAT may test you on scientific notation.

The number of organisms in a liter of water is approximately 6.0×10^{23}. Assuming this number is correct, about how many organisms exist in a covered Petri dish that contains $\frac{1}{200}$ liters of water?

(A) 6.9

(B) 3.0×10^{21}

(C) 6.0×10^{22}

(D) 3.0×10^{23}

(E) 1.2×10^{26}

This question uses many words to ask you to the find the answer to $6.0 \times 10^{23} \div 200$. If a liter of water contains a certain number of organisms, $\frac{1}{200}$ liter of water would contain the same number of organisms divided by 200. Try not to let the wording of the question confuse you.

So if 6.0 divided by 200 equals 0.03, the answer is 0.03×10^{23}, but that's not scientific notation because the decimal point is in the wrong place. Move the decimal point two places to the right and decrease the power by two (remember that when you move the decimal point to the right, the exponent is negative, so you subtract). The answer is Choice (B), 3.0×10^{21}.

Chapter 11

Considering All the Variables: Algebra

. . . .

In This Chapter
▶ Defining variables and other fundamental algebra terms
▶ Solving your problems with algebraic operations
▶ Simplifying your life with factoring
▶ Getting functions to function
▶ Cracking the mysteries of solving algebraic equations and inequalities

. . . .

Algebra is the study of properties of operations carried out on sets of numbers. That may sound like mumbo-jumbo, but the idea is that algebra is really just a form of arithmetic in which symbols (usually letters) stand for numbers. You use algebra to solve equations and to find the value of a variable. For example, how often have you heard the command, "Solve the equation for x"?

The algebra concepts tested on the GMAT are limited to the ones you'd use in a first-year algebra course, so you're at no disadvantage if you've never taken Algebra II. But many GMAT math problems involve basic algebra, and this chapter provides what you need to know to excel on all of them.

Defining the Elements: Algebraic Terms

Before we jump into solving algebra problems, we define some terms you need to know in the following sections. Although the GMAT doesn't specifically test you on the definitions of *variable, constant,* and *coefficient,* it does expect you to know these concepts when they crop up in the questions.

Braving the unknowns: Variables and constants

You'll see a lot of *variables* in algebra problems. They're the symbols that stand for numbers. Usually the symbols take the form of letters and represent specific numeric values. True to their name, variables' values can change depending on the equation they're in.

Think of variables as abbreviations for discrete things. For example, if a store charges different prices for apples and oranges and you buy two apples and four oranges, the clerk can't ring them up together by simply adding 2 + 4 to get 6. That would be incorrectly comparing apples and oranges! So to express the transaction in algebraic terms, you use variables to stand in for the price of apples and oranges, something like 2*a* and 4*o*.

In contrast, *constants,* as their name implies, are numbers with values that don't change in a specific problem. Letters may also be used to refer to constants, but they don't change their value in an equation as variables do (for example, *a, b,* and *c* stand for fixed numbers in the formula $y = ax^2 + bx + c$).

Coming together: Terms and expressions

Single constants and variables or constants and variables grouped together form *terms;* terms are any set of variables or constants you can multiply or divide to form a single unit in an equation. You can combine these single parts in an equation that applies addition or subtraction. For example, the following algebraic expression has three terms: $ax^2 + bx + c$. The first term is ax^2, the second term is bx, and the third term is c.

Terms often form *expressions.* An algebraic expression is a collection of terms that are combined by addition or subtraction and are often grouped by parentheses, such as $(x + 2)$, $(x - 3c)$, and $(2x - 3y)$. Although an expression can contain just one term, it's more common to think of expressions as combinations of two or more terms. So in the apples and oranges scenario we presented earlier, you can make an expression for combining two apples and four oranges, which may look something like this: $2a + 4o$.

A *coefficient* is a number or symbol that serves as a measure of a property or characteristic. In $2a + 4o$, the variables are a and o, and the numbers 2 and 4 are the coefficients of the variables. This means that the coefficient of the variable a is 2 and the coefficient of the variable o is 4.

In an algebraic expression, terms involving the same variable, even if they have different coefficients, are called *like terms.* For example, in the expression $3x + 4y - 2x + y$, $3x$ and $-2x$ are like terms because they both contain the single x variable; $4y$ and y are also like terms because they both contain the y variable and only the y variable.

The variables must be exact matches with the same powers; for example, $3x^3y$ and x^3y are like terms, but x and x^2 aren't like terms, and neither are $2x$ and $2xy$.

You can combine (add/subtract) like terms together, but you can't combine unlike terms. So in the expression $3x + 4y - 2x + y$, you can subtract the terms with the common x variable: $3x - 2x = x$. And you can add the like terms with the common y variable: $4y + y = 5y$ (if a variable has no visible numerical coefficient, it's understood that its coefficient is 1; therefore, y is understood to be $1y$). All this combining results in the final expression of $x + 5y$, which is a much simpler expression to work with. We work with many more algebraic expressions in the section "Maintaining an Orderly Fashion: Algebraic Operations," later in this chapter.

Knowing the nomials: Kinds of expressions

Expressions carry particular names depending on how many terms they contain. On the GMAT, you'll work with monomials and polynomials.

A *monomial* is an expression that contains only one term, such as $4x$ or ax^2. A monomial is, therefore, also referred to as a term in an algebraic expression.

Poly means many, so we bet you've already figured out that a *polynomial* is an expression that has more than one term. These multiple terms can be added together or subtracted from one another. Here are a couple of examples of polynomials:

$$a^2 - b^2$$

$$ab^2 + 2ac + b$$

Polynomials can have more specific designations, depending on how many terms they contain. For example, a *binomial* is a specific kind of polynomial, one that contains two terms, such as $a + b$ or $2a + 3$. And a *trinomial* is a polynomial with three terms, like $4x^2 + 3y - 8$.

A famous trinomial that you should be very familiar with for the GMAT is the expression known as a *quadratic polynomial,* which is this trinomial expression:

$$ax^2 + bx + c$$

We discuss this very important expression in the "Solving quadratic equations" section, later in this chapter.

Maintaining an Orderly Fashion: Algebraic Operations

Symbols like $+$, $-$, $\times$, and $\div$ are common to arithmetic and algebra. They symbolize the operations you perform on numbers. Arithmetic uses numbers with known values, such as $5 + 7 = 12$, in its operations (visit Chapter 10 for more on basic arithmetic operations), but algebraic operations deal with unknowns, like $x + y = z$. This algebraic equation can't produce an exact numerical value because you don't know what x and y represent, let alone z. But that doesn't stop you from solving algebra problems as best you can with the given information. In the following sections, we show you how to add, subtract, multiply, and divide expressions with unknowns.

Adding to and taking away

From arithmetic, you know that 3 dozen plus 6 dozen is 9 dozen, or

$$(3 \times 12) + (6 \times 12) = (9 \times 12)$$

In algebra, you can write a somewhat similar equation by using a variable to stand in for the dozen: $3x + 6x = 9x$. And you can subtract to get the opposite result: $9x - 6x = 3x$.

Remember to combine positive and negative numbers according to the rules of arithmetic (see Chapter 10 if you need a refresher). If you add two or more positive numbers in an expression, they keep the positive sign. If you add a positive to a negative number, it's as though you're subtracting.

For example, to tackle the expression $7x + (-10x) + 22x$, you find the sum of the two positive numbers ($7x$ and $22x$) and then subtract the value of the negative number (because adding a negative is the same as subtracting a positive), like this:

$$7x + (-10x) + 22x$$

$$= 29x - 10x$$

$$= 19x$$

That's fine for adding and subtracting like terms, you may say, but what about working with unlike terms? You can't combine terms with different symbols or variables the same way you can when the symbols are the same. For instance, take a look at this example:

$$7x + 10y + 15x - 3y$$

If you simply combine the whole expression by adding and subtracting without accounting for the different variables, you'd come up with a wrong answer, something like $29xy$. (And you can bet the GMAT will offer this incorrect figure as one of the answer choices to try to trap you.) Instead, you first separate the x's from the y's and add and subtract to get something more manageable, like this:

$$7x + 15x = 22x$$
$$10y - 3y = 7y$$

which gives you this final expression:

$$22x + 7y$$

If you want to get tricky and add two or more expressions, you can set them up just as you would an addition problem in arithmetic. Remember, only like terms can be combined together this way.

$$3x + 4y - 7z$$
$$2x - 2y + 8z$$
$$\underline{-x + 3y + 6z}$$
$$4x + 5y + 7z$$

Here's how an algebra problem may look on the GMAT.

For all x and y, $(4x^2 - 6xy - 12y^2) - (8x^2 - 12xy + 4y^2) = ?$

(A) $-4x^2 - 18xy - 16y^2$

(B) $-4x^2 + 6xy - 16y^2$

(C) $-4x^2 + 6xy - 8y^2$

(D) $4x^2 - 6xy + 16y^2$

(E) $12x^2 - 18xy - 8y^2$

The easiest way to approach this problem is to distribute the negative sign to the second expression (see the later section "Distributing terms") and combine the two expressions with like terms by following these steps:

1. **Distribute the negative sign (multiply each term in the second expression by –1).**

   Remember that subtracting is the same as adding a negative number. So your problem is really $(4x^2 - 6xy - 12y^2) + -1(8x^2 - 12xy + 4y^2)$. Distributing the negative sign changes the second expression to $-8x^2 + 12xy - 4y^2$, because a negative times a positive makes a negative and two negatives make a positive.

2. **Combine the expressions with like terms together:**

   $$4x^2 - 8x^2 - 6xy + 12xy - 12y^2 - 4y^2$$

3. **Add and subtract like terms:**

   $$4x^2 - 8x^2 = -4x^2; -6xy + 12xy = 6xy; -12y^2 - 4y^2 = -16y^2$$

4. Put the terms back into the polynomial:

$-4x^2 + 6xy - 16y^2$

So the answer is $-4x^2 + 6xy - 16y^2$, which is Choice (B). If you chose any of the other answers, you either distributed the negative sign improperly or you added and subtracted the like terms incorrectly.

After you've combined like terms, double-check that you've used the correct signs, particularly when you change all the signs like you did in the second expression. The other answer choices for the sample problem are very similar to the correct choice. They're designed to trap you in case you make an addition or subtraction error. Add and subtract carefully, and you won't fall for these tricks.

Multiplying and dividing expressions

Multiplying and dividing two or more variables works just as though you were performing these same operations on numbers with known values. So if $2^3 = 2 \times 2 \times 2$, then $x^3 = x \times x \times x$. Likewise, if $2^2 \times 2^2 = 2^4$, then $x^2 \times x^2 = x^4$. Similarly, if $2^6 \div 2^4 = 2^2$, then $y^6 \div y^4 = y^2$.

The process is pretty simple for monomials, but polynomials may be a little more complicated. In the next sections, we explore the different methods for multiplying and dividing polynomials.

Distributing terms

You can distribute terms in algebra just like you do in arithmetic. For example, when you multiply a number by a binomial, you multiply the number by each term in the binomial. In this example, you multiply $4x$ by each term inside the parentheses:

$4x(x - 3) = 4x^2 - 12x$

With division, you do the same operation in reverse.

$(16x^2 + 4x) \div 4x = 4x + 1$

Here's an example of a GMAT question that you can use distribution to answer.

For all x, $12x - (-10x) - 3x(-x + 10) = ?$

(A) $10x$

(B) $-3x^2 - 10x$

(C) $3x^2 - 52x$

(D) $3x^2 + 8x$

(E) $3x^2 - 8x$

This question tests your ability to add, subtract, and multiply terms in an algebraic expression. First, use distribution to multiply $-3x$ by $(-x + 10)$: $-3x \times -x = 3x^2$ and $-3x \times 10 = -30x$, so $-3x (-x + 10) = 3x^2 - 30x$.

Now the equation looks like this:

$12x - (-10x) + 3x^2 - 30x = ?$

Combine the terms that contain the *x* variable:

$$12x + 10x - 30x = -8x$$

So the answer to the equation is Choice (E): $3x^2 - 8x$

Stacking terms

One easy way to multiply polynomials is to stack the two numbers to be multiplied on top of one another. Suppose you have this expression: $(x^2 + 2xy + y^2) \times (x - y)$.

You can stack this expression just like an old-fashioned multiplication problem. Just remember to multiply each of the terms in the second line by each term in the first line.

$$
\begin{array}{r}
x^2 + 2xy + y^2 \\
x - y \\
\hline
x^3 + 2x^2y + xy^2 \\
-x^2y - 2xy^2 - y^3 \\
\hline
x^3 + x^2y - xy^2 - y^3
\end{array}
$$

Line up like terms during the first round of multiplication so they match up before you add the products.

The GMAT may ask you to divide a polynomial by a monomial. Simply divide each term of the polynomial by the monomial. Here's how you'd divide the expression $\dfrac{60x^4 - 20x^3}{5x}$:

$$
\begin{aligned}
\frac{60x^4 - 20x^3}{5x} &= \frac{60x^4}{5x} - \frac{20x^3}{5x} \\
&= \left(\frac{60}{5} \times \frac{x^4}{x} \right) - \left(\frac{20}{5} \times \frac{x^3}{x} \right) \\
&= \left(12 \times x^{4-1} \right) - \left(4 \times x^{3-1} \right) \\
&= 12x^3 - 4x^2
\end{aligned}
$$

Taking a shine to the FOIL method

You can multiply binomials by using the *FOIL* method. FOIL is an acronym for *first, outer, inner, last*, which indicates the order that you multiply the terms from one binomial by the terms of the second binomial before adding their products. Take a look at this example:

$$(4x - 5)(3x + 8) =$$

Multiply the first terms in each binomial — $4x$ and $3x$.

$$4x \times 3x = 12x^2$$

Then multiply the outer terms ($4x$ and 8) to get $32x$ and the inner terms ($3x$ and -5) to get $-15x$. You can add the products at this point because they're like terms.

$$32x - 15x = 17x$$

Last, multiply the last terms.

$$-5 \times 8 = -40$$

Combine the products to form the resulting expression.

$$12x^2 + 17x - 40$$

You may recognize this expression as the quadratic polynomial we discussed in the earlier section "Knowing the nomials: Kinds of expressions." To save time on the GMAT, you may want to commit the following factors and their resulting equations to memory:

$$(x + y)^2 = x^2 + 2xy + y^2$$
$$(x - y)^2 = x^2 - 2xy + y^2$$

So if you're asked to multiply $(x + 3)(x + 3)$, you know without using FOIL that the answer is $x^2 + 2(3x) + 9$ or $x^2 + 6x + 9$. And $(x - 3)(x - 3) = x^2 - 6x + 9$.

If you're able to keep track of the terms, you can use FOIL to multiply terms in the proper order without taking the time to stack them. The FOIL method comes in handy for solving GMAT problems like the next one.

When the polynomials $3x + 4$ and $x - 5$ are multiplied together and written in the form $3x^2 + kx - 20$, what is the value of k?

(A) 2

(B) 3

(C) –5

(D) –11

(E) –20

This question asks you for the constant in the middle term of the quadratic expression formed by multiplying $3x + 4$ and $x - 5$. Remember with FOIL, you multiply the first, outer, inner, and last. The problem gives you the first term: $3x^2$. The last is also there: –20. Because the problem provides the product of the first terms and last terms, all you have to do to get the middle term is to multiply the outer and inner numbers of the two expressions and then add them together.

1. **Multiply the outer numbers:**

    $3x \times -5 = -15x$

2. **Multiply the inner numbers:**

    $4 \times x = 4x$

So the middle term of the quadratic is $-15x + 4x = -11x$. The constant k must equal –11, which is Choice (D).

Extracting Information: Factoring Polynomials

Factors are the numbers you multiply together to get a product. So factoring a value means you write that value as a product of its factors. For the GMAT, you should know how to pull out the common factors in expressions and the two binomial factors in a quadratic polynomial. We show you how to do both in the following sections.

Something in common: Finding common factors

To simplify polynomials for complex problems, extract their common factors by dividing each term by the factors that are common to every term. You can think of the process as the opposite of distributing terms. For example, to find the common factors of the terms in the expression $-14x^3 - 35x^6$, follow these steps:

1. **Consider the coefficients.**

   Because -7 is common to both -14 and -35, take this factor out of the expression by dividing both terms by -7. Then put the remaining expression in parentheses next to the common factor: $-7(2x^3 + 5x^6)$.

2. **Now look at the variables.**

   Because x^3 or a multiple of it is common to both terms, divide both terms in parentheses by x^3, multiply x^3 by the other common factor (-7), and put the remaining expression in parentheses: $-7x^3(2 + 5x^3)$.

So $-14x^3 - 35x^6 = -7x^3(2 + 5x^3)$.

Two by two: Factoring quadratic polynomials

The GMAT also expects you to know how to factor quadratic polynomials. To accomplish this task, you have to perform the FOIL operations in reverse to come up with a couple of binomial factors that look something like this: $(x \pm a)(x \pm b)$.

For example, look at the following quadratic polynomial:

$x^2 + 5x + 6$

To find its factors, draw two sets of parentheses: ( )( ). The first terms of the two factors have to be x and x because x^2 is the product of x and x. So you can add x as the first term for both sets of parentheses:

$(x \pm\ )(x \pm\ )$

To find the second terms for the two factors, ask yourself which two numbers have a product of 6 (the third term of the quadratic) and add up to the number 5 (the coefficient of the quadratic's second term). The only two factors that meet these two criteria are 2 and 3. The other factors of 6 (6 and 1, -6 and -1, -2 and -3) don't add up to 5. So the binomial factors of the quadratic equation are $(x + 2)$ and $(x + 3)$.

Because you do just the opposite of what you do when you multiply binomials using the FOIL method, you can use the FOIL method to make sure the binomial factors result in the original quadratic when you multiply them together.

There's a timesaving way to factor binomials that are made up of a difference of perfect squares, such as $x^2 - 4$. Factors for these types of quadratic polynomials result in the following form:

$(x - a)(x + a)$

The variable x is the square root of the first term, and a is the square root of the second term. So the factors of $x^2 - 4$ are $(x - 2)(x + 2)$.

This factoring technique is very easy to memorize and can help you answer some algebra questions much more quickly than if you were to take the time to carry out long calculations. For example, if you're asked to multiply factors $(x - 5)(x + 5)$, you can use the FOIL method to figure out the answer, but spotting that the correct answer will be the difference of two perfect squares is much faster. You know the correct answer is $x^2 - 25$ without performing time-consuming calculations.

Likewise, if you need to factor $x^2 - 25$, all you do is figure the square root of x^2 and the square root of 25 and enter those values into the proper factoring form for perfect square quadratics. You know right away that the factors are $(x - 5)(x + 5)$. When you break down the quadratic polynomial, you'll be able to solve quadratic equations. For more about how to do this, see the section "Solving quadratic equations," later in this chapter.

Minding Your Ps and Qs: Functions

Some of the GMAT math questions involve functions. Simply put, *functions* are relationships between two sets of numbers; each number you put into the formula gives you only one possible answer. Functions may sound complicated, but they're really pretty simple. A function problem looks something like this:

$f(x) = 2x^2 + 3$. What is $f(2)$?

We explore the terminology of functions and how to find the domain and range of functions in the following sections.

Standing in: Understanding function terminology

Before we show you how to solve function problems, you need to know a few definitions. Table 11-1 gives you the terms we use when we discuss functions.

Table 11-1	Defining Terms for Functions
Term	*Definition*
Function	A rule that turns each member of one set of numbers into a member of another set.
Independent variable (input)	The number you want to find the function of; the x in $f(x)$.
Dependent variable (output)	The result of substituting the independent value into the function, $f(x)$. (This is like your y variable.)
Domain	The set of all possible values of the independent variable.
Range	The set of all possible values of the dependent variable.

Functions on the GMAT are usually displayed with the letters f or g. For example, $f(x)$ is used to indicate the function of x, and it simply means "f of x."

Don't let this language confuse you. All you really have to do is substitute the indicated value for x in the function.

Don't think that the parentheses in the function notation mean multiplication like they do in algebraic operations. The expression $f(x)$ doesn't mean $f \times x$.

To see how functions work, consider the earlier example:

$f(x) = 2x^2 + 3$. What is $f(2)$?

The initial expression means that the function of x is to square x, multiply the result by 2, and then add 3. To calculate the function exercise with the number $f(2)$, you just substitute 2 for x in the expression and solve.

$f(2) = 2(2)^2 + 3$

$f(2) = 2(4) + 3$

$f(2) = 8 + 3$

$f(2) = 11$

So when x is 2, $f(x)$ is 11. That's all there is to it! The function notation is really just a fancy way of telling you to perform a substitution.

Here's another example.

If $g(x) = 2x^2 + 17$, what is $g(12)$?

(A) 12

(B) 17

(C) 100

(D) 288

(E) 305

If you quickly consider the situation, you can eliminate Choices (A), (B), and (C) right away. When you substitute 12 for x in the function, you square 12, which is 144. The answer then results from multiplying by and adding to that number, so you know the result will be greater than 100. Furthermore, the answer in Choice (D), 288, is just 2×144. You still have to add 17, so the answer probably isn't Choice (D) either. Without much calculation, you can eliminate enough answers to determine that Choice (E) is correct. But to do the calculations, just substitute 12 for x and solve:

$g(12) = 2(12)^2 + 17$

$g(12) = 288 + 17$

$g(12) = 305$

The answer is definitely Choice (E).

That was a pretty simple problem. But functions can get more complicated on the GMAT. Check out this example.

If $f(x) = (x - 2)^2$, find the value of $f(2x - 2)$.

(A) $4x^2 - 4$

(B) $4x^2 + 4$

(C) $4x^2 - 8x + 16$

(D) $4x^2 - 16x + 16$

(E) $4x^2 - 16x - 16$

Don't try to do this one in your head. Begin by plugging in $(2x - 2)$ for x. Then solve.

$$f(2x-2) = (2x-2-2)^2$$
$$= (2x-4)^2$$
$$= (2x-4)(2x-4)$$
$$= 4x^2 - 8x - 8x + 16$$
$$= 4x^2 - 16x + 16$$

So the correct answer is Choice (D).

Taking it to the limit: Domain and range of functions

The *domain of a function* is the set of all numbers that can possibly be an input of a function, the x in $f(x)$. The *range of a function* is the set of all numbers that can possibly be an output of a function, the value for $f(x)$. In other words, if you think of the domain as the set of all possible independent variables you can put into a function, the range is the set of all possible dependent variables that can come out of any particular function. Domain and range questions aren't difficult, but you need to be aware of some basic rules to determine the proper limits of the domain and range. The GMAT also tests you on graphing functions on the coordinate plane, but we discuss that in Chapter 13.

Mastering the territory: Domain

Unless a problem specifies otherwise, the domain of a function includes all real numbers, which means that the only numbers that aren't included in the domain are numbers that aren't real (see Chapter 10 for more info on imaginary and real numbers). Here are some properties of numbers that *aren't* real and, therefore, can't be part of the domain of a function:

- A real number can't be a fraction with a denominator of 0, because then the number would be undefined.

- A real number can't be an even-numbered root of a negative number. Even-numbered roots of negatives aren't real numbers because any number that's squared or has an even-numbered power can't result in a negative number.

  For example, there's no such thing as $\sqrt{-4}$ because there's no one number that you can square that results in a negative 4. So -2×-2 will always equal positive 4.

To see how the first rule affects domain, look at this function:

$$f(x) = \frac{x+4}{x-2}$$

Normally, the domain of x in a function can contain an unlimited number of values. In the preceding example, though, you have a fraction in the function, which puts the variable x in the denominator. Because your denominator can't add up to 0, the denominator of $x - 2$ can't equal 0. This means that x can't equal 2. In terms of functions, the domain of $f(x)$ is, therefore, $\{x \neq 2\}$. That's all there is to it!

Here's a function that relates to the second rule:

$$g(n) = 3\sqrt[4]{n+2}$$

In this function, you have an even-numbered radical sign with the variable n within it. You know that the root of an even-numbered radical, in this case, the 4th root, can't be a negative number. Otherwise, you wouldn't have a real number as your final answer. Therefore, the number under the radical sign can't be less than 0. So $n \geq -2$. The result is that the domain of the function $g(n)$ is $\{n \geq -2\}$.

The GMAT may test your knowledge of domain with a problem such as the following.

Determine the domain of the function $f(x) = \dfrac{4}{x^2 - x - 2}$.

(A) $\{x \neq -1, 2\}$

(B) $\{x \neq 1, -2\}$

(C) $\{x = -1, 2\}$

(D) $\{x = -4, 2\}$

(E) $\{x \neq -4, 2\}$

This problem involves simple algebra. You know the denominator can't equal 0, so set the trinomial in the denominator equal to 0, and solve for x to find out what x can't be. We show you how to solve trinomials later in the "Solving quadratic equations" section.

$$x^2 - x - 2 = 0$$
$$(x+1)(x-2) = 0$$
$$x + 1 = 0$$
$$x = -1$$
$$x - 2 = 0$$
$$x = 2$$

You're not finished! If you picked Choice (C) as your answer, your factoring would have been absolutely right, but your answer would be absolutely wrong. Answer Choice (C) gives you only the values for x that make the denominator equal to 0. You're trying to find the values that make the denominator *not* equal to 0.

So the correct answer is Choice (A); x can be any real number other than -1 and 2 because if x were equal to -1 or 2, the denominator would be 0, and the value would be undefined. If you chose Choice (B), you switched the signs of the factors. If you chose Choices (D) or (E), you found the correct factors of the denominator but mistakenly divided the numerator by each root of the denominator.

Roaming the land: Range

Just as the domain of a function is limited by certain laws of mathematics, so, too, is the range. Here are the rules to remember when you're determining the range of a function:

✔ An absolute value of a real number can't be a negative number.

✔ An even exponent or power can't produce a negative number.

Check out some situations where these rules come into play. Look at the following functions:

$$g(x) = |x|$$
$$g(x) = x^2$$

Each of these functions can result only in an output that's a positive number or 0. So in each case, the range of the function of g is greater than or equal to 0. Here's a question that puts the range rules to work.

What is the range of the function $g(x) = 1 - \sqrt{x-2}$?

(A) $g(x) \geq -2$

(B) $g(x) \leq -2$

(C) $g(x) \geq 2$

(D) $g(x) \geq -1$

(E) $g(x) \leq 1$

First, you have to make the radical a real number. The value within the square root sign has to be equal to or greater than 0. So x has to be equal to or greater than 2 because any value less than 2 would make the radical a negative value. To check the possible outputs, consider several values for x.

If x is the lowest value, 2, you'd figure the output of the function like this:

$$1 - \sqrt{2-2} = 1 - \sqrt{0}$$
$$= 1 - 0$$
$$= 1$$

So you know that $g(x)$ can be equal to 1.

If x is a higher value than 2, say 6, then you'd calculate the output like this:

$$1 - \sqrt{6-2} = 1 - \sqrt{4}$$
$$= 1 - 2$$
$$= -1$$

Now you know that any value for x that's higher than 2 results in a lower value for the output of the function. Therefore, $g(x)$ has to equal 1 or be less than 1, and the correct answer is Choice (E).

Getting confused and looking for the domain when you should be finding the range is very easy. If you chose Choice (C), you solved for the domain of x. If you chose Choices (A) or (B), you're hung up trying to make the number under the radical a positive number. If you chose Choice (D), you simply don't know how to solve for range, so be sure to review this section.

Putting On Your Thinking Cap: Problem Solving

You may be wondering how the GMAT tests your knowledge of algebra concepts. Well, wonder no more. The following sections present you with many of the ways you'll use algebra to solve GMAT math problems.

Isolating the variable: Linear equations

A *linear equation* is an algebra equation that contains an unknown variable and no exponent greater than 1. In other words, these equations are fairly easy.

In its simplest form, a linear equation is expressed as $ax + b = 0$, where x is the variable and a and b are constants. Here are two things to keep in mind when you're solving linear equations:

✔ Isolate the variable in the equation you're trying to solve, which means you work to get it all by itself on one side of the equation. In other words, you're solving for x.

✔ Whatever operation you perform on one side of the equation, you must do to the other side.

This easy question asks you to solve a linear equation: If $4x + 10 = -38$, what is the value of x?

Solve for x by isolating the variable on one side of the equation:

1. **Eliminate 10 from the left side of the equation by subtracting it.**

   (Remember that if you do something to one side of the equation, you need to do the same thing to the other side. Otherwise, your math teacher is liable to rap you on the knuckles with a slide rule.) Here's what happens when you subtract 10 from both sides:

   $$4x + 10 - 10 = -38 - 10$$
   $$4x = -48$$

2. **Next, divide both sides by 4, and you have your answer.**

   $$\frac{4x}{4} = \frac{-48}{4}$$
   $$x = -12$$

The value of x is -12.

You tackle division problems the same way. So if you're asked to solve for x in the problem $\frac{x}{4} = -5$, you know what to do. Isolate x to the left side of the equation by multiplying both sides of the equation by 4:

$$\frac{x}{4} \times 4 = -5 \times 4$$
$$x = -20$$

 If the equation includes multiple fractions, you can simplify things and save precious time by eliminating the fractions. Just multiply each fraction by the *least common denominator* (which is the lowest positive whole number that each fraction's denominator divides into evenly). For example, you may have to solve for x in a problem like this:

$$\frac{3x}{5} + \frac{8}{15} = \frac{x}{10}$$

The lowest number that 5, 15, and 10 go into evenly is 30, so that's your least common denominator. Multiply each fraction by a fraction equivalent to 1 that will give you 30 in the denominators, like this:

$$\left(\frac{3x}{5} \times \frac{6}{6}\right) + \left(\frac{8}{15} \times \frac{2}{2}\right) = \left(\frac{x}{10} \times \frac{3}{3}\right)$$
$$\frac{18x}{30} + \frac{16}{30} = \frac{3x}{30}$$

Now you can eliminate the fractions by multiplying both sides of the equation by 30:

$$18x + 16 = 3x$$

Then just solve for x:

$$18x + 16 - 3x = 3x - 3x$$
$$15x + 16 = 0$$
$$15x + 16 - 16 = 0 - 16$$
$$15x = -16$$
$$\frac{15x}{15} = \frac{-16}{15}$$
$$x = -\frac{16}{15}$$

Bringing in the substitution: Simultaneous equations

Solving for x is simple when it's the only variable, but what if your equation has more than one variable? When you have another equation that contains at least one of the variables, you can solve for either variable. These two equations are called *simultaneous equations*. You just solve one of the equations for one of the variables and then plug the answer into the other equation and solve. Here's a simple example.

If $4x + 5y = 30$ and $y = 2$, what is the value of x?

Because the second equation tells you that y is 2, just substitute 2 for the value of y in the first equation and you're on your way:

$$4x + 5y = 30$$
$$4x + 5(2) = 30$$
$$4x + 10 = 30$$
$$4x = 20$$
$$x = 5$$

That's all there is to it!

You can also solve simultaneous linear equations by stacking them. This method works when you have as many equations as you have possible variables to solve for. So you can stack these two equations because they contain two variables.

$$6x + 4y = 66$$
$$-2x + 2y = 8$$

Your goal is to find a way to remove one of the variables. Here's how:

1. **Examine the equations to determine what terms you can eliminate through addition or subtraction.**

   If you multiply the entire second equation by 3, you can eliminate the x terms in both equations because $-2x \times 3 = -6x$, and $6x - 6x = 0$. Just be sure to multiply each term in the equation by the same value. So the second equation becomes $-6x + 6y = 24$.

2. **Stack the equations, combine like terms, and solve for *y*.**

$$6x + 4y = 66$$
$$\underline{-6x + 6y = 24}$$
$$0 + 10y = 90$$
$$y = 9$$

3. **Plug the value of one variable into one of the equations and solve for the other value.**

You've found that $y = 9$, so substitute 9 for the value of *y* in one of the equations to solve for *x*.

$$-2x + 2y = 8$$
$$-2x + 2(9) = 8$$
$$-2x + 18 = 8$$
$$-2x = -10$$
$$x = 5$$

Therefore, the solutions, also referred to as *roots,* to the simultaneous equations are $x = 5$ and $y = 9$.

Not playing fair: Inequalities

An inequality is a statement such as "*x* is less than *y*" or "*x* is greater than or equal to *y*."

In addition to the symbols for add, subtract, multiply, and divide, mathematics also applies standard symbols to show how the two sides of an equation are related. You're probably pretty familiar with these symbols, but a little review never hurts. Table 11-2 gives you a rundown of the symbols you'll deal with on the GMAT.

Here are some of the more common symbols used in algebra to signify equality and inequality.

Table 11-2	Mathematical Symbols for Equality and Inequality
Symbol	*Meaning*
$=$	Equal to
$\neq$	Not equal to
$\approx$	Approximately equal to
$>$	Greater than
$<$	Less than
$\geq$	Greater than or equal to
$\leq$	Less than or equal to

Performing operations with inequalities

You treat inequalities a lot like equations. Isolate the variable to one side and perform the same operations on both sides of the inequality. The only difference is that if you multiply or divide by a negative number, you need to reverse the direction of the inequality sign. So here's how you solve this inequality:

$$-2x \leq 10$$
$$x \geq -5$$

Working with ranges of numbers

You can also use inequalities to show a range of numbers. For example, the GMAT may show the range of numbers between –6 and 12 as an algebraic inequality, like this:

$$-6 < x < 12$$

To show the range between –6 and 12 including –6 and 12, you use the ≤ sign:

$$-6 \leq x \leq 12$$

You can add or subtract values within a range. For example, you add 5 to each part of $-6 < x < 12$, like this:

$$-6 < x < 12$$
$$-6 + 5 < x + 5 < 12 + 5$$
$$-1 < x + 5 < 17$$

And you can perform operations between different ranges, such as $4 < x < 15$ and $-2 < y < 20$. To find the sum of these two ranges, follow these steps:

1. **Add the smallest values of each range:**

   $$4 + (-2) = 2$$

2. **Add the largest values of each range:**

   $$15 + 20 = 35$$

3. **Create a new range with the sums:**

   $$2 < x + y < 35$$

   This means that the range of values of $x + y$ is $2 < x + y < 35$.

Here's an example of how the GMAT may ask you to deal with inequalities.

If $x^2 - 1 \leq 8$, what is the smallest real value x can have?

(A) –9

(B) –6

(C) –3

(D) 0

(E) 3

This problem asks you to determine the smallest real value of x if $x^2 - 1$ is less than or equal to 8. Solve the inequality for x:

$$x^2 - 1 \leq 8$$
$$x^2 - 1 + 1 \leq 8 + 1$$
$$x^2 \leq 9$$
$$x \leq \sqrt{9}$$

Remember that the square root of a number may be positive or negative. The square root of 9 is either 3 or –3. Because –3 is less than 3, –3 must be the smallest real value of x.

To make sure you're right, you can eliminate answer choices by using common sense. For example, –9 in Choice (A) would make x^2 equal 81, and –6 in Choice (B) would make x^2 equal 36. So neither Choices (A) nor (B) can be a solution for x. In Choice (D), 0 is a solution for x, but it isn't the smallest solution, because you know that –3 is a possibility. Choice (E) can't be right because it's larger than two other possible solutions, –3 and 0. So Choice (C) is the correct answer.

Solving quadratic equations

When you set a quadratic polynomial equal to 0, you get what's called a quadratic equation. An example of the classic quadratic form is $ax^2 + bx + c = 0$, where a, b, and c are constants and x is a variable that you have to solve for. Notice that 0 is on one side of the equation and all non-zero terms are on the other side.

Quadratic equations may appear in slightly different forms. For example, all the following equations are quadratic equations because they contain a squared variable and equal 0:

$$x^2 = 0$$
$$x^2 - 4 = 0$$
$$3x^2 - 6x + 5 = 0$$

Factoring to find x

The GMAT may give you a quadratic equation and ask you to solve for x. The simplest way to solve a quadratic equation is to try to factor the equation into two binomials, just like we did earlier in the section "Two by two: Factoring quadratic polynomials."

$$x^2 - 6x + 5 = 0$$

To factor this trinomial, consider what numbers multiply together to become 5 that also have a sum of –6.

The two factors of 5 are 5 and 1 or –5 and –1. To get a sum of –6, you need to go with the negative values. Doing so gives these two binomial factors: $(x - 5)$ and $(x - 1)$. So the resulting equation is $(x - 5)(x - 1) = 0$.

To solve for x, you set each of the binomial factors equal to 0. You can do so because you know that one of the factors must equal 0 if their product is 0.

$$x - 5 = 0$$
$$x = 5$$

and

$$x - 1 = 0$$
$$x = 1$$

Now the solutions (or roots) to the equation are clear: $x = 1$ and $x = 5$. Both 1 and 5 are possible solutions for x in this quadratic equation.

Quadratic equations usually have two possible solutions.

Determining solutions for the difference of perfect squares

Finding the solution set for a quadratic equation made up of the difference of perfect squares (like $x^2 - y^2 = 0$) is simple if you remember that $x^2 - y^2 = (x + y)(x - y)$. If the GMAT presents you with the task of solving for x in an equation where the difference of perfect squares is equal to 0, you know that x equals the positive and negative values of the square root of y^2 (which is the second term).

So if you're told to find the solution set for $x^2 - 49 = 0$, you'd determine the square root of the second term (49), which is 7. The factors, then, are $(x + 7)$ and $(x - 7)$. Therefore, the solution set for this problem is $x = -7$ and $x = 7$, which is indeed the positive and negative values of the second term's square root!

Using the quadratic formula

Solving quadratic equations is easy when the solutions come out to be nice, round numbers. But what if the ultimate solutions are harsh-looking radicals or perhaps not even real roots? When you can't simply solve a quadratic equation by factoring, you may have to use the quadratic formula, which is a rearrangement of the classic equation: $ax^2 + bx + c = 0$. It looks like this:

$$x = \frac{-b \pm \sqrt{b^2 - 4ac}}{2a}$$

Although this formula may look mighty unmanageable, it may be the only way to find the solution to x for quadratic equations that aren't easily factored. Here's how you'd apply the formula when asked to solve $3x^2 + 7x - 6 = 0$ for x. In this equation, $a = 3$, $b = 7$, and $c = -6$. Plug these numbers into the quadratic formula:

$$x = \frac{-7 \pm \sqrt{7^2 - 4(3)(-6)}}{2(3)}$$

$$x = \frac{-7 \pm \sqrt{49 + 72}}{6}$$

$$x = \frac{-7 \pm \sqrt{121}}{6}$$

$$x = \frac{-7 \pm 11}{6}$$

$$x = \frac{-18}{6} \text{ or } -3$$

$$x = \frac{4}{6} \text{ or } \frac{2}{3}$$

The solutions for x are $\frac{2}{3}$ and -3. Whew! Luckily, the GMAT won't give you many quadratic equations that require you to apply this formula. But you'll know what to do if you encounter one of the few.

Reading between the lines: Word problems

The GMAT tests algebra and arithmetic concepts in word problems as well as mathematical equations. In fact, word problems are more common on the GMAT than straightforward equation solving. So you have to know how to translate the English language into mathematical expressions. (You'll probably see a few geometry word problems, too, but algebra is more common on the GMAT.)

To help you with the translation, Table 11-3 provides some of the more common words you'll encounter in word problems and tells you what they look like in math symbols.

Table 11-3	Common Words and Their Math Equivalents
Plain English	**Math Equivalent**
More than, increased by, added to, combined with, total of, sum of	Plus (+)
Less than, fewer than, decreased by, diminished by, reduced by, difference between, taken away from	Minus (−)
Of, times, product of	Multiply (×)
Ratio of, per, out of, quotient	Divide (÷ or /)
x percent of y	$(x \div 100) \times y$
Is, are, was, were, becomes, results in	Equals (=)
How much, how many, a certain number	Variable (x, y)

Here's an example of how you play foreign language interpreter on GMAT word problems.

On the first day of an alpine slalom competition, the total combined time of Grace's two runs was 1 minute and 57 seconds. If twice the number of seconds in her first run was 30 seconds more than the number of seconds in her second run, what was her time in seconds for the first run?

(A) 15

(B) 30

(C) 49

(D) 68

(E) 147

Focus on what you're supposed to figure out. The question asks for the time of Grace's first run in seconds. So you know you have to convert her total time to seconds so you're working in the correct units. A minute has 60 seconds, which means that Grace's total time was 60 + 57, or 117 seconds.

You can immediately eliminate Choice (E) because Grace's first run couldn't have been longer than the sum of her two runs. Now apply your math translation skills. You have two unknowns: the time of Grace's first run and the time of her second run. Let x stand for the first unknown and y for the second.

You can solve a problem with two variables when you know two equations that involve those two variables. So search the problem for two equations.

For the first equation, the problem tells you that the total time of the two runs is 117 seconds. According to the English-to-math-translation dictionary, that means $x + y = 117$. You've got one equation!

You also know that 2 times (×) the number of seconds in her first run (x) was (=) 30 seconds more (+) than her time for the second run (y). Translation please? $2x = 30 + y$.

After you have the two equations, you can use substitution or stacking to solve for x. For this problem, stacking is faster. Notice that $2x = 30 + y$ is the same as $2x - y = 30$. When you stack and add the two equations, you can eliminate the y variable because $y - y = 0$.

$$x + y = 117$$
$$2x - y = 30$$
$$3x + 0 = 147$$
$$x = 49$$

So Grace ran her first race in 49 seconds, which is Choice (C). If you chose Choice (D), you solved for *y* instead of *x*. Grace's second run was 68 seconds.

Burning the midnight oil: Work problems

Work problems ask you to find out how much work gets done in a certain amount of time. You use this formula for doing algebra work problems.

Production = Rate of Work × Time

Production means the amount of work that gets done. Because you get that quantity by multiplying two other numbers, you can say that production is the product of the rate times the time.

Here's how you'd apply the formula on a GMAT work problem.

There are two dock workers, Alf and Bob. Alf can load 16 tons of steel per day, and Bob can load 20 tons per day. If they each work 8-hour days, how many tons of steel can the two of them load in one hour, assuming they maintain a steady rate?

(A) 2.5

(B) 4.5

(C) 36

(D) 160

(E) 320

This question asks you to find the amount of production and gives you the rate and the time. But to calculate the rate properly, you must state the hours in terms of days. Because a workday is eight hours, one hour is $\frac{1}{8}$ of a day. Figure out how much Alf loads in one hour ($\frac{1}{8}$ of a day) and add it to what Bob loads in one hour.

Total Production = Alf's Production + Bob's Production

Total Production = $\left(16 \times \frac{1}{8}\right) + \left(20 \times \frac{1}{8}\right)$

Total Production = 2 + 2.5

Total Production = 4.5

So Alf and Bob load 4.5 tons of steel in one hour ($\frac{1}{8}$ of a day), which is Choice (B). If you chose Choice (C), you figured out the total production for one day rather than one hour.

Going the distance: Distance problems

Distance problems are a lot like work problems. The formula for computing distance or speed problems is this:

Distance = Rate × Time

Any problem involving distance, speed, or time spent traveling can be boiled down to this equation. The important thing is that you have your variables and numbers plugged in properly. Here's an example.

Abby can run a mile in seven minutes. How long does it take her to run $\frac{1}{10}$ of a mile at the same speed?

(A) 30 sec

(B) 42 sec

(C) 60 sec

(D) 360 sec

(E) 420 sec

Before you do any calculating, you can eliminate Choice (E) because 420 seconds is 7 minutes, and you know it takes Abby less time to run $\frac{1}{10}$ of a mile than it does for her to run a mile.

The problem tells you that Abby's distance is $\frac{1}{10}$ of a mile. You can figure her rate to be $\frac{1}{7}$ because she runs 1 mile in 7 minutes. The problem is asking how long she runs, so you need to solve for time. Plug the numbers into the distance formula:

$$\text{Distance} = \text{Rate} \times \text{Time}$$

$$\frac{1}{10} = \frac{1}{7} \times t$$

You need to isolate t on one side of the equation, so multiply both sides by 7:

$$\frac{1}{10} \times 7 = t$$

$$\frac{7}{10} = t$$

So Abby runs $\frac{1}{10}$ of a mile in $\frac{7}{10}$ of a minute. Convert minutes to seconds. There are 60 seconds in a minute, and $\frac{7}{10} \times 60$ seconds is 42 seconds. The correct answer must be Choice (B).

Chapter 12

Getting the Angle on Geometry: Planes and Solids

Geometry starts with the basics — plane geometry — which is the study of lines and shapes in two dimensions. From that foundation, geometry constructs increasingly complex models to more accurately portray the real world. Three-dimensional, or solid, geometry is almost as simple as plane geometry, with the added dimension of depth.

The GMAT tends to have fewer math questions about planes and solids than about algebra and statistics. Those of you who aren't particularly fond of manipulating shapes and figures can rejoice! But 20 percent of GMAT math questions cover geometry concepts, and this chapter is designed to make sure you're ready for them.

Fishing for the Answers: Lines and Angles

The building blocks for geometric forms are lines and angles, so we start by defining these fundamental elements. Understanding the meanings of these terms is an important part of solving problems on the GMAT. Here are the common terms that pop up on the test:

  ✔ **Line:** A straight path of points that extends forever in two directions. A line doesn't have any width or thickness. Arrows are sometimes used to show that the line goes on forever. See line *AB* in Figure 12-1.

  ✔ **Line segment:** The set of points on a line between any two points on the line. Basically it's just a piece of a line from one point to another that contains those points and all the points between. See line segment *CD* in Figure 12-1.

  ✔ **Ray:** A ray is like half of a line; it starts at an endpoint and extends forever in one direction. You can think of a ray as a ray of light extending from the sun (the endpoint) and shining as far as it can go. See ray *EF* in Figure 12-1.

  ✔ **Midpoint:** The point halfway (equal distance) between two endpoints on a line segment.

✔ **Bisect:** To cut something exactly in half, such as when a line, or *bisector,* cuts another line segment, angle, or polygon into two equal parts.

✔ **Intersect:** Just like it sounds — *intersect* simply means to cross; that is, when one line or line segment crosses another line or line segment.

✔ **Collinear:** A set of points that lie on the same line.

✔ **Vertical:** Lines that run straight up and down.

✔ **Horizontal:** Lines that run straight across from left to right.

✔ **Parallel:** Lines that run in the same direction, always remaining the same distance apart. Parallel lines never cross one another.

✔ **Perpendicular:** When two lines intersect to form a square corner. The intersection of two perpendicular lines forms a right, or 90 degree, angle.

✔ **Angle:** The intersection of two rays (or line segments) sharing a common endpoint. The common endpoint is called the *vertex.* The size of an angle depends on how much one side rotates away from the other side. An angle is usually measured in degrees or radians.

✔ **Acute angle:** Any angle measuring less than 90 degrees. Like an acute, or sharp, pain, the acute angle has a sharp point. See Figure 12-2.

✔ **Right, or perpendicular, angle:** An angle measuring exactly 90 degrees. It makes up a square corner. See Figure 12-3.

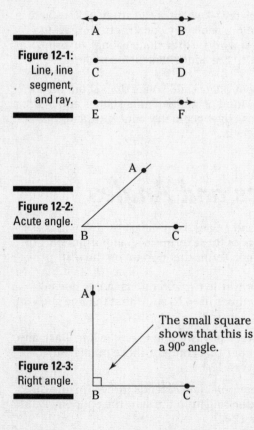

Figure 12-1:
Line, line segment, and ray.

A   B

C   D

E   F

Figure 12-2:
Acute angle.

A

B   C

Figure 12-3:
Right angle.

A

The small square shows that this is a 90° angle.

B   C

✔ **Obtuse angle:** An angle that measures more than 90 degrees but less than 180 degrees. The opposite of an acute angle, an obtuse angle is dull rather than sharp. See Figure 12-4.

✔ **Straight angle:** An angle that measures exactly 180 degrees. A straight angle appears to be a straight line or line segment.

✔ **Complementary angles:** Two angles that add together to total 90 degrees. Together, they form a right angle.

✔ **Supplementary angles:** Two angles that add together to total 180 degrees. They form a straight angle.

✔ **Similar:** Objects that have the same shape but may have different sizes.

✔ **Congruent:** Objects that are equal in size and shape. Two line segments with the same length, two angles with the same measure, and two triangles with corresponding sides of equal lengths and angles that have equal degree measures are congruent.

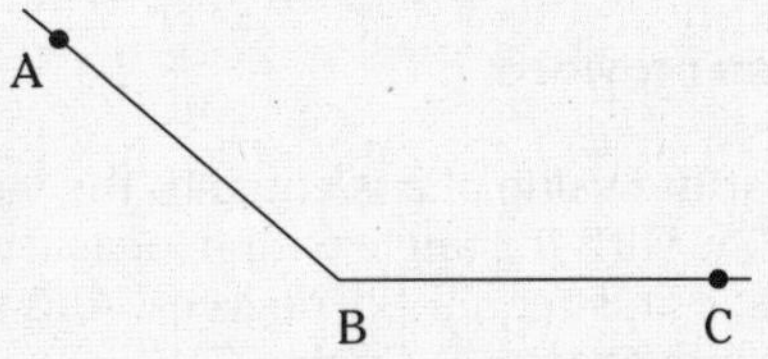

Figure 12-4:
Obtuse
angle.

Two important rules for lines and angles arise from these basic definitions. You can read all about them in Table 12-1.

Table 12-1	Rules for Lines and Angles	
Condition	**Rule**	**Sample Figure**
Intersecting lines	When two lines intersect, the opposite angles (across from each other) are always congruent or equal, and the adjacent angles are always supplementary. Opposite angles are also known as *vertical angles*. Adjacent angles have a common side, so they're right next to each other. In the sample figure, ∠ABC and ∠DBE are congruent; ∠ABC and ∠CBD form a straight line and are, therefore, supplementary.	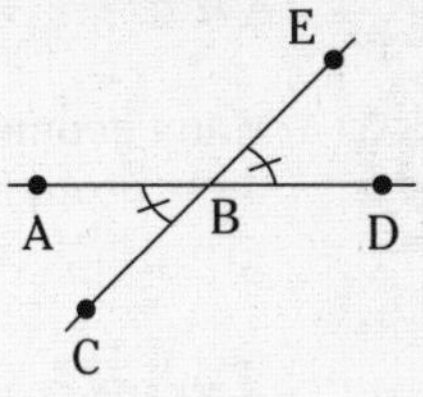
Parallel lines intersected by a transversal	When parallel lines are crossed by a third line that's not perpendicular to them (called a *transversal*), the resulting small and large angles share certain properties. Each of the small angles is equal; the large angles are also equal to each other. The measurement of any small angle added to that of any large angle equals 180°.	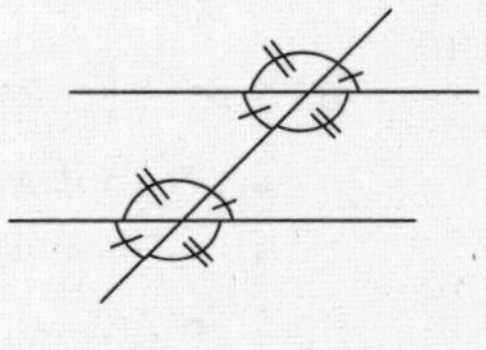

Here's how lines and angles may be tested on the GMAT math section.

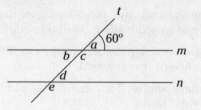

In the preceding figure, line *m* is parallel to line *n* and line *t* is a transversal crossing both lines *m* and *n*. Given the information contained in this figure, what is the value of *e*?

(A) 30°

(B) 60°

(C) 100°

(D) 120°

(E) It cannot be determined from the information provided.

Because lines *m* and *n* are parallel, you know that the value of *e* is equal to the value of *c*. The angle with a value of *c* lies along a straight line with the angle with a measure of *a*, so *a* + *c* = 180 degrees. Because *a* equals 60 degrees, *c* must equal 120 degrees. And because *c* equals *e*, *e* must also equal 120 degrees. The correct answer is Choice (D).

Trusting Triangles

Lines and angles form figures, and one of the most commonly tested GMAT figures is the triangle. A triangle has three sides, and the point where two of the sides intersect is called a *vertex.* You name triangles by their vertices, so a triangle with vertices *A, B,* and *C* is called Δ*ABC*.

Many geometry questions on the GMAT involve triangles, so pay particular attention to their properties and rules.

Triple treat: Types of triangles

You can identify triangle types by the measurements of their sides and angles:

- ✔ A *scalene triangle* has no equal sides and no equal angles.

- ✔ An *isosceles triangle* has two equal sides, and the measures of the angles opposite those two sides are also equal to each other.

- ✔ An *equilateral triangle* has three sides of equal lengths and three 60-degree angles.

- ✔ A *right triangle* has one angle that measures 90 degrees. The side opposite the right angle is called the *hypotenuse.*

These rules hold true for all types of triangles:

- ✔ The measures of the three angles add up to 180 degrees.

- ✔ The sum of the lengths of two sides is always greater than the length of the third side.

> ✔ The side that's opposite of a given angle in a triangle is proportionate to that angle, as you can see in Figure 12-5. So the smallest angle faces the shortest side of the triangle. If two or more angles have the same measurement, their opposite sides are also equal.

Figure 12-5:
Angles of a
triangle are
in propor-
tion to their
opposite
sides.

If angles $a < b < c$,
then sides A < B < C

Here's an example of how this information may be tested on the GMAT.

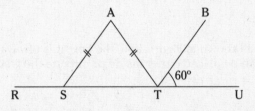

In the preceding figure, line *SA* is parallel to line *TB*. If the measure of ∠*BTU* is 60 degrees, what is the measure of ∠*ATB?*

(A) 30°

(B) 40°

(C) 50°

(D) 60°

(E) 80°

Like a bridge over troubled water, line *RU* traverses the parallel lines *SA* and *TB*. Therefore, ∠*BTU* and ∠*AST* are corresponding angles and have the same measurement. Because the value of ∠*BTU* is 60 degrees, ∠*AST* must also measure 60 degrees.

You also know that line segment *SA* equals line segment *TA,* so Δ*SAT* is isosceles, and the angles opposite these two line segments have the same measure. One of these angles is ∠*AST.* ∠*AST* measures 60 degrees; ∠*STA* has the same measurement as ∠*AST;* therefore, ∠*STA* also measures 60 degrees.

The measures of the angles along a straight line add up to 180 degrees, so the measure of ∠*ATB* = 180 – the value of ∠*BTU* – the value of ∠*ATS.* ∠*BTU* and ∠*ATS* each measure 60 degrees, so the measure of ∠*ATB* = 180 – 60 – 60, which is also 60. The correct answer is Choice (D).

The area of a triangle

The GMAT will likely ask you to determine the area of a triangle, so you better be ready. Memorize this formula:

$$A = \frac{1}{2}bh$$

A stands for (what else) area, *b* is the length of the base or bottom of the triangle, and *h* stands for the height (or altitude), which is the distance that a perpendicular line runs from the base to the angle opposite the base. For a visual, check out Figure 12-6.

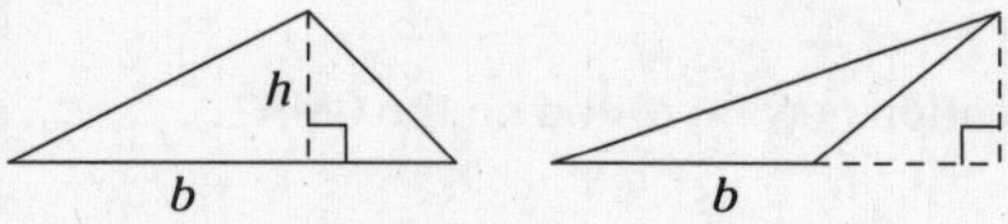

Figure 12-6:
The base
and height
of a triangle.

Notice that, as shown in Figure 12-6, the height is always perpendicular to the base and that the height can be placed either inside or outside the triangle.

The Pythagorean theorem and other cool stuff about right triangles

You can solve GMAT problems for the lengths of the sides of right triangles by using a groovy little formula called the Pythagorean theorem and by memorizing some common right triangle side lengths.

Digging Pythagoras and his theorem

The Pythagorean theorem simply states that the sum of the squares of the legs of a right triangle is equal to the square of the hypotenuse, or $a^2 + b^2 = c^2$, where *a* and *b* represent the two sides or legs of the right triangle and *c* is the hypotenuse. The legs of a right triangle are simply the sides that form the right angle, and the hypotenuse is the side opposite it. (It's always the biggest side of the right triangle.) If you know the lengths of two sides of a right triangle, you can easily find the length of the other side by using this handy formula.

Keep in mind that the Pythagorean theorem works only with right triangles. You can't use it to find the lengths of sides of triangles that don't have a right angle in them.

Which of the following is the length, in inches, of the remaining side of a right triangle if one side is 7 inches long and the hypotenuse is 12 inches long?

(A) $\sqrt{5}$

(B) 5

(C) 7

(D) 12

(E) $\sqrt{95}$

You may find it helpful to draw a right triangle on your paper to visualize the problem, but doing so isn't necessary. If the hypotenuse is 12 inches and one side is 7 inches, you figure the measurement of the remaining side by applying the formula:

$$a^2 + b^2 = c^2$$
$$7^2 + b^2 = 12^2$$
$$49 + b^2 = 144$$
$$b^2 = 95$$

You know that b^2 is 95, but the question asks for the value of b, not b^2. That means the measurement of the remaining side is the square root of 95, which is Choice (E).

Getting hip to the common ratios of right triangles

You may find it handy to memorize some ratios based on the Pythagorean theorem. That way, you don't have to work out the whole theorem every time you deal with a right triangle.

The most common ratio of the three sides of a right triangle is 3:4:5 (3 is the measure of the short leg, 4 is the measure of the long leg, and 5 is the measure of the hypotenuse). Related multiples are 6:8:10, 9:12:15, and so on. As soon as you recognize that two sides fit the 3:4:5 ratio or a multiple of the 3:4:5 ratio, you'll automatically know the length of the third side.

Other proportions of right triangles you should try to remember are 5:12:13, 8:15:17, and 7:24:25. Knowing these proportions may allow you to more quickly solve problems like the following one on the GMAT.

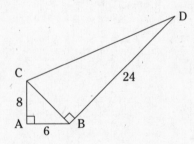

In the preceding figure, *AB* is 6 units long, *AC* is 8 units long, and *BD* is 24 units long. How many units long is *CD?*

(A) 26

(B) 32

(C) 80

(D) 96

(E) 100

This problem would be time consuming to solve if you didn't know the common ratios of right triangles. To determine the length of line segment *CD,* you first need to know the length of *CB*. You could use the Pythagorean theorem, but you know an easier, faster way. Because *AB* = 6 and *AC* = 8, △*ABC* is a 3:4:5 triangle times 2 — a 6:8:10 triangle. Therefore, the length of the hypotenuse, *BC,* is 10.

This makes △*BCD* a 5:12:13 triangle times 2 — a 10:24:26 triangle. So the length of *CD* = 26, and the correct answer is Choice (A).

Knowing what's neat about the 30:60:90 degree triangle

Some other handy right triangles exist. One is the 30:60:90 degree triangle. When you bisect any angle in an equilateral triangle, you get two right triangles with 30, 60, and 90 degree angles. In a 30:60:90 degree triangle, the hypotenuse is 2 times the length of the shorter leg, as shown in Figure 12-7. The ratio of the three sides is $s : s\sqrt{3} : 2s$, where s = the length of the shortest side.

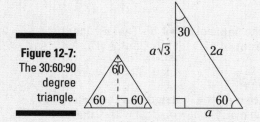

Figure 12-7:
The 30:60:90
degree
triangle.

Feeling the equilibrium of a 45:45:90 degree triangle

If you bisect a square with a diagonal line, you get two triangles that both have two 45 degree angles. Because the triangle has two equal angles (and, therefore, two equal sides), the resulting triangle is an isosceles right triangle, or 45:45:90 degree triangle. Its hypotenuse is equal to $\sqrt{2}$ times the length of a leg. It's important to recognize this also means that the length of a leg is equal to the length of the hypotenuse divided by $\sqrt{2}$. The ratio of sides in an isosceles right triangle is, therefore, $s : s : s\sqrt{2}$ (where s = the length of one of the legs) or $\frac{s}{\sqrt{2}} : \frac{s}{\sqrt{2}} : s$ (where s = the length of the hypotenuse). Figure 12-8 shows the formula.

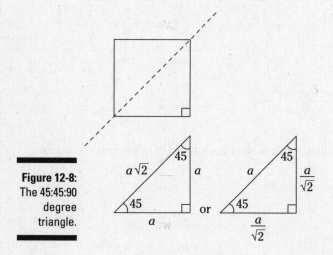

Figure 12-8:
The 45:45:90
degree
triangle.

This example question shows just how helpful your knowledge of special triangles can be.

In $\triangle STR$, $\angle TSR$ measures 45 degrees and $\angle SRT$ is a right angle. If SR is 20 units long, how many units is TR?

(A) 10

(B) $10\sqrt{2}$

(C) 20

(D) $20\sqrt{2}$

(E) 40

You could draw the triangle, but with what you know about 45:45:90 degree triangles, you don't need to.

Because ∠*SRT* is a right angle, you know that the triangle in this question is a right triangle. If ∠*TSR* measures 45 degrees, then ∠*RTS* must also measure 45 degrees, and this is a 45:45:90 degree triangle. So *SR* must equal *TR*. The length of line segment *SR* = 20, so *TR* = 20. The correct answer is Choice (C).

A striking resemblance: Similar triangles

Triangles are *similar* when they have exactly the same angle measures. Similar triangles have the same shape, even though their sides may have different lengths. The corresponding sides of similar triangles are in proportion to each other. The heights of the two triangles are also in proportion. Figure 12-9 provides an illustration of the relationship between two similar triangles.

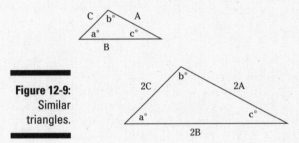

Figure 12-9:
Similar
triangles.

Knowing the properties of similar triangles helps you answer GMAT questions like the next one.

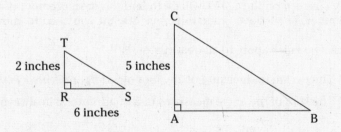

Δ*RTS* and Δ*ACB* in the preceding figure are similar right triangles with side lengths that measure as indicated. What is the area of ΔACB?

(A) 10

(B) 15

(C) 30

(D) 37.5

(E) 75

To find the area of Δ*ACB*, you need to know the measurements of its base and height. The figure gives you the length of its height (5), so you need to find the base.

Because the two triangles are similar (and proportionate to each other), you can use what you know about $\triangle RTS$ to find the base measurement of $\triangle ACB$. TR is proportionate to CA, and RS is proportionate to AB. Set up a proportion with x representing the measure of AB, cross-multiply, and solve:

$$\frac{2}{5} = \frac{6}{x}$$
$$2x = 6 \times 5$$
$$2x = 30$$
$$x = 15$$

The base of $\triangle ACB$ is 15 inches.

Don't stop there and choose Choice (B). The question asks for the area of $\triangle ACB$, not the length of AB.

Substitute the base and height measurements for $\triangle ACB$ into the formula for the area of a triangle ($\frac{1}{2}$ of the base times the height) and solve:

$$A = \frac{1}{2}(5)(15)$$
$$A = \frac{1}{2}(75)$$
$$A = 37.5$$

The correct answer is Choice (D).

Playing Four Square: Quadrilaterals

A quadrilateral is a four-sided polygon, and several types of quadrilaterals exist. Your primary concern on the GMAT will be to find the measurement of a quadrilateral's area and perimeter. The following sections review what you need to know to accomplish this goal.

These two rules apply to all quadrilaterals:

- ✔ The perimeter measure of any four-sided figure is always the sum of its side lengths.
- ✔ The sum of the angle measures of a quadrilateral is always 360 degrees.

Drawing parallels: Parallelograms

Most of the quadrilaterals that appear on the GMAT are parallelograms.

Parallelograms have properties that are very useful for solving GMAT problems:

- ✔ The opposite sides are parallel and equal in length.
- ✔ The opposite angles are equal in measure to each other.
- ✔ The measures of the adjacent angles add up to 180 degrees, so they're supplementary to each other.
- ✔ The diagonals (designated by d) of a parallelogram bisect each other. In other words, they cross at the midpoint of both diagonals.

Figure 12-10 provides a visual representation of the very important properties of parallelograms.

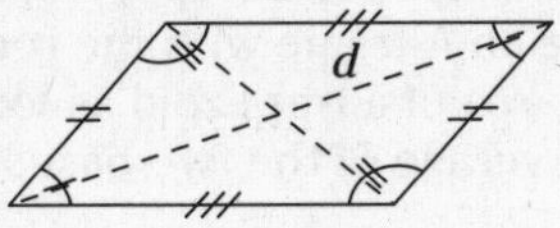

Figure 12-10:
A parallelogram.

The area of any parallelogram is its base times its height ($A = bh$). You determine the height pretty much the same way you determine the height of a triangle. The difference is that you draw the perpendicular line from the base to the opposite side (instead of to the opposite angle, as in the case of a triangle). See Figure 12-11.

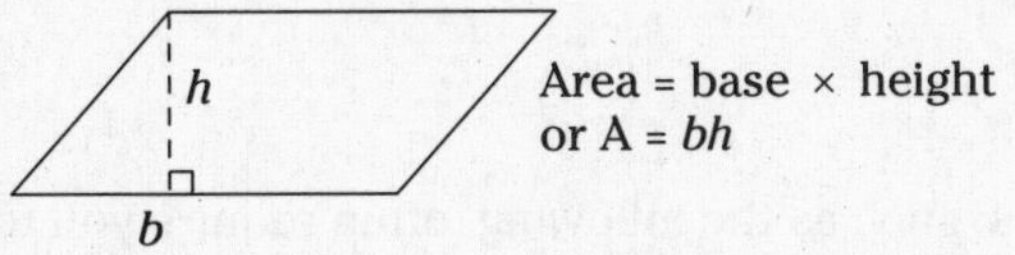

Figure 12-11:
Finding the area of a parallelogram.

Area = base × height
or A = bh

You can use the Pythagorean theorem to help you find the height of a parallelogram. When you drop a perpendicular line from one corner to the base to create the height, the line becomes the leg of a right triangle. If the problem gives you the length of other sides of the triangle (or information you can use to determine the length), you can use the formula to find the height measurement.

Parallelograms come in various types:

✔ A *rectangle* is a parallelogram with four right angles. The formula for the area of a rectangle is $A = bh$, where the base and height are the measures of the rectangles' length and width.

✔ A *square* is a rectangle with four equal sides, which means you can easily find its area when you know the length of only one side. Keep these formulas in mind:

• The area is $A = s^2$, where s is the length of a side.

• The perimeter is $4s$.

• When you know the length of a square's diagonal (d), you can use this formula $A = \dfrac{d^2}{2}$ to find the area.

✔ A *rhombus* has four equal sides but not necessarily four right angles. Find the area of a rhombus by multiplying the lengths of its two diagonals (designated as d) and then dividing by 2:

$$A = \tfrac{1}{2}d_1 d_2$$

Raising the roof: Trapezoids

A *trapezoid* is a quadrilateral with just one set of parallel sides. The parallel sides are called the bases, and the other two sides are called the legs. In an isosceles trapezoid, the legs of the quadrilateral are the same length. It looks kind of like an A-frame with the roof cut off. Check out Figure 12-12 for an example. You can find the area of a trapezoid as long as you know the length of both bases and the height. Take the average of the two bases and multiply by the height:

$$A = \frac{1}{2}(b_1 + b_2)h$$

Figure 12-12: The base and height of a trapezoid.

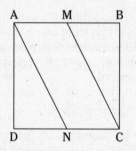

GMAT questions about quadrilaterals, such as the following, often require you to apply the formulas for area and perimeter and what you know about triangles.

In the preceding figure, square *ABCD* has sides the length of 4 units, and *M* and *N* are the midpoints of *AB* and *CD,* respectively. What is the perimeter, in units, of *AMCN*?

(A) 6

(B) $6\sqrt{5}$

(C) $2 + 2\sqrt{3}$

(D) $4 + 4\sqrt{5}$

(E) $8\sqrt{5}$

This question asks you to determine the perimeter of parallelogram *AMCN*. To solve it, rely on what you know about triangles and simplifying radicals.

If *M* and *N* are the midpoints, then *AM* = 2 (which is $\frac{4}{2}$) and *NC* = 2. Now you know the short sides of *AMCN* = 2. You can see that each of the long sides of the parallelogram is the hypotenuse of the right triangles within the square. The lengths of the legs of the right triangles measure 2 and 4, which doesn't fit with any of the special ratios associated with right triangles. So use the Pythagorean theorem:

$$2^2 + 4^2 = c^2$$
$$4 + 16 = c^2$$
$$20 = c^2$$
$$\sqrt{20} = c$$
$$\sqrt{4 \times 5} = c$$
$$2\sqrt{5} = c$$

Each of the short sides of *AMCN* measures 2 units and each long side measures $2\sqrt{5}$. Add the sides to get its perimeter:

$$P = 2(2) + 2(2\sqrt{5})$$
$$P = 4 + 4\sqrt{5}$$

The answer provided by Choice (D).

Showing Their Good Sides: Other Polygons

The GMAT may throw in some other types of polygons to make things interesting. Here are some of the common ones:

✔ **Pentagon:** A five-sided figure

✔ **Hexagon:** A six-sided figure (the *x* makes it sound like *six*)

✔ **Heptagon:** A seven-sided figure

✔ **Octagon:** An eight-sided figure (like *oct*opus)

✔ **Nonagon:** A nine-sided figure

✔ **Decagon:** A ten-sided figure (like *dec*athlon)

In general, GMAT polygons will be regular polygons, which means that all the sides are the same length and all the angles are equal. Polygons with exactly the same shape and same angle measurements have proportional corresponding side lengths.

No set formula exists for determining the area of a polygon. You need to create quadrilaterals and triangles within the polygon, find their areas, and add them together to get the total area of the polygon. In addition to determining its area, you may have to come up with the sum of a polygon's interior angles.

The formula for determining the sum of the interior angles of any polygon is simple:

Sum of the Angles = $(n - 2) \times 180$ degrees, where *n* is equal to the number of sides.

Works every time! If the polygon's regular, you can also determine the measure of each of the angles. You divide the sum of the angles by the total number of angles. So each angle in a regular pentagon measures $540 \div 5 = 108$ degrees.

The formula for determining the measure of an angle in a polygon works only if the GMAT tells you that the polygon is regular.

Eating Up Pieces of Pi: Circles

A circle, by technical definition, is a set of points in a plane that are at a fixed distance from a given point. That point is called the *center*. The following sections go into detail about the kinds of questions the GMAT will ask you about circles, from knowing the measures of the circle's radius, diameter, and circumference to working with arcs, chords, inscribed figures, and tangents.

Ring measurements: Radius, diameter, and circumference

Almost any GMAT problem regarding circles requires you to know or find its radius, diameter, circumference, and area.

- ✔ The *radius* of a circle is the distance from the center of the circle to any point on the circle. The radius is usually indicated by the letter *r*, as shown in Figure 12-13.

- ✔ The *diameter* of a circle is the length of a line that goes from one side of the circle to the other and passes through the center. The diameter is twice the length of the radius, and it's the longest possible distance across the circle. Diameter usually is indicated by the letter *d*, as shown in Figure 12-13.

- ✔ The *circumference* of a circle is the distance around the circle. The formula for finding circumference is 2 times the radius times pi: $C = 2\pi r$. Because twice the radius is the measure of the diameter, you can also figure circumference by multiplying the diameter by pi: $C = d\pi$.

- ✔ The *area* of a circle is the measure of the space inside the circle. The formula for finding area is $A = \pi r^2$.

Figure 12-13:
Radius and diameter of a circle.

Blueprints for Noah: Arcs

When it comes to angles and arcs on a circle, you should have a basic understanding of the following terms so you aren't running in circles on the GMAT math section:

- ✔ An *arc* of a circle is a portion along the circumference of the circle. See Figure 12-14.

  - • A *minor arc* is less than 180 degrees.

  - • A *major arc* is greater than 180 degrees. In fact, the arc of the entire circle is 360 degrees. You're more likely to work with minor arcs than major ones on the GMAT.

✔ A *central angle* of a circle is an angle that's formed by two radii; it's called a central angle because its vertex is the center of the circle. The measurement of the central angle is the same as that of the arc formed by the endpoints of its radii. So a 90 degree central angle (like the one in Figure 12-14) intercepts one-quarter of the circle, or a 90 degree arc.

Figure 12-14:
An arc and central angle.

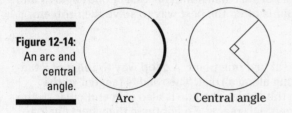

Arc   Central angle

Line 'em up: Chords, inscribed and circumscribed figures, and tangents

The GMAT may toss in some extra lines and figures when it questions you about circles. The extra features may appear within or outside the circle. The next sections describe each of these extras.

Striking a chord

A *chord* is a line segment cutting across a circle that connects two points on the edge of a circle. Those two points at the end of the chord are also the endpoints of an intercepted arc. See Figure 12-15.

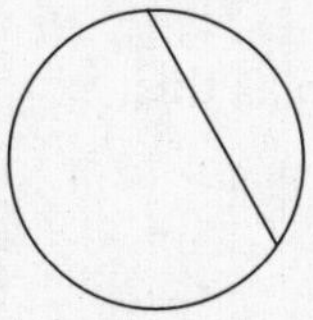

Figure 12-15:
A chord.

Moving in: Inscribed and circumscribed figures

An *inscribed figure* is any figure (angle, polygon, and so on) that's drawn inside another figure. For example, you could draw a triangle inside a circle so that all its vertices touch at points on the circle, just like Figure 12-16.

A *circumscribed figure* is one that is drawn around the outside of another shape, such as a circle drawn around a triangle so that all the vertices of the triangle touch the circle. You'd say the circle in Figure 12-16 is circumscribed around the triangle.

Figure 12-16:
Inscribed and circumscribed figures.

The only difference between an inscribed and a circumscribed figure hinges on the reference. You refer to the figure on the outside of another figure as a circumscribed figure and the figure on the inside of another figure as an inscribed figure.

The GMAT may use circumscribed and inscribed figures to ask you to calculate the area of a shaded area. When you get a "shaded area" problem, calculating the area of both figures and then subtracting the area of one from the other is often the best way to solve the problem.

Going off on a tangent

A *tangent line* is one that intersects the circle at just one point. A good way to think of a tangent line in the real world is like a wheel rolling along a road. The road is tangent to the wheel. Figure 12-17 shows line *AB* tangent to the circle. The line is also perpendicular to the radius that touches the circle where the tangent intersects. To continue the wheel analogy, if that wheel had an infinite number of spokes coming from its center, only one spoke would touch (be perpendicular to) the ground at any one time.

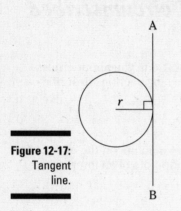

Figure 12-17:
Tangent
line.

The GMAT may test your knowledge of circles with a question such as this:

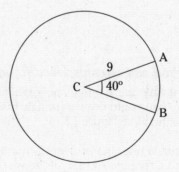

In the preceding figure, *A* and *B* lie on the circle with center *C*. *CA* is 9 units long, and the measure of ∠*ACB* is 40 degrees. How many units long is minor arc *AB*?

(A) π

(B) 2π

(C) 9π

(D) 18π

(E) 36π

First, determine how many degrees are in arc *AB*. Because *CA* and *CB* are radii of the circle, the degree measurement of the central angle *ACB* is the same as the measurement of the arc the ends of the radii form on the circle. So the minor arc *AB* is 40 degrees. How does that help you determine the length of the arc? Well, you know that a circle is 360 degrees, and 40 degrees is $\frac{1}{9}$ of 360 degrees. That means that arc *AB* is $\frac{1}{9}$ of the circumference of the circle. Determine the circumference:

$$C = 2\pi r$$
$$C = 2\pi 9$$
$$C = 18\pi$$

Then figure out $\frac{1}{9}$ of that length:

$$\frac{1}{9} \times 18\pi = x$$
$$2\pi = x$$

The correct answer must be Choice (B).

Getting a Little Depth Perception: Three-Dimensional Geometry

Three-dimensional geometry, or solid geometry, adds some depth to plane geometrical figures. You'll likely encounter no more than a handful of solid geometry questions on the GMAT, and they'll likely concern only rectangular solids and cylinders, which we discuss in the following sections.

Chipping off the old block: Rectangular solids

You make a rectangular solid by taking a simple rectangle and adding depth. Good examples of rectangular solids are bricks, cigar boxes, or boxes of your favorite cereal. A rectangular solid is also known as a *right rectangular prism* because it has 90 degree angles all around. *Prisms* have two congruent polygons on parallel planes that are connected to each other by their corresponding points. The two connected polygons make up the bases of the prism, as shown in Figure 12-18.

A rectangular solid has three dimensions: length, height, and width. You really need to worry about only two basic measurements of rectangular solids on the GMAT: total surface area and volume.

Finding volume

The volume (*V*) of a rectangular solid is a measure of how much space it occupies, or to put it in terms everyone can appreciate, how much cereal your cereal box holds. You measure the volume of an object in cubic units. The formula for the volume of a rectangular solid is simply its length (*l*) × width (*w*) × height (*h*): *V* = *lwh*.

Another way of saying this formula is that the volume is equal to the base times the height (*V* = *Bh*), where *B* is the area of the base. See what we mean in Figure 12-18.

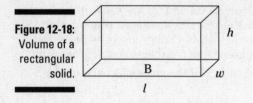

Figure 12-18:
Volume of a
rectangular
solid.

Determining surface area

You can find the surface area (*SA*) of a rectangular solid by simply figuring out the areas of all six sides of the object and adding them together.

First you find the area of the length (*l*) times height (*h*), then the area of length times width (*w*), and finally width times height (see Figure 12-19). Now multiply each of these three area measurements times 2 (after you find the area of one side, you know that the opposite side has the same measurement). The formula for the surface area of a rectangular solid is $SA = 2lh + 2lw + 2wh$.

You can visualize the surface area of a rectangular solid, or any solid figure for that matter, by mentally flattening out all the sides and putting them next to each other. It's sort of like taking apart a cardboard box to get it ready for recycling; only now you get to measure it. Lucky you!

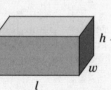

Figure 12-19:
Surface
area of a
rectangular
solid.

Working with cubes

You can use the same formulas you used with rectangular solids to find the area and volume of a three-dimensional square, called a *cube*, shown in Figure 12-20. Because all the faces on a cube are perfect squares, you can find its measurements with some simple formulas.

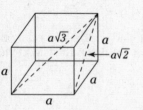

Figure 12-20:
A cube.

✔ The volume of a cube with an edge *a* is a^3: $V = a^3$.

✔ The surface area of a cube is simply the area of one side times 6: $SA = 6a^2$.

✔ The diagonal of a face on a cube (a square) measures $a\sqrt{2}$, as shown in Figure 12-20.

✔ Figure 12-20 also shows that the diagonal of a cube itself measures $a\sqrt{3}$.

Sipping from soda cans and other cylinders

A cylinder is a circle that grows straight up into the third dimension to become the shape of a can of soda. The bases of a cylinder are two congruent circles on different planes. The cylinders you see on the GMAT are right circular cylinders, which means that the line segments that connect the two bases are perpendicular to the bases. Figure 12-21 shows a right circular cylinder. All the corresponding points on the circles are joined together by line segments. The line segment connecting the center of one circle to the center of the opposite circle is called the axis.

Figure 12-21:
A right circular cylinder.

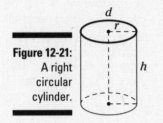

A right circular cylinder has the same measurements as a circle. That is, a right circular cylinder has a radius, diameter, and circumference. In addition, a cylinder has a third dimension: its height, or altitude.

To get the volume of a right circular cylinder, first take the area of the base (a circle), which is πr^2, and multiply by the height (h) of the cylinder: $V = \pi r^2 h$.

If you want to find the total surface area of a right circular cylinder, you have to add the areas of all the surfaces. Imagine taking a soda can, cutting off the top and bottom sections, and then slicing it down one side. You then spread out the various parts of the can. If you measure each one of these sections, you get the total surface area.

When you measure the surface area of a right circular cylinder, don't forget to include the top and bottom of the can in your calculation.

Here's the formula for the total surface area (*SA*) of a right circular cylinder — the diameter (*d*) is 2 times the radius (*r*):

$$SA = \pi dh + 2\pi r^2$$

Here's a sample question that shows how the GMAT may try to find out how much you know about three-dimensional shapes.

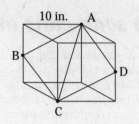

The preceding figure shows a cube with an edge that measures 10 inches. If points *B* and *D* are midpoints of two of the edges, what is the measure in inches of the straight line that joins point *A* to point *C*?

(A) $5\sqrt{5}$

(B) $10\sqrt{2}$

(C) $10\sqrt{3}$

(D) $20\sqrt{5}$

(E) 125

Answering this question is easy when you know the formula for the diagonal of a cube. Each edge of the cube measures 10 inches, and the diagonal of a cube is the edge length $\times \sqrt{3}$. So line *AC* measures $10\sqrt{3}$ inches, which is Choice (C).

Make sure you apply the correct formula. If you pick Choice (B), you're using the formula for the diagonal of a square.

Chapter 13

Keeping in Step: Coordinate Geometry

• •

In This Chapter

▶ Taking off on the coordinate plane

▶ Using formulas to find slope, graph lines, and determine midpoints and distances

▶ Evaluating functions

• •

Coordinate geometry involves working with points on a graph that's officially known as the *Cartesian coordinate plane*. This perfectly flat surface has a system that allows you to identify the position of points by using pairs of numbers. In this chapter, you figure out how equations and numbers relate to geometric forms and shapes, such as a straight line or a parabola, and review the formulas you need to know to fly high on questions about the coordinate plane.

You can expect to encounter coordinate geometry questions on roughly 10 percent of the problems on the GMAT. So if you're not particularly savvy about coordinate geometry, it won't significantly affect your GMAT math score.

Taking Flight: The Coordinate Plane

The coordinate plane doesn't have wings, but it does have points that spread out infinitely. You may not have encountered the coordinate plane in a while (it isn't something most people deal with in everyday life), so take just a minute to refresh your memory about a few relevant terms that may pop up on the GMAT. Although you won't be asked to define the terms in the following sections, knowing what they mean is absolutely essential to answering GMAT math questions.

Line dancing: Understanding coordinate geometry

Before you get too engrossed in the study of coordinate geometry, ground yourself with an understanding of these essential terms:

✔ **Coordinate plane:** The coordinate plane is a perfectly flat surface where points can be identified by their positions, using ordered pairs of numbers. These pairs of numbers represent the points' distances from an origin on perpendicular axes. The coordinate of any particular point is the set of numbers that identifies the location of the point, such as (3, 4) or (x, y).

✔ **x-axis:** The *x*-axis is the horizontal axis (number line) on a coordinate plane. The values start at the origin, which has a value of 0. Numbers increase in value to the right of the origin and decrease in value to the left. The *x* value of a point's coordinate is listed first in its ordered pair.

✔ **y-axis:** The y-axis is the vertical axis (number line) on a coordinate plane. Its values start at the origin, which has a value of 0. Numbers increase in value going up from the origin and decrease in value going down. The y value of a point's coordinate is listed second in its ordered pair.

✔ **Origin:** The origin is the point (0, 0) on the coordinate plane. It's where the x- and y-axes intersect.

✔ **Ordered pair:** Also known as a *coordinate pair,* this duo is the set of two values that expresses the distance a point lies from the origin. The horizontal (x) coordinate is always listed first, and the vertical (y) coordinate is listed second.

✔ **x-intercept:** The value of x where a line, curve, or some other function crosses the x-axis. The value of y is 0 at the x-intercept. The x-intercept is often the *solution* or *root* of an equation.

✔ **y-intercept:** The value of y where a line, curve, or some other function crosses the y-axis. The value of x is 0 at the y-intercept.

✔ **Slope:** Slope measures how steep a line is and is commonly referred to as *the rise over the run.*

What's the point? Finding the coordinates

You can identify any point on the coordinate plane by its coordinates, which designate the point's location along the x- and y-axes. For example, the ordered pair (2, 3) has a coordinate point located two units to the right of the origin along the horizontal (x) number line and three units up on the vertical (y) number line. In Figure 13-1, point A is at (2, 3). The x-coordinate appears first, and the y-coordinate shows up second. Pretty simple so far, huh?

On all fours: Identifying quadrants

The intersection of the x- and y-axes forms four quadrants on the coordinate plane, which just so happen to be named Quadrants I, II, III, and IV (see Figure 13-1). Here's what you can assume about points based on the quadrants they're in:

✔ All points in Quadrant I have a positive x value and a positive y value.

✔ All points in Quadrant II have a negative x value and a positive y value.

✔ All points in Quadrant III have a negative x value and a negative y value.

✔ All points in Quadrant IV have a positive x value and a negative y value.

✔ All points along the x-axis have a y value of 0.

✔ All points along the y-axis have an x value of 0.

Quadrant I starts to the right of the y-axis and above the x-axis. It's the upper-right portion of the coordinate plane. As shown in Figure 13-1, the other quadrants move counterclockwise around the origin. Figure 13-1 also shows the location of coordinate points A, B, C, and D:

✔ Point A is in Quadrant I and has coordinates (2, 3).

✔ Point B is in Quadrant II and has coordinates (−1, 4).

✔ Point C is in Quadrant III and has coordinates (−5, −2).

✔ Point D is in Quadrant IV and has coordinates (7, −6).

The GMAT won't ask you to pick your favorite quadrant, but you may be asked to identify which quadrant a particular point belongs in.

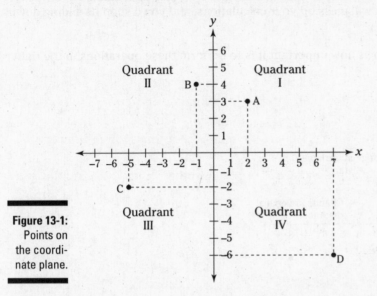

Figure 13-1:
Points on the coordinate plane.

Slip-Sliding Away: Slope and Linear Equations

One of the handiest things about the coordinate plane is that it graphs the locations of lines and linear equations. In fact, questions that expect you to know how to graph lines and equations are some of the most common GMAT coordinate geometry questions. You should know the formulas for finding the slope and the slope-intercept equation and for determining the midpoint and the distance between two points on the plane. Lucky for you, we discuss all those formulas in the following sections.

Taking a peak: Defining the slope of a line

If a line isn't parallel to one of the coordinate axes, it either rises or falls from the left-hand side of the coordinate plane to the right-hand side. The measure of the steepness of the line's rising or falling is its *slope*. In the following sections, we explain how to find the slope of a line and explore the different types of slopes on a coordinate plane.

The formula for slope

You can think of the slope as the value of the rise over the value of the run. In more mathematical terms, the slope formula looks like this:

$$\text{Slope}(m) = \frac{\text{Change in Vertical Coordinates}}{\text{Change in Horizontal Coordinates}} = \frac{y_2 - y_1}{x_2 - x_1}$$

The x and y values in the equation stand for the coordinates of two points on the line. The formula is just the ratio of the vertical distance between two points and the horizontal distance between those same two points. You subtract the y-coordinate of one point from the y-coordinate of the other point to get the numerator. Then you subtract the x-coordinate of the one point from the x-coordinate of the other point to get the denominator.

When you subtract the values, remember to subtract the x and y values of the first point from the respective x and y values of the second point. Don't fall for the trap of subtracting $x_2 - x_1$ to get your change in the run but then subtracting $y_1 - y_2$ for your change in the rise. That kind of backward math will mess up your calculations, and you'll soon be sliding down a slippery slope.

The graph in Figure 13-2 shows how important it is to perform these operations in the right order.

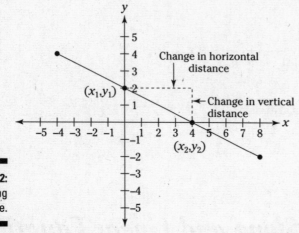

Figure 13-2:
Finding slope.

Figure 13-2 shows coordinate point (0, 2) as (x_1, y_1), and the coordinate point (4, 0) as (x_2, y_2). You may be tempted to subtract the 0 in each coordinate point from the corresponding greater number in the other coordinate point, but doing that switches the order of how you subtract the x and y values in the two coordinate points.

For the slope formula to work, you calculate $0 - 2$ for your $y_2 - y_1$ operation (which gives you –2), and then you take $4 - 0$ for your $x_2 - x_1$ (which gives you 4). The resulting ratio, or fraction, is $-\frac{2}{4}$, or $-\frac{1}{2}$. This gives you a slope of $-\frac{1}{2}$.

Types of slope

The line in Figure 13-2 falls from left to right. This nice ski-slope image is your visual clue that the line has a negative slope. Figure 13-3 shows how you can quickly eyeball a line to get a good idea of what kind of slope a line has.

In Figure 13-3, line m has a negative slope; line n has a positive slope; a line on the horizontal x-axis has a slope of 0; and a line on the vertical y-axis has an undefined slope.

- ✔ A line with a negative slope falls from left to right (its left side is higher than its right), and its slope is less than 0.

- ✔ A line with a positive slope rises from left to right (its right side is higher than its left), and its slope is greater than 0.

- ✔ A horizontal line has a slope of 0; it neither rises nor falls and is parallel to the x-axis.

- ✔ The slope of a vertical line is undefined because you don't know whether it's rising or falling; it has no slope and is parallel to the y-axis.

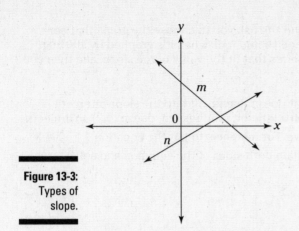

Figure 13-3:
Types of
slope.

Using the slope-intercept form to graph lines

The characteristics of a line can be conveyed through a mathematical formula. The equation of a line (also known as the *slope-intercept form*) generally shows y as a function of x, like this:

$$y = mx + b$$

In the slope-intercept form, the coefficient m is a constant that indicates the slope of the line, and the constant b is the y-intercept (that is, the point where the line crosses the y-axis). The equation of the line in Figure 13-2 is $y = -\frac{1}{2}x + 2$, because the slope is $-\frac{1}{2}$ and the y-intercept is 2. The equation $y = 2$ indicates a horizontal line that intersects the y-axis at point (0, 2). The equation $x = 3$ indicates a vertical line that intersects the x-axis at point (3, 0). A line with the formula $y = 4x + 1$ has a slope of 4 (which is a rise of 4 and run of 1) and a y-intercept of 1. The line is graphed in Figure 13-4.

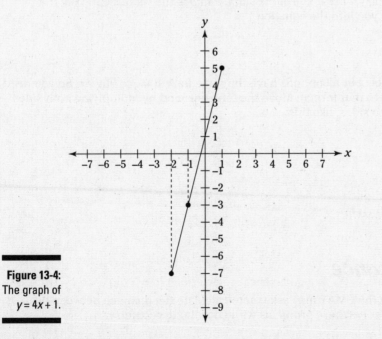

Figure 13-4:
The graph of
$y = 4x + 1$.

The GMAT may give you an equation of a line and ask you to choose the graph that correctly grids it. You can figure out how the line should look when it's graphed by starting with the value of the *y*-intercept, marking points that fit the value of the slope, and then connecting these points with a line.

Whenever you get an equation for a line that doesn't neatly fit into the slope-intercept format, go ahead and play with the equation a little bit (sounds fun, doesn't it?) so it meets the $y = mx + b$ format that you know and love. For instance, to put the equation $\frac{1}{3}y - 3 = x$ in slope-intercept form, you simply manipulate both sides of the equation and solve for *y*, like this:

$$\frac{1}{3}y - 3 = x$$
$$\frac{1}{3}y = x + 3$$
$$y = 3(x + 3)$$
$$y = 3x + 9$$

The new equation gives you the slope of the line, 3, as well as the *y*-intercept, 9. Pretty handy! Here's a sample question to give you a taste of how the slope-intercept form may be tested on the GMAT.

What is the equation of a line with a slope $-\frac{3}{4}$ and a *y*-intercept of 8?

(A) $4x + 3y = 32$

(B) $-3x + 4y = 16$

(C) $3x - 4y = 32$

(D) $3x + 4y = 16$

(E) $3x + 4y = 32$

In the slope-intercept form, $y = mx + b$, *m* is the slope and *b* is the *y*-intercept. Plug the values the problem gives you into the equation:

$$y = -\frac{3}{4}x + 8$$

This isn't an answer choice, but all options have the same format of $ax + by = c$. So you need to convert your equation to that format. Move the terms around by multiplying both sides by 4 and adding $3x$ to both sides, like this:

$$y = -\frac{3}{4}x + 8$$
$$4y = -3x + 32$$
$$4y + 3x = 32$$

Choice (E) is the correct answer.

Going the distance

Some of the questions on the GMAT may ask you to calculate the distance between two points on a line. You can solve these problems with coordinate geometry.

To answer these questions, use the *distance formula.* Assume you have two points, A (x_1, y_1) and B (x_2, y_2), on a line. The formula to find the distance between A and B is this:

$$AB = \sqrt{(x_2 - x_1)^2 + (y_2 - y_1)^2}$$

Look at the graph in Figure 13-5 to see how the distance formula actually works.

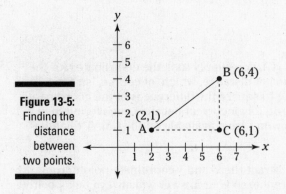

Figure 13-5: Finding the distance between two points.

Notice that point A has coordinates (2, 1) and point B has coordinates (6, 4). To find the distance between these two points, you plug these numbers into the distance formula:

$$AB = \sqrt{(x_2 - x_1)^2 + (y_2 - y_1)^2}$$
$$AB = \sqrt{(6 - 2)^2 + (4 - 1)^2}$$
$$AB = \sqrt{(4)^2 + (3)^2}$$
$$AB = \sqrt{16 + 9}$$
$$AB = \sqrt{25}$$
$$AB = 5$$

If you're thinking this formula looks familiar, you're absolutely right. It's another use for the good old Pythagorean theorem. (If this theorem is vaguely familiar to you, check out Chapter 12.) Connecting points A and B to a third point C, as shown in Figure 13-5, gives you a right triangle, which in this case happens to be your tried and true 3:4:5 right triangle.

Here's a sample problem that asks you to find the distance between two points.

What is the distance in units of a line segment that connects the origin to the coordinate point (–2, –3)?

(A) $\sqrt{5}$

(B) $\sqrt{13}$

(C) 5

(D) 8.94

(E) 13.42

Use the distance formula to figure out the distance between the coordinates of the origin $(0, 0)$ and the endpoint $(-2, -3)$:

$$AB = \sqrt{(x_2 - x_1)^2 + (y_2 - y_1)^2}$$
$$AB = \sqrt{(-2 - 0)^2 + (-3 - 0)^2}$$
$$AB = \sqrt{(-2)^2 + (-3)^2}$$
$$AB = \sqrt{4 + 9}$$
$$AB = \sqrt{13}$$

Choice (B) is the answer. If you chose Choice (C), you simply took the coordinates for the endpoint, $(-2, -3)$, and added them together to get distance, which, of course, isn't the proper method. Choice (A) results from failing to square the differences of the coordinates. You can guess that Choices (D) and (E) are probably incorrect because uncovering their values requires using a calculator, which you won't have available on the GMAT quantitative section.

Notice that order doesn't matter when you subtract the x- and y-coordinate points from each other — you end up squaring their difference, so your answer will always be a positive number.

Keep in mind that, in the end, the distance between two points is always a positive number. If you ever see zero or a negative number as an answer choice for a distance question, just let your mouse scoot on by.

Fully Functioning: Graphing Functions

Coordinate geometry and functions are connected. You can actually evaluate functions on the coordinate plane. By looking at a graph of a function, you can tell something about the function and its domain and range. The GMAT may give you a graph of a function and ask you to determine whether a statement about the function is true or false. In the following sections, we give you the info you need to know to get these questions right.

When you graph a function $f(x)$ on the coordinate plane, the x value of the function (the input, or the domain, of the function) goes along the horizontal (x) axis, and the $f(x)$ value of the function goes along the vertical (y) axis. Anytime you see a coordinate pair that represents a function, for example (x, y), the x value is the domain, or input, of the function and the y value is the output, or range, of the function. (For more info on functions, see Chapter 11.)

Passing the vertical line test

A function is a distinct relationship between the x (input) value and the y or $f(x)$ (output) value. For every x value, there's a distinct y value, and only one y value, that corresponds to the x value. The vertical line test is one way to look at a graph and tell whether it's a graph of a function. This test states that no vertical line intersects the graph of a function at more than one point.

For example, the graphs in Figure 13-6 show two straight lines that pass the vertical line test and, therefore, represent functions.

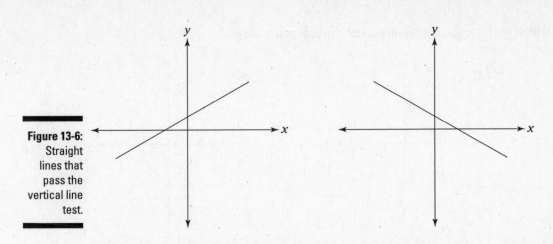

Figure 13-6:
Straight
lines that
pass the
vertical line
test.

The two lines in Figure 13-6 go on infinitely in both directions. Any vertical line you draw on the graph intersects the graphed line at only one point. For every *x* value along the line in each of these graphs, a separate and distinct *y* value corresponds to it. These lines pass the vertical line test, which means they represent functions.

You probably already know that most lines are functions — after all, the equation of a line is $y = mx + b$. Now you can see it for yourself graphically, The only straight line that isn't a graph of a function is a vertical line. A bazillion *y* values exist along a vertical line, but the line has only one *x* value.

Not all lines are straight. Sometimes you see graphs of curved lines. Take a look at the two graphs in Figure 13-7 and determine which of them graphs a function.

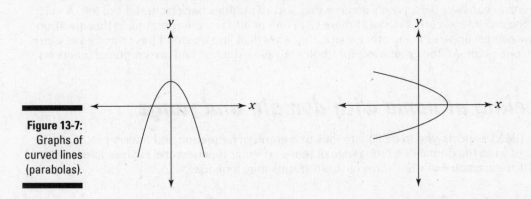

Figure 13-7:
Graphs of
curved lines
(parabolas).

The curves in Figure 13-7 are parabolas, a shape we discuss in more detail in the upcoming section about graphing domain and range. The curve in the left graph opens downward, so it goes on infinitely downward and outward. For every *x* value on that curve, there's a separate and distinct *y* value. This curve passes the vertical line test and, therefore, graphs a function. The curve in the right graph is almost like the first one, except that it opens sideways. One vertical line *can* cross the path of this curve in more than one place. Therefore, this curve isn't the graph of a function.

Questions that ask you to recognize the graph of a function appear rarely on the GMAT, but if you see one, you'll know what to do.

Which of the following graphs is *not* a graph of a function?

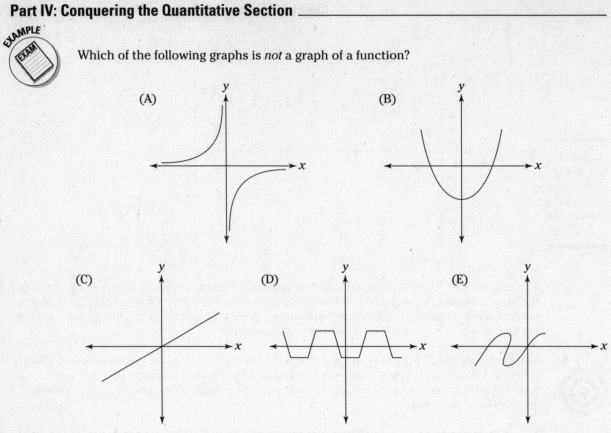

This question is easy when you're familiar with the vertical line test. Choice (E) has to be the correct answer because it's a curve that sort of doubles back from right to left. A vertical line can intersect that curve at more than one point. The other graphs in this question show curves, lines, or some other shape that a vertical line wouldn't pass through at more than one point. All the graphs except Choice (E) pass the test and are graphs of functions.

Feeling at home with domain and range

The GMAT expects you to be able to look at a graph of a function and have a pretty good idea of what the domain and the range of that particular function are. Figures 13-8, 13-9, and 13-10 are examples of what some of these graphs may look like.

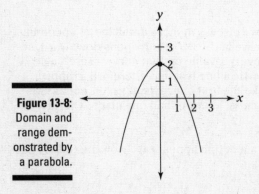

Figure 13-8:
Domain and range demonstrated by a parabola.

Figure 13-8 shows you a parabola. Its vertex is the coordinate point (0, 2). The graph extends outward infinitely from side to side, so this function contains all possible values of *x*, which means its domain is all real numbers. The graph also extends downward infinitely, but because the *y* value in this function is limited on the upward side and doesn't extend above the point (0, 2), its range is {*y*: *y* ≤ 2}

In Figure 13-9, you see a straight line that goes on forever from left to right. This line also extends infinitely upward on the left side and infinitely downward on the right side. The domain and range of this linear function are also all real numbers. There's no artificial limit to the *x* and *y* values in this graph.

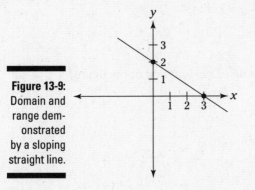

Figure 13-9: Domain and range demonstrated by a sloping straight line.

In Figure 13-10, the horizontal line extends infinitely from right to left, but it has only one value on the *y*-axis. Its *y* value is limited to –3, so the equation for this line is *y* = –3, and the range is limited to simply {*y*: *y* = –3}. Because the line goes on forever from left to right, it includes every possible *x* value, which means the domain of this linear function is all real numbers.

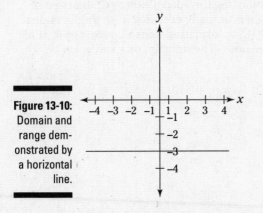

Figure 13-10: Domain and range demonstrated by a horizontal line.

That's really all there is to it. See how easy determining domain can be with this question.

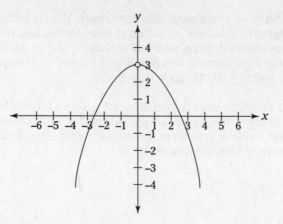

Which of the following answers could be the domain of the function of the figure?

(A) $\{x: x \neq 0\}$

(B) $\{x: x \neq 3\}$

(C) $\{x: x = 0\}$

(D) $\{x: x \leq 3\}$

(E) $\{x: x < 0 < x\}$

This question asks for the *domain,* not the *range,* so don't let the fact that the upper limit of the y value is just shy of 3 distract you from looking for all the possible x values that make up the domain. You should toss out any answer choice that refers to the value 3, so get rid of Choices (B) and (D) right away.

The empty circle point (0, 3) means that you don't count that point in your answer. So Choice (C) is exactly the opposite of what you're looking for. Also, Choice (C) limits your domain to only one value: 0. Because the value of 0 is actually *excluded* from the function, Choice (C) simply can't be right. The way Choice (E) is formatted doesn't make sense at all. Set your sights on Choice (A) as the answer of the hour. The domain, or x value, isn't equal to 0.

Chapter 14

Manipulating Numbers: Statistics and Sets

● ●

In This Chapter

▶ Getting a grip on group problems

▶ Excelling with sets and Venn diagrams

▶ Arranging groups with permutations and combinations

▶ Managing means, modes, and medians

▶ Solving standard deviations

▶ Prospering on probability problems

● ●

From the time you mastered the ability to tie your shoes, you had to figure out how to work and play in groups. The GMAT tests what you know about groups of numbers, or sets. These question types are usually pretty easy, so you could probably work out the answers to most of the GMAT set questions given enough time. But, of course, you don't have all the time in the world on the GMAT, so in this chapter, we provide some shortcuts to help you answer set questions quickly.

You may find the statistics and probability questions on the GMAT a little more challenging. But don't worry: In this chapter, we go over the concepts you need to know, which include determining probability, statistical averages, and variations from the average. The statistics questions you'll encounter on the GMAT aren't particularly complex, but giving this subject your full attention will pay off.

Joining a Clique: Groups

Group problems regard populations of persons or objects and the way these populations are grouped together into categories. The questions generally ask you to either find the total of a series of groups or determine how many people or objects make up one of the subgroups.

You can find the answer to most group problems by using your counting skills, but counting is time-consuming, and you want to work smarter, not harder, to solve these questions. Solving group problems comes down to applying simple arithmetic in a handy formula and nothing else.

Here's the formula for solving group problems:

Group 1 + Group 2 − Both Groups + Neither Group = Grand Total

So if you're told that out of 110 students, 47 are enrolled in a cooking class, 56 take a welding course, and 33 take both cooking and welding, you can use the formula to find out how many students take neither cooking nor welding. Let Group 1 be the cooks and Group 2 the welders. The variable is the group that doesn't take either the cooking or welding class. Plug the known values into the formula and set up an equation to solve:

$$\text{Group } 1 + \text{Group } 2 - \text{Both Groups} + \text{Neither Group} = \text{Grand Total}$$
$$47 + 56 - 33 + x = 110$$
$$70 + x = 110$$
$$x = 40$$

Of the 110 students, 40 take neither the cooking class nor the welding class. Here's an example of how group problems may appear on the GMAT.

One-third of all United States taxpayers may deduct charitable contributions on their federal income tax returns. Forty percent of all taxpayers may deduct state income tax payments from their federal returns. If 55 percent of all taxpayers may not deduct either charitable contributions or state sales tax, what portion of all taxpayers may claim both types of deductions?

(A) $\frac{3}{20}$

(B) $\frac{9}{50}$

(C) $\frac{1}{5}$

(D) $\frac{7}{25}$

(E) $\frac{17}{60}$

Use the formula to determine the correct percentage of taxpayers who may claim both deductions. Group 1 can be the $\frac{1}{3}$ who claim charitable deductions, and Group 2 can be those who deduct state income tax payments. The unknown is those who make up both groups.

Before you begin calculating, check the answer choices. Every answer appears as a fraction. Because your final answer will be in the form of a fraction, change references to percentages into fractions. Converting percentages to fractions is easy; put the value of the percentage over a denominator of 100.

So 40 percent is the same as $\frac{40}{100}$, which reduces to $\frac{2}{5}$. Fifty-five percent is the same as $\frac{55}{100}$, which equals $\frac{11}{20}$. Plug in the values and solve the formula:

$$\text{Group } 1 + \text{Group } 2 - \text{Both Groups} + \text{Neither Group} = \text{Grand Total}$$
$$\frac{1}{3} + \frac{2}{5} - x + \frac{11}{20} = 1$$

To add and subtract fractions, you have to find a common denominator for all fractions and then convert the fractions so all of them have the same denominator (see Chapter 10 for more about performing operations with fractions). The common denominator for this problem is 60.

$$\frac{20}{60} + \frac{24}{60} - x + \frac{33}{60} = \frac{60}{60}$$

$$\frac{77}{60} - x = \frac{60}{60}$$

$$x = \frac{17}{60}$$

The correct answer is Choice (E).

 Compute accurately. Another reason for working with fractions instead of percentages in this problem is that it helps you perform accurate calculations. You may be fooled into thinking that the one-third of the taxpayers who can claim charitable contributions equals 33 percent of taxpayers. Although one-third is very close to 33 percent, it isn't exactly that amount. If you used 33 percent instead of one-third, you may have calculated the group as $0.33 + 0.4 + 0.55 + x = 1$ and incorrectly chosen Choice (D). If you convert $\frac{1}{3}$ to 33 percent, you're sacrificing accuracy to save time.

Setting Up Sets

Groups are related to sets. A *set* is a collection of objects, numbers, or values. The objects in a set are the *elements,* or *members,* of the set. An *empty set,* or *null set,* means that nothing is in that set. GMAT questions about sets are usually pretty simple to answer as long as you know a little terminology and how to read a Venn diagram. The following sections explore all you need to know about sets.

Set terminology

The terms *union, intersection, disjoint sets,* and *subset* describe how two or more sets relate to one another through the elements they contain.

- **A *union* of two sets contains the set of all elements of both sets.** For example, the union of sets $A = \{0, 1, 2, 3, 4, 5, 6, 7, 8, 9\}$ and $B = \{2, 4, 6, 8, 10\}$ is $S = \{0, 1, 2, 3, 4, 5, 6, 7, 8, 9, 10\}$.

- **An *intersection* of two sets is the set of the elements that are common to both sets.** For example, the intersection of sets $A = \{0, 1, 2, 3, 5, 6, 7, 8, 9\}$ and $B = \{2, 4, 6, 8, 10\}$ is $S = \{2, 6, 8\}$.

- **Disjoint sets are two or more sets with no elements in common.** For example, set A and set B are disjoint sets if set $A = \{0, 2, 6, 8\}$ and set $B = \{1, 3, 5, 7\}$.

- **A subset is a set whose elements appear in another, larger set.** If all the elements of set $B = \{2, 3, 5, 7\}$ also appear in set $A = \{0, 1, 2, 3, 5, 6, 7, 8, 9\}$, you'd say that set B is a *subset* of set A.

Getting a visual: Venn diagrams

The GMAT often illustrates the concept of sets with Venn diagrams, such as those presented in Figure 14-1. Venn diagrams provide visual representations of union, intersection, disjoint sets, and subset. You can draw Venn diagrams to help you answer GMAT questions about sets.

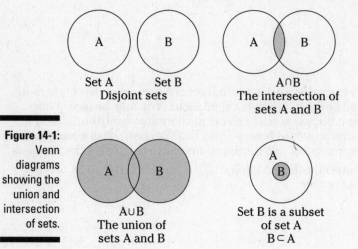

Figure 14-1: Venn diagrams showing the union and intersection of sets.

Set A   Set B
Disjoint sets

A∩B
The intersection of sets A and B

A∪B
The union of sets A and B

Set B is a subset of set A
B⊂A

GMAT quantitative reasoning questions regarding sets are usually pretty straightforward. Here's an example.

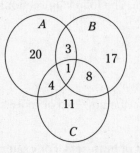

Given the Venn diagram, what are the number of elements in the intersection of sets *A* and *B*?

(A) 0

(B) 3

(C) 4

(D) 16

(E) 53

The number of elements in the intersection of sets *A* and *B* is the number of elements that are common to both sets. The portion of the diagram that represents the intersection is where the *A* circle and the *B* circle overlap. When you add the values in this intersection, you find that the number of elements that are common to both set *A* and set *B* is 4 (3 + 1 = 4). The correct answer is Choice (C).

If you chose Choice (B), you ignored the one element that's common to all three sets. You must include that one element, however, because it's a common element of sets *A* and *B*. Choice (E) conveys the number of elements in the union of sets *A* and *B* rather than their intersection.

Making Arrangements: Permutations and Combinations

The GMAT may test you on the arrangement of groups and sets, so you're likely to see some permutation and combination problems. When you calculate *permutations,* you figure out the number of ways the elements of a set can be arranged in specific orders. Determining *combinations* is similar to finding permutations, except that the order of the arrangements doesn't matter. In the following sections, we provide explanations and examples of each type of problem.

Positioning with permutations

Permutations problems ask you to determine how many arrangements of numbers are possible given a specific set of numbers and a particular order for the arrangements. For example, figuring out the number of possible seven-digit telephone numbers you can create is a permutation problem. And the answer is huge (10^7) because you have 10 possible values (the integers between 0 and 9) to fill each of the seven places.

Order matters when you set up permutations. Even though two different phone numbers may have the same combination of numbers, such as 345-7872 and 543-7728, the phone numbers ring two different lines because you input them into the phone in a different order.

Consider the elements of $S = \{a, b, c\}$. You can arrange these three elements in six different ways:

$$a\,b\,c \quad a\,c\,b \quad b\,a\,c \quad b\,c\,a \quad c\,a\,b \quad c\,b\,a$$

Even though each group contains the same elements, these groupings are completely different permutations because they convey different orderings of the three elements. Writing out the number of possible orderings of a set of three letters isn't too difficult, but what if you had to figure out the number of orderings for a set of 11 numbers? That problem would take more time than anyone would care to spend and certainly more time than you have to finish the GMAT. Luckily, you can rely on factorials to figure out permutations.

A *factorial* is the product of all natural numbers in the set of numbers from 1 through a particular number (n), which is the number of the factorial. The number of permutations of n objects is expressed as $n!$. The ! symbol indicates a *factorial,* and you read the expression as "n factorial." So 5! is a way of expressing $5 \times 4 \times 3 \times 2 \times 1$.

Instead of writing the possible permutations for the set of three letters $\{a, b, c\}$, use a factorial. Three different elements (the letters in the set) arranged in as many different orders as possible look like this: 3!, which is equal to $3 \times 2 \times 1$, which is equal to 6. So 3! = 6. The three elements have six permutations.

Suppose you have more than three elements. Maybe a photographer wants to know how many different ways she can arrange five people in a single row for a wedding photo. The number of possible arrangements of the five-person wedding party is 5! or 5! = $5 \times 4 \times 3 \times 2 \times 1 = 120$.

The factorial of 0 is written as 0!, which always equals 1.

As you can see, more possible arrangements exist as the number of objects in the arrangement increases. That's the basic information you need to know to answer basic permutation questions, such as the following one. Give it a shot!

Alice received a bracelet with four distinct removable charms. How many different ways can she arrange the four charms on her new bracelet?

(A) 4

(B) 8

(C) 24

(D) 100

(E) 40,320

Because the bracelet has four charms, the number of arrangements or permutations is 4!: $4 \times 3 \times 2 \times 1$.

Then just multiply the numbers to get the number of possible arrangements (the order you multiply them in doesn't matter): $4 \times 3 = 12$, and $12 \times 2 = 24$. Because $24 \times 1 = 24$, the correct answer is Choice (C).

You can eliminate Choices (A) and (B) because they're too small. You know that more than four arrangements must exist, because you have four charms. Choice (B) is 4×2, which isn't much better. In permutations, you know the number gets pretty large in a hurry, but not as large as Choice (E), which is 8!.

Permutations get a little more challenging when you have a fixed number of objects, n, to fill a limited number of places, r, and you care about the order the objects are arranged in.

For example, consider the predicament of the big-league baseball coach of a 20-member baseball team who needs to determine the number of different batting orders that these 20 ball players can fill in a 9-slot batting lineup. The coach could work this permutation out by writing all the factors from 20 back 9 places (because 20 players can fill only 9 slots in the batting order), like this:

$$20 \times 19 \times 18 \times 17 \times 16 \times 15 \times 14 \times 13 \times 12 = x$$

But this time-consuming process isn't practical in the middle of a game. Luckily, the coach can rely on a permutation formula.

The number of permutations of n things taken r at a time is stated as $_nP_r$. (To help you remember the formula, think of a certain public radio station that has these call letters.) The permutation formula for n objects taken r at a time looks like this:

$$_nP_r = n! \div (n-r)!$$

Apply the formula to figure out the possible number of batting orders:

$$_nP_r = \frac{n!}{(n-r)!}$$

$$_{20}P_9 = \frac{20!}{(20-9)!}$$

$$_{20}P_9 = \frac{20!}{11!}$$

The GMAT doesn't allow you to use calculators, so it won't expect you to calculate the permutation beyond this point. Here's an example of how complex permutations may appear on the GMAT.

A lawn care company has five employees that it schedules on a given day to work the lawns of any ten possible homes. How many different ways can the company assign the five employees to the ten homes if each employee provides lawn care service for just one home?

(A) 50

(B) $\frac{2!}{1!}$

(C) 120

(D) $\frac{10!}{5!}$

(E) 10!

This question may seem counterintuitive to the formula, which calculates *n* number of things taken *r* at a time to get the number of permutations. This problem appears to be taking a smaller number of things, *r* (the number of employees), and finding out how many times they can be spread around a greater number of places. That's what makes this question a little tricky.

This problem may look backward, but it really follows the same formula. Rather than thinking of how to spread five workers over ten houses, think of how many ways you can arrange the ten houses over the more limited number of workers and apply the formula:

$$_nP_r = \frac{n!}{(n-r)!}$$

$$_{10}P_5 = \frac{10!}{(10-5)!}$$

$$_{10}P_5 = \frac{10!}{5!}$$

The correct answer is Choice (D). With a calculator, you can figure out that 30,240 ways exist to assign employees. If you chose Choice (A), you simply multiplied the number of workers times the number of houses. But that's not the correct calculation. Choice (C) is what you get if you calculated 5!, which isn't the complete answer. Likewise, Choice (E) is incomplete.

Don't let Choice (B) trip you up. You can't simplify factorials like you can common fractions: $\frac{10!}{5!} \neq \frac{2!}{1!}$.

If this problem was difficult for you, take heart: You won't see too many of these kinds of questions on the GMAT.

Coming together: Combinations

Combinations are a lot like permutations, only easier. You form a *combination* by extracting a certain number of persons or things from a larger total sample of persons and things. Unlike permutations, the order doesn't matter with combinations, so combinations result in fewer possibilities than permutations.

A combination problem may ask you to find how many different teams, committees, or other types of groups can be formed from a set number of persons. For example, if you're asked to select as many teams as you can from a set number of people and the order of the team members doesn't matter, you're finding the total number of combinations of different teams.

Consider how many three-member committees you can form with Tom, Dick, and Harry. Tom, Dick, and Harry don't line up in any particular order while they're convening, so the way you list them doesn't matter. A committee composed of Tom, Dick, and Harry is the same as a committee composed of Tom, Harry, and Dick or one composed of Dick, Tom, and Harry. So only one possible combination exists of this three-member committee. If Tom, Dick, and Harry were asked to participate in a lineup, you'd have a permutation and six different possible arrangements, but because order doesn't matter when you're forming the committee, you have only one possible combination.

You can apply a formula to figure out the number of combinations. The formula is the number of ways to choose *r* objects from a group of *n* objects when the order of the objects doesn't matter, and it looks like this:

$$_nC_r = \frac{n!}{r!(n-r)!}$$

You can see right away that this formula is different from the one for permutations. Because you have a larger number in the denominator than you'd have with a permutation, the final number will be smaller.

Suppose a pollster randomly approaches three different people from a group of five mall walkers. To figure out how many possible combinations of three different people the pollster can annoy, use the combination formula:

$$_nC_r = \frac{n!}{r!(n-r)!}$$

$$_5C_3 = \frac{5!}{3!(5-3)!}$$

The factorial of 5! is 120 ($5 \times 4 \times 3 \times 2 \times 1$), and the factorial of 3! is 6 ($3 \times 2 \times 1$). So here's the resulting equation:

$$_5C_3 = \frac{120}{6(5-3)!}$$

Subtract the values in the parentheses to get 2!. The value of 2! is 2 (because 2×1 is 2):

$$_5C_3 = \frac{120}{6(2)}$$

$$_5C_3 = \frac{120}{12}$$

$$_5C_3 = 10$$

Therefore, from the five mall walkers, the pollster can create ten different combinations of three people to poll.

Because you can't use a calculator, GMAT combination problems won't get too complex. The test-makers won't make you perform overly complex calculations on your low-tech noteboard.

Here's an example of what you can expect from GMAT combination problems.

Some fourth graders are choosing foursquare teams at recess. What is the total possible number of combinations of four-person teams that can be chosen from a group of six children?

(A) 6

(B) 15

(C) 120

(D) 360

(E) 98,280

Apply the formula for combinations and see what happens:

$$_nC_r = \frac{n!}{r!(n-r)!}$$

$$_6C_4 = \frac{6!}{4!(6-4)!}$$

$$_6C_4 = \frac{6!}{(4!)(2!)}$$

$$_6C_4 = \frac{720}{24 \times 2}$$

$$_6C_4 = \frac{720}{48}$$

$$_6C_4 = 15$$

After you perform the calculations, you find that the correct answer is Choice (B).

If you went for Choice (D), you calculated a permutation instead of a combination.

Meeting in the Middle: Mean, Median, and Mode

At least a few GMAT math problems will require you to evaluate sets of numbers. To evaluate data correctly, you need to know the *central tendency* of numbers and the dispersion of their values. A measurement of central tendency is a value that's typical, or representative, of a group of numbers or other information. Common tools for describing a central tendency include average (arithmetic mean), median, mode, and weighted mean.

✔ *Average* (also referred to as *arithmetic mean*) is the most commonly tested tendency value. To find the average (arithmetic mean) of a set of numbers, add the numbers and divide by the quantity of numbers in the group:

$$\text{Average (Arithmetic Mean)} = \frac{\text{Sum of All Numbers in the Set}}{\text{Number of Members in the Set}}$$

You can plug known values into this formula to solve for the other values. For example, if the GMAT gives you the average and the sum of a group of numbers, you can use the formula to figure out how many numbers are in the set.

✔ **The *median* is the middle value among a list of several values or numbers.** To find the median, put the values or numbers in order, usually from low to high, and choose the value that falls exactly in the middle of the other values. If you have an odd number of values, just select the middle value. If you have an even number of values, find the two middle values and average them. The outcome is the median.

✔ **The *mode* is the value that occurs most frequently in a set of values.** Questions about mode may contain words like *frequency* or ask you how often a value occurs. For example, you may be asked what income occurs most frequently in a given population or sample. If more people in the population or sample have an income of $30,000 than any other income amount, the mode is $30,000.

✔ **You determine a *weighted mean* when some values in a set contribute more to the final average than others.** Multiply each individual value by the number of times it occurs in a set of numbers. Then, you add these products together and divide the sum by the total number of times all the values occur.

For example, suppose you're asked to calculate Becky's overall grade point average from Table 14-1, which charts the grades in all her classes and the amount of credits for each.

Table 14-1	The Weighted Mean of Grade Point Averages		
Class	*Number of Credits*	*Grade*	*Total Grade Points*
Statistics	5	3.8	19
English	5	1.9	9.5
Speech	4	2.3	9.2
Bowling	1	4.0	4
Total	15	2.78 GPA	41.7

First, you multiply the individual values (the grades) by the number of times they each occur (the credits) to get total grade points for each class. Then, you add the total grade points for all classes (41.7) and divide by the total number of times they all occur (which is the number of total credits, 15): 41.7 ÷ 15 = 2.78 GPA.

You'll likely see a bunch of questions on the GMAT that ask you to figure out the central tendency of a set of values. Here's an example of one that asks for mean.

George tried to compute the average (arithmetic mean) of his eight statistics test scores. He mistakenly divided the correct sum of all his test scores by 7 and calculated his average to be 96. What was George's actual average test score?

(A) 80

(B) 84

(C) 96

(D) 100

(E) 108

The question asks you for George's average score on eight tests and gives the average of those eight scores when they're divided by 7. You know that his average must be less than 96 because you're dividing by a larger number, so you can automatically eliminate Choices (C), (D), and (E). Just use the formula for averages to determine George's average score for eight tests.

1. **Figure out the sum of all George's test scores, using what you know from his incorrect calculation.**

$$96 = \frac{\text{Sum of All Scores}}{7}$$
$$96 \times 7 = \text{Sum of All Scores}$$
$$672 = \text{Sum of All Scores}$$

2. **Find George's actual average based on the sum of all his scores.**

$$\text{Average} = \frac{672}{8}$$
$$\text{Average} = 84$$

The correct answer is Choice (B).

Straying from Home: Range and Standard Deviation

Besides knowing the main concepts of central tendency, you also need to know about *variation* or *dispersion* of values in statistics. The two types of dispersion you'll deal with on the GMAT are *range* and *standard deviation,* which we explore in the following sections. Dispersion tells you how spread out the values are from the center. If dispersion is small, the values are clustered around the mean. But a wide dispersion of values tells you that the mean average isn't a reliable representative of all the values.

Scouting out the range

The easiest measure of dispersion to calculate is the *range*. You can say that the range is the difference between the highest and lowest values in the set of data. The range of values in statistics can come from either a population or a sample. The *population* is the set of all objects or things, that is, the total amount of all data considered. A *sample* is just a part of the population.

Here's an example of how to find the range of a set of values: If the highest test score in a math class was 94 percent and the lowest was 59 percent, you'd subtract the low from the high to get the score range (94 − 59 = 35). The range of test scores is 35. Simple as that!

Watching out for wanderers: Standard deviation

Another form of dispersion you need to know for the GMAT is *standard deviation.* The standard deviation expresses variation by measuring how spread out the distribution is from the mean. Although the range (see preceding section) can give you an idea of the total spread, standard deviation is a more reliable indicator of dispersion because it considers all the data, not just the two on each end. Standard deviation is the most widely used figure for expressing how much the data is dispersed from the mean.

For example, suppose you get a grade of 75 on a test where the mean grade is 70 and the vast majority of all the other grades fall between 60 and 80. Your score is comparatively better in this situation than if you get a 75 on the same test, where the mean grade is still 70, but most of the grades fall between 45 and 95. In the first situation, the grades are more tightly clustered around the central tendency. A standard deviation in this case is a small number. Your grade is higher compared to all the other test-takers' grades in the first group than your grade would be in the second scenario. In the second scenario, the standard deviation is a bigger number, and a grade of 75 isn't as good relative to the others.

You've probably had a statistics class by this time in your career, and you probably had to calculate standard deviation in that class. The GMAT won't ask you to actually calculate standard deviation, but it will expect you to know how to use standard deviation.

It's a good idea to be able to recognize that a *normal distribution* creates a symmetrical bell curve such as the one in Figure 14-2. The standard deviation in a normal distribution is a constant. The average (arithmetic mean) appears as an X with a line over it and appears in the exact middle of all the values. If you stray 1 standard deviation in either direction from the mean, you'll have netted 68 percent of all the values. Going another standard deviation away from the center, you pick up another 27 percent of all values, giving you about 95 percent of all values. Finally, when you go ± 3 standard deviations from the mean, you now have about 99.7 percent of all the values in your population or sample.

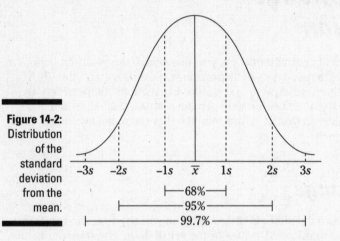

Figure 14-2: Distribution of the standard deviation from the mean.

If the curve in Figure 14-2 showed a group of test scores, it would mean that more than a majority of test-takers scored within 1 standard deviation of the mean (68 percent is more than 51 percent). The vast majority scored within 2 standard deviations, and virtually everyone scored within 3 standard deviations. Say that the mean test score is 80, and one standard deviation may be 10 points on either side. This means that 68 percent of the students scored between 70 and 90. If the second standard deviation was another 5 test points in either direction, you could say that 95 percent of the students scored between 65 and 95 on the test. Finally, you could say that the third standard deviation is another 4 points away from the mean, which means that 99.7 percent of the students scored between 61 and 99.

A small value for the standard deviation means that the values of the group are more tightly clustered around the mean. A greater standard deviation means that the numbers are more scattered away from the mean. The greater the standard deviation for a group of values, the easier deviating from the center is. The less the standard deviation, the harder it is to deviate from the center.

Here's what a standard deviation question on the GMAT may look like.

   I. {55, 56, 57, 58, 59}

  II. {41, 57, 57, 57, 73}

 III. {57, 57, 57, 57, 57}

Which of the following lists sets I, II, and III in order from least standard deviation to greatest standard deviation?

(A) I, II, III

(B) I, III, II

(C) II, III, I

(D) III, I, II

(E) III, II, I

The set with the least standard deviation is the one that has the least amount of difference from the highest to the lowest values. The values in Set III are all the same, so Set III has the least standard deviation and should be listed first. Eliminate Choices (A), (B), and (C) because they don't list Set III first.

Set II (41 and 73) has a greater difference between the high and low values than Set I (55 and 59). So the set with the greatest standard deviation is Set II, which means it should be listed last. Choice (D) lists the sets in their proper order from least standard deviation to greatest standard deviation, so it's the correct answer.

Predicting the Future: Probability

Probability is the measure of how likely a particular event will occur, but figuring probability is a bit more scientific than telling fortunes and reading tarot cards. You express probability as a percentage, fraction, or decimal. You'd say that the probability of an event's occurring falls between 0 percent and 100 percent or between 0 and 1. If the probability of an event's occurrence is 0, or 0 percent, it's impossible for the event to occur. If the probability is 1, or 100 percent, the event is certain to occur. Few things in life are certain, other than death and taxes. For an event to be impossible is also rare. Therefore, the probability of the occurrence of an event usually falls somewhere between 0 and 1, or 0 and 100 percent.

Probability questions may ask you to determine the probability of one event or multiple events. We show you how to determine the probability for each type of question in the following sections.

Finding the probability of one event

Probability deals with *outcomes* and *events*. For situations where all possible outcomes are equally likely, the probability (*P*) that an event (*E*) occurs, represented by $P(E)$, is defined as

$$P(E) = \frac{\text{Number of Outcomes Involving Occurences of } E}{\text{Total Possible Number of Outcomes}}$$

Because you express probability as a fraction, it can never be less than 0 or greater than 1. Getting both heads and tails with one flip of a coin is impossible, so the probability of that particular event occurring is 0. If you used a coin with heads on both sides, the probability of getting heads on one flip would be 1, because the number of possible outcomes is exactly the same as the number of outcomes that will occur.

Finding the probability of many events

You can find the probability of multiple events by following several rules. Table 14-2 lists and describes each rule, shows the corresponding formula, and provides an example of when you'd use it.

Table 14-2	Finding the Probability of the Occurrence of Multiple Events		
Rule	*Circumstance*	*Formula*	*Example*
Special Rule of Addition	The probability of the occurrence of either of two possible events that are mutually exclusive	$P(A \text{ or } B) = P(A) + P(B)$	The probability of rolling a 5 or 6 on one roll of one die
General Rule of Addition	The probability of the occurrence of either of two possible events that can happen together	$P(A \text{ or } B) = P(A) + P(B) - P(A \text{ and } B)$	The probability of drawing a playing card that displays a club or a queen
Special Rule of Multiplication	The probability of the occurrence of two events at the same time when the two events are independent of each other	$P(A \text{ and } B) = P(A) \times P(B)$	The probability of rolling a 5 and a 6 on one roll of two dice.
General Rule of Multiplication	The probability of the occurrence of two events when the occurrence of the first event affects the outcome of the second event	$P(A \text{ and } B) = P(A) \times P(B|A)$	The probability of first drawing the queen of clubs from a pack of 52 cards, keeping the queen of clubs out of the pack, and then drawing the jack of diamonds on the next try

Applying the special rule of addition

You use the special rule of addition to figure out the probability of rolling a die and coming up with either a 1 or a 2. You can't get both on one roll, so the events are mutually exclusive. Therefore, the probability of rolling a 1 or a 2 in one roll is $P(A) + P(B)$:

$$P(A \text{ or } B) = \frac{1}{6} + \frac{1}{6}$$

$$P(A \text{ or } B) = \frac{2}{6}$$

$$P(A \text{ or } B) = \frac{1}{3}$$

Applying the general rule of addition

You use the general rule of addition to figure probability in the case of choosing sodas from a cooler. Imagine that three types of sodas are in a cooler. Colas are numbered consecutively 1 through 5, orange sodas are numbered 1 through 7, and grape sodas are numbered 1 through 8. Let event *A* stand for when a cola is taken out of the cooler and event *B* represent when a can with a number 2 is taken out. You want to know the probability of picking out *either* a cola *or* a can with the number 2 on it but *not* specifically a cola with the number 2 on it. Five of the 20 cans are sodas, three display the number 2, and only one can is a cola with the number 2. So $P(A)$ is $\frac{5}{20}$, $P(B)$ is $\frac{3}{20}$, and $P(A$ and $B)$ is $\frac{1}{20}$. Plug the values in to the formula: $P(A$ or $B) = P(A) + P(B) - P(A$ and $B)$.

$$P(A \text{ or } B) = \frac{5}{20} + \frac{3}{20} - \frac{1}{20}$$
$$P(A \text{ or } B) = \frac{7}{20}$$

You can also express this probability as 0.35 or as 35 percent.

Applying the special rule of multiplication

The probability of multiple events occurring together is the product of the probabilities of the events occurring individually. For example, if you're rolling two dice at the same time, here's how you find the probability of rolling a 1 on one die and a 2 on the other:

$$P(A \text{ and } B) = \frac{1}{6} \times \frac{1}{6}$$
$$P(A \text{ and } B) = \frac{1}{36}$$

Applying the general rule of multiplication

Suppose the outcome of the second situation depends on the outcome of the first event. You then invoke the general rule of multiplication. The term $P(B|A)$ is a conditional probability, where the likelihood of the second event depends on the fact that *A* has already occurred. For example, to find the odds of drawing the ace of spades from a deck of 52 cards on one try and then drawing the king of spades on the second try — with the ace out of the deck — apply the formula, like this: $P(A$ and $B) = P(A) \times P(B|A)$.

The line between the *B* and *A* stands for "*B* given *A*"; it doesn't mean divide!

$$P(A \text{ and } B) = \frac{1}{52} \times \frac{1}{51}$$
$$P(A \text{ and } B) = \frac{1}{2,652}$$

We wouldn't bet against the house on that outcome! The probability of drawing the king of spades on the second draw is slightly better than the probability of drawing the ace on the first draw, because you've already removed one card from the deck on the first draw. Here's a sample of how the GMAT may test your knowledge of probability rules.

A candy machine contains gumballs: three blue, two red, seven yellow, and one purple. The machine distributes one gumball for each dime. A child has exactly two dimes with which she will purchase two gumballs. What is the chance that the child will get two red gumballs?

(A) $\frac{2}{169}$

(B) $\frac{1}{13}$

(C) $\frac{2}{13}$

(D) $\frac{1}{156}$

(E) $\frac{1}{78}$

You need to treat getting the two red gumballs as two events. The occurrence of the first event affects the probability of the second because after the child extracts the first red gumball, the machine has one fewer gumball. So you apply the general rule of multiplication.

The chance of getting a red gumball with the first dime is 2 (the number of red gumballs) divided by 13 (the total number of gumballs in the machine), or $\frac{2}{13}$. If the child tries to get the second gumball, the first red gumball is already gone, which leaves only 1 red gumball and 12 total gumballs in the machine, so the chance of getting the second red gumball is $\frac{1}{12}$. The probability of both events happening is the product of the probability of the occurrence of each event:

$$P(A \text{ and } B) = P(A) \times P(B \mid A)$$

$$P(A \text{ and } B) = \frac{2}{13} \times \frac{1}{12}$$

$$P(A \text{ and } B) = \frac{2}{156}$$

$$P(A \text{ and } B) = \frac{1}{78}$$

Choice (E) is the correct answer. Choice (A) is $\frac{2}{13} \times \frac{1}{13}$, which would look right if you didn't subtract the withdrawn red gumball from the total number on the second draw. Choice (B) is the chance of drawing one red gumball from a machine with 13 gumballs and only 1 red gumball. In this problem, $\frac{1}{13}$ is also the chance of drawing the purple gumball. If you picked Choice (C), you found the chance of drawing the first red gumball.

Chapter 15

It's All in the Presentation: GMAT Quantitative Question Types

---

In This Chapter

▶ Diving into data sufficiency questions

▶ Probing problem-solving questions

You need more than just math skills to excel on the quantitative section; you also need to know how to approach the questions. This chapter tells you what to expect from the math sections and how to work through the unique ways the GMAT presents the questions.

The kinds of math questions that appear on the GMAT test your ability to reason and think on your feet as you make use of the information you're given.

Two basic types of questions are intermingled throughout the quantitative section of the GMAT: data sufficiency questions and problem-solving questions. Both types of questions require similar skills, but they demand different approaches. In this chapter, we show you how to ace both kinds of questions.

Enough's Enough: Data Sufficiency Questions

The quantitative section has 37 questions, and about half of them are presented in a unique form called data sufficiency. These questions aren't particularly hard if you understand how to approach them before you walk into the testing center. However, if you don't know much about these questions, getting confused and making careless mistakes are easy. Fortunately, you've decided to read this book to get a sneak peek. Your knowledge should be more than sufficient for data sufficiency!

You don't need the solution to find the answer

Unlike the traditional math problems you've seen throughout your life, data sufficiency questions don't actually require you to solve the problem. Instead, you have to evaluate two statements and determine which of those statements provides *sufficient* information for you to answer the question.

For each data sufficiency problem, you have a question and two statements, labeled (1) and (2). Your job is to decide whether each of the statements gives you enough information to answer the question with general math skills and everyday facts (such as the number of days in a month and the meaning of *clockwise*). If you need a refresher in the math concepts tested on the GMAT, read Chapters 10, 11, 12, 13, and 14.

Don't make foolish assumptions when you answer data sufficiency questions. Keep in mind that your job is to determine whether the information given is sufficient, not to try to make up for the lack of data! You're used to having to come up with an answer to every math problem, so if the statements lack just a little information, you may be tempted to stretch the data to reach a solution. Don't give in to temptation. For example, if a data sufficiency question provides a four-sided figure, don't assume that it's a square unless the data tells you it's a square — even if knowing that the figure is a square would allow you to solve the problem. Deal only with the information expressly as it's stated without making unwarranted assumptions.

The answer choices for data sufficiency questions are the same for each question:

(A) Statement (1) *alone* is sufficient, but Statement (2) alone is not sufficient to answer the question asked.

(B) Statement (2) *alone* is sufficient, but Statement (1) alone is not sufficient to answer the question asked.

(C) *Both* Statements (1) and (2) *together* are sufficient to answer the question asked, but *neither* statement *alone* is sufficient.

(D) *Each* statement *alone* is sufficient to answer the question asked.

(E) Statements (1) and (2) *together* are *not* sufficient to answer the question asked, and additional data are needed.

The computer doesn't actually designate the answer choices with the letters A through E, but the choices appear in this order (you choose the correct one with your mouse or keyboard), and we refer to them as A, B, C, D, and E to make the discussion simpler.

It's possible that just one of the statements gives enough data to answer the question, that the two statements taken together solve the problem, that both statements alone provide sufficient data, or that neither statement solves the problem, even with the information provided by the other one. That's a lot of information to examine and apply in two minutes! Don't worry. You can eliminate brain freeze by following a step-by-step approach to these questions.

Steps to approaching data sufficiency problems

Take a methodical approach to answering data sufficiency questions, and follow this series of steps:

1. **Evaluate the question to make sure you know exactly what you're supposed to solve, and, if you can, decide what kind of information you need to solve the problem.**

2. **Examine one of the statements and determine whether the data in that one statement is enough to answer the question.**

   Start with the first statement or whichever one seems easier to evaluate. Record your conclusion on the noteboard.

3. **Examine the other statement and determine whether it has enough information to answer the question.**

   Record your conclusion on the noteboard.

4. **Evaluate what you've written on your noteboard.**

   - If you recorded *yes* for both statements, pick the fourth answer, which we designate as Choice (D).

   - If you recorded *yes* for (1) and *no* for (2), select the first answer, Choice (A) in this book.

   - If you recorded *no* for (1) and *yes* for (2), choose the second answer, Choice (B) for our purposes.

   - If you've written *no* for both statements, go on to the next step.

5. **Examine the statements together to determine whether the data given in both is enough information to answer the question.**

   - If the answer is *yes,* select the third answer, our Choice (C).

   - If the answer is *no,* choose the last answer, the one we've designated as Choice (E).

You can boil this method down to a nice, neat chart, like the one shown in Figure 15-1.

Data Sufficiency Answer Elimination Chart

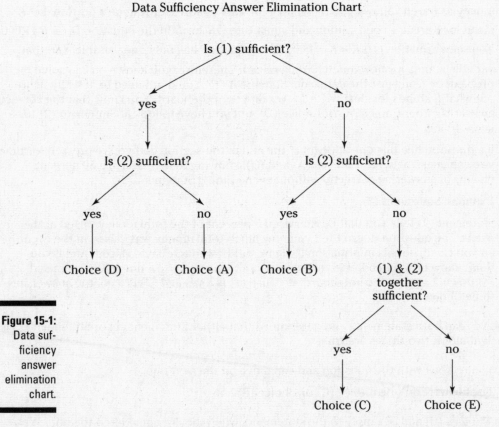

Figure 15-1:
Data suf-
ficiency
answer
elimination
chart.

Don't think *too* hard about whether an answer provides sufficient information to solve a problem. Data sufficiency questions aren't necessarily designed to trick you. For example, you deal only with real numbers in these questions, and if a line looks straight, it is.

A statement is sufficient to answer the question if it provides only one possible answer for the question. If the information in a statement allows for two or more answers, the statement isn't sufficient.

David and Karena were among a group of runners who were raising money for a local charity. If David and Karena together raised $1,000 in the charity race, how much of the money did Karena raise?

(1) David raised $\frac{4}{5}$ as much money as Karena did.

(2) David raised 5 percent of the total money raised at the event.

Use the steps and/or the chart in Figure 15-1 to solve the problem:

1. Know what you have to solve for.

The question asks you to figure out how much money Karena raised for charity. The question gives you the total money raised by David and Karena together ($D + K = $1,000$) but doesn't specify how much David raised. Check out the statements to see whether either or both of them let you know how much David came up with. If you have David's figure, you only need to subtract it from $1,000 to get Karena's figure.

2. Consider Statement (1) to determine whether it lets you solve for Karena's total.

You determined that you needed data that would allow you to separate the money raised by Karena from that raised by David. Knowing that David raised $\frac{4}{5}$ as much money as Karena allows you to set up a formula to solve for Karena's portion. Let K stand for Karena's contribution and substitute $\frac{4}{5}K$ for D in the equation $D + K = $1,000$. Your new equation is $\frac{4}{5}K + K = 1,000$. This equation has only one variable, and that variable stands for how much Karena raised. Therefore, you know you can solve the problem by using just the data from Statement (1). You don't need to actually figure out what K stands for. Just write *1 = yes* on your noteboard. You know that the correct answer is either Choice (A) or Choice (D), but you have to look at Statement (2) to know which.

If a question like this one appears at the end of the section and you're pressed for time, you can guess between Choices (A) and (D), knowing that you have a 50 percent chance of answering correctly without even reading Statement (2).

3. Examine Statement (2).

Statement (2) tells you that David raised 5 percent of the total money raised at the event. The question doesn't tell you how much total money was raised at the event, so you can't use this information to figure out how much David raised. And if you don't know how much David raised, you can't figure out how much Karena raised. Jot down *2 = no* on the noteboard. Because (1) is a *yes* and (2) is a *no,* the answer has to be Choice (A).

If you've read both statements and determined that either Statement (1) or Statement (2) is sufficient alone, two things are true:

- ✔ You're done with the question and can move on the next one.

- ✔ The answer can't be Choice (C) or Choice (E).

Both Choices (C) and (E) apply to the statements when they're considered together. You don't need to consider the statements together if either statement is sufficient alone. Your only possible choices if *either* statement is sufficient are Choice (A) if only Statement (1) is sufficient, Choice (B) if only Statement (2) is sufficient, and Choice (D) if each statement alone is sufficient.

Don't evaluate whether both statements together answer the problem unless you've determined that neither is sufficient alone. The only time you consider (1) and (2) together is when you've answered *no* to both statements. For instance, say the example question replaced Statement (1) with this data: "The event raised a total of $10,000." Statement (1) wouldn't be enough to answer the question. But because Statement (2) tells you that David raised 5 percent of the total event money, you can answer the question using the data from both statements. Statement (1) provides the total amount, and Statement (2) allows you to figure out how much David raised based on that amount. If you subtract that amount from $1,000, you'll have Karena's total.

Choice (E) would be correct if Statement (1) said, "The event raised more money this year than last year." In this case, neither statement, nor the two together, could answer the question.

Don't waste time trying to come up with the actual numeric answer if you don't have to. When you look at a question like the example, you may be tempted to solve the equation and figure out how much Karena raised. Don't give in! Finding the number just wastes precious time, and no one gives you extra credit for solving the problem! Instead, use your valuable time to solve other questions in the quantitative section.

Taking a Look at Data Sufficiency Practice Problems

The best way to master the steps for solving data sufficiency questions is to practice on sample problems. Use the set of questions in this section to hone your skills. Make sure you have a piece of scratch paper nearby to simulate the noteboard. You can check your answers by reading through the explanations that follow the questions.

Practice questions

The GMAT gives you about two minutes to answer each quantitative question. So set your timer for ten minutes to get a feel for the time limit you'll be facing on the actual test. Follow the chart in Figure 15-1 to work your way through the answer choices. If you need to refresh your memory of the answer choices before you begin, see the earlier section "You don't need the solution to find the answer."

1. What's the value of the two-digit integer *x?*

   (1) The sum of the two digits is 5.

   (2) *x* is divisible by 5.

   (A) (B) (C) (D) (E)

2. Office Solutions employs both male and female workers who work either full time or part time. What percentage of its employees work part time?

   (1) Twenty percent of the female employees at Office Solutions work part time.

   (2) Thirty percent of the workforce at Office Solutions is male.

   (A) (B) (C) (D) (E)

3. What is the value of $2(x + y)$ in the preceding figure?

   (1) $y = 120$

   (2) $BC \parallel AD$

   (A) (B) (C) (D) (E)

4. Joe uses three different modes of transportation to travel a total of 225 kilometers to visit his aunt. How many kilometers does Joe travel by bus?

   (1) Joe rides his bike 5 kilometers to the bus station where he boards the bus to take him to the train station. He then takes the train 10 times the distance he has traveled by bus.

   (2) The distance Joe travels by bike is $\frac{1}{4}$ the distance he travels by bus, and his train ride is 40 times longer than his bike ride.

   (A) (B) (C) (D) (E)

5. If x and y are positive integers and $(a)^{2x}(a)^{2y} = 81$, what is the value of $x + y$?

   (1) $a = 3$

   (2) $x = y$

   (A) (B) (C) (D) (E)

Answer explanations

The following answer explanations provide not only the correct answer for the data sufficiency practice questions in the preceding section but also additional insight into how to approach this unique question type. So be sure to read all the info provided here.

1. **C.** Apply the steps:

   1. **Find out what to solve for.**

      This short question gives you little information about x; all you know is that it's a two-digit integer.

   2. **Examine Statement (1).**

      Statement (1) tells you that the sum of the digits is 5. Several two-digit numbers are composed of digits that when added together equal 5: 14, 23, 32, 41, and 50. Statement (1) narrows the field of two-digit numbers down to just these five possibilities, but that's not good enough. Because you don't have a single answer, Statement (1) isn't sufficient. Write down *1 = no.* You've just eliminated Choices (A) and (D).

3. Evaluate Statement (2).

Statement (2) says that x is divisible by 5. You probably realize immediately that every two-digit number ending in 0 or 5 is divisible by 5, so the possibilities are 10, 15, 20, 25, and so on. Clearly, Statement (2) isn't sufficient, because $\frac{1}{5}$ of all two-digit numbers are divisible by 5. Write down *2 = no.* You've just eliminated Choice (B).

4. Check out what you've written.

You have double *nos,* so you have to consider both statements together.

5. Evaluate the two statements together.

Statement (1) narrows the two-digit numbers down to five possibilities: 14, 23, 32, 41, and 50. Statement (2) narrows the list to those numbers that are divisible by 5. The only possibility from Statement (1) that ends in 0 or 5 is 50. Because 50 is divisible by 5 and the digits add up to 5, it answers the question. The two statements together provide enough information to answer the question. *Correct answer:* Choice (C).

You'll notice that, for this question, you had to find the actual answer to the question to determine whether the information was sufficient. Sometimes doing so is the quickest way to determine whether statements provide enough data. An equation may exist that you could've set up (and not solved) that would have told you that you had sufficient information. However, on questions like this one, just applying the information to the question is often simpler and quicker. Solving the actual problem is okay *if it's the quickest way to determine that you have enough information.* Just remember to stop solving the problem as soon as you determine whether the information is sufficient!

2. **E.** Here's an example of how word problems may appear as data sufficiency questions. Apply the steps in the same way you do for solving linear equations:

1. **Find out what to solve for.**

The question asks you to find the percentage of part-time employees at Office Solutions. You know two facts at this point: (1) Office Solutions employs a certain number of males (m) and a certain number of females (f), and (2) a certain number of employees work either full time (F) or part time (P). That creates four unknown variables. The question doesn't tell you anything about how many total people (T) Office Solutions employs, so you have another unknown. Here's what you know in mathematical terms: $F + P = T$ and $f + m = T$.

2. **Examine Statement (1).**

The first statement gives you the percentage of female part-time employees but tells you nothing about the percentage of male part-time employees. It takes care of only two of the unknown variables; you're missing half of what you need to solve the problem. Statement (1) isn't sufficient. Write down *1 = no,* and eliminate Choices (A) and (D).

3. **Evaluate Statement (2).**

This statement concerns male employees at Office Solutions, but not females, so it's insufficient by itself. Record your finding as *2 = no.* The answer can't be Choice (B).

4. **Check out what you've written.**

You have double *nos,* so consider Statement (2)'s sufficiency when paired with Statement (1).

5. **Evaluate the two statements together.**

One statement provides a percentage for females and the other offers a percentage for males. You may be on your way to finding the percentage for both.

Read the statements carefully. You may be tempted to think that Statement (2) offers the other half of the solution, but this statement tells you the percentage of *all* males who work at the company, not just the ones who work part time.

You can't determine the total percentage of part-time workers if you don't know the ratio of male full-time to male part-time workers. Neither statement is sufficient and the two together don't cut it. *Correct answer:* Choice (E).

3. **B.** For this problem, you evaluate a four-sided geometric figure:

1. **Find out what to solve for.**

   You know that the sum of the interior angles of four-sided figures is 360 degrees and that x and y are the measures of two of these interior angles, but that's not enough to determine the value of $2(x + y)$. But you knew that. Data sufficiency questions never give you enough information to solve them without considering the statements. So check out what they have to offer.

2. **Examine Statement (1).**

   Statement (1) gives you the value of y. You may have examined the figure, assumed that it was a parallelogram, and deduced that x and y are, therefore, angles formed by parallel lines cut by a transversal. That makes them supplementary angles that add to 180 degrees. So if $y = 120$, $x = 60$, and $2(x + y) = 360$. Problem solved!

   Not so fast. You can't assume information about a GMAT figure by looking at it. If the figure is supposed to be a parallelogram, the GMAT will give you the information you need to know that. Nothing to this point has indicated that BC and AD are parallel lines, so you have to write *no* next to Statement (1).

3. **Evaluate Statement (2).**

   Well, here you go. Now you know expressly that AB is a transversal that passes through two parallel lines. The two angles x and y are supplementary.

   Were you tempted at this point to pick Choice (C)? It's true that both statements together give you the value of x, but you aren't looking for the value of x. You're asked to find the value of $2(x + y)$. All you need is Statement (2). If the value of $x + y$ is 180, the value of $2(x + y)$ is 360. Write *yes* next to Statement (2) on your noteboard and pick Choice (B). You're done!

   You only pick Choice (C) if *neither* of the two statements by itself solves the problem. After you've determined that one of the statements works and the other doesn't, you know the answer can't be Choice (C). Follow the line of questions in the chart in Figure 15-1 and you'll be fine.

4. **D.** This data sufficiency question is essentially a simple addition problem.

1. **Find out what to solve for.**

   You know the total distance Joe travels to his aunt's is 225 kilometers and that he takes different types of transportation, one of which is a bus. Lucky guy! The question asks for the length of Joe's bus ride. That's your unknown, or x value.

2. **Examine Statement (1).**

   From the first statement, you learn that the other modes of transportation are bike (b) and train (t). Great news! It also tells you the exact length of Joe's bike ride (5 kilometers) and that his train ride is 10 times his bus ride. So $t = 10x$. You can set up an equation with this information: $5 + x + 10x = 225$. The equation has only one variable, the unknown length of the bus ride. You know you can solve a linear equation with only one variable, so Statement (1) is sufficient. Write *yes* next to (1) on your noteboard and eliminate Choices (B), (C), and (E).

3. **Evaluate Statement (2).**

Create an equation from the information in the second statement. If Joe's bike ride (k) is $\frac{1}{4}$ as long as his bus ride (b), then $k = \frac{1}{4}b$. If the train trip (x) is 40 times the length of the bike ride (k), then $x = 40k$. This gives simultaneous equations. Substitute $\frac{1}{4}b$ for k in the train ride equation: $x = 40\left(\frac{1}{4}b\right)$. So the equation for the bike ride plus the bus ride plus the train trip is this:

$$\frac{1}{4}b + b + 40\left(\frac{1}{4}b\right) = 225$$

This equation has only one variable, so you know you can solve for b. After you know the value of b, you can substitute that value in the equation for x, and you'll know the length of Joe's train trip. You don't have to actually solve for x; you just need to know that you can to know that Statement (2) is also sufficient. Write *yes* next to (2). *Correct answer:* Choice (D).

5. **A.** The last question in the practice set contains a bunch of unknown variables, so you may think you can't solve for much. You may be surprised!

1. **Find out what to solve for.**

Take a few seconds to evaluate the equation. You're given two factors with exponents and their product is equal to a perfect square. Both factors have the same base (a) and both contain an exponent with a factor of 2. The problem asks you to find the sum of the other two factors in the exponents of the terms.

2. **Examine Statement (1).**

From the information in the first statement, you can substitute 3 for a in the equation:

$$(3)^{2x}(3)^{2y} = 81$$

The terms have the same base, so you add the exponents when you multiply the terms:

$$3^{2x+2y} = 81$$

Now extract the common factor in the exponent:

$$3^{2(x+y)} = 81$$

Square 3 to get 9:

$$9^{(x+y)} = 81$$

Because $9^2 = 81$, you know that the exponent ($x + y$) must equal 2. The information in Statement (1) is sufficient to tell you the value of $x + y$. Write *yes* next to (1) on your noteboard and eliminate Choices (B), (C), and (E).

3. **Evaluate Statement (2).**

This statement tells you that x and y are equal, so you may be tempted to draw from the information in the last statement and assume that x and y each equal 1. Well, that could be true if $a = 3$. But you no longer know that $a = 3$.

You can't carry over the information from one statement to evaluate the sufficiency of the other. Start fresh with each statement.

It's true that x and y could each equal 1, but they could also each be equal to 0.5:

$$(a)^{2x}(a)^{2y} = 81$$
$$\left[a^{(2)(0.5)}\right]\left[a^{(2)(0.5)}\right] = 81$$
$$\left(a^1\right)\left(a^1\right) = 81$$
$$a^2 = 81$$
$$a = 9$$

In that case, $x + y$ would be equal to 1. Because Statement (2) results in more than one value for $x + y$, it can't be sufficient to answer the question. Write *no* next to (2) on your noteboard. *Correct answer:* Choice (A).

Houston, We Have a Problem: Problem-Solving Questions

About half of the 37 math problems on the GMAT quantitative section are data sufficiency. The other half are problem-solving questions, which (not surprisingly!) require you to apply your mathematical skills to solve a problem. These questions are more like the ones you've seen on other standardized tests, like the SAT and ACT. They present you with a question and provide five possible answer choices from which you select the correct answer.

The approach to regular old problem-solving questions is less clear-cut than the one for data sufficiency problems, but you should still follow an approach. Arriving at the test center with a practice problem-solving plan not only provides you with a groovy little alliteration but also gives you a real edge for answering standard math questions. These techniques apply more directly to some questions than others, but learn all of them so you're prepared for all types of problem-solving questions:

- ✔ **Examine all the data the question provides to make sure you know exactly what you're asked to do.** Some problems present you with figures, graphs, and scenarios, and some with just an equation with an equal sign. Don't jump into the answer choices until you've given the question a little thought. Isolate exactly what the problem asks you to solve for and what information the problem provides you. Especially for more complex questions and word problems, use your noteboard to keep track of what you know and what you have to find out.

- ✔ **Eliminate obviously incorrect answer choices if possible.** Before you begin solving a more complex math problem, look at the answer choices to root out any clearly illogical options. You can then focus your problem solving, and you won't pick these answers later through mistaken calculations. You can find more tips for eliminating answer choices in Chapter 2.

- ✔ **Use the information in the problem.** The GMAT rarely presents you with the answer choice that states, "It cannot be determined from the information." Almost every problem-solving question contains enough information for you to figure out the correct answer. But you need to use what you're given. Pull out the numbers and other terms in a problem and write them on your noteboard in a way that makes the numbers meaningful. Depending on the problem, you may show relationships between quantities, draw simple diagrams, or organize information in a quick table.

- ✔ **Find the equation.** Some GMAT problems provide the equation for you. Others, such as word problems, require you to come up with an equation using the language in the problem. Whenever possible, formulate an equation to solve from the information provided in the problem and write it down on your noteboard.

- ✔ **Know when to move on.** Sometimes you may confront a question that you just can't solve. Relax for a moment and reread the question to make sure you haven't missed something. If you still don't know what to do or if you can't remember the tested concept, eliminate all the answers you can and record your best guess.

Apply the process to a sample problem.

A survey reveals that the average income of a company's customers is $45,000 per year. If 50 customers responded to the survey and the average income of the wealthiest 10 of those customers is $75,000, what is the average income of the other 40 customers?

(A) $27,500

(B) $35,000

(C) $37,500

(D) $42,500

(E) $50,000

Scan the question to get an idea of what it's asking of you. The word problem talks about surveys and averages, so it's a statistics question. It asks for the average income of 40 out of 50 customers when the average of the other 10 is $75,000 and that the average of all 50 is $45,000.

You can eliminate Choice (E) off the bat because there's no way that the 40 customers with lower incomes have an average income that's more than the average income of all 50 customers. Choice (D) is probably wrong, too, because the top ten incomes carry such a high average compared to the total average. You know the answer is either Choice (A), (B), or (C), and you haven't even gotten down to solving yet!

Quickly eliminating answers before you begin can save you from choosing an answer that comes from making a math error. Sometimes, the test-makers are tricky; they anticipate the kinds of little mistakes you'll make and offer the resulting wrong answers as distracters in the answer choices. So be sure to eliminate illogical answers before you begin a problem.

You can find the total income of all 50 customers and the total income of the wealthiest 10 customers by using the formula for averages. The average equals the sum of the values in a group divided by the number of values in the group. Apply the formula to find the total income for the group of 50. Then find the total income for the group of 10. Subtract the total income of the 10 from the total income of the 50 to find the total income of the 40. Then you can divide by 40 to get the average income for the group of 40. Here's how you do it:

Your calculations may be easier if you drop the three zeroes from the salaries. For this problem, shorten $45,000 to $45 and $75,000 to 75. Just remember to add the zeroes back on to your solution when you find it!

1. **Find the total income for the group of 50.**

   The average income is $45 and the number of group members is 50, so use the formula to find the sum of all incomes (x):

   $$\text{Average} = \frac{\text{Sum of Values}}{\text{Number of Values}}$$

   $$45 = \frac{x}{50}$$

   $$2{,}250 = x$$

2. **Find the total income for the group of 10.**

   The average income is $75 and the number of group members is 10, so use the formula to find the sum (y):

   $$\text{Average} = \frac{\text{Sum of Values}}{\text{Number of Values}}$$

   $$75 = \frac{y}{10}$$

   $$750 = y$$

3. **Find the total income for the group of 40.**

   Subtract the total income of the group of 10 (y) from the total income for the group of 50 (x):

   $$2{,}250 - 750 = 1{,}500$$

4. **Find the average income of the group of 40.**

   The sum of the incomes in the group is $1,500, and the number of group members is 40, so apply the average formula:

   $$\text{Average} = \frac{\text{Sum of Values}}{\text{Number of Values}}$$

   $$\text{Average} = \frac{1{,}500}{40}$$

   $$\text{Average} = 37.5$$

Add three decimal places for the three zeroes you excluded in your calculations, and you have your answer. The average income of the 40 customers is $37,500, which is Choice (C).

Trying Out Some Problem-Solving Practice Problems

Here are a few practice questions to help you master the approach to problem-solving questions in the quantitative section. When you're finished answering them, read through the answer explanation to see how you've fared.

Practice questions

Try to answer these practice problems in the same amount of time you'll experience on the actual GMAT (give yourself about ten minutes to answer all five questions). Remember to keep track of the information you know and the information you have to figure out as you work through the problems. Use a piece of scratch paper to simulate the noteboard as you work out the answers.

1. An electronics firm produces 300 units of a particular MP3 player every hour of every day. Each unit costs the manufacturer $60 to produce, and retailers immediately purchase all the produced units. What is the minimum wholesale price (amount the manufacturer receives) per unit that the manufacturer should charge to make an hourly profit of $19,500?

   (A) $60

   (B) $65

   (C) $95

   (D) $125

   (E) $145

2. What is the value for x in the equation $\frac{2x}{4+2x} = \frac{6x}{8x+6}$?

   (A) –3

   (B) 1

   (C) 2

   (D) 3

   (E) 6

3. $g(r) = \begin{cases} 4|r| & \text{if } r \geq 2 \\ -|r| & \text{if } r < 2 \end{cases}$

   Given the above, evaluate $g(-r)$ if $r = -7$.

   (A) –28

   (B) –14

   (C) –7

   (D) 7

   (E) 28

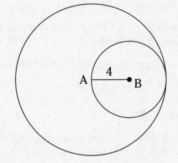

4. In the preceding figure, the circle centered at B is internally tangent to the circle centered at A. The smaller circle passes through the center of the larger circle and the length of AB is 4 units. If the smaller circle is removed from the larger circle, how many square units of the area of the larger circle will remain?

   (A) 16π

   (B) 36π

   (C) 48π

   (D) 64π

   (E) 800π

5. A line with the equation $y - 2x + 3 = 0$ for all real numbers would pass through which quadrants on the coordinate plane?

   (A) I, II and III only

   (B) III and IV only

   (C) I, II, III and IV

   (D) I, III and IV only

   (E) II and IV only

Answer explanations

1. **D.** Note what the question gives and what it's asking for. It provides units per hour and cost per unit. It also tells you the total desired hourly profit. You're supposed to find the price per unit.

   The first thing to do is eliminate obviously incorrect answer choices. You know that you're looking for the wholesale price that will yield a profit (which results from price minus cost to produce) of $19,500 per hour. Because the answers given are wholesale prices, you can eliminate Choices (A) and (B). The cost to produce each unit is $60. If the company charged the same amount for the MP3 players as it spent to produce them, it would make no profit, so Choice (A) is obviously incorrect. Choice (B) isn't much better. At a profit of just $5 per unit and 300 units per hour, the firm would make only $1,500 per hour.

   You've eliminated two answer choices. Evaluate the data to find the correct answer from the remaining three. You know that 300 units are produced every hour and that those 300 units have to net a profit of $19,500. If you knew the amount of profit per unit, you could add that to the amount each unit costs to produce and get the minimum wholesale price. Set up an equation with x as the profit per unit. Remember that *per* means to *divide*:

   $$x = \$19{,}500 \div 300$$

   $$x = 65$$

   The firm needs to make a profit of $65 per unit.

   You can't stop here and pick Choice (B). You're not done yet, but you know that because you've already eliminated Choice (B).

   You have to add profit to the per-unit production cost to get the final wholesale price:

   $$\$60 + \$65 = \$125.$$

   Correct answer: Choice (D).

   You could use estimation to solve this problem by rounding $19,500 up to the nearest convenient multiple of 300, which is $21,000, and then dividing 21 by 3 in your head and getting 7. This would tell you that you need a little less than $70 profit from each unit, or a little under $130 as the wholesale price (because $60 + $70 = $130).

2. **D.** Here's a relatively simple question that asks you to solve for x. The only element that makes it a little complex is that you're dealing with variables in fractions. Take a moment to consider the equation. The numerator in the fraction on the right is 3 times the numerator in the fraction on the left. Multiplying the numerator of the left-side fraction would make it equal to the numerator on the right side.

   When the numerators of two fractions are equal, their denominators are also equal, so creating equal numerators allows you to set the denominators equal to each other. Then just solve for x.

   1. **Multiply the left-side fraction by $\frac{3}{3}$.**

      This doesn't change the value of the fraction, because multiplying by $\frac{3}{3}$ is the same as multiplying by 1.

      $$\frac{2x}{4+2x} \times \frac{3}{3} = \frac{6x}{12+6x}$$

   2. **Set the denominators equal to each other and solve for x:**

      $$12 + 6x = 8x + 6$$

      $$6x = 8x - 6$$

      $$-2x = -6$$

      $$x = 3$$

   Correct answer: Choice (D).

You can also solve this question by cross-multiplying opposite numerators and denominators, but that's more complicated and time-consuming. You're in a race against the clock on the GMAT, so using shortcuts gives you the edge.

3. **E.** This function problem provides you with two outputs depending on the value of the input. If the input is greater than or equal to 2, the output is 4 times the absolute value of the input. If the input is less than 2, the output is the negative of the absolute value of the input.

Don't let the negative signs mess you up. If $r = -7$, then $g(-r)$ is the same as saying $g(7)$, because $-(-7)$ is 7. So the value of the input in this problem is 7.

Because 7 is greater than 2, you'll look to the first rule of the function $g(r)$. The solution to $g(r) = 4$ times the absolute value of 7 is simply 4×7, or 28. *Correct answer:* Choice (E).

If you confuse the signs, you'll come up with the negative version of the correct answer, which is Choice (A). You get the other answer choices when you use the incorrect rule.

4. **C.** This geometry question asks you to find the area of the large circle less the area of the small circle. Apply the formula for finding the area of a circle: $A = \pi r^2$.

Because the smaller circle passes through the center of the larger one, the radius of the larger circle is two times the radius of the smaller one: The radius of the larger circle equals 8. Apply the area formula to the larger circle:

$A = \pi(8^2)$

$A = 64\pi$

Determine the area of the smaller circle in the same way:

$A = \pi(4^2)$

$A = 16\pi$

Now subtract the two areas:

$64\pi - 16\pi = 48\pi$

Correct answer: Choice (C).

5. **D.** This coordinate geometry problem requires you to know the slope-intercept form: $y = mx + b$. But before you do any calculations, go ahead and eliminate Choice (C). No way can a straight line pass through all four quadrants of the coordinate plane. When you rearrange the equation into the slope-intercept form by isolating the y variable on the left side, you get $y = 2x - 3$. The slope-intercept form gives you the y-intercept and slope of the line. The value of b is the y-intercept, and the value of m is the slope.

For this kind of question, you may want to draw on your noteboard a coordinate plane graph and label the quadrants I, II, III, and IV. Nothing fancy, mind you, just enough to get your bearings. Now, draw a point below the origin on the y-axis representing –3, the y-intercept. Then draw a line that travels upward from left to right rising two units toward the top of the paper for every one to the right. Your figure doesn't have to be perfect. From a rudimentary drawing, you can immediately see that the line passes through Quadrants I, III, and IV.

So Choice (D) is your best choice. Choice (A) would be correct if you had a parallel line with a positive y-intercept. Choice (B) is possible for a line parallel to the x-axis with a negative y-intercept. Choice (E) would require a line with a negative slope passing through the origin.

Any line must travel through at least two quadrants, unless the line runs directly on top of either the x- or y-axis. A line that lies directly on top of an axis doesn't go *through* any quadrant. The lines that travel through only two quadrants are those that pass through the origin or are parallel to either the x- or the y-axis. All other lines must eventually travel through three quadrants.

Correct answer: Choice (D).

Chapter 16

All Together Now: A Mini Practice Quantitative Section

In This Chapter

▶ Honing your GMAT math skills by working through practice questions

▶ Taking a look at the answer explanations to understand what you did wrong — and right

---

Here's a chance to test your GMAT math skills before your embark on the real adventure of taking the test. This chapter contains only the types of math questions you'll see on the GMAT, so it's kind of like a mini practice test. To get a better idea of the time restrictions you'll face on test day, try to complete the questions in the following section in about 38 minutes. If you want to avoid the time pressure for now, feel free to just focus on answering the questions. You'll have the opportunity to time yourself again when you take the full-length practice tests included with this book.

If the question is a data sufficiency type (questions 3, 5, 7, 8, 11, 12, 14, 16, and 18 in the next section), choose one of the following choices:

▶ Choice (A) if Statement (1) *alone* is sufficient to answer the question but Statement (2) isn't

▶ Choice (B) if Statement (2) *alone* is sufficient but Statement (1) isn't

▶ Choice (C) if *both* Statements (1) and (2) *together* are sufficient to answer the question asked, but *neither* statement *alone* is sufficient

▶ Choice (D) if *each* statement *alone* is sufficient to answer the question asked

▶ Choice (E) if Statements (1) and (2) taken *together* still aren't sufficient (in other words, you need more information to answer the question)

Read through all the answer explanations (even the ones for the questions you answered correctly), because you want to make sure you know why you got the answer you did and because you may see something in the explanations that can help you with other questions.

Tackling GMAT Math Practice Questions

Here are 18 practice questions for the GMAT math section. Grab your pencil, set your timer for 38 minutes, and get started. (Try not to peek at the answers until you've come up with your own.)

1. If $\left(\dfrac{3}{y} + 2\right)(y - 5) = 0$ and $y \neq 5$, then $y =$

   (A) $-\dfrac{3}{2}$

   (B) $-\dfrac{2}{3}$

   (C) $\dfrac{2}{3}$

   (D) $\dfrac{3}{2}$

   (E) 6

2. If Esperanza will be 35 years old in 6 years, how old was she x years ago?

   (A) $41 - x$

   (B) $x - 41$

   (C) $35 - x$

   (D) $x - 29$

   (E) $29 - x$

3. What is the value of $\dfrac{x}{3} + \dfrac{y}{3}$?

   (1) $\dfrac{x + y}{3} = 6$

   (2) $x + y = 18$

   (A) (B) (C) (D) (E)

4. Sofa King is having "a sale on top of a sale!" The price of a certain couch, which already had been discounted by 20%, is further reduced by an additional 20%. These successive discounts are equivalent to a single discount of which of the following?

   (A) 40%

   (B) 38%

   (C) 36%

   (D) 30%

   (E) 20%

5. If x is a member of the set {44, 45, 47, 52, 55, 58}, what is the value of x?

   (1) x is even.

   (2) x is a multiple of 4.

   (A) (B) (C) (D) (E)

6. In a given year, the United States census estimated that there were approximately 6.5 billion people in the world and 300 million in the United States. Approximately what percentage of the world's population lived in the United States that year?

    (A) 0.0046%

    (B) 0.046%

    (C) 0.46%

    (D) 4.6%

    (E) 46%

7. The symbol © represents one of the following operations: addition, subtraction, multiplication, or division. What is the value of 4 © 5?

    (1) 0 © 1 = 0

    (2) 0 © 1 = 1

    (A) (B) (C) (D) (E)

8. How many burritos did Dave's Wraps sell today?

    (1) A total of 350 burritos was sold at Dave's Wraps yesterday, which is 100 fewer than twice the number sold today.

    (2) The number of burritos sold at Dave's Wraps yesterday was 20 more than the number sold today.

    (A) (B) (C) (D) (E)

9. To boost sales around the holidays, the government of the fictional country of Capitalistamia dictates that a citizen may purchase goods up to a total value of $1,000 tax-free but must pay a 7% tax on the portion of the total value in excess of $1,000. How much tax must be paid by a citizen who purchases goods with a total value of $1,220?

    (A) $14.00

    (B) $15.40

    (C) $54.60

    (D) $70.00

    (E) $87.40

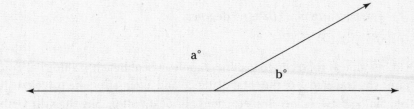

10. In the preceding figure, $\frac{a+b}{b} = \frac{5}{2}$, what does b equal?

    (A) 108

    (B) 99

    (C) 81

    (D) 72

    (E) 63

11. Is the value of x closer to 75 than it is to 100?

    (1) $100 - x > x - 75$

    (2) $x > 85$

    (A) (B) (C) (D) (E)

12. How long did it take Ms. Nkalubo to drive her family nonstop from her home to Charlestown, West Virginia?

    (1) Ms. Nkalubo's average speed for the trip was 45 miles per hour.

    (2) If Ms. Nkalubo's average speed for the trip had been $1\frac{1}{4}$ times faster, the trip would have taken three hours.

    (A) (B) (C) (D) (E)

13. The arithmetic mean and standard deviation for a certain normal distribution are 9.5 and 1.5, respectively. Which of these values is more than 2.5 standard deviations from the mean?

    (A) 5.75

    (B) 6

    (C) 6.5

    (D) 13.25

    (E) 13.5

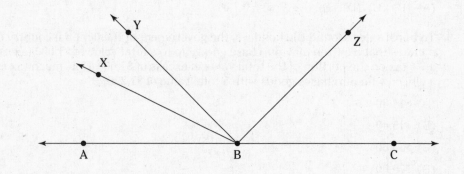

14. What is the measure of $\angle ABX$ in the preceding figure?

    (1) *BX* bisects $\angle ABY$ and *BZ* bisects $\angle YBC$.

    (2) The measure of $\angle YBZ$ is 60 degrees.

    (A) (B) (C) (D) (E)

15. On her annual road trip to visit her family in Seal Beach, California, Traci stopped to rest after she traveled $\frac{1}{3}$ of the total distance and again after she traveled $\frac{1}{4}$ of the distance remaining between her first stop and her destination. She then drove the remaining 200 miles and arrived safely at her destination. What was the total distance in miles from Traci's starting point to Seal Beach?

    (A) 250

    (B) 300

    (C) 350

    (D) 400

    (E) 550

16. In the fraction $\frac{a}{b}$, where a and b are positive integers, what is the value of b?

    (1) The lowest common denominator of $\frac{a}{b}$ and $\frac{1}{5}$ is 10.

    (2) $a = 3$

    (A) (B) (C) (D) (E)

17. If n is a positive integer and $x + 3 = 4^n$, which of the following could *not* be a value of x?

    (A) 1

    (B) 13

    (C) 45

    (D) 61

    (E) 253

18. A downtown theater sells each of its floor seats for a certain price and each of its balcony seats for a certain price. If Matthew, Linda, and Jake each buy tickets for a particular performance at this theater, how much did Jake pay for one floor seat and one balcony seat?

    (1) Matthew bought four floor seats and three balcony seats for $82.50.

    (2) Linda bought eight floor seats and six balcony seats for $165.

    (A) (B) (C) (D) (E)

Checking Out the Answer Explanations

1. **A.** The GMAT usually starts with a question of medium difficulty, and this one is in that range. If the product of two factors equals 0, then at least one of the factors must be 0 (because anything times 0 equals 0). Therefore, one of the factors in this equation must equal 0. You know it isn't the second one, because y doesn't equal 5, and y would have to equal 5 for the second term to result in 0.

   Therefore, you need to create an equation that sets the first factor equal to 0 and then solve for y. Here's what you get for the first factor:

   $$\frac{3}{y} + 2 = 0$$

   $$\frac{3}{y} = -2$$

   Cross-multiply (because $-2 = -\frac{2}{1}$) and solve:

   $$3 = -2y$$

   $$-\frac{3}{2} = y$$

2. **E.** If Esperanza will be 35 years old in 6 years, she is 29 right now ($35 - 6 = 29$). Therefore, to determine how old she was x years ago, simply subtract x from her current age of 29: $29 - x$.

3. **D.** This problem is simple when you recognize that because the two fractions have a common denominator, $\frac{x}{3} + \frac{y}{3}$ is the same thing as $\frac{x + y}{3}$.

Statement (1) says that $\frac{x+y}{3} = 6$, and because $\frac{x}{3} + \frac{y}{3} = \frac{x+y}{3}$, $\frac{x}{3} + \frac{y}{3}$ must also equal 6. So you know that Statement (1) is sufficient to answer the question and that the answer must be either Choice (A) or Choice (D). To figure out which it is, consider Statement (2). If it's sufficient, the answer is Choice (D). If not, the answer is Choice (A).

Because $\frac{x}{3} + \frac{y}{3} = \frac{x+y}{3}$, and Statement (2) tells you the value of $x + y$, you can substitute 18 for $x + y$ in the expression and solve for a known value (18 ÷ 3 = 6) So Statement (2) also provides sufficient information to answer the question.

4. **C.** This is a percent decrease question. You can apply a formula to solve it, but a faster and easier method is to apply actual numbers to the circumstances. To simplify your life, use a nice, round figure like $100.

If the couch originally cost $100 but was discounted by 20 percent, you'd multiply $100 by 20 percent (0.20) and subtract that from $100 to find the price after the first discount (100 × 0.20 = 20, and 100 – 20 = 80). After the first round of discounts, the couch cost $80.

However, the couch was discounted an additional 20 percent. Now, you have to repeat the process, this time using $80 as the original price (80 × 0.20 = 16, and 80 – 16 = 64). After both discounts, the couch cost $64.

But you're not finished yet. You need to calculate the total discount. The couch originally cost $100 and later cost $64. The discount, in dollars, is 100 – 64, which is $36. To find the percentage of the full discount, simply divide $36 by the original price of $100 ($\frac{36}{100} = 0.36$ or 36 percent).

5. **E.** Evaluate Statement (1). Knowing that x is even doesn't help you much. Three numbers in the set are even: 44, 52, and 58. So Statement (1) doesn't allow you to narrow down the value of x to one number. The answer can't be Choice (A) or Choice (D).

Consider Statement (2). Two numbers in the set are multiples of 4: 44 and 52. So even when you know that x is a multiple of 4, you can't come up with a fixed value for x. Statement (2) by itself isn't sufficient, so the answer can be only Choice (C) or (E). You still have one more evaluation: whether the two statements together provide sufficient information.

Multiples of 4 are always even, so the two statements together don't point you to the value of x. So the correct answer is Choice (E).

6. **D.** This question requires you to work with very large numbers, so you need to know what large numbers look like.

One billion = 1,000,000,000, and 1 million = 1,000,000. In other words, 1 billion is 1,000 million.

Now, look at the question at hand: 6.5 billion is written as 6,500,000,000. Writing out 6 billion is obvious, and 0.5 billion is one-half of 1,000 million, which is 500 million, or 500,000,000. You write 300 million like 300,000,000. To solve for the percentage, simply divide 300,000,000 by 6,500,000,000, using the fraction form:

$$\frac{300,000,000}{6,500,000,000}$$

Simplify things by canceling out eight zeros on the top and bottom. (This step is legal because you're just reducing your fraction.) Then divide 3 by 65.

You don't actually have to complete the mathematical calculation, because all the answer choices are derivatives of 46. You do need to know, though, that when you divide 3 by 65, your answer will have three places after the decimal. If you can't figure this in your head, quickly set up the division problem on your noteboard and mark where the decimal will be in your answer.

So 3 ÷ 65 = 0.046, but the question asks for a percentage. To convert the decimal to a percentage, move the decimal point two places to the right and add a percentage sign. The answer is 4.6 percent.

7. **B.** To determine the value of 4 © 5, you have to figure out which of the four operations the symbol represents. The way to do so is to plug each of the operations into the equations offered by each of the two statements and see whether either of them allows you to narrow the symbol down to just one operation.

Statement (1) gives you 0 © 1 = 0. Plug in each operation to see whether any make the equation true. You know addition and subtraction don't work because you can't add or subtract 1 to or from a number and end up with the same number. Both multiplication and division work: 0 × 1 = 0, and 0 ÷ 1 = 0. So Statement (1) isn't sufficient because it doesn't allow you to narrow the symbol down to just one operation. The answer, then, can't be Choice (A) or Choice (D).

Statement (2) offers 0 © 1 = 1. The only difference between this equation and the one in Statement (1) is the answer. You know that multiplication and division don't work, because they already produced an answer of 0. Subtraction results in –1, so the only operation that works is addition (0 + 1 = 1). This means that Statement (2) alone gives you enough information to determine which operation the symbol stands for, which allows you to figure out the value of 4 © 5.

Data sufficiency questions don't ask for the actual numeric answer, so don't take the time to determine the actual value of the operation (not that it would take you long to do so for this question).

8. **A.** Evaluate each statement to determine whether it allows you to figure out the exact number of burrito sales for the day.

You can construct a mathematical equation from the language in Statement (1). The unknown is the total number of today's burrito sales. Let b = today's burritos. *Fewer* means subtraction, so yesterday's sales equal $2b - 100$. The equation then looks like this:

$$350 = 2b - 100$$

This equation has only one variable, so you know you can easily solve this equation to find out how many burritos left the shop today. (Don't take the time to actually figure it out, though!) Statement (1) is sufficient, and the answer is either Choice (A) or Choice (D). To determine which it is, evaluate Statement (2).

Statement (2) tells you that the number of burritos sold at Dave's Wraps yesterday was 20 more than the number sold today, but this statement gives you two variables. You don't know how many burritos were sold today, *and* you don't know how many went out the door yesterday. If y stands for yesterday's burrito sales, the equation would look something like this: $y = 20 + b$. You can't definitively solve an equation with two variables without more information, so Statement (2) isn't sufficient. The correct answer is Choice (A).

(Oh, and if you won't be able to sleep unless we confirm for you the number of burritos sold today, it's 225: 450 = 2b, so 225 = b. Now be sure to get your sleep; you need it for the GMAT!)

9. **B.** The first thing that should jump out at you is that the first $1,000 of purchases is tax-free, so you don't need to consider the first $1,000. Subtract $1,000 from $1,220 to get the value of purchases that will actually be taxed: $220.

To find the amount of tax due, you multiply 220 by 7 percent (or 0.07), but you don't have to take the time to fully work out the calculation. To make things simple, you can estimate: 200 is close to 220, and 200 × 0.07 is 14.00, so the amount has to be just a little more than $14.

The only answer that's just a little more than $14 is Choice (B). If you take the time to multiply 220 and 0.07, you'll find that it's exactly $15.40. But because this is a test where saving time is crucial, avoid making full calculations whenever possible.

10. **D.** The key to solving this problem is to recognize that a and b are supplementary angles, which means they add up to 180 degrees: $a + b = 180$. (Chapter 12 has more information on shapes and angles.)

Now all you have to do is substitute 180 for $a + b$ in the original equation and solve:

$$\frac{a+b}{b} = \frac{5}{2}$$
$$\frac{180}{b} = \frac{5}{2}$$
$$5b = 360$$
$$b = 72$$

So the correct answer is Choice (D).

11. **A.** To solve this problem, recognize that the halfway point between 100 and 75 is 87.5, so if x is greater than 87.5, it's closer to 100. If it's less than 87.5, it's closer to 75. (If it equals 87.5, it's the same distance from both.)

If the difference between 100 and x $(100 - x)$ is greater than the difference between x and 75 $(x - 75)$, then x must be less than 87.5, because values greater than 87.5 would make $100 - x$ less than $x - 75$. Therefore, you absolutely know from Statement (1) that x is closer to 75. It's sufficient to answer the question, and the answer is either Choice (A) or Choice (D).

Now, look at Statement (2). Knowing that $x > 85$ doesn't help, because values above 87.5 would make x closer to 100 and values between 85 and 87.5 would make it closer to 75. Statement (2) isn't sufficient. For more about inequalities, consult Chapter 11.

12. **B.** This is a distance problem, so to determine the time of Ms. Nkalubo's trip, you have to use the distance equation.

The formula for distance is $r \times t = d$, which stands for Rate × Time = Distance (see Chapter 11 for details about this formula).

Statement (1) is pretty easy to evaluate. Knowing that her average speed was 45 miles per hour gives you the rate value for the equation but nothing more, so you're left with an unknown distance and an unknown amount of time. You can't solve an equation with two variables without more information. Therefore, you can't calculate her time. Statement (1) isn't sufficient, so the answer can't be Choice (A) or Choice (D).

Statement (2) takes a little more thought. At first it may not appear to give you enough information to figure out time. But if you look further, you'll see that it enables you to set up two simultaneous equations, and when you have two simultaneous equations with two variables, you can find the value of either variable. Here's how: The first equation is for Ms. Nkalubo's actual trip, which you can denote as Trip 1 (we've used a subscript 1 to show the values for Trip 1). Use the standard formula for distance:

$$r_1 \times t_1 = d_1$$

That's as much as you know about Trip 1 for now.

The second equation is for the theoretical trip proposed in the problem, which you can call Trip 2 (which we've denoted with a subscript 2). Start with the standard distance formula:

$$r_2 \times t_2 = d_2$$

Take the equation further with the information provided by Statement (2). Begin with the easy value. Trip 2 would take 3 hours, so $r_2 \times 3 = d_2$. You also know that Ms. Nkalubo's rate for Trip 1 was $\frac{5}{4}$ the rate of Trip 2. So $r_2 = \frac{5}{4}r_1$. Substitute this value for rate into the equation for Trip 2:

$$\frac{5}{4}r_1 \times 3 = d_2$$

You should also recognize that d_1 and d_2 have the same value because the distances of the two trips are the same (it's the same trip!). Therefore, you can set the left side of the first equation equal to the left side of the second and divide the rate variable from both sides.

At this point, you have an equation with only one variable, so you know you can solve for the exact length of Ms. Nkalubo's trip. Statement (2)'s information is sufficient to answer the question, so the correct answer is Choice (B).

For those of you who hate to be left hanging and need to see how the equation turns out, we'll finish the calculations. Just remember, you shouldn't do this part for the test; it's a waste of time. Here's what the solution looks like:

$$r_1 \times t_1 = \frac{5}{4} r_1 \times 3$$

$$t_1 = \frac{5}{4} \times 3$$

$$t_1 = \frac{15}{4}$$

That's equal to 3 hours and 45 minutes. The family was probably ready for some action after almost four hours in the car!

13. **E.** Don't let the language of this problem scare you. You're really just applying basic operations.

The arithmetic mean is 9.5 and the standard deviation is 1.5, so you'll use a deviation of 1.5 to find values that stray from the mean. This means that the values that are 1 standard deviation from the mean are 11 and 8, which is the mean (9.5) plus or minus the standard deviation (1.5). The values that are 2 standard deviations from the mean are 12.5 and 6.5, which you get from adding and subtracting 3 (2×1.5) from the mean of 9.5. The values that are 3 standard deviations from the mean are 14 and 5, which you derive by adding and subtracting 4.5 (3×1.5) from the mean.

So to solve this problem, you find that the values that are 2.5 standard deviations from the mean are 13.25 and 5.75, because 2.5×1.5 is 3.75. Look for an answer choice that's more than 13.25 or less than 5.75. The answer is 13.5, Choice (E).

14. **C.** The four angles lie along a straight line, so they add up to 180 degrees. (If you need a refresher on the properties of angles, read Chapter 12.)

Although it's lovely to know that *BX* bisects (which means cuts exactly in half) the two angles on the left side and that *BZ* bisects the two angles on the right side, without the measure of at least one of the angles, you have no way of knowing the measurements of any of the angles. So Statement (1) isn't sufficient, and the answer has to be Choice (B), Choice (C), or Choice (E).

Statement (2) gives you only one of the angle measures, which by itself doesn't clarify the measure of $\angle ABX$ any better than Statement (1) does. Statement (2) isn't sufficient.

But remember that we said that for Statement (1) to work, you just need a value for at least one of the angles. Well, Statement (2) provides that value. Taken together, the two statements allow you to solve for the measure of $\angle ABX$. You can stop right there. The correct answer is Choice (C).

You don't have to actually figure out the measurement of the angle, but because we're so thorough, we're going to go through the calculations for you anyway. This step is unnecessary on test day. Knowing that *BZ* bisects $\angle YBC$ and that $\angle YBZ$ measures 60 degrees allows you to deduce that $\angle ZBC$ is also 60 degrees. Additionally, you've now accounted for 120 of the total 180 degrees allotted for the four angles, which leaves you 60 degrees to play with. Finally, because *BX* bisects $\angle ABY$, two equal angles remain. Two equal angles that together equal 60 degrees must equal 30 degrees each, because $60 \div 2 = 30$.

15. **D.** To find the total distance of Traci's trip, set up an equation that expresses the sum of the three separate trip portions. Let x equal the total distance in miles. Traci stopped to rest after she traveled $\frac{1}{3}$ of the total distance, so the first part of the trip is $\frac{1}{3}x$. She stopped again after she traveled $\frac{1}{4}$ of the distance remaining between her first stop and her destination, which is the total distance she traveled minus the first part of her trip. You can represent the second part of the trip mathematically, like this:

$$\frac{1}{4}\left(x - \frac{1}{3}x\right)$$

The third part of the trip is the remaining 200 miles. Add up the three parts of the trip to set up the equation and solve for total distance:

$$x = \frac{1}{3}x + \frac{1}{4}\left(x - \frac{1}{3}x\right) + 200$$

$$x = \frac{1}{3}x + \frac{1}{4}\left(\frac{3}{3}x - \frac{1}{3}x\right) + 200$$

$$x = \frac{1}{3}x + \frac{1}{4}\left(\frac{2}{3}x\right) + 200$$

$$x = \frac{1}{3}x + \frac{1}{6}x + 200$$

At this point, you can make it easier on yourself by multiplying each expression on both sides by 6 to get rid of the fractions:

$$2x + x + 1{,}200 = 6x$$

$$3x + 1{,}200 = 6x$$

$$1{,}200 = 3x$$

$$400 = x$$

Traci traveled a total distance of 400 miles, so the correct answer is Choice (D).

16. **E.** This problem seems simple, but if you try to solve it too quickly, you may miss something. So consider all possibilities.

Evaluating Statement (1) can be tricky. Don't jump to the conclusion that if the lowest common denominator (LCD) of the two fractions is 10, then $\frac{a}{b}$ must have a denominator of 10 and, therefore, $b = 10$.

The value of b could also equal 2, and the two fractions would still have an LCD of 10. Because b has two possible values, Statement (1) is insufficient. Therefore, the answer is Choice (B), Choice (C), or Choice (E).

Statement (2) is easier to evaluate. The value of the numerator has no bearing on the value of the denominator, so the fact that $a = 3$ is irrelevant to the value of b. Statement (2) is also insufficient, which means the answer is either Choice (C) or Choice (E).

Knowing that $a = 3$ tells you nothing about whether b is 10 or 2, which means that the two statements together are still insufficient to answer the question.

17. **C.** You could try to solve for n, but a faster and easier way to approach this problem is to plug each of the answer choices into the given equation and pick the one that doesn't make the expression true:

   ✔ Choice (A) gives you 1. Plug in 1 for x in the equation: $1 + 3 = 4^n$. Doing so makes $n = 1$, which is a positive integer. Because 1 is a possible value for x, Choice (A) is wrong.

   ✔ If you substitute 13 from Choice (B), you get $13 + 3 = 4^n$. And $13 + 3$ is 16 and 4^2 is 16. If $n = 2$, it's a positive integer, so eliminate Choice (B).

✔ For Choice (C), you substitute 45 into the equation: $45 + 3 = 4^n$. The equation comes out to $48 = 4^n$, and although it may seem like 4 could be a root of 48, it's not. There's no way n could be a positive integer when $x = 45$. Choice (C) is the correct answer. You can choose Choice (C) and go on, or you can check the last two answers just to be sure. Your decision depends on how much time you have remaining.

✔ If you plug in 61 from Choice (D) into the equation, you get $61 + 3 = 4^n$. And $61 + 3 = 64$, which is 4^3. But 3 is a positive integer, so Choice (D) can't be right.

✔ Choice (E) is 253, and $253 + 3 = 256$. And 256 is 4^4, which would make $n = 4$, a positive integer. Choice (E) makes the equation true, so it's the wrong answer.

WARNING!

Be careful when you answer questions that ask you to find the answer that *can't* be true. In these cases, if an answer choice works, you have to eliminate it rather than choose it. Keep reminding yourself of your goal.

18. **E.** This is the last question, and it happens to be one of the most difficult ones of the bunch. At first, you may think that you can solve this question with two simultaneous equations. However, when you take a closer look, you see this isn't the case. To get started, let f = the cost of a floor seat and b = the cost of a balcony seat. Then evaluate the statements.

If you write out Matthew's information in Statement (1) in mathematical terms, you get an equation with two variables: $4f + 3b = 82.50$. As we've said before, you can't solve an equation with two variables without additional information. This statement alone isn't sufficient, so the answer is either Choice (B), (C), or (E).

Likewise, Statement (2)'s information leads to an equation with two variables: $8f + 6b = 165$. This equation alone isn't enough to solve the problem, so the answer has to be Choice (C) or Choice (E).

Here's where you may have gotten prematurely excited. You may have thought that Statements (1) and (2) provided simultaneous equations that could be manipulated to give you the value of one of the variables. But if you look more closely, you'll see that the equations are exactly the same. When you reduce the second equation or expand the first, you have identical equations. Look at the second equation:

$$8f + 6b = 165$$

Divide both sides by 2:

$$4f + 3b = 82.50$$

You don't have simultaneous equations at all, and the two statements together won't enable you to solve the problem. Mark Choice (E).

Part V

Excelling on the Integrated Reasoning Section

The 5th Wave   By Rich Tennant

"I'm studying for the new section of the GMAT,
Integrated Reasoning with Parents, Boyfriend,
and Little Brother."

In this part . . .

The second section of the GMAT contains question types that you've likely never experienced before on a standardized test. To answer these questions, you apply analytical reasoning and math skills to real-life situations. Only 12 questions appear in this section, but almost every question has at least two or three parts, and you have to answer each part correctly to receive credit for the question. So half the battle of this section is mastering time management.

This part relates how to approach each of the four question types (multi-source reasoning, table analysis, graphics interpretation, and two-part analysis) and reviews the crucial math, analytical, and data interpretation skills you need to successfully reason your way through this section. The mini practice test for this part is featured on the CD so that you can see just how this section works on the computerized test.

Chapter 17

Best of Both Worlds: The Integrated Reasoning Section

. . . .

In This Chapter

▶ Discovering what to expect from the integrated reasoning section

▶ Understanding how the integrated reasoning section is scored

▶ Planning how to use your time wisely to answer questions

▶ Working through the four integrated reasoning question types

. . . .

Integrated reasoning (IR) questions appear right after the analytical writing section. The IR section throws you something completely different from the five-answer multiple-choice questions you're probably used to. The 12 questions in the integrated reasoning section are formatted in a variety of ways and include tables and graphs to test how well you apply reasoning skills to different scenarios. A lot goes on at once in this section, and this chapter gives you the information you need to manage it all successfully within the 30-minute time limit.

Understanding What the IR Section Is All About

True to its name, the integrated reasoning section combines the critical reasoning skills tested in the verbal reasoning section with some of the math skills you use to solve quantitative reasoning questions. Therefore, if you're well prepared for the GMAT's math and verbal sections, you should do well in the IR section, too. We explain the details of the IR section and the purpose behind it in the next two sections.

Skills tested

The most common math computations in the IR section involve these areas:

✔ Basic statistics, such as average, median, mode, and range

✔ Percentages

✔ Rate and distance

✔ Functions

✔ Geometry formulas

You'll need to apply these essentials of critical reasoning:

✔ Basic elements of logical arguments: premises, conclusions, and assumptions

✔ How to strengthen and weaken an argument

✔ Argument types: cause and effect, analogy, and statistical

You can review the necessary math concepts in Chapters 12, 13, and 14. Read more about evaluating logical arguments in Chapter 5.

Question format

The IR section presents you with 12 questions, one question at a time, and you have 30 minutes to answer them. Almost every question has multiple parts. To get credit for answering a question correctly, you have to answer *all* its parts correctly. You don't receive partial credit for getting one part of the question correct. Unlike the verbal and quantitative reasoning sections, the IR section isn't computer adaptive. So the order in which you receive questions is preordained and not based on your performance.

Your IR score is based on your answers to four types of questions. On average, you can expect to come across about three of each question type on the GMAT, but the actual number of questions of each type and the order in which they appear may vary. So count on seeing at least a couple of each of these four question types crop up on your test:

- ✔ **Table analysis:** This three-part IR question offers you a spreadsheet of values that you can order in different ways by clicking the heading of each column. You use the data to make judgments about three pieces of information; each of your judgments has to be correct to get credit for the question.

- ✔ **Two-part analysis:** Based on a short written explanation of a phenomenon, situation, or mathematical problem, you come up with the proper assertions or mathematical expressions that meet the two interrelated criteria presented in the question.

- ✔ **Graphics interpretation:** A graph or chart gives you all the data you need to complete the two missing pieces of information in one or two statements. You choose from a pull-down menu of several answer options to record your answers.

- ✔ **Multi-source reasoning:** These properly named questions present you with several sources of information, such as short passages, graphs and charts, and business documents, from which you draw logical conclusions to answer questions in either of two formats: standard five-answer multiple choice questions and three-part questions that ask you to evaluate statements.

Using the GMAT calculator

The calculator in the GMAT IR section looks a lot like the calculator you can purchase at your local dollar store or the one that appears when you access the Microsoft calculator accessory. It has minimal features but everything you need to work out the calculations in the IR section. When you click on *Calculator* at the top of your screen, the tool pops up. You can move it anywhere on the screen by dragging it with your mouse. It stays open until you close it by clicking the *X* in the upper right corner of the tool.

The number and operation keys work just like a regular calculator. You can clear a single entry with the CE key or just the right digit with the ← key. Start over again from scratch by clicking the C key, which wipes out the entry and all its associated computations.

Unlike a scientific calculator, the GMAT calculator doesn't follow the order of operations. So if you enter 4 + 5 * 10, you get 90 instead of 54. To get the right value, you have to enter the values in the proper order, 5 * 10 + 4.

The MS key stores a value to the memory. You can add values to the memory with the M+ key and subtract them with the M- key. To access the value in the memory, click MR. To clear it, click MC.

The ± changes a positive value to negative and a negative value to positive. The / key means divide, and the * key multiples. To find the square root of 34, you enter 34 and click on √. To find 35 percent of 70, you enter 70 * 35 and hit the % key. Though we doubt you'll use it much, the 1/x key finds the reciprocal of any integer. To find the value of the reciprocal of 4, for example, you enter 4 and click the 1/x key — voila! — 0.25 appears.

We cover the steps to answering each question type in the section "Approaching Each Question Type," later in this chapter.

To assist you with the mathematical computations you may need to make for some of the IR questions, the GMAT software provides you with a simple calculator. Whenever you need it, you click the box labeled *Calculator* and something that looks like Figure 17-1 appears. You select its functions by using your mouse. Don't get too attached to it, though; the calculator is available only for IR questions, so you won't be able to use it in the quantitative reasoning section. If you want more information on the calculator's features, see the nearby sidebar "Using the GMAT calculator."

CALCULATOR	X

123.45

MC	MR	MS	M+	M-
←	CE	C	±	√
7	8	9	/	%
4	5	6	*	1/x
1	2	3	-	=
0		.	+	

Figure 17-1: GMAT calculator.

Illustration by Wiley, Composition Services Graphics

 Because using a computer calculator can be awkward, you'll likely answer most IR questions more quickly by using estimation or working out calculations by hand on your noteboard. Save the calculator for only the most complex or precise computations.

Figuring Out How the IR Section Is Scored

Like the score you receive for the analytical writing section, your integrated reasoning score has no influence on your overall GMAT score, which consists of the combination of only your quantitative reasoning and verbal reasoning scores. Based on your performance in the IR section, your raw score is converted to a scaled score that ranges in whole numbers from 1 to 8 and is recorded separately from all the other scores.

MBA programs decide how they use your IR score and may choose to disregard it altogether. So your IR score is unlikely to make much of an impression unless it's unusually low, in the 1 to 3 score range, or really high, such as the rare 7 or 8. A midrange score of 4, 5, or 6 likely won't significantly hurt or help your chances of admission.

Making the Most of Your Time

If you've already calculated that answering 12 questions in 30 minutes gives you 2.5 minutes to answer each question, you may be celebrating the fact that that gives you even more time per question than you have for the quantitative and verbal reasoning sections. Don't get too excited just yet. Almost every IR question has multiple parts, and you have to answer all parts of the question correctly to be credited with a correct answer. When you consider the average number of sub-questions contained within each of those 12 questions, the actual number of IR answers you have to come up with in 30 minutes may be as high as 30. Therefore, you have to use your time wisely as you move through the section.

You'll likely feel the time crunch more fiercely in this section than the others. We provide some coping skills to help you through it:

- ✔ **Conceal the timer.** To maintain your sanity, refrain from constant clock-watching. Hide the timer on the computer by clicking on it. After you answer about three questions, reveal the timer by clicking on it again. It counts down from 30 minutes, so if you're at 22 minutes, you're cruising comfortably. If you're at 21 or fewer, you may need to make some more calculated guesses to move through the section at a successful pace.

- ✔ **Know when to move on.** Discipline yourself to submit your best stab at an answer if you find yourself spending more than several minutes on any one question. You don't want to sacrifice getting to an easy, less time-consuming question because you've worked too long on a harder question. You can't go back and revisit questions after you submitted your answers, so this practice may be difficult for you, especially if you tenaciously seek perfection. Take a deep breath, mark your best guess, and move on to what lies ahead.

- ✔ **Write stuff down.** Don't be afraid to spend a little time upfront analyzing the loads of data in some IR questions. Unless you're someone who can juggle a lot of details in your head, you should write on your noteboard as you think. A little note-taking may save you from reading information over again, which is a real time waster.

- ✔ **Whisper to yourself.** Studies show that processing information is easier if you speak out loud. Don't be afraid to whisper your way through some of the more complex problems the IR section throws at you. You'll likely take the test in a cubicle-like setting, so if you speak quietly, you won't disturb anyone.

Approaching Each Question Type

Each of the four IR question types tests your analytical ability in a slightly different way, so your approach depends on the question format. This section outlines the important considerations for handling each type.

Table analysis

Table analysis questions present you with a table that contains several columns of data, similar to the one in Figure 17-2. As you can see, a little bit of explanatory material precedes the table, but don't waste too much time reading those words. Usually, everything you need to answer the question appears in the data table.

The *Sort By* feature at the top of the table allows you to organize the information by column heading, an element that comes in handy when you analyze the three statements that follow the table. When you click on *Sort By,* a drop-down menu of all column headings appears. Clicking on the column heading in the menu causes the table to rearrange its data by that category. So if you click on *Cuisine Type* in the drop-down menu in Figure 17-2, the table would rearrange the order of the rows alphabetically so that all the American restaurants would be listed first, followed by the Asian, Italian, Latin, Mexican, Steakhouse, and Seafood restaurants, respectively.

Using the information in the table, you decide whether the proper response to each statement is *True* or *False, Inferable* or *Not Inferable,* or *Yes* or *No,* or some other similar either/or answer choice dictated by the specifications of the question. Then you indicate your choice by clicking on the circle next to the appropriate answer.

During Lexington Restaurant Week, participating eateries design a three-course meal that they will offer throughout the week at a set price of either $20, $30, or $40 a person, excluding drinks (unless otherwise noted), tax, and tip, as reported on the following table.

Sort By:	Restaurant
	Cuisine Type
	Price Per Meal
	Neighborhood
	Wine Included? (Y/N)
	Average Daily Number of Meals Sold

Restaurant	Cuisine Type	Price Per Meal	Neighborhood	Wine Included? (Y/N)	Average Daily Number of Meals Sold
Bendimere's	Steakhouse	$40	Downtown	N	150
Big Ben's Bistro	American	$30	Central	Y	175
Chang's	Asian	$20	Chinatown	N	142
Frank's House	American	$20	Downtown	N	175
Hadley's on the Beach	Seafood	$40	Uptown	Y	160
Meritage	American	$40	Uptown	N	152
Ocean View	Seafood	$40	Uptown	N	151
Pesce Blue	Seafood	$40	Downtown	Y	164
The Purple Parrot	Latin	$30	Northwest	Y	134
Sorbello's	Italian	$40	Old Town	Y	175
Sushi Fusco	Asian	$30	Old Town	N	100
Thai Time	Asian	$20	Northwest	N	87
Valenzuela's	Mexican	$20	Downtown	N	113

Figure 17-2: Sample table analysis format.

Illustration by Wiley, Composistion Services Graphics

These questions require you to manipulate data and make observations and calculations. Some of the most common calculations are statistical ones, such as percentages, averages, medians, and ratios, so table analysis questions can be some of the easiest questions to answer in the IR section. Here's how to make sure you get them right:

- ✔ **Jump to the question immediately.** Most of the information you need appears in the table, so you rarely need to read the introductory paragraph that comes before the table. Glance at the column headings to get an idea of the type of information the table provides, and then move promptly to the question.

- ✔ **Read the question carefully.** You're most likely to get tripped up on these questions simply because you haven't read them carefully enough to figure out exactly what data they ask you to evaluate.

- ✔ **Isolate the relevant column heading.** Often, the key to answering a table analysis question is ordering the data properly. Quickly figure out which column provides you with the best way to arrange the data and sort by that column. For example, if you were asked for the neighborhood on the list with the most participating restaurants, you'd sort by *Neighborhood*.

- ✔ **Make accurate computations.** Determine exactly what calculations the question requires and perform them accurately, either in your head or on the calculator. Based on Figure 17-2, for example, you could easily figure the restaurant with the greatest average daily number of meals sold by sorting by that column and glancing at the highest number. However, calculating which participating restaurant in the Downtown neighborhood brought in the greatest average daily gross revenue may require the calculator to multiply each restaurant's price per meal by its average daily number of meals sold.

✔ **Make use of your noteboard.** Keep track of more complex calculations on your noteboard. As you calculate each Downtown restaurant's average daily gross revenue, for example, record the results on your noteboard. Then you can easily compare the four values without having to memorize them.

You can apply these strategies to a sample question.

For each of the following statements, select *Yes* if the statement is true based on the information provided in Figure 17-2. Otherwise, choose *No*.

Yes	No	
○	○	A. The average price per meal for all participating restaurants in the Downtown neighborhood was approximately $30.
○	○	B. The average price per meal for participating restaurants in the Old Town neighborhood was less than the average price per meal in the Downtown neighborhood.
○	○	C. Participating restaurants that included wine with the meal in the Uptown neighborhood sold more meals on average per day than participating restaurants that did not include wine with the meal.

Statement (A) references two columns, *Price Per Meal* and *Neighborhood*. Sorting by *Neighborhood* makes more sense because it lists all Downtown restaurants together so that you may better view and compare each Downtown restaurant's price per meal. After you've sorted by *Neighborhood,* the table looks like this:

Restaurant	Cuisine Type	Price Per Meal	Neighborhood	Wine Included? (Y/N)	Average Daily Number of Meals Sold
Big Ben's Bistro	American	$30	Central	Y	175
Chang's	Asian	$20	Chinatown	N	142
Bendimere's	Steakhouse	$40	Downtown	N	150
Frank's House	American	$20	Downtown	N	175
Pesce Blue	Seafood	$40	Downtown	Y	164
Valenzuela's	Mexican	$20	Downtown	N	113
The Purple Parrot	Latin	$30	Northwest	Y	134
Thai Time	Asian	$20	Northwest	N	87
Sorbello's	Italian	$40	Old Town	Y	175
Sushi Fusco	Asian	$30	Old Town	N	100
Hadley's on the Beach	Seafood	$40	Uptown	Y	160
Meritage	American	$40	Uptown	N	152
Ocean View	Seafood	$40	Uptown	N	151

This arrangement allows you to see that two participating restaurants in the Downtown neighborhood charged $20 per meal and two charged $40 per meal. The number of $20 meals sold by both restaurants is 288, and the number of $40 meals sold at the two other restaurants is 314. To find the weighted average, multiply $20 by 288 and $40 by 314. Add the two products and divide by the total number of meals sold (602):

$$A = \frac{(20 \times 288) + (40 \times 314)}{602}$$
$$A = \frac{5,760 + 12,560}{602}$$
$$A = 30.43$$

Because $30.43 is approximately $30, you can say that the average price of a Downtown meal was $30. The answer is *Yes*.

You've already figured out the second calculation for Statement (B). The average price per meal at a Downtown restaurant is about $30. You can write D = 30 on your noteboard to remind you. All the Uptown restaurants charged $40 per meal, so the average price per meal in Uptown is greater than the average price in Downtown. Select *No*.

Statement (C) again focuses on one neighborhood, so you don't have to resort the table. The one restaurant that included wine in the meal price sold 160 meals on average per day, which is more than the 152 and 151 sold by the other two restaurants in the neighborhood. The answer is *Yes*.

Table analysis questions may not require that you use all the data provided. For example, you didn't need to evaluate *Cuisine Type* for any of the question parts in the example question. Don't worry if you don't use the data in some columns at all. Part of the task in answering table analysis questions is knowing what data is important and what's irrelevant.

Two-part analysis

When you see a paragraph or two of information that sets you up to choose two pieces of information from a table with three columns, you know you're dealing with a two-part analysis question. You select the answer for the first part of the question in the first column and the answer to the second part in the second column. The third column provides the set of possible answer choices for each part.

Reading the explanatory paragraph for these questions is absolutely essential. It provides the conditions you need to consider and clarifies what each part of the question asks for. Read each possibility in the third column carefully. Often, the differences among the options are subtle.

The GMAT usually uses the two-part analysis question to test mathematical skills (such as figuring functions and the properties of geometric shapes) and verbal logical reasoning abilities (such as strengthening and weakening arguments). Often the best way to figure out the answer for the math variety is to try each of the possible values to see which ones fulfill the requirements. Usually, the best way to answer the verbal type is by process of elimination.

The following two sample questions give you an example of a math two-part analysis and a verbal two-part analysis.

EXAMPLE

A set of expressions consists of a total of four expressions: these three expressions {$2n + 8$, $n + 4$, $6n - 2$} and one additional expression. From the following expressions, select the one that could be the fourth expression in the set and the one that could be the resulting arithmetic mean of the four expressions in the set. Make only one selection per column.

Fourth Expression of the Set	Arithmetic Mean of the Set	
○	○	A. $2n$
○	○	B. $3n + 2$
○	○	C. $3n - 2$
○	○	D. $12n + 8$
○	○	E. $48n + 32$
○	○	F. $4n + 8$

Approach this question by trying out the possible answer choices as potential fourth expressions to see which, when it's included with other expressions in the set, results in an arithmetic mean that's another of the possible answer choices.

First, evaluate the three provided expressions. All contain one-digit values that are multiplied by n and then have a one-digit value added or subtracted from that term. So evaluate similar expressions, such as Choices (B), (C), and (F) before you consider less similar expressions, such as Choices (A), (D), and (E).

If Choice (B), $3n + 2$, were the fourth expression, the average mean of the set would be the result of applying the average formula:

$$\frac{(2n+8)+(n+4)+(6n-2)+(3n+2)}{4} = A$$

$$\frac{12n+12}{4} = A$$

$$3n + 3 = A$$

Because $3n + 3$ isn't one of the answer choices, you know that $3n + 2$ can't be the fourth expression.

Try Choice (C), $3n - 2$. If you wrote your calculations for $3n + 2$ on your noteboard, you know that the first term of the average mean is the same because the $3n$ doesn't change.

$$\frac{(2n+8)+(n+4)+(6n-2)+(3n-2)}{4} = A$$

$$\frac{12n+8}{4} = A$$

$$3n + 2 = A$$

This value is a possible option. When the fourth expression in the set is $3n - 2$, the average mean of the set is $3n + 2$. Select Choice (C) for the first column and Choice (B) for the second. Only one possible set of answers exists, so if you're confident about your calculations, you don't have to consider the other expressions. Submit your answer and move on.

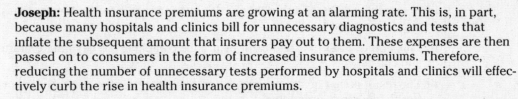

Joseph: Health insurance premiums are growing at an alarming rate. This is, in part, because many hospitals and clinics bill for unnecessary diagnostics and tests that inflate the subsequent amount that insurers pay out to them. These expenses are then passed on to consumers in the form of increased insurance premiums. Therefore, reducing the number of unnecessary tests performed by hospitals and clinics will effectively curb the rise in health insurance premiums.

Ronald: Often, the unnecessary diagnostics that you speak of are the result of decisions made by doctors on behalf of their patients. Doctors usually choose the diagnostics that allow them to bill insurers for more money but may not necessarily benefit the patient in a meaningful way or influence the course of treatment chosen. As a result, in order to succeed in reducing the number of unnecessary tests, patients should be allowed to decide which course of diagnostics they would like to undergo.

In the following table, identify the unique assumption upon which each argument depends. Make only one selection in each column: one in the first column for the best representation of Joseph's assumption in his argument and one in the second column for the best representation of Ronald's.

Joseph	Ronald	
O	O	A. Doctors are generally able to determine with great reliability which diagnostic procedures and tests will yield the most effective results.
O	O	B. Tests and diagnostic procedures make up a significant portion of the bills that are sent to insurers.
O	O	C. Insurance companies in other industries, such as auto and home, have been able to reduce costs by reducing the number of unnecessary repairs and replacements on claims for automobiles and homes.
O	O	D. Patients are not as likely as doctors to choose the most expensive diagnostics and tests.
O	O	E. Health insurance premiums have increased twice as fast in the past 5 years than they have over an average of the past 25 years.

Whereas the sample math two-part analysis question required you to figure out the answers to both parts at the same time, this verbal reasoning sample question is more easily handled one column at a time. First, consider the assumption that's most likely part of Joseph's argument. Then consider the one that pertains to Ronald's.

The assumption is usually the statement that best links the premises of the argument to its conclusion. For details on evaluating arguments, see Chapter 5.

Following are the premises of Joseph's argument:

- ✔ Hospitals and clinics are billing health insurance companies for unnecessary and expensive tests.

- ✔ This practice has caused health insurance companies to pay inflated rates to hospitals and clinics.

- ✔ The result is that health insurance companies are compensating by raising consumers' health insurance premiums.

Based on these premises, Joseph concludes that reducing unnecessary tests will significantly control the rise in health insurance premiums.

To find the assumption that provides a link between the cessation of the unnecessary tests and a significant effect on increasing healthcare premiums, begin by narrowing your options. Joseph doesn't mention doctors in his argument, so you can eliminate Choices (A) and (D). Choice (E) addresses healthcare premiums but not unnecessary tests, so it's out. Choice (C) concerns other insurance industries, so it has nothing to do with Joseph's argument about healthcare premiums. The best option for Joseph is the assumption that unnecessary tests make up a significant portion of insurance billing. If they make up just a small portion, eliminating tests wouldn't have a significant impact on the rising cost of healthcare premiums. Mark Choice (B) in the column for Joseph.

Now evaluate Ronald's argument. Here are his premises:

- ✔ Doctors order unnecessary tests to increase their earnings.

- ✔ Patients should be able to choose their tests.

- ✔ Putting the decision regarding diagnostics and tests in the patients' control would reduce the number of unnecessary tests.

So you're looking for the assumption that links patients' decisions to fewer unnecessary tests.

Notice that Ronald doesn't address healthcare premiums at all, so you can confidently eliminate Choice (E). Choice (B) is out because you've already attributed it to Joseph. Choice (C) doesn't work for the same reason that it doesn't work for Joseph. Ronald's argument concerns only healthcare. Of the two remaining options (Choices [A] and [D]), only Choice (D) relates to patients' decisions. Only if patients make decisions differently than doctors do would putting patients in control lessen the number of unnecessary tests. So you mark Choice (D) in the column for Ronald.

Graphics interpretation

Not surprisingly, graphics interpretation questions require you to interpret graphs. You may see line graphs, bar graphs, pie charts, Venn diagrams, and so on. Based on the information displayed in the graph, you fill in two separate blanks by selecting the best option from a drop-down menu for each blank. (In the example question later in this section, we include the answer options in parentheses.) You have to complete both blanks correctly to get credit for one graphics interpretation question.

The information you need to fill in the blanks comes primarily from the graph, so make sure you know how to read charts and graphs. Chapter 18 provides a review of the most common GMAT charts and graphs to refresh your memory.

Here are some other tips to help you efficiently move through graphics interpretation questions:

> ✔ **Analyze the graph or chart to determine exactly what information it provides and how.** Observe the labels and examine the numerical increments carefully.

> ✔ **Click on Select One to view all the answer options.** To see the possible answers in the drop-down menu for each blank, you have to click on the box that says Select One. Filling in the blank is much easier when you're limited to just the several available choices. Don't attempt to answer the question without seeing the answer choices first.

> ✔ **Eliminate illogical answer choices.** Approach the two parts of a graphics interpretation question much like you would a standard multiple-choice question. Eliminate obviously incorrect options and use your reasoning skills to select the best answer from the remaining choices.

> ✔ **Make estimations.** The data in charts and graphs are rarely precise, so most of your calculations are estimates or approximations that you can work out on your noteboard or in your head rather than on the calculator.

Here's a sample graphics interpretation question to consider.

Scientists, health professionals, and life insurance agents are interested in examining the percentage of people in a population who will live to a certain age. One way to measure this information is to look at the percentage of the population who has died after a certain number of years. The following graph displays the results of such a study.

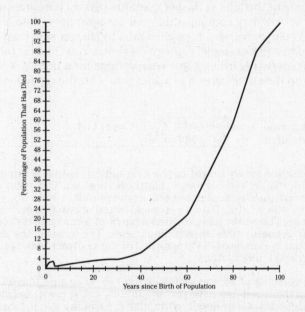

Approximately, _____ (10, 40, 60, 80) percent of the population lives to at least 80 years of age. A person who was a member of the study population would still have an 80 percent chance of being alive at around a maximum age of _____ (15, 35, 55, 80) years.

Filling the first blank in the question tests your graph reading skills. Find 80 years of age on the horizontal axis. Move your finger from the 80-year mark upward on the graph until you reach the plotted curve. Move your finger to the left to see that at 80 years, about 60 percent of people have died. Don't stop there and choose 60 percent, however. The question asks for how many are alive at the 80-year mark. Subtract 60 from 100 to get that approximately 40 percent of the population lives to at least 80 years. The correct answer is 40 percent.

To complete the second blank, make sure you look at the answer choices first. Because the statement concerns the *maximum* value, consider higher ages first. The oldest option is 80, but it's very unlikely that 80 percent of people are alive at age 80, so try the next highest age, 55. Move along the graph until you reach 55 years. At 55 years of age, 20 percent have died, leaving a maximum of 80 percent alive. Ages above 55 can't be right, so 55 is the correct answer.

If you started with the first option of 15 years, you may be misled. Note that the graph shows you that at about 15 years of age, less than 5 percent of people have died, which means that more than 95 percent of the population are still alive. That's more than 80 percent, but the statement regards the *maximum* age where 80 percent of the population is still kicking, so 15 can't be correct.

Multi-source reasoning

The only IR question type with more than one question that pertains to a set of data is the multi-source reasoning question. For this question type, the GMAT presents different kinds of information in a series of two or three tabs. Each tab conveys a relevant aspect of a set of circumstances. The topics of the scenarios vary greatly. You may have information concerning a certain scientific phenomena, such as black holes or plant photosynthesis, or you may be asked to apply data that relates to business situations, such as hiring decisions or event planning.

At least one of the tabs in the set contains several paragraphs of written information on a subject. Others may contain additional paragraphs or data contained in tables, charts, or graphs. You use the resources in all tabs to answer several questions, most of which have several parts. For example, Figure 17-3 shows you the first tab for a sample multi-source reasoning scenario regarding guest reservations for a hotel's wedding block. The e-mail in this tab sets up the situation and provides you with the guidelines for the reservation.

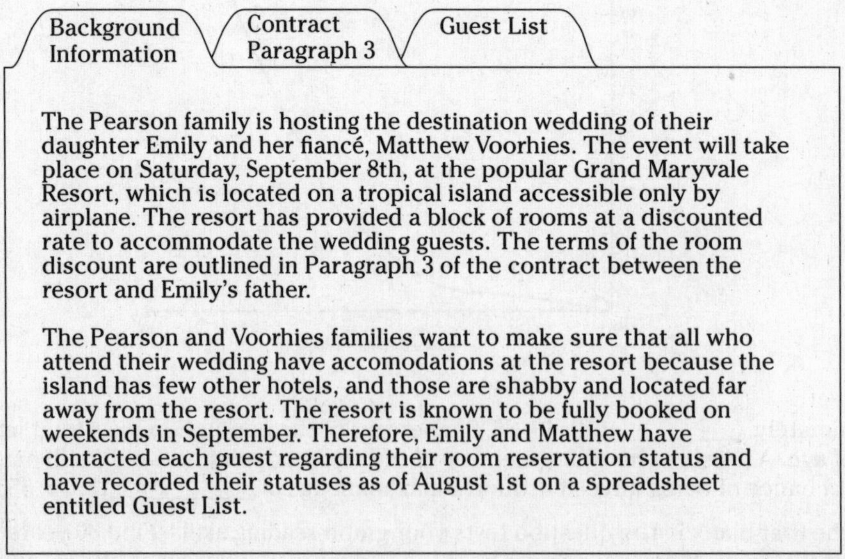

| Background Information | Contract Paragraph 3 | Guest List |

The Pearson family is hosting the destination wedding of their daughter Emily and her fiancé, Matthew Voorhies. The event will take place on Saturday, September 8th, at the popular Grand Maryvale Resort, which is located on a tropical island accessible only by airplane. The resort has provided a block of rooms at a discounted rate to accommodate the wedding guests. The terms of the room discount are outlined in Paragraph 3 of the contract between the resort and Emily's father.

The Pearson and Voorhies families want to make sure that all who attend their wedding have accomodations at the resort because the island has few other hotels, and those are shabby and located far away from the resort. The resort is known to be fully booked on weekends in September. Therefore, Emily and Matthew have contacted each guest regarding their room reservation status and have recorded their statuses as of August 1st on a spreadsheet entitled Guest List.

Figure 17-3:
Sample
multi-source
reasoning
format,
background
tab.

Illustration by Wiley, Composition Services Graphics

Figure 17-4 shows what you find when you click on the second tab: language from the contract between the Pearson family and the resort.

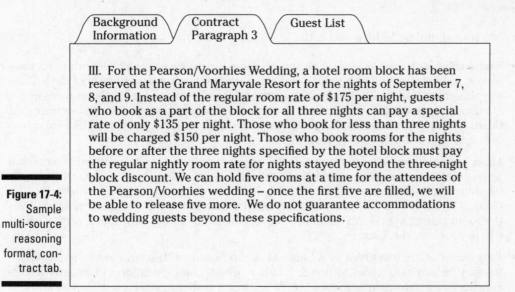

| Background Information | Contract Paragraph 3 | Guest List |

III. For the Pearson/Voorhies Wedding, a hotel room block has been reserved at the Grand Maryvale Resort for the nights of September 7, 8, and 9. Instead of the regular room rate of $175 per night, guests who book as a part of the block for all three nights can pay a special rate of only $135 per night. Those who book for less than three nights will be charged $150 per night. Those who book rooms for the nights before or after the three nights specified by the hotel block must pay the regular nightly room rate for nights stayed beyond the three-night block discount. We can hold five rooms at a time for the attendees of the Pearson/Voorhies wedding – once the first five are filled, we will be able to release five more. We do not guarantee accommodations to wedding guests beyond these specifications.

Figure 17-4: Sample multi-source reasoning format, contract tab.

Illustration by Wiley, Composition Services Graphics

When you click on the final tab, you may see a table with relevant data, such as the one in Figure 17-5, which shows the wedding guest list and their reservation status.

| Background Information | Contract Paragraph 3 | Guest List |

Name	Number Attending	Number of Rooms Needed	Nights Staying at Resort	Reservations Made?
The Rose Family	4	1	3	N
The Crawford Family	6	2	2	Y
The Fishers	2	1	1	Y
The Ball Family	5	2	3	Y
The Ranks Family	6	2	3	N
The Keppners	2	1	1	Y
The Albertsons	4	1	1	N
....	....	....	....	....

Figure 17-5: Sample multi-source reasoning format, guest list tab.

Illustration by Wiley, Composition Services Graphics

The multi-source reasoning questions appear in one of two formats: three-part table (similar to table analysis questions) or standard five-answer multiple-choice. Keep in mind that you have to answer all three parts of the first format to get credit for the one question. The multiple-choice format may be one of the easiest questions to answer in the IR section. You can use the process of elimination to narrow the answers, and you have to choose only one correct answer to get full credit for the question.

The trickiest aspect of answering multi-source reasoning questions is sifting through the plethora of information to discover what's relevant. Depending on the scenario, you may have to juggle information in tables, diagrams, articles, and so on to come up with correct answers.

Here are some pointers to help you with the task:

- **Summarize each tab.** As you read through the information in each tab for the first time, record pertinent points to help you remember which tab holds what type of data. That way you don't have to continually flip back and forth between screens as you answer questions. For example, summarize the contract details in Figure 17-4 on your noteboard with quick notations, such as *9/7, 8, & 9 = $135/night; < 3 nights = $150/night; before/after 9/7 or 9/9 = $175/night.*

- **Make connections.** After you've seen the information in each tab, synthesize facts and figures from one tab with correlative data from another. Keep track of your findings on your noteboard. For example, you should notice as you read the information in Figures 17-4 and 17-5 that you can correlate the data in the table in the final tab with the room charge specifications in the second tab to figure out how much each guest will pay for resort rooms.

- **Rely on what the test gives you.** Some of the topics in multi-source reasoning scenarios may be familiar to you. Although familiarity may make the information more accessible to you, it may also influence you to answer questions based on what you know instead of what the exam tells you. For example, you shouldn't answer any questions about the Pearson wedding sample scenario based on what you know about hotel booking from your own experience as a front desk manager.

Here's another sample multi-source scenario with a couple of questions to help you get more acquainted with the question type. This scenario has only two tabs, each conveying an opposing opinion from two scientists on a specific scientific phenomenon.

Scientist 1

Ancient ice cores from Antarctica indicate that the concentration of carbon dioxide in the atmosphere and global mean temperatures have followed the same pattern of fluctuations in levels over the past 160,000 years. Therefore, the increase in atmospheric carbon dioxide concentration from 280 parts per million to 360 parts per million that has occurred over the past 150 years points to significant and detrimental climatic changes in the near future. The climate has already changed: The average surface temperature of the earth has increased 0.6°C in the past hundred years, with the ten hottest years of that time period all occurring since 1980. Although 0.6°C may not seem large, changes in the mean surface temperature as low as 0.5°C have dramatically affected crop growth in years past. Moreover, computer models project that surface temperatures will increase about 2.0°C by the year 2100 and will continue to increase in the years after even if concentration of greenhouse gases is stabilized by that time. If the present trend in carbon dioxide increase continues, though, carbon dioxide concentration will exceed 1,100 parts per million soon after 2100 and will be associated with a temperature increase of approximately 10.0°C over the present mean annual global surface temperature.

Scientist 2

The observed increases in minor greenhouse gases such as carbon dioxide and methane will not lead to sizeable global warming. Water vapor and clouds are responsible for more than 98% of the earth's greenhouse effect. Current models that project large temperature increases with a doubling of the present carbon dioxide concentration incorporate changes in water vapor, clouds and other factors that would accompany a rise in carbon dioxide levels. The way these models handle such feedback factors is not supported by current scientific knowledge. In fact, there is convincing evidence that shows that increases in carbon dioxide concentration would lead to changes in feedback factors that would diminish any temperature increase associated with more carbon dioxide in the atmosphere. The climatic data for the last hundred years show an irregular pattern in which many of the greatest jumps in global mean temperature were too large to be associated with the observed increase in carbon dioxide. The overall increase of 0.45°C in the past century is well under what the models would have predicted given the changes in carbon dioxide concentration. As with the temperature models, recent increases in atmospheric carbon dioxide have not risen to the extent predicted by models dealing solely with carbon dioxide levels. The rate of carbon dioxide concentration increase has slowed since 1973. Improved energy technologies will further dampen the increase so that the carbon dioxide concentration will be under 700 parts per million in the year 2100.

Consider each of the following statements about atmospheric carbon dioxide levels and determine whether Scientists 1 and 2 are both likely to agree by marking either *Yes* or *No:*

Yes	*No*	
O	O	A. Increasing carbon dioxide levels affect other factors.
O	O	B. Humans will never be able to stabilize atmospheric carbon dioxide levels.
O	O	C. The rate of increase in carbon dioxide levels will rise throughout the next 100 years.

Statement (A) is a nice, noncontroversial statement with which both scientists would agree. Scientist 1 stresses that rising carbon dioxide is linked to higher temperature (another factor), while Scientist 2 discusses *feedback factors,* which are factors that respond to carbon dioxide changes and will, in turn, affect the carbon dioxide. Select *Yes* for Statement (A).

To answer Statement (B), notice that Scientist 2, who refers to improved energy technology, clearly disagrees with the statement, but so does Scientist 1, who mentions the possibility that carbon dioxide levels will stabilize. Neither scientist would agree with Statement (B), so the answer is *No.*

Scientist 2 disagrees with Statement (C) and actually discusses a slowing down in the rate of carbon dioxide level increase. Because at least one of the scientists would disagree with the statement, the answer to Statement (C) is *No.*

The next question is in multiple-choice format.

Which of the following statements does only Scientist 1 support?

(A) A change in atmospheric water vapor could significantly affect global temperatures.

(B) The increase in atmospheric carbon dioxide concentration from 280 parts per million to 360 parts per million that has occurred over the last 150 years is not expected to affect climactic change negatively in the future.

(C) Recent increases in atmospheric carbon dioxide have surpassed those predicted by temperature models dealing solely with carbon dioxide models.

(D) Temperature fluctuations will match carbon dioxide changes when carbon dioxide changes are abrupt.

(E) Increases in carbon dioxide concentration would lead to changes in feedback factors that would compound any temperature increase associated with more carbon dioxide in the atmosphere.

Focus on the information in the first tab. Scientist 1 mentions a match between carbon dioxide and temperature variations and then uses the recent large change in carbon dioxide levels as evidence that significant changes in temperature will occur. Scientist 1 goes on to discuss how continued sharp increases in atmospheric carbon dioxide will lead to similar dramatic temperature increases. Scientist 1 implies that the recent carbon dioxide changes have been unprecedented. The data during the past 160,000 years show a correspondence between temperature and carbon dioxide fluctuations, but this correspondence has occurred in the absence of the dramatic changes the earth is now and soon will be experiencing. For Scientist 1 to use the fluctuation correspondence as evidence for what will soon happen, she must assume that the correspondence will continue in light of current and near-future sharp changes. So Choice (D) is correct.

Choice (A) is supported by Scientist 2, and neither scientist would support the Choices (B), (C), or (E). In fact, Scientist 1 actually says that an increase in atmospheric carbon dioxide concentration from 280 parts per million to 360 parts per million can cause "significant and detrimental climactic changes in the near future."

Chapter 18

Deciphering Data in Charts and Graphs

• •

In This Chapter

▶ Recognizing the different charts and graphs the integrated reasoning section may toss at you

▶ Discovering how to interpret and apply data displayed in charts and graphs

• •

*N*ot every integrated reasoning question relies on a chart or graph, but most do. This chapter reviews the characteristics of the ways the GMAT represents data in the integrated reasoning section and explains how to read each type in the most efficient way.

The charts and graphs you'll encounter on the GMAT integrated reasoning section display data in a variety of formats. You interpret the data provided in tables, bar graphs, line graphs, scatter plots, pie charts, or Venn diagrams, and then you apply your analysis to draw conclusions about a bunch of scenarios. You get to compare statistics, identify trends or lapses in trends, make predictions for the future, and so on.

Approaching Integrated Reasoning Data in Five Easy Steps

Most integrated reasoning questions contain a chart or graph. You won't have much time to waste, so it's a good idea to know how to extract data from the various types of charts and graphs before you sit down in front of the computer on exam day. Regardless of the graph or chart you're working with, you'll follow a similar, five-step approach:

1. **Identify the type of chart or graph.**

   Graphs display data in different ways, so start by recognizing which graph or chart type you're dealing with. To make this step easy, we provide detailed information on each of the most common charts and graphs on the GMAT in this chapter.

2. **Read the accompanying question and determine what it asks.**

   Before you attempt to read the chart or graph, examine the question to figure out exactly what kind of information you need to answer it.

3. **Isolate what you need to get out of the chart or graph to successfully answer the question.**

   Refer to the chart or graph to discover where it conveys the specific data you need to answer the question.

4. **Read the chart or graph properly.**

   Examine the chart or graph carefully to spot trends and note where the quantities associated with each variable appear and how the value of each increment is displayed.

5. **Solve the problem.**

   Use the data you've carefully extracted from the chart or graph to come up with the correct answer to the question.

The remaining sections in this chapter show you how to apply this approach to reading a variety of charts and graphs. You can practice answering questions about charts and graphs, using the integrated reasoning mini practice test on the CD (or if you're using a digital or enhanced digital version of this book, go to http://booksupport.wiley.com for access to the additional content).

Translating Information in Tables

Tables report, organize, and summarize data and allow you to view and analyze precise values. For example, a table can be an effective way of presenting average daily high and low temperatures in a given area, the number of male and female births that occur each year within a population, or the ranking of a band's top-ten hits.

The sample table in Figure 18-1 records the four individual event and all-around scores for five gymnasts in a local meet. Its data is precise rather than approximated, which allows you to come up with accurate analyses of the values. For example, you can see from the table that Kate just barely edged out Jess on the balance beam by a 0.005 difference in scores.

Figure 18-1: You're likely to see a table like this one as part of a GMAT integrated reasoning question.

Bayside Gymnastics Club Score Report					
Name	Vault Score	Uneven Bars Score	Balance Beam Score	Floor Exercise Score	All-Around Score
Kelsea Moore	16.25	15.5	15.1	14.985	61.835
Adrianne Rizzo	15.9	14.975	15.225	15.325	61.425
Kate McCaffery	16.0	14.6	15.0	13.995	58.595
Jess Hartley	15.875	13.966	14.995	15.0	59.836
Maggie Birney	16.1	13.92	15.1	13.87	58.990

Illustration by Wiley, Composition Services Graphics

When you evaluate a table, pay particular attention to the column labels to determine exactly what kind of information and values it displays. Read carefully to differentiate values and determine, say, whether the numbers represent percentages or actual figures. For example, a few seconds of careful consideration of the values in the sample table in Figure 18-1 tells you that the gymnasts' all-around score is the sum of the other scores rather than their average. So if a question asked you about a particular gymnast's average score for all events, you'd know you'd have to compute this calculation rather than report the provided all-around score.

Not surprisingly, tables are the primary source of information in the integrated reasoning table analysis question type. These questions use tables to display data, usually a lot of it. You may also find tables in multi-source reasoning and two-part analysis questions. (Chapter 17 provides more detail on how to answer all four integrated reasoning question types.)

Making Comparisons with Bar Graphs

Bar graphs (also sometimes called *bar charts*) have a variety of uses. They're especially good for comparing data and approximating values. As the name suggests, they use rectangular bars to represent different categories of data (either horizontally or vertically); the height or length of each bar indicates the corresponding quantity for that category of data.

You see bar graphs most frequently on the GMAT in graphics interpretation questions, but they may also appear in multi-source reasoning and two-part analysis questions. Simple bar graphs present the relationship between two variables. More complex bar graphs show data for additional data by displaying additional bars or by segmenting each individual bar. We show you how to read simple and complex bar graphs in the following sections.

Simple bar graphs

Bar graphs provide an excellent way to visualize the similarities and differences among several categories of data. Even a simple bar graph, such as the one in Figure 18-2, can convey a whole bunch of information.

The chart heading in Figure 18-2 defines the overall category of information: 2009 activity ticket sales for Pleasantdale High School by group. You don't need a title for the horizontal axis. It's obvious from the chart heading that each bar provides the data for each school group. From the vertical axis title, you discover that the data represents number of tickets sold rather than the total revenue from those tickets. *In Thousands* means that each major horizontal gridline represents 1,000 tickets. Each of the four minor gridlines between each major gridline represents 200 tickets (the four lines divide the segments between the whole number into five parts, and $1,000 \div 5$ is 200). So the graph indicates that the number of drama club tickets sold was approximately 3,700 because the *Drama Club* bar ends between the third and fourth minor gridlines above the 3,000 mark. To find the total number of drama club tickets sold, add 200 for each of the three minor gridlines and half of that (100) as represented by the half space between the third and fourth minor gridlines: $3,000 + 3(200) + 100 = 3,700$.

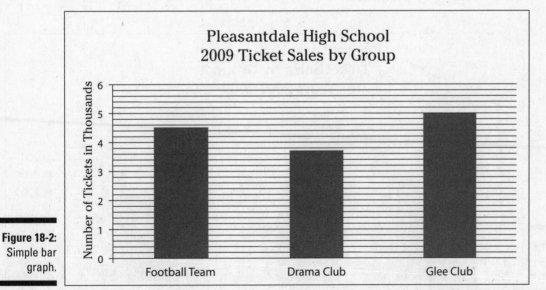

Figure 18-2: Simple bar graph.

Some GMAT bar graphs may display information for a range of values. An example appears in Figure 18-3. Based on this graph, you can figure that the minimum total number of tickets sold by all groups in 2009 was the sum of the lowest number for each group (4,000 + 5,000 + 6,000), or 15,000 tickets. The maximum possible total of tickets sold by the three groups combined was the sum of the highest value for each category: 5,000 + 6,000 + 7,000, or 18,000.

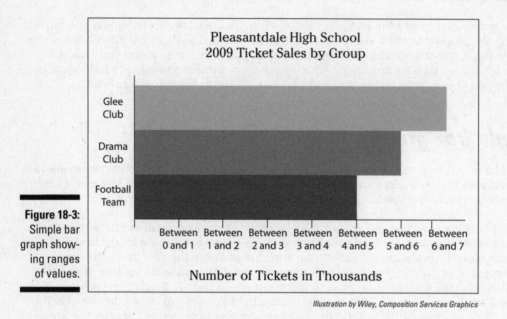

Figure 18-3:
Simple bar graph showing ranges of values.

Illustration by Wiley, Composition Services Graphics

Graphs with many bars

Altering the design of a bar graph allows you to convey even more information. Graphs with multiple bars reveal data for additional categories. For example, Figure 18-4 compares the ticket sales totals for the three groups by year for three years.

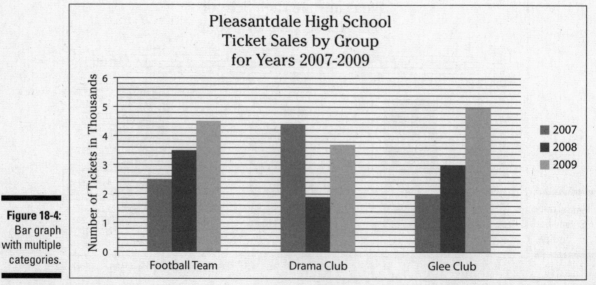

Figure 18-4:
Bar graph with multiple categories.

Illustration by Wiley, Composition Services Graphics

The legend designates which group the bars stand for. This graph allows you to easily make comparisons over the years and among the three groups. For example, it's easy to see that in 2009, glee club ticket sales were not only greater than they had been in previous years but also exceeded sales for either of the other two groups. Perhaps sales were influenced by the launch of a popular TV show featuring a high-school glee club!

Segmented bar graphs

Graphs with segmented bars display the characteristics of subcategories. Each bar is divided into segments that represent different subgroups. The height of each segment within a bar represents the value associated with that particular subgroup. For example, Pleasantdale High can provide more specific comparisons of the ticket sales during different times of the year by using a segmented bar graph, such as the one in Figure 18-5.

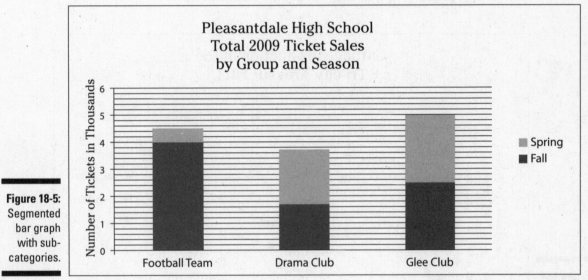

Figure 18-5: Segmented bar graph with sub-categories.

You apply subtraction to read a segmented graph. The top of each bar is the total from which you subtract the designations for each subcategory. So for the *Football Team* bar in Figure 18-5, the total number of tickets sold in 2009 was 4,500. The number of tickets sold in the fall is represented by the lower segment, which climbs up to about the 4,000 mark. The number of tickets sold in the spring is the difference between the approximate total number of tickets (4,500) and the approximate number of fall tickets (4,000), which is about 500. The graph also reveals that activity sales for the glee club and drama club occur more consistently across both seasons than for the football team, which sells many more tickets in the fall than it does in the spring.

Whenever you reference data from a bar graph, you speak in estimates. Bar graphs don't provide exact values; that's not their job. They allow you to make comparisons based on approximations.

Evaluating Line Graphs

Another graph that crops up frequently in GMAT graphics interpretation questions is the *line graph*. Line graphs display information that occurs over time or across graduated measurements and are particularly effective in highlighting trends, peaks, or lows. Typically (but not always), the *x*-axis displays units of time or measurement (the independent variable), and the *y*-axis presents the data that's being measured (the dependent variable).

Basic line graphs

The line graph in Figure 18-6 shows the garbage production for three cities for each of the four quarters of 2011. You can tell from the graph that Plainfield produced more garbage in every quarter than the other two cities did, and it's evident that all three cities produced less garbage in Quarter 3 than they did in the other quarters.

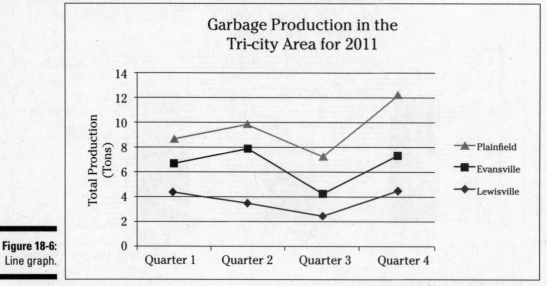

Figure 18-6: Line graph.

Illustration by Wiley, Composition Services Graphics

Scatter plots

Line graphs are extensions of *scatter graphs,* or *scatter plots,* which display the relationship between two numerical variables. These graphs display a bunch of points that show the relationship between two variables, one represented on the *x*-axis and the other on the *y*-axis. For example, the scatter plot in Figure 18-7 plots each city's population on the *x*-axis and its garbage production on the *y*-axis. Scatter plots show you trends and patterns. From Figure 18-7, you can figure out that, generally, a direct or positive relationship exists between a city's population and the amount of garbage it produces. The graph indicates that, because the data points tend to be higher on the *y*-axis as they move to the right (or increase) on the *x*-axis. You can also surmise that of the 20 cities listed, more have fewer than 200,000 people than have greater than 200,000 people. That's because the graph shows a greater number of points that fall to the left of the 200,000 population line than to the right.

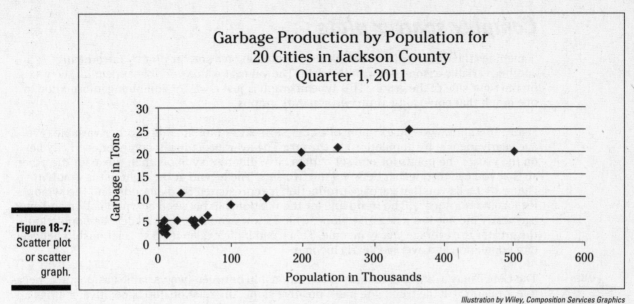

Illustration by Wiley, Composition Services Graphics

Figure 18-7:
Scatter plot
or scatter
graph.

Scatter plots also convey trend and pattern deviations. The GMAT may provide a scatter plot with or without a *trend line*. The trend line shows the overall pattern of the data plots and reveals deviations. The scatter plot in Figure 18-7 doesn't display a trend line, so you have to imagine one. You can lay your noteboard along the graph to help you envision the trend line if one isn't provided. Figure 18-8 shows you the trend line for the garbage production graph. With the trend line in place, you can more easily recognize that the largest city in the county deviates from the trend somewhat considerably. Its garbage production is less in proportion to its population than for most other cities in the county. You know that because its data point is considerably below the trend line.

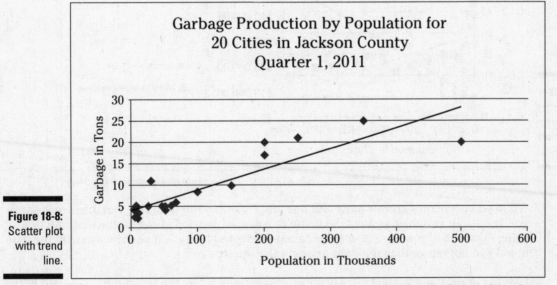

Figure 18-8:
Scatter plot
with trend
line.

Illustration by Wiley, Composition Services Graphics

Complex scatter plots

Sometimes the GMAT crams even more information on a scatter plot by introducing another variable associated with the data. The values for this variable appear on the *y*-axis on the right side of the graph. This type of graph is just a way of combining information in one graph that could appear on two separate graphs.

Figure 18-9 shows you an example of a complex scatter plot. It adds another variable (average yearly income by population) to the mix. The average annual income for each city lies on the *y*-axis. The points for one set of data have different symbols than those for the other so that you can distinguish between the two sets. The legend at the right of the graph in Figure 18-9 tells you that garbage production is represented by diamonds, and the symbol for income is a square. The trend line for the relationship between city population and average yearly income has a negative slope, which shows you that the smaller the population, the greater the average yearly income. This trend indicates an inverse relationship between city population and average yearly income.

The GMAT may ask you to identify the relationship between two variables as positive, negative, or neutral. If the trend line has a positive slope, the relationship is positive; if it has a negative slope, the relationship is negative. If the trend line is horizontal or the points are scattered without any recognizable pattern, the relationship is neutral, meaning that no correlation exists between the variables.

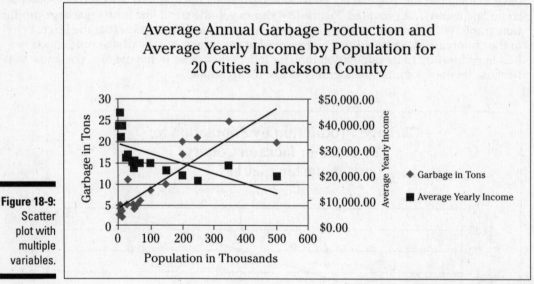

Figure 18-9:
Scatter plot with multiple variables.

Illustration by Wiley, Composition Services Graphics

When you encounter scatter plots and line graphs with more than two variables, make sure you keep your variables straight. So if you're asked a question about garbage production, using Figure 18-9, you have to use the data represented by the left vertical axis and the diamond symbol rather than the right axis and the squares.

Like bar graphs, line graphs display approximate values. Use the technique explained in the earlier section "Simple bar graphs" to help you estimate the values associated with each data point from the axes labels and grid marks on these graphs.

Clarifying Circle Graphs (A.k.a. Pie Charts)

Circle graphs, also known as *pie charts,* show values that are part of a larger whole, such as percentages. The graphs contain divisions called *sectors,* which divide the circle into portions that are proportional to the quantity each represents as part of the whole 360-degree circle. Each sector becomes a piece of the *pie;* you get information and compare values by examining the pieces in relation to each other and to the whole pie.

When a graphics interpretation question provides you with a circle graph and designates the percentage values of each of its sectors, you can use it to figure out actual quantities. The circle graph in Figure 18-10 tells you that Plainfield has more Republican affiliates than Democrat and that Democrats constitute just over twice as many Plainfield residents as Independents do.

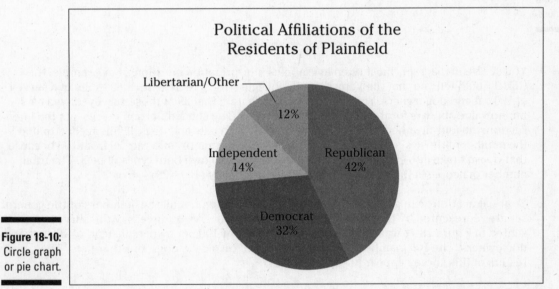

Figure 18-10: Circle graph or pie chart.

Political Affiliations of the
Residents of Plainfield

Libertarian/Other — 12%

Independent 14%

Republican 42%

Democrat 32%

Illustration by Wiley, Composition Services Graphics

When you know one of the quantities in a circle graph, you can find the value of other quantities. For example, if a multi-source reasoning question in the integrated reasoning section provides you with both the line graph in Figure 18-7 and the circle graph in Figure 18-10 and tells you that the city of Plainfield was the city in Figure 18-7 with the highest population, you can use information from both graphs to discover the approximate number of Plainfield residents who are registered Democrats. The city with the largest population in Figure 18-7 has around 500,000 residents. Figure 18-10 tells you that 32 percent of Plainfield residents are Democrats. So just about 160,000 ($500,000 \times 0.32$) Democrats reside in Plainfield.

Extracting Data from Venn Diagrams

Venn diagrams, such as the one in Figure 18-11, are made of interconnected circles — usually two or three — and are a great way to show relationships that exist between sets of data. Each data set is represented by a circle; the interaction of the circles shows how the data relates.

Individuals Surveyed: 100

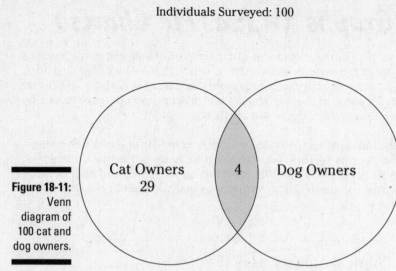

Illustration by Wiley, Composition Services Graphics

Figure 18-11:
Venn
diagram of
100 cat and
dog owners.

You see Venn diagrams most often in graphics interpretation questions. For example, the GMAT could tell you that the Venn diagram in Figure 18-11 represents the results of a survey of 100 cat and dog owners. You know from the diagram that 29 of those surveyed own cats, but no value appears for the number of dog owners. The shaded portion represents the intersection: the four members of the survey who own both cats and dogs. If you needed to find the number of those surveyed who own dogs, you can't simply subtract 29 from 100 because that doesn't take into consideration the four people who own both types of pets. The total number of people in the survey who own dogs is actually (100 – 29) + 4, or 75.

Your calculations can get a little more complicated when not all the members of the general set are represented by the circles in the Venn diagram. For example, say the survey represented in Figure 18-11 was modified a bit to represent 100 pet owners instead of 100 cat and dog owners. The 100 members of the survey could own cats, dogs, or other pets. The results of this survey appear in Figure 18-12.

Individuals Surveyed: 100

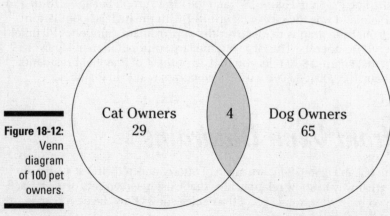

Figure 18-12:
Venn
diagram
of 100 pet
owners.

Illustration by Wiley, Composition Services Graphics

Based on this diagram, the GMAT could pose questions that ask for the number of people who own only cats but not dogs, the number of people who own at least one cat or one dog, or the number of those surveyed who own neither a cat nor a dog. Here's how you'd solve for these three cases:

- ✔ The number of people who own cats but not dogs is simply the difference between the quantity in the cat owner circle and the quantity of members who own both cats and dogs: 29 − 4 = 25. Of the 100 people surveyed, 25 own cats but don't own dogs.

- ✔ To find how many of the surveyed pet owners own at least a cat or a dog, you just need to add the values in each circle and subtract the quantity in the shaded intersection: (29 + 65) − 4 = 90. Of the 100 people surveyed, 90 owned at least one cat or one dog.

- ✔ Figuring the number of pet owners who own neither a cat nor a dog means that you're looking for the quantity that exists outside of the two circles. The number of people represented inside the circles plus the number of people outside of the circles is equal to 100, the total number of people surveyed. You know the number of people represented by the space inside the circle; it's the same number as those who own at least a cat or a dog (90). If x represents the number of pet owners who don't have a cat or a dog, the equation would be $90 + x = 100$. When you solve for x, you figure out that 10 people in the survey owned some pet other than a dog or cat.

So to evaluate Venn diagrams correctly, keep track of the total members in the set and what they represent. Information in the question will allow you to assess whether the circles represent the total number of members or whether a subset of members resides outside of the circle, so reading carefully will allow you to accurately interpret the Venn diagram. When you've successfully figured out the general set and the subsets, extracting information from Venn diagrams is easy.

Part VI
Practice Makes Perfect

The 5th Wave   By Rich Tennant

"I always get a good night's sleep the day before a test so I'm relaxed and alert the next morning. Then I grab my pen, eat a banana, and I'm on my way."

In this part . . .

The best way to prepare for any standardized test is to practice, and this part provides you with a bunch of questions to test your knowledge. We give you a complete GMAT practice test, with tips on how to score yourself. Before you sit down with your pencil and scratch paper, though, make sure you have at least three and a half uninterrupted hours to devote so you can get the full mind-numbing effect of plugging through the GMAT.

The chapter immediately following the test provides explanations of the answer choices for each of the questions. You find out why the right answers are right and why the wrong answers are wrong. We provide a lot of valuable information in each of the explanations, so we suggest you read through all of them, even the ones for questions you answered correctly. When you're ready for more, you can pop the CD into your computer. It contains four additional full-length practice tests with answer explanations.

Chapter 19

GMAT Practice Test

● ●

The more practice you get answering GMAT questions before you take the test, the better you'll do on exam day. Increase your chances for a top score with the following practice exam, consisting of three sections of multiple-choice questions and an analytical writing prompt. You have to write an essay in 30 minutes, finish 12 integrated reasoning questions (located only on the CD version of this test) in 30 minutes, complete 37 math questions in 75 minutes, and answer 41 verbal questions in 75 minutes. (*Note:* If you're using a digital or enhanced digital version of this book, please go to http://booksupport.wiley.com for access to the additional content.)

To make the most of this practice exam, take the test under conditions similar to those you'll face on test day:

- ✔ Find a place where you won't be distracted (preferably as far from your refrigerator as possible).

- ✔ If possible, take the practice test at approximately the same time of day as when you'll be taking the actual GMAT.

- ✔ Use a timer to keep track of the time limits for each section.

- ✔ Take no more than two eight-minute breaks.

- ✔ Mark your answers by circling the appropriate letters in the text. (On the actual GMAT, you'll mark your answer by clicking the oval next to the correct answer.)

- ✔ Use a blank piece of paper to simulate the noteboard for keeping notes and making calculations.

- ✔ If possible, complete your essay on a computer with the grammar and spelling correction functions turned off.

- ✔ When your time is up for each section, put down your pencil and stop working.

After you finish, turn to Chapter 20 to check your answers with the answer key and read through the answer explanations — even the ones for the questions you got right. The explanations may present a way of approaching a problem that you haven't considered.

Section 1: Analytical Writing Assessment

Time: 30 minutes for one essay

Directions: In this section, you're asked to write a critique of the argument presented. The prompt requests only your critique and does not ask you for your opinions on the matter.

Think for a few minutes about the argument and organize your response before you start writing. Leave time for revisions when you're finished.

You'll be scored based on your ability to accomplish these tasks:

✔ Organize, develop, and express your thoughts about the given argument.

✔ Provide pertinent supporting ideas with examples.

✔ Apply the rules of standard written English.

  Essay Topic: A number of states have installed photo radar cameras on major highways to help control speeds and minimize accidents. But these cameras are often inaccurate and prone to errors and create an additional danger by often startling motorists with their bright flashbulbs. They also fail to account for many of the other major causes of accidents, like drinking and driving and driver cellphone use. The installation of photo radar cameras represents just another way the government infringes on civil liberties and causes unnecessary stress and strife on citizens; the cameras should, therefore, be removed from all major highways in America.

Examine this argument and present your judgment on how well reasoned it is. In your discussion, analyze the author's position and how well the author uses evidence to support the argument. For example, you may need to question the author's underlying assumptions or consider alternative explanations that may weaken the conclusion. You can also provide additional support for or arguments against the author's position, describe how stating the argument differently may make it more reasonable, and discuss what provisions may better equip you to evaluate its thesis.

STOP DO NOT TURN THE PAGE UNTIL TOLD TO DO SO.
DO NOT RETURN TO A PREVIOUS TEST.

Section 2: Integrated Reasoning

Time: 30 minutes for 12 questions

Directions: Follow these directions for each of the four question types:

1. For graphics interpretation questions, examine the graph or chart and select the answer from the list that most accurately completes the statement.

2. The two-part analysis questions have two solutions. Select one choice from the list in the first column and one choice from the list in the second column to provide a complete answer for the question.

3. Analyze the data in the table analysis problems to determine which of the two opposing answer choices most clearly defines the accuracy of the statements.

4. The multi-source reasoning questions present you with several sets of different data. Read through the data and select the information you need to answer the questions.

Note: To simulate the look and feel of the integrated reasoning section on the actual GMAT, we include these questions in "Section 2: Integrated Reasoning" of Practice Exam 3 on the CD. If you're using a digital or enhanced digital version of this book, please go to http://booksupport.wiley.com for access to the additional content.

STOP — DO NOT TURN THE PAGE UNTIL TOLD TO DO SO. DO NOT RETURN TO A PREVIOUS TEST.

Section 3: Quantitative

Time: 75 minutes for 37 questions

Directions: Choose the best answer from the five choices provided.

Use the following answer choices to answer the data sufficiency questions (those questions that list the answer letters only):

(A) Statement (1) *alone* is sufficient, but Statement (2) alone is not sufficient to answer the question asked.

(B) Statement (2) *alone* is sufficient, but Statement (1) alone is not sufficient to answer the question asked.

(C) *Both* Statements (1) and (2) *together* are sufficient to answer the question asked, but *neither* statement *alone* is sufficient.

(D) *Each* statement *alone* is sufficient to answer the question asked.

(E) Statements (1) and (2) *together* are *not* sufficient to answer the question asked, and additional data are needed.

1. The population of Townsville doubles every ten years. In approximately what year will Townsville's population exceed 300,000 if the population was 5,000 in 1970?

   (A) 2010
   (B) 2020
   (C) 2030
   (D) 2040
   (E) 2050

2. What is 75% of $\frac{6}{13}$ of 104?

   (A) 27
   (B) 36
   (C) 54
   (D) 72
   (E) 108

3. Jackie can take two separate trails from the base of a mountain to its peak. One trail covers a shorter distance than the other. If Jackie must also take one of these two trails on the way back from the peak to the base, what is the distance of the longer route?

   (1) When Jackie hikes from the base to the peak and back by using the shorter route, she hikes a total of 12 miles.

   (2) When she hikes from the base to the peak by the longer route and hikes from the peak to the base by the shorter route, she hikes a total of 16 miles.

   (A)   (B)   (C)   (D)   (E)

4. What is the value of *x?*

   (1) $x = -|x|$
   (2) $x^3 = -27$

   (A)   (B)   (C)   (D)   (E)

5. The value of $\frac{7}{10} - \frac{2}{5}$ is how many times greater than the value of 0.1 – 0.05?

   (A) 5.5
   (B) 6
   (C) 6.5
   (D) 7
   (E) 7.5

Go on to next page ⟹

6. If x and y are nonzero numbers, what is the value of x^y?

(1) $x = 3$

(2) $x^2 = y^2$

(A)　　(B)　　(C)　　(D)　　(E)

7. What is the value of $(x + y)^2$?

(1) $x + y = 3 - y$

(2) $x + y = \dfrac{4}{x + y}$

(A)　　(B)　　(C)　　(D)　　(E)

8. If $a + b + c + d = 24e$, what is the average (arithmetic mean) of a, b, c, d, and e in terms of e?

(A) $10e$

(B) $\dfrac{e}{5}$

(C) $4e + 1$

(D) $\dfrac{5e}{4}$

(E) $5e$

9. If n is an integer, is $\dfrac{80 + n}{n}$ also an integer?

(1) $n > 9$

(2) $n^2 = 100$

(A)　　(B)　　(C)　　(D)　　(E)

10. In the preceding figure, is the length of $PQ + RS$ greater than the length of QR?

(1) $PQ = RS$

(2) $PS = 40$

(A)　　(B)　　(C)　　(D)　　(E)

11. What is the value of x?

(1) $-2x + 8 = -4x + 2$

(2) $x^2 + 1 = 10$

(A)　　(B)　　(C)　　(D)　　(E)

12. If Sherry invests $1 at an interest rate of 5% compounded quarterly, what would be the total value in dollars of Sherry's investment at the end of three years?

(A) $(1.125)^{12}$

(B) $(1.0125)^{12}$

(C) $4(1.125)^3$

(D) $1.0125(4)^3$

(E) $1 + (0.05)^{12}$

13. College A has 800 senior students, and College B has 700 senior students. If 90% of the seniors who attend College A will graduate this year and 80% of all the senior students from both colleges combined will graduate this year, how many seniors will graduate this year from College B?

(A) 300

(B) 380

(C) 450

(D) 480

(E) 500

14. If x is a positive integer and the value of $\dfrac{x^2}{72}$ is a positive integer, what is the largest of the following numbers that must result in a positive integer when it is divided by x?

(A) 2

(B) 4

(C) 6

(D) 12

(E) 32

15. If $p = \dfrac{8q}{2r}$ and $r \neq 0$, is p an integer?

(1) $q = 2r$

(2) $q = \dfrac{2}{5}$

(A)　　(B)　　(C)　　(D)　　(E)

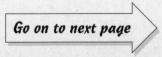

Go on to next page

16. A baker purchased x kilograms of white flour at \$1.40 per kilogram and y kilograms of wheat flour at \$2 per kilogram. If the baker spent a total of \$350 on 190 kilograms of flour, how many kilograms of wheat flour did she purchase?

    (A) 110

    (B) 120

    (C) 130

    (D) 140

    (E) 150

17. A radio station fundraiser brought in a total of \$349 in donations from listeners. If the minimum donation was \$5, what is the greatest possible number of listeners that could have donated to the fundraiser?

    (A) 62

    (B) 63

    (C) 69

    (D) 70

    (E) 71

18. If $x = -1$, what is the value of $\dfrac{x^3 + x^4 - x^3}{2x - 2}$?

    (A) $-\dfrac{1}{2}$

    (B) $-\dfrac{1}{4}$

    (C) 0

    (D) $\dfrac{1}{4}$

    (E) $\dfrac{1}{2}$

19. How long is the route from Mike's house to the grocery store?

    (1) It takes Mike six fewer minutes to bike from his home to the grocery store when he bikes at a speed of 10 miles per hour than when he travels at a speed of 5 miles per hour.

    (2) It takes Mike 30 minutes traveling at 4 miles per hour to bike on the route from his house to the store and back to his house.

    (A)   (B)   (C)   (D)   (E)

20. Is the product $qrst$ equal to -1?

    (1) $\dfrac{q}{r} = \dfrac{s}{t}$

    (2) $q = -\dfrac{1}{r}$ and $s = -\dfrac{1}{t}$

    (A)   (B)   (C)   (D)   (E)

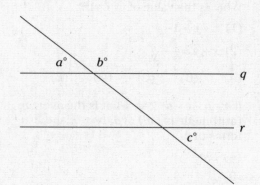

21. In the preceding figure, the lines q and r are parallel. What is the degree measure of angle c?

    (1) Angle b measures 140 degrees.

    (2) Angle a measures 40 degrees.

    (A)   (B)   (C)   (D)   (E)

22. If a, b, and c are positive, is $a^2 = \dfrac{b^3}{c^2}$?

    (1) $a = \sqrt{\dfrac{b^3}{c^2}}$

    (2) $c = \dfrac{b^3}{a^2 c}$

    (A)   (B)   (C)   (D)   (E)

23. The ages of four dogs are 3, 5, 7, and 11 years, respectively. Of the following values, which *cannot* be the total age in years of a combination of any two of the four dogs?

    (A) 8

    (B) 9

    (C) 10

    (D) 12

    (E) 16

Go on to next page

24. If it takes a painter 12 hours to paint $\frac{2}{5}$ of the walls in the house, how many hours will it take the painter to paint the rest of the walls in the house?

    (A) 18

    (B) 20

    (C) 26

    (D) 28

    (E) 30

25. A bacterial colony contains 203.78 billion cells. Of these cells, 595.02 million cells contain mutation X. Which of the following values is the best approximation of the percentage of cells within the colony that contain mutation X?

    (A) 30

    (B) 3

    (C) 0.3

    (D) 0.03

    (E) 0.003

26. The positive integer x is divisible by 15. If $\sqrt{x} < 15$, which of the following values could be the quotient of $\frac{x}{15}$?

    (A) 14

    (B) 15

    (C) 16

    (D) 17

    (E) 18

27. Kim has a number of coins in her pocket composed of p pennies, d dimes, n nickels, and q quarters. If Kim adds an additional 3 pennies, 2 dimes, and 1 nickel to her pocket, what is the probability that she will pick a penny when she randomly removes a single coin from her pocket?

    (A) $\frac{p}{d+n+q}$

    (B) $\frac{p}{p+d+n+q}$

    (C) $\frac{p+3}{d+n+q+3}$

    (D) $\frac{p+3}{p+d+n+q+3}$

    (E) $\frac{p+3}{p+d+n+q+6}$

28. $\dfrac{\frac{1}{4}}{\frac{1}{2}+\frac{1}{6}} = ?$

    (A) $\frac{1}{12}$

    (B) $\frac{1}{6}$

    (C) $\frac{3}{8}$

    (D) $\frac{1}{2}$

    (E) 2

29. A square yard has an area of $2x$ square feet. In terms of x, what is the shortest distance in feet from the northwest corner of the yard to the southeast corner?

    (A) $2x$

    (B) $x\sqrt{2}$

    (C) $2\sqrt{x}$

    (D) $4\sqrt{x}$

    (E) $\sqrt{2x}$

30. Is n closer to 60 than it is to 95?

    (1) $n - 60 \le 95 - n$

    (2) $n < 80$

    (A)　　(B)　　(C)　　(D)　　(E)

31. Is the value of $a > 0$?

    (1) $ab < 0$ and $bc > 0$

    (2) $c < 0$

    (A)　　(B)　　(C)　　(D)　　(E)

32. In the decimal $7.4\Diamond\Delta 3$, $\Diamond$ and Δ each represent one digit. What is the value of $\Diamond$?

    (1) When rounded to the nearest hundredth, the decimal becomes 7.45.

    (2) When rounded to the nearest tenth, the decimal becomes 7.4.

    (A)　　(B)　　(C)　　(D)　　(E)

Go on to next page

33. Tim has $94 with which to purchase cans of soup. The cans are sold at $36 for a pack of 24, $12 for a pack of 6, and $2.50 for a single can. What is the greatest number of cans that Tim can buy?

    (A) 52

    (B) 54

    (C) 56

    (D) 58

    (E) 60

34. What is the value of $\dfrac{(0.5)^6}{(0.5)^9}$?

    (A) $\dfrac{1}{8}$

    (B) $\dfrac{2}{3}$

    (C) $\dfrac{3}{2}$

    (D) 6

    (E) 8

35. A jar can hold a total of how many jelly beans?

    (1) There are 800 jelly beans presently in the jar.

    (2) If 400 jelly beans are added to the jar when the jar is a third full, the number of jelly beans in the jar increases by 50%.

    (A)   (B)   (C)   (D)   (E)

36. What is the ratio of $a{:}b{:}c$?

    (1) $\dfrac{a}{b} = \dfrac{2}{5}$ and $\dfrac{c}{b} = 3$

    (2) $c = 2$ and $a = \dfrac{32}{b}$

    (A)   (B)   (C)   (D)   (E)

37. If a circular pizza is made so that 55% of the pizza is topped with cheese only and the remaining portion is topped with pepperoni, what is the degree measure of the portion of the pizza that is topped with pepperoni?

    (A) 225

    (B) 198

    (C) 162

    (D) 135

    (E) 120

Section 4: Verbal

Time: 75 minutes for 41 questions

Directions: Follow these directions for each of the three question types:

✔ **Sentence correction questions:** Choose the answer choice that best phrases the underlined words according to the rules of standard English. The first answer choice duplicates the phrasing of the underlined portion; the other four choices provide alternative phrasings. Choose the one that rephrases the sentence in the clearest, most grammatically correct manner.

✔ **Reading comprehension questions:** Choose the best answer to every question based on what the passage states directly or indirectly.

✔ **Critical reasoning questions:** Pick the answer choice that best answers the question about the argument provided.

1. SpeedyTrim claims to be the most effective weight loss supplement available today without a prescription. To back up this claim, company executives offered a free trial to 12 people exercising at a popular gym. All 12 trial members confirmed that SpeedyTrim was the best weight loss supplement they had ever taken.

   Which of the following, if true, would most seriously weaken SpeedyTrim's claim?

   (A) The trial at the popular gym was conducted by a company other than SpeedyTrim.

   (B) All 12 people in the trial confirmed that SpeedyTrim was the only weight loss supplement they had ever taken.

   (C) Another test of weight loss supplements revealed that the prescription drug Nogain was more effective in promoting weight loss than was SpeedyTrim.

   (D) All 12 people involved in the trial at the popular gym were extremely overweight when they began taking SpeedyTrim.

   (E) SpeedyTrim's primary ingredient is highly addictive.

2. The federal government estimates that per mile traveled, the ratio of the number of motorcycle deaths to automobile deaths is 37 to 1. Therefore, to protect the safety of their citizens, most states have implemented laws that mandate some sort of helmet use for motorcycle riders. Opponents of motorcycle helmet laws maintain that in a free country, people should have the right to engage in potentially dangerous behavior at their discretion as long as they aren't harming others. They think it should be a matter of individual choice whether to wear a helmet when riding a motorcycle.

   Which of the following, if true, most weakens the helmet opponents' argument?

   (A) More head injuries are reported by motorcycle riders who don't wear helmets than by those who do.

   (B) Head injuries from motorcycle accidents exceed head injuries from auto accidents.

   (C) Most states have laws that require bicycle riders under the age of 18 to wear helmets.

   (D) Some states do not require motorcycle riders to wear helmets, leaving the decision of whether to wear a helmet up to the individual.

   (E) Motorcycle insurance rates for all motorcycle owners have risen by 5 percent over the last decade to offset the medical costs associated with head injuries incurred by motorcycle riders who fail to wear helmets.

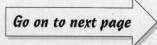
Go on to next page

3. Executives of several large and small businesses have united in an effort to oppose proposed legislation that would prohibit them from requesting access to potential employees' social media accounts. Proponents of the new law state that requesting access to job applicants' social media pages is an egregious invasion of personal privacy and claim that what applicants post on their social media sites is no indication of how they would perform on the job.

   The position of the group of executives would be most strengthened if it were true that

   (A) studies have indicated that the level of discretion and common sense people exhibit when they use social media directly mirrors their use of the same in day-to-day personal and business interactions

   (B) requesting and requiring access to another's social media page is a clear violation of First Amendment rights

   (C) potential employers have the right to request access to anything they want from applicants, and the potential employee, in turn, has the right to deny access and pursue employment elsewhere

   (D) individuals who have a strong social media presence tend to be better informed than those who do not

   (E) no level of privacy whatsoever can be assumed when it comes to the Internet

4. Studies show that nearly one-third of women in America today give birth via Cesarean section, a far more expensive procedure than a regular birth. In 1965, fewer than 5 percent of all babies were born by using this method. This proves that hospitals today are motivated primarily by money and do not have the best interests of their patients at heart.

   Which of the following, if true, best refutes the claim of the argument?

   (A) Studies have shown that increasingly greater numbers of women are choosing elective Cesarean section deliveries for cosmetic and other personal reasons.

   (B) There were fewer surgeons trained in the Cesarean section procedure in 1965 than there are today.

   (C) Midwives were far more popular in 1965 than they are today.

   (D) Doctors are required to take a solemn oath that they will perform their duties with a primary focus on the patient's best interests.

   (E) Statistics regarding medical procedures are far more accurate and readily available today than they were in 1965.

5. The homeschooling association met on the third Thursday of each month to discuss issues concerning the homeschooling community, introduce new members, and for organizing group field trips.

   (A) for organizing group field trips

   (B) to organize group field trips

   (C) organizing group field trips

   (D) it determined how group field trips should be organized

   (E) organize group field trips

Go on to next page

6. Many surfers <u>seem to be avoiding the Sunset/Waimea Bay area because they are experiencing</u> an increase in shark attacks.

   (A) seem to be avoiding the Sunset/Waimea Bay area because they are experiencing

   (B) seem to avoid the Sunset/Waimea Bay area because they are experiencing

   (C) avoid the Sunset/Waimea Bay area seemingly because they are experiencing

   (D) seem to be avoiding the Sunset/Waimea Bay area because it is experiencing

   (E) seemingly avoid the Sunset/Waimea Bay area when it experiences

7. Law enforcement officials believe that roughly 600 incidents of runaways have occurred in the city this year, with most of these incidents <u>resulting from violence at home, disagreements with parents or legal guardians, parents' divorce, or the addition of a new child to the home</u>.

   (A) resulting from violence at home, disagreements with parents or legal guardians, parents' divorce, or the addition of a new child to the home

   (B) being the result of violence at home, disagreements with parents or legal guardians, or parents divorcing or adding a new child to the home

   (C) occurrences being the result of violence at home, disagreements with parents or legal guardians, or parents divorcing or adding a new child to the home

   (D) being abused runaways, runaways who have not got along with their parents, or runaways whose parents got divorced or added a new child to the home

   (E) having been the result from violence at home, disagreements with parents or legal guardians, parental divorce, or the adding of a new child to the home

Questions 8–12 refer to the following passage, which is excerpted from Anatomy and Physiology For Dummies, *2nd Edition, by Maggie Norris and Donna Rae Siegfried (Wiley).*

Scientifically speaking, human biology isn't more or less complex, specialized, or cosmically significant than the biology of any other species, and all are interdependent. Every species of animal, plant, and fungus on the planet has both anatomy and physiology. So does each species of *protist* (one-celled creatures, like amoebae and the plasmodia that cause malaria). At the cellular level, all these groups are astoundingly similar. At the levels of tissues, organs, and organ systems (the provenance of anatomy and physiology), plants are very different from animals, and both plants and animals are equally dissimilar to fungi.

Each of these major groups, called a *kingdom,* has its own characteristic anatomy and physiology. It's evident at a glance to everyone at the beach that a starfish and a human are both animals, while the alga in the tide pool and the cedar tree on the shoreline are both plants. Obvious details of anatomy (the presence or absence of bright green tissue) and physiology (the presence or absence of locomotion) tell that story. The different forms within each kingdom have obvious differences as well: The cedar must stand on the shore but the alga would die there. The starfish can move from one place to another within a limited range, while humans can (theoretically) go anywhere on the planet and, with the appropriate accoutrements of culture (a human adaptation), survive there for at least a while. (That is, assuming the cedar and the alga keep on photosynthesizing.) Scientists use these differences to classify organisms into smaller and smaller groups within the kingdom, until each organism is classified into its own "specie-al" group.

8. The primary purpose of the passage is to

   (A) discuss the biology of humans, plants, and animals, and the ways that species can be categorized

   (B) show the similarities and differences between the biology of humans and that of plants and animals

   (C) explain how kingdoms can be further subcategorized

   (D) explore the complexities of human biology

   (E) examine why humans are the superior species

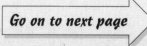
Go on to next page

9. The authors make all the following assertions about biology *except*

(A) The biology of humans is not any more intricate than that of other species.

(B) The biology of humans is strikingly like that of plants and fungi on the cellular level.

(C) The biological makeup of humans enables them to subsist for at least some amount of time essentially anywhere on the planet.

(D) Starfish have limited mobility because their biological structure is less elaborate than that of humans.

(E) Animals, plants, and fungi have both anatomy and physiology.

10. According to the passage, all but which of the following are true about kingdoms?

(A) The kingdoms depend upon one another.

(B) They are somewhat similar in their anatomy and physiology.

(C) Different forms within the same kingdom can have substantial differences.

(D) Organisms within a kingdom can be classified into smaller and smaller groups.

(E) Kingdoms have their own characteristic organ systems.

11. The authors compare human beings to starfish primarily to demonstrate

(A) that human beings are more adaptive than starfish

(B) the ways that human biology is more complex than that of other species

(C) that there are still substantial differences among members of the same kingdom

(D) the ways that species depend on each other

(E) the significant cellular differences that can exist within the same kingdom

12. The authors are most likely to agree with which of the following statements?

(A) The genetic makeup of a human being is far more intricate than that of a starfish.

(B) All species share very similar anatomy and physiology.

(C) Although plants and animals are different from one another, they are more similar to each other than either one is to fungi.

(D) Animals, plants, and fungi are somewhat similar in the provenance of their anatomy and physiology.

(E) Organisms within the same kingdom are generally classified into smaller groups that reflect their obvious differences.

13. Since the 1993 release of *Jurassic Park,* paleontologists around the world have studied the validity of the movie's premise that dinosaurs could have possibly been cloned if their DNA was extracted from a fossilized insect's last meal.

(A) could have possibly been cloned

(B) could be cloned

(C) might have possibly been cloned

(D) could clone

(E) cloning could occur

14. According to written accounts from residents of Salem, Massachusetts, scholars find that much of the horror of the Salem witch trials that has been depicted in movies like *The Crucible* does not stray too far from the truth.

(A) According to written accounts from residents of Salem, Massachusetts,

(B) In accordance with written accounts from residents of Salem, Massachusetts,

(C) With written accounts of residents of Salem, Massachusetts, used as a basis,

(D) With the written accounts of residents of Salem, Massachusetts, having been used,

(E) Using accounts from residents of Salem, Massachusetts,

Go on to next page

15. Berry & Westfall, LLC, and Atredies, Inc., merged in 2010 to create Berry, Westfall, and Atredies, Inc., <u>and they're now the most successful zoning law firm in the region</u>.

    (A) and they're now the most successful zoning law firm in the region

    (B) and it is now the region's more successful zoning law firm

    (C) and they're now the most successful zoning law firms in the region

    (D) which is now the region's most successful zoning law firm

    (E) and its now one of the most successful zoning law firms in the region

16. The meadows, ponds, and wetlands created by a beaver dam <u>increases biodiversity and improves overall environmental quality</u>.

    (A) increases biodiversity and improves overall environmental quality

    (B) increase biodiversity and improves overall environmental quality

    (C) contribute to increasing biodiversity and improving overall environmental quality

    (D) increase biodiversity and improve overall environmental quality

    (E) has increased biodiversity and improved overall environmental qualities

17. Studies show that the more people are exposed to a particular sport, the more they like it. The four most popular and successful professional sports in the United States are basketball, baseball, hockey, and American football. Soccer is less popular in the United States, but it experiences tremendous popularity and success in other countries.

    Which of the following provides the most reasonable explanation for the information in the preceding prompt?

    (A) Americans tend to dislike soccer because other countries are better at it.

    (B) Americans have no room in their hearts for another major league sport.

    (C) American television and other media sources devote less time to soccer coverage than media outlets in other countries do.

    (D) Other countries have fewer professional sports to choose from, so they tend to watch and follow soccer.

    (E) Americans find soccer to be less exciting than American football.

18. Chris and Laurie are servers at the same restaurant. Chris believes that because he is a male server, he earns larger tips from female customers, and Laurie believes that her bigger tips come from males. To maximize profits, Chris is going to take all the predominantly female tables, and Laurie will serve the tables that are primarily occupied by males.

    Chris and Laurie's plan is based on which of the following assumptions?

    (A) Both male and female restaurant patrons are inherently sexist.

    (B) Chris and Laurie are equally capable servers.

    (C) A representative of the predominant gender at a given table is most likely to pick up the check.

    (D) Males are generally more likely to leave larger tips when they are served by a female.

    (E) If a table is made up of both males and females, one of the males is more likely to pay the check.

19. Studies have repeatedly shown that children in a daycare setting thrive best when the child to caregiver ratio is low. Therefore, when the time comes to place my child in daycare, I will ensure that he ends up in one with a small number of children.

    The reasoning in the argument is flawed because the author fails to acknowledge which of the following?

    (A) Children perform better and are better behaved when they have more than one primary authority figure.

    (B) The quality of childcare depends more on the age of the caregiver than the number of children.

    (C) Children in daycare are more likely to thrive when they are forced to be independent.

    (D) A small number of children does not necessarily ensure a low child to caregiver ratio.

    (E) Parental desires regarding a choice of daycare facility are not as important as statistical evidence concerning what is best for their children.

Go on to next page ⟹

Questions 20–23 refer to the following passage, which is excerpted from Native America: A History, *by Michael Leroy Oberg (Wiley).*

So many accounts of this continent's past begin with Europeans striding ashore, claiming this "new found land" and its human inhabitants for their respective empires. These arrogant assertions always have been challenged by native peoples, but nonetheless jurists and scholars have inscribed them in American law and in the written histories from which the law springs. And with heads bowed, or with a bounteous welcome, too many native peoples in too many of these accounts prepare to greet their colonizers as saviors, whatever their initial misgivings. When the Algonquian-speaking peoples of the Carolina Sounds first saw the English colonists sent to occupy Roanoke Island in 1585, for instance, the astute English observer Thomas Harriot reported that they "began to make a great and horrible crye as people which never before had seene men appareled like us." Confused and savage, "they made out," Harriot continued, "cries like wild beasts or men out of their wits." Soon they calmed themselves, in Harriot's eyes, and stopped acting like beasts, and regained their wits, but only after the newcomers presented them with gifts that demonstrated and confirmed their benevolent intent. These native peoples soon would debate amongst themselves, as they considered the great power these newcomers seemed to possess, whether they were "gods or men."

That is how Harriot saw it, yet today many Americans still believe that it is with the arrival of Europeans that their nation's history begins. We could find, if we looked, dozens of accounts of "discovery" that differed from Harriot's only in their details. These moments of encounter, depicted so often over the years in the work of American artists, historians, and myth-makers, represent the opening of a grand story — the growth and development of the United States. All that happened before these seminal moments, as a result, has been ignored or trivialized by earlier generations of American historians, who celebrated the progress of a new nation.

20. The author of this passage is primarily concerned with

(A) discussing the impact the arrival of European settlers to the North American continent had on existing native peoples

(B) disputing the claims made by many jurists and scholars that the native inhabitants of North America welcomed European settlers with open arms

(C) verifying the accuracy of Harriot's account of the 1585 English arrival on Roanoke Island

(D) demonstrating how Harriot's account of the 1585 English arrival on Roanoke Island differed from those of other English historians and scholars

(E) distinguishing myth from reality in regard to the reception early European settlers received from North America's native peoples

21. Upon whom does the author place blame for perpetuating the inaccuracies in the depictions of the arrival of European settlers on the land that is now North America?

(A) Harriot

(B) American historians

(C) Europeans

(D) Algonquin-speaking peoples

(E) English colonizers

Go on to next page

22. It can be inferred from the passage that the author's primary issue with early accounts of the arrival of European settlers on the North American continent is that

    (A) they fail to accurately depict the way the native people reacted to the European settlers after the settlers showed their benevolence

    (B) despite being disputed by native peoples, they still influence American art, written history, and law

    (C) they create the image that native peoples welcomed the English colonists ashore and viewed them as saviors without reporting how the colonists felt about seeing the native inhabitants

    (D) much of what has made its way into American law and history books strays substantially from the accounts of English settlers who were present to observe the events

    (E) they largely ignore the native peoples' initial response to the arrival of European settlers

23. Which of the following is *not* a description Harriot used to depict the native peoples' initial reaction to him and other settlers of Roanoke Island?

    (A) witless

    (B) bewildered

    (C) savage

    (D) benevolent

    (E) beast-like

24. Despite rampant criticism by parental groups and some religious organizations, reality shows that focus on teen motherhood have not been linked to an increase in teen pregnancy, this seems as if to suggest that they may in fact have the opposite effect.

    (A) this seems as if to suggest that

    (B) which seems suggestive of

    (C) this seems like a suggestion that

    (D) which seems like it is suggesting that

    (E) suggesting that

25. When naming your child, be sure to imagine what the name will look like on a business card 20 to 25 years from now. The real world is far less likely to take colleagues' opinions seriously when they're named something like Candy or Bambi.

    The preceding argument would be most strengthened if it were true that

    (A) unemployed women named Candy and Bambi outnumber those with names like Susan and Kathleen

    (B) name trends come and go

    (C) before they even meet someone, people form mental images of others based on their first name

    (D) studies show that people are more likely to form opinions of others based on their family background than on the way they dress

    (E) names like Candy and Bambi will be considered old-fashioned 20 to 25 years from now

26. As incidents of employee theft skyrocketed during the last decade, more and more businesses have implemented stiffer penalties and zero tolerance policies. Yet most of these businesses are not seeing a decrease in the number of incidents of employee theft, so the stiffer penalties clearly aren't working.

    Which of the following, if true, would most weaken the preceding conclusion?

    (A) All new employees have been forced to undergo theft prevention training.

    (B) Businesses have redefined their definition of theft.

    (C) Businesses' theft prevention efforts in general have been reduced due to budget constraints.

    (D) At the same time that businesses began imposing stiffer sanctions for employee theft, the average number of employees per business increased.

    (E) Businesses have fewer employees now than they did ten years ago.

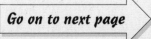
Go on to next page

27. The increase in the number of underage celebrities being photographed stumbling out of bars is evidence that bar and club owners care more about being the latest "hot spot" than following federal laws that prohibit bars and clubs from serving alcohol to those who are underage. With today's technology, machines exist that effectively detect falsified IDs.

Which of the following does the argument assume to properly reach its conclusion?

(A) The only way to become a hip hot spot is to make sure celebrities frequent your establishment.

(B) Bars and clubs that attract celebrities also attract underage patrons.

(C) Bar and club owners have likely paid off local authorities in hopes that they will "look the other way" when underage patrons drink in their clubs.

(D) The underage celebrities were not intoxicated.

(E) The bars and clubs that are frequented by underage celebrities also have access to technology that successfully scans methods of identification.

28. Arguments have been made time and time again about the dangers associated with tanning. An advocate for the tanning industry, however, is working tirelessly to change this notion by spreading the word that spray tanning does not share the same risk factors and, therefore, should not be put in the same category and undergo the same scrutiny as tanning booths.

The tanning industry advocate makes the assumption that

(A) the viability of the tanning industry as a whole is in danger due to elevated concerns about its health risks

(B) industry advocates should be compensated for their efforts

(C) spray tanning has fewer inherent risk factors than does booth tanning

(D) those who argue against tanning are not aware of the benefits of spray tanning

(E) the arguments against tanning are directed toward the tanning industry

29. Evolutionists believe that the recently discovered prosauropods from Madagascar are nearly 2 million years <u>as old as any of their</u> Argentinean relatives.

(A) as old as any of their

(B) older than any of they're

(C) as old as their

(D) older than any of their

(E) older than there

30. Conservationists in Indonesia have discovered a tree frog they've dubbed the *spike nosed tree frog,* one <u>that they believe is</u> a type previously unknown to scientists.

(A) that they believe is

(B) that they believe is to be

(C) they believe that it is of

(D) they believe is

(E) they believe to be of

Go on to next page

31. In the 1970s, researchers on a small island nation conducted a study, using a sample of pregnant women who resided there. Of those sampled, 35 were daily smokers of marijuana and 35 had never smoked. The study indicated that the babies of the marijuana smokers were just as healthy as those of nonsmokers and concluded that smoking marijuana has little effect on the health of a woman's unborn child.

Which of the following, if true, most weakens the conclusion of the researchers?

(A) The women in the study who smoked daily reported less cramping and nausea throughout their pregnancies than those who did not smoke.

(B) The women in the study who smoked marijuana were from the same village, one whose residents were of a substantially higher socioeconomic status than the rest of the country, with better access to prenatal care.

(C) The women in the study who smoked marijuana were from the same village, one that cultivated 85 percent of the country's supply of marijuana and whose residents used marijuana at a higher rate than residents of other villages.

(D) The women in the study who smoked regularly were generally farther along in their pregnancies when the study began than those in the nonsmoking group.

(E) Marijuana has been shown to be far less damaging to an unborn fetus than tobacco is.

Questions 32–35 refer to the following passage, which is excerpted from Content Rules: How to Create Killer Blogs, Podcasts, Videos, Ebooks, Webinars (and More) That Engage Customers and Ignite Your Business, *by Ann Handley and C.C. Chapman (Wiley).*

Marcus Sheridan is one of three owners of River Pools and Spa in Warsaw, Virginia. The company installs swimming pools and hot tubs throughout Maryland and Virginia. Since joining the business in 2002, Marcus has spearheaded tremendous growth at the company. Despite years of record rainfall, a housing slump, and the slacker economy, River Pools continues to grow: In 2009, it sold more fiberglass pools than any other company in the United States, where it's among the top 5 percent of all in-ground pool companies.

A big reason for that, Marcus says, is his company's approach to business. "I used to see my company as a 'pool company.' [We] installed lots of swimming pools and therefore we were a pool company.

"In hindsight, though, this mentality was all wrong," he says. "Today, I see my business as a content marketing company. In other words, my entire goal is to give more valuable, helpful, and remarkable content to consumers than anyone else in my field, which will in turn lead to more sales."

Through a steady stream of blog posts and videos (the company publishes one to three a week) and an ebook on the subject of "how to buy a pool" (with the subtext "without getting ripped off"), Marcus set out to create the most educational and informative swimming pool web site on the Internet.

"I want our web site to be an encyclopedia of pool buying," he says, not unlike a business trade magazine publisher might seek to have similar authority in any given industry. "I want someone with a question to come to our site and get an answer by reading it or watching it."

The swimming pool industry is dominated by larger manufacturers, which makes it difficult for a small, young company like the nine-year-old River Pools to compete online for general search terms like *swimming pool* or *in-ground pool*. (When a potential customer searches for swimming pool information online using such terms, Google is more likely to return results for one of the big guys, not a small outfit like River Pools.)

Go on to next page

32. Based on the information in the passage, which of the following would be the wisest next step in marketing River Pools?

    (A) Starting a business trade magazine

    (B) Increasing the frequency of blog posts and video streams from several times a week to daily

    (C) Purchasing ads and billboards in states bordering Maryland and Virginia

    (D) Increasing web presence through search engine optimization

    (E) Hosting in-person seminars at major retailers that sell pool supplies

33. Which of the following would be the best potential heading for this passage?

    (A) Marketing Made Easy

    (B) The Value of Internet Marketing

    (C) Creating a Competitive Advantage with Content

    (D) River Pools: A Small Fish in a Big Pond

    (E) How to Buy a Pool without Getting Ripped Off

34. Which of the following best describes what Marcus means when he says, "I used to see my company as a 'pool company'"?

    (A) He did not see the bigger picture when considering items River Pools could sell to its customer base.

    (B) Initially, he did not fully understand that River Pools was different from others in the nationwide industry of pool manufacturers.

    (C) He had failed to recognize how the Internet could allow a small company like River Pools to successfully expand its business beyond its home turf.

    (D) He had overestimated the amount of knowledge the general public had about pools.

    (E) He had failed to consider the less tangible services his business offered.

35. The author cites all but which of the following as a goal of River Pools?

    (A) To have its website serve as a comprehensive online information source on pool buying

    (B) To expand its customer base beyond Maryland and Virginia

    (C) To provide valuable content to website visitors

    (D) To establish the most informative swimming pool website available online

    (E) To produce additional sales

36. Our state's students would benefit tremendously if the state government would allow for a school voucher system, where students are allotted a certain amount of money to spend for tuition at any school they like, public or private.

    Which of the following, if true, would most weaken the preceding argument?

    (A) Vouchers can help minimize the disparity between private and state education, a major divider in the current class system.

    (B) History has shown time and time again that without outside incentives, schools are unlikely to change.

    (C) A school voucher program would increase competitiveness among schools and force underperforming schools to up their game in order to attract enough students to stay afloat.

    (D) Students in poorer neighborhoods cannot afford the transportation costs required to attend schools that are not located nearby.

    (E) Public schools tend to provide an overall better educational experience than private schools.

Go on to next page

37. In our state, methamphetamine abuse is the single largest cause of death among young people. Currently, residents on the North Side are seeing more meth-related deaths than are residents of the West Side, but fewer than those on the East Side. The West Side has a substantially older population than the East Side.

    If the information in the prompt is true, what also must be true?

    (A) Meth-related deaths occur more frequently on the East Side than the West Side.

    (B) The population of the North Side is, on average, older than that of the West Side.

    (C) Residents on the West Side must have a greater access to methamphetamines.

    (D) The East Side has the highest concentration of meth-producing laboratories in the city.

    (E) The West Side experiences a lower death rate from methamphetamine use because the average age of its population is older than that of the rest of the city.

38. Studies indicate that some individuals never fully recover from the damaging effects of violence <u>occurring when a child</u>.

    (A) occurring when a child

    (B) that occurred when they were children

    (C) that occurred when a child

    (D) occurring when children

    (E) that has occurred when each was a child

39. <u>Each of the West Memphis Three — Damian Echols, Jason Baldwin, and Jessie Misskelley, Jr. — were freed from prison in August 2011,</u> nearly two decades after they were wrongly convicted of the brutal murder of three young boys in Arkansas.

    (A) Each of the West Memphis Three — Damian Echols, Jason Baldwin, and Jessie Misskelley, Jr. — were freed from prison in August 2011,

    (B) Damian Echols, Jason Baldwin, and Jessie Misskelley, Jr., each of whom were members of the West Memphis Three, were freed from prison in August 2011,

    (C) The West Memphis Three — Damian Echols, Jason Baldwin, and Jessie Misskelley, Jr. — were freed from prison in August 2011,

    (D) Freed from prison in August 2011, Damian Echols, Jason Baldwin, and Jessie Misskelley, Jr., were members of the West Memphis Three

    (E) Freed from prison in August 2011 — Damian Echols, Jason Baldwin, and Jessie Misskelley, Jr. — every one a member of the West Memphis Three,

 *Go on to next page*

40. Regarded as one of the "greenest" presidents to ever hold the position, <u>Teddy Roosevelt's environmental projects included preserving 150 million acres of land and the creation of 50 wildlife refuges and five national parks.</u>

   (A) Teddy Roosevelt's environmental projects included preserving 150 million acres of land and the creation of 50 wildlife refuges and five national parks

   (B) Teddy Roosevelt's environmental projects included the preservation of 150 million acres of land and the creation of 50 wildlife refuges and five national parks

   (C) Teddy Roosevelt's environmental projects included 50 wildlife refuges and five national parks being created and 150 million acres of land being preserved

   (D) Teddy Roosevelt carried out environmental projects that included preserving 150 million acres of land and creating 50 wildlife refuges and five national parks

   (E) Teddy Roosevelt put into operation environmental projects that included preserving 150 million acres of land and the creation of five wildlife refuges and 50 national parks

41. Jameson, Bender, and Co., a manufacturer of auto parts, made the switch this year to using a computer software program rather than manpower to screen potential new hires, <u>and it's been able to substantially minimize overall company expenditures as a result.</u>

   (A) and it's been able to substantially minimize overall company expenditures as a result

   (B) they've been able to minimize overall company expenditures substantially as a result

   (C) and its been able to minimize substantially overall company expenditures as a result

   (D) which makes them able to substantially minimize overall company expenditures as a result

   (E) and as a result, they've been able to substantially minimize their overall company expenditures

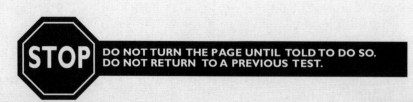

Chapter 20

Practice Test Answers and Explanations

• •

You've finished the test, but you're not done yet. Reading through the following explanations may be the most important part of taking the practice exam. Examine the information for the questions you missed as well as those you answered correctly. You may find tips and techniques you haven't thought of before in one of the answer explanations. If you're short on time or just want to quickly check your answers, head to the end of this chapter for an abbreviated answer key.

Section 1: Analytical Writing Assessment

Scoring the practice analytical writing task is a little different than scoring the other sections. Your job is to honestly analyze the essay you've written and assign yourself a score. You can also ask a friend or composition teacher to look over your essay and give you an opinion. Refer to the scoring considerations in Chapters 7 and 9 for guidance on what readers are looking for. To help you determine your score for this section, we've included a sample essay and an explanation of its strengths and weaknesses. Use these tools to identify your own essay's strengths and weaknesses and improve your essay response before you take the actual test.

Here's a sample response to the essay prompt:

> The author of this statement argues that photo radar cameras cause more harm than good and combat only one small component of the many dangers of highway driving. He also asserts that they are an infringement of civil liberties, and yet another way citizens are under government control in their daily lives.

> While he offers a number of reasons as to why he doesn't support camera use, there are a number of additions he could have made to make his argument more convincing. For example, he notes that the cameras are "inaccurate" and "prone to errors"; yet, he fails to cite the problems these inaccuracies can cause. Perhaps people are receiving speeding tickets in the mail as a result of the cameras that say they were traveling faster than they actually were. When this happens with a normal, police officer-issued ticket, one can "challenge" the ticket and the officer who issued it in court. But how does one challenge a machine?

> He could have also strengthened his argument by noting that the cameras are unable to make the distinction between regular travelers and emergency vehicles like ambulances and fire trucks. While a cop on the hunt for speeders is not going to pull over an ambulance for going 80 MPH in a 65, cameras are unable to make this distinction and that ambulance is just as likely to receive a ticket in the mail as a regular motorist traveling at the same speed.

> Furthermore, while he notes that the cameras fail to recognize many of the other common causes of highway accidents, like cellphone use and driving while intoxicated, he could have strengthened this argument by including some statistics about how the other factors he noted, aside from speed, are more likely to cause crashes. He might

have referenced that, in the 1980s, highway deaths decreased substantially long before the introduction of highway cameras, because the country was more focused on preventing drunk and distracted driving and other common causes of accidents than in combating speeding.

The author also fails to consider arguments in favor of speed cameras. While he states that their use is an infringement on civil liberties and a cause of unnecessary stress and strife among citizens, he fails to consider the fact that their technology can also potentially help citizens by tracking stolen vehicles and getaway vehicles or catching people using their cellphones while driving in states where this is illegal. He notes that there are other factors that often cause highway accidents, but fails to consider evidence that supports their effectiveness in improving safety. Many countries that have instituted the use of traffic cameras have seen substantial declines in the number of highway deaths in only a short amount of time since the cameras were installed.

While the author makes some solid points, his lack of statistical evidence, real life examples and consideration for the other side weakens his overall argument. He also fails to offer any alternative solutions to helping minimize speeds on highways, like improving driver's education curriculum or enacting a national advertising campaign intended to raise awareness of the dangers of speeding on highways. Had he backed up his statements with solid evidence and figures, considered the arguments frequently made by his opposition and offered his own ideas to help combat the problem, his argument would be far more likely to convince.

This essay effectively takes on the arguments against speed cameras made in the essay prompt and assesses their validity. It recognizes that, while the original argument isn't entirely terrible, it could be strengthened and improved in order to be more convincing. Most importantly, the essay provides specific examples as to how the author could have improved the argument. The essay uses solid reasoning throughout as it considers each point made in the prompt and also demonstrates that the author has the ability to focus on the topic at hand and has a solid grasp of general writing and organizational skills. This essay would likely score a solid 5.

Section 2: Integrated Reasoning

Refer to "Section 2: Integrated Reasoning" of Practice Exam 3 on the CD to check your answers for the 12 questions in this section. (*Note:* If you're using a digital or enhanced digital version of this book, please go to http://booksupport.wiley.com for access to the additional content.)

Section 3: Quantitative

1. **C.** You'd need to use a calculator that computes logarithms to find the exact answer to this question, but the question asks for an approximate year. You can easily estimate the answer by using the formula for exponential increase or decrease.

Here's the formula for repeated percent increase, where n stands for the number of changes: Final Amount = Original Amount $\times (1 + \text{Rate})^n$.

The problem tells you that Townsville's population doubles every ten years. This doubling may be represented by 2^n, where the 2 represents the doubling event and n is the number of times the population will double. In terms of the formula, $1 + \text{Rate} = 1 + 1 = 2$, or 200 percent.

The rate is 1 because the doubling event adds a 100 percent increase to the value. The total population, P, may be represented by the starting population times the number of times this original population doubles:

$$P = (5,000)(2^n)$$

Because you want to know how much time it'll take to reach 300,000, set P equal to the desired population and solve for n:

$$300,000 = 5,000(2^n)$$
$$60 = 2^n$$

You can now easily solve for n by successively multiplying 2 by itself until you reach or exceed 60: $2^1 = 2$, $2^2 = 4$, $2^3 = 8$, $2^4 = 16$, $2^5 = 32$, $2^6 = 64$.

You can see that sometime just before $n = 6$, the population has reached 300,000. So you know the population must double, an event that takes ten years, six times: 6×10 is 60. It will take 60 years for the population to reach 300,000. Add 60 years to 1970, and you find that 2030 is the approximate year that Townsville's population will reach 300,000.

TIP

If applying the formula seems overwhelming, you can simply list the population amounts in ten-year increments until you get to 300,000 or greater. In 1970, the population was 5,000; double that to see that in 1980, Townsville had 10,000 residents. Carry the process along every ten years, and you see that the population in 2030 will be 320,000.

2. **B.** Because dividing 6 by 13 would create a nasty decimal to deal with, you're better off solving this problem by converting 75 percent to a fraction. So 75 percent becomes $\frac{75}{100}$ or $\frac{3}{4}$. Because *of* means *multiply* in math language, the equation translates to $\frac{3}{4} \times \frac{6}{13} \times 104 =$.

TIP

You can just multiply the terms, but because you don't have access to a calculator, doing some factoring before you multiply is probably quicker. You can factor 2 from the numerator and denominators of the first two fractions:

$$\frac{3}{\underset{2}{\cancel{4}}} \times \frac{{}^{3}\cancel{6}}{13} = \frac{9}{26}$$

That gives you $\frac{9}{26} \times \frac{104}{1}$. Because 26 is a factor of 104, you can divide the numerator and denominator by 26 to get $\frac{9}{1} \times \frac{4}{1}$, which is 36.

3. **C.** To solve this data sufficiency problem, figure out what you know, what you don't know, and the value you're supposed to find. The problem tells you that Jackie climbs up and down the mountain by one of two possible trails, and one is longer than the other. You don't know the lengths of either of the trails, but you're supposed to find the length of the longer route. Look for information that gives you the length of the longer route or allows you to figure it out from additional information about the shorter route.

All by itself, Statement (1) gives you only the distance of the shorter route ($2s = 12$, where s is the distance of the shorter route one way), but you can't solve for the distance of the longer route without more information. Because Statement (1) alone doesn't provide sufficient information, eliminate Choices (A) and (D).

Statement (2) gives you another equation, $s + l = 16$, but you can't solve an equation with two variables without additional information. The sum of an infinite number of pairs of numbers would give you a total of 16. So eliminate Choice (B), which leaves you with Choices (C) and (E) as possible answers.

You've probably already noticed that the two statements together give you two equations with two variables. Now you know the answer is Choice (C).

Whenever you have as many linear equations as you have variables, you have enough information to find the value of any variable.

You don't need to actually solve for *l* to answer the question, but if you solve for *s* in the first equation, you get *s* = 6. Then, you can substitute 6 for *s* in the second equation to find *l*: 6 + *l* = 16, so *l* = 10.

4. **B.** The question doesn't give you much; all it asks for is the value of *x*. Jump right into the statements: Because negative values are less than zero, Statement (1) simply tells you that $x \le 0$, so all you know about the value of *x* is that it's negative. An infinite number of negative values exist for *x*, so rule out Choices (A) and (D).

   Check out Statement (2) — now we're talking! You can easily solve this equation for a definite value for *x*. The only value with a cubed value of –27 is –3: $-3 \times -3 = 9$ and $9 \times -3 = -27$. The answer must be Choice (B).

5. **B.** To solve this problem, follow these steps:

   1. Find the difference between the first two fractions by finding the common denominator (10), converting the fractions, and subtracting:

      $$\frac{7}{10} - \frac{2}{5} = \frac{7}{10} - \frac{4}{10} = \frac{3}{10}$$

   2. Find the difference between the decimals: $0.1 - 0.05 = 0.05$.

   3. To compare the resulting values, convert them to the same form. Changing the decimal to a fraction may be easier:

      $$0.05 = \frac{5}{100}$$

   4. Then divide:

      $$\frac{3}{10} \div \frac{5}{100} = \frac{3}{10} \times \frac{100}{5} = \frac{300}{50} = 6$$

   The answer is Choice (B).

6. **E.** To answer this data sufficiency question, you need to have enough information to solve for both *x* and *y*. Check out the statements:

   ✔ Statement (1) gives you the value of *x*, but you know nothing about the value of *y*. You can eliminate Choices (A) and (D).

   ✔ Statement (2) just tells you that when you square both *x* and *y*, you get the same value, but you don't know what that value is. Eliminate Choice (B) and check whether both statements together give you definite values for the two variables.

   Don't be fooled into thinking that Statement (2) tells you that *x* and *y* are equal. If you made the mistake of thinking that *y* has to be 3 if *x* is 3, you forgot that finding the square root of an unknown value gives you two possible values, a negative and a positive. So, *y* can equal either 3 or –3 if *x* is 3.

   The two statements together don't give you a finite value for *y*, so the answer is Choice (E).

7. **B.** You can figure out the value of $(x + y)^2$ if you know the values of both *x* and *y* or the value of *x* + *y*.

   When you manipulate the information in Statement (1), you can easily determine that $x = 3 - 2y$, but that just gives you a value for *x* in terms of *y* or *y* in terms of *x*. Because Statement (1) isn't sufficient to answer the question, get rid of Choices (A) and (D) and move to the second statement.

   When you multiply both sides of the equation in Statement (2) by $(x + y)$, you discover that $(x + y)^2 = 4$. End your work right there — that's all you need to know, so the answer must be Choice (B).

8. **E.** This question is easy when you apply the formula for finding averages.

To find the average of a set of numbers, divide the sum of the numbers by the number of elements in the set. Don't be intimidated by the variables.

The sum of the set of values is $a + b + c + d + e$, and the problem tells you that $a + b + c + d = 24e$. Just substitute $24e$ for $a + b + c + d$ and set up the equation, remembering that the set has five values: $\frac{24e + e}{5} = A$. A quick glance at the answers shows you that you just need to solve in terms of e, so all that's left for you to do is solve the equation:

$$\frac{24e + e}{5} = A$$

$$\frac{25e}{5} = A$$

$$5e = A$$

The answer is Choice (E).

9. **B.** This data sufficiency question requires that you deal with an inequality and an exponent. The quickest way to answer it is to simply plug in values that meet the qualifications for n that each statement provides to see whether $\frac{80 + n}{n}$ always results in an integer.

Statement (1) says that n must be greater than 9, so substitute some integers that follow 9. Try both odd and even options, say, 10 and 11:

When $n = 10$, the result is an integer, 9: $\frac{80 + 10}{10} = \frac{90}{10} = 9$.

When $n = 11$, the result isn't an integer: $\frac{80 + 11}{11} = \frac{91}{11} = 8.\overline{27}$.

Because the two possibilities give you two different answers (*yes* when the integer is 10, *no* when the integer is 11), you can rule out Choices (A) and (D).

Statement (2) narrows down the possible value for n to two. When you know that $n^2 = 100$, n must be either 10 or –10. You already know from analyzing Statement (1) that the result is an integer when $n = 10$, so just try –10:

$$\frac{80 + (-10)}{-10} = \frac{70}{-10} = -7$$

An integer can be positive or negative, so both solutions for n in Statement (2) give you an integer. You can definitively answer *yes* to the question based on Statement (2), so the answer is Choice (B).

10. **E.** To solve this question, you need to determine whether the sum of the lengths of arcs PQ and RS is greater than the length of arc QR alone.

When answering this question and others like it, remember that figures aren't necessarily drawn to scale unless otherwise stated. Rely only on what the problem gives you about the arc lengths.

Statement (1) tells you that the lengths of the arcs PQ and RS are equal, but you still don't know how they relate to the length of QR. You need more information to figure out whether $PQ + RS > QR$, so eliminate Choices (A) and (D).

Statement (2) gives the length of the entire curve but again tells nothing of the relative length of QR to that of PQ and RS. Disregard Choice (B) and check whether both statements together give you the ability to get a straight yes or no answer to the question.

You know from Statement (1) that PQ and RS are the same length and from Statement (2) that the length of PS is 40 units long. So for $PQ + RS > QR$ to be true, $PQ + RS$ must be greater than half the entire length of PS. Because you don't know how the shorter lengths relate to the entire length of the arc, you can't answer the question with any certainty. For example, if *PQ* and *RS* were each 5 units long, *QR* would be 30 units and the answer would be *no*. However, if *PQ* and *RS* each measures 15 units, their sum of 30 would be greater than *QR*'s length of 10 units, and the answer would be *yes*. When you come up with more than one answer to the question, the information is insufficient. Taking both statements into consideration doesn't work, so the answer is Choice (E).

11. **A.** Remember that you don't have to solve for *x* to determine whether you have enough information to get a unique solution. Statement (1) has one variable, so you can solve for one value for *x*. The solution is –3, but you don't need to figure that out to know that Statement (1) is sufficient and the answer is either Choice (A) or Choice (D). Check out Statement (2) to see which it is.

Statement (2) is an equation with only one variable, but that variable is squared, so it's unlikely that *x* has only one value. An *x* value of either –3 or 3 would satisfy the equation. The answer has to be Choice (A).

12. **B.** You should notice two things about this interest problem:

✔ You're dealing with compounded interest.

✔ The interest is compounded quarterly.

You know that Sherry's investment of $1 is compounded quarterly at an annual interest rate of 5 percent. Because Sherry's rate compounds four times a year, her investment increases by 5 percent ÷ 4, or 1.25 percent, each quarter. You can work out by hand the gain for each quarter over three years, but applying the compound interest formula is faster:

$$FV = P\left(1+\frac{r}{n}\right)^{Yn}$$

FV stands for the future value of the investment, *P* is the principal or initial investment, *r* is the interest rate expressed as a decimal, *n* is the number of times interest is compounded per year, and *Y* indicates the number of years. Substitute the figures for Sherry's investment and solve for *FV*:

$$FV = P\left(1+\frac{r}{n}\right)^{Yn}$$
$$FV = 1\left(1+\frac{0.05}{4}\right)^{(3)(4)}$$
$$FV = 1(1+0.0125)^{12}$$
$$FV = (1.0125)^{12}$$

Choice (B) is the answer.

13. **D.** Here's what the problem gives you:

✔ The total number (800) of senior students in College A

✔ The total number (700) of senior students in College B

✔ The percentage (90) of the total number of students in College A that graduated

✔ The percentage (80) of the total number of students in both colleges that graduated

What you're supposed to find is the total number of graduates from College B, and because this isn't a data sufficiency problem, you know you have all you need to figure out the solution. Start with the easy calculation: You can find out how many students graduated from College A by multiplying the total number by 90 percent: $800 \times 0.9 = 720$. Then, if you like setting up math equations (and let's face it — who doesn't?), here's what you can do: Figure that the number of College B graduates (*B*) is equal to the number of total graduates (*T*) less the number of College A graduates (720), or $B = T - 720$.

The equation for finding the total number of graduates is the sum of the total students from College B (700) and the students from College A (800) multiplied by 80 percent: $(700 + 800) \times 0.80 = T$. Solve for T: $1,500 \times 0.80 = 1,200$. Then substitute 1,200 for T in the first equation and solve for B: $B = 1,200 - 720$ or 480. So Choice (D) is the correct answer.

14. **D.** The hardest part about this question is figuring out what it's asking. Essentially, you have to find a possible value for x and then find the answer from the list of choices that's the largest multiple of x. All cleared up now? If the waters still appear muddy, take the problem one step at a time.

    You know that x is a positive integer (which means it's a whole number), so when you square x, you get a whole number — a perfect square. You also know that when you square x and divide by 72, you get a whole number. So 72 is a factor of x^2. Play around with multiples of 72 to find a perfect square: 72×2 is 144 — that's a perfect square ($12^2 = 144$). So x could be 12. Now, look at the answer choices. Which answer is the largest multiple of 12? Choice (E), 32, is the largest number, but it isn't a multiple of 12. Choices (A), (B), and (C) are smaller than 12, so they can't be multiples of 12. The only choice that's a multiple of 12 is Choice (D); and $12 \div 12 = 1$, which is a positive integer.

15. **A.** To know enough about the value of p to determine whether it's an integer, you must have values for both q and r or know the value of q in terms of r or r in terms of q.

    Happy day! Statement (1) tells you the value of q in terms of r. You don't have to solve the equation to know that the first statement is sufficient to determine whether p is an integer and that the answer is either Choice (A) or Choice (D). But if you're not convinced by what we tell you, we'll just go ahead and show you.

    When you substitute $2r$ for q in the equation, you get $p = \dfrac{(8)2r}{2r}$. The $2r$ in the numerator and denominator cancel each other out, so the value of p is 8, an integer. So the answer to the question is *yes*.

    You have a 50-50 chance of answering this question correctly, but to increase your odds to 100 percent, check out Statement (2). It gives the value of q but doesn't relate it to r. When you substitute $\dfrac{2}{5}$ for q, the equation still contains two unknowns, so you can't get a definite value for p. Statement (2) alone isn't enough to answer the question of whether p is an integer, so the answer is Choice (A).

16. **D.** This problem has two unknowns: the quantity of white flour, x, and the quantity of wheat flour, y.

    To solve a problem with two variables, you need two equations:

    ✔ The first equation represents the total cost of the baker's purchase. You know that the price of white flour times the quantity of white flour (x) plus the price of wheat flour times the quantity of wheat flour (y) equals \$350. Translated to math language, this becomes $1.4x + 2y = 350$.

    ✔ To create the second equation, consider that the total quantity of flour purchased, 190 kilograms, must equal the quantity of white flour plus the quantity of wheat flour: $x + y = 190$.

    Solve for x in terms of y in the second equation: $x = 190 - y$. Then substitute this value for x in the first equation and solve for y:

$$1.4(190 - y) + 2y = 350$$
$$266 - 1.4y + 2y = 350$$
$$266 + 0.6y = 350$$
$$0.6y = 84$$
$$y = 140$$

If coming up with equations takes you longer than finishing a game of Monopoly, you may get through this one more quickly if you substitute answer choices for *y* to see which works best. Start with the middle value first. If it doesn't work, you'll know to try the bigger values or the smaller values.

If *y* were 130, Choice (C), the quantity of white flour would be 60 (190 – 130 is 60). See whether 130($2) + 60($1.40) = $350. You know that 130 × 2 = 260. Figure that 60 × 1 is 60 and 60 × 0.40 is 24, so 60 × 1.40 = 84. And 260 + 84 = 344, which is less than 350. Try a slightly greater value for *y*. Choice (D) gives you 140($2) + 50(1.40) = 350, or 280 + 70 = 350. That's true! The correct answer is Choice (D).

17. **C.** If every listener who donated gave $5 (instead of, say, $10, $20, or $100), you'd have the maximum number of listeners who could donate $5. So simply divide $349 by $5 to get 69.8. You can't have 0.8 of a listener. The maximum number of whole-bodied listeners who could have donated $5 is 69, which is Choice (C).

18. **B.** This one's easy. No tricks here. Simply substitute –1 for all values of *x*. Just remember the operation rules for positive and negative numbers (see Chapter 10):

$$\frac{(-1)^3+(-1)^4-(-1)^3}{2(-1)-2}=?$$

$$\frac{-1+1-(-1)}{(-2)-2}=?$$

$$-\frac{1}{4}=?$$

The correct answer is Choice (B).

19. **D.** To answer this data sufficiency question, you must determine whether you have enough information in each statement to solve for the distance of the route. That sounds a lot like a rate problem. As long as you have the components of the formula, you can find the distance.

The formula for finding distance is Rate × Time: *d = rt*.

Statement (1) says that it takes Mike six minutes (which is the same as 0.1 hours) less to bike the full distance of the route when his rate is 10 miles per hour than when his rate is 5 miles per hour. That information gives you all you need to find the rate and the time, so it's sufficient to find the distance. Narrow the answers to Choice (A) or Choice (D). If you need more proof, here's the solution:

1. Let *t* stand for the time it takes Mike to complete the route at a rate of 5 miles per hour: *d = 5t*.

2. The same route takes Mike *t* – 0.1 hours when he bikes at a rate of 10 miles per hour: *d = 10(t – 0.1)*.

3. The distance is the same for both rates, so you can set the two equations equal to each other and solve for *t*:

$$5t = 10(t-0.1)$$
$$5t = 10t-1$$
$$-5t = -1$$
$$t = \frac{1}{5}$$

4. Substitute $\frac{1}{5}$ for *t* in the first equation, and you get $d = 5 \times \frac{1}{5}$, so the distance is 1 mile.

Aren't you glad you didn't have to go through all those calculations to know that Statement (1) is sufficient?

That Statement (2) gives you values for rate and time is more obvious. At a rate of 4 miles per hour, Mike travels twice the distance of the route in the time of 30 minutes (0.5 hours). You have concrete values for rate and time in both statements, so the answer must be Choice (D).

20. **D.** Analyze the problem. For the product of *q, r, s,* and *t* to be negative, one or three of the values has to be negative. Keep that in mind as you evaluate the first statement. It gets complicated.

    When you cross-multiply the values in Statement (1), you get *qt = rs.* If *qt = rs,* the terms *qt* and *rs* must have the same sign. Because *qt* and *rs* have the same sign, the product of (*qt*) (*rs*), which is the same as *qrst,* must be positive. Statement (1) allows you to rule out –1 as the product of *qrst* and is, therefore, sufficient to answer the question. The correct answer has to be either Choice (A) or Choice (D).

    Now look at Statement (2). You can rearrange the equations to find that *qr* = –1 and *st* = –1. Therefore, the product of the two terms must be positive 1: (–1)(–1) = 1. Statement (2) provides another clear answer to the question of whether *qrst* is equal to –1. Because both Statements (1) and (2) are sufficient to answer the question, the answer is Choice (D).

21. **D.** This data sufficiency question deals with angles formed when a transversal intersects parallel lines. You can review the properties of these angles in Chapter 12. Examining the figure tells you that the measure of angle *a* is equal to the measure of angle *c* because they're alternate exterior angles. You also know that the measure of angles *a* and *b* add up to 180 degrees, because they form a straight line. So when you know the measures of either angle *a* or angle *b,* you know that you can find the measure of angle *c.* Statement (1) gives you the measure of angle *b,* which means you can find out the measure of angle *a* and, therefore, the measure of angle *c.* The answer is either Choice (A) or Choice (D).

    Statement (2) tells you the measure of *a,* which means you know the measure of *c.* Both Statements (1) and (2) alone are sufficient to find the measure of angle *c,* so the answer is Choice (D).

22. **D.** To solve this data sufficiency question, see whether you can easily manipulate the equations provided in each statement to come up with the equation in the question. Notice that if you square the terms on both sides of the equation in Statement (1), you get $a^2 = \frac{b^3}{c^2}$.

    That settles it quickly. The first statement is sufficient, and the answer is either Choice (A) or Choice (D).

    When you multiply both sides of the equation in the second statement by $\frac{a^2}{c}$, you also come up with $a^2 = \frac{b^3}{c^2}$. Therefore, both statements alone provide sufficient data to answer the question, and the answer is Choice (D).

    Did you hesitate to pick Choice (D) because it was the fourth Choice (D) in a row? Don't worry about how many times a particular answer choice appears on the GMAT. The answers are randomized by the computer, so you won't find patterns.

23. **B.** To quickly solve this simple problem, apply what you know about adding odd numbers. The dogs' ages are odd numbers. The sum of any two odd numbers is even, so the answer here must be even. The only answer choice that isn't an even number is Choice (B).

    If you haven't memorized the properties of odd and even numbers, this question is still easy to answer. Just eliminate any answer choice that *is* a sum of two of the dogs' ages. Choice (A) is the sum of 3 and 5, so ignore that answer. You can't get 9 by adding any of the ages, so Choice (B) is the likely answer. Check the other three just to be sure: 10 is the result of adding 3 and 7; you get 12 when you take 5 + 7; and 5 + 11 is 16. The answer that *can't* be a sum of a couple of the ages is Choice (B).

24. **A.** The painter takes 12 hours to paint $\frac{2}{5}$ of the walls in the house, so 12 hours is $\frac{2}{5}$ of the time it takes to paint all the walls (t): $\frac{2}{5}t = 12$. Solve for t to figure out how long it takes to complete the entire painting job:

$$\frac{2}{5}t = 12$$
$$2t = 60$$
$$t = 30$$

Be sure to read carefully, though. The question doesn't ask for the time it takes to paint the entire job, so the answer isn't Choice (E). To find the remaining time, subtract 12 from 30. The answer is 18 hours, Choice (A).

25. **C.** This problem deals with large numbers, and you can't use a calculator.

To avoid some very long division, write the values given for cell populations in scientific notation (see Chapter 10), and then solve. Write 203.78 billion as 203.78×10^9 and 595.02 million as 595.02×10^6. The fraction of cells with mutation X within the cell colony is this:

$$\frac{595.02 \times 10^6}{203.78 \times 10^9} = \frac{595.02}{203.78 \times 10^3}$$

Notice that the question asks for an approximation, so you may round the numbers to make calculating more manageable:

$$\frac{595.02}{203.78 \times 10^3} \approx \frac{600}{200 \times 10^3} \approx \frac{6}{2,000} \approx \frac{3}{1,000}$$

When you convert that to a percent, you get 0.3 percent, which is Choice (C).

26. **A.** To solve this problem, first find the value for x that fulfills the requirement of $\sqrt{x} < 15$. To eliminate the radical in the inequality, square both sides to get $x < 15^2$. Because $15^2 = 225$, $x < 225$. When you substitute 225 for x in the fraction, you get $\frac{225}{15}$. Because $225 \div 15$ is 15, the quotient has to be less than 15. The only value in the answer choices that's less than 15 is 14. The correct answer is Choice (A).

27. **E.** To solve this problem, you need to find the ratio of the number of pennies in Kim's pocket to the number of all coins in Kim's pocket. Because Kim initially has p pennies in her pocket and then adds 3 more pennies, you can say the number of pennies is $p + 3$. The total number of coins in Kim's pocket is the sum of all the coins in her pocket initially ($p + d + n + q$) plus the coins she adds ($3 + 2 + 1$). So Kim has a total of $p + d + n + q + 6$ coins in her pocket, and the probability of selecting a penny at random is this:

$$\frac{\text{Total Number of Pennies}}{\text{Total Number of All Coins}} = \frac{p + 3}{p + d + n + q + 6}$$

That's Choice (E).

If working through this problem makes doing laundry sound fun, try assigning values to the variables and calculate the answer choices to see which one fits. Sometimes, the quickest and easiest way to answer a math question is to analyze each answer choice to see which one works.

Say Kim has 2 pennies ($p = 2$), 3 dimes ($d = 3$), 5 nickels ($n = 5$), and 4 quarters ($q = 4$). Write these values on your noteboard. When Kim adds the new coins to the stash, she has 5 pennies, 5 dimes, 6 nickels, and 4 quarters. The probability that Kim will select a penny at random is 5 out of 20 or $\frac{1}{4}$. Then see which answer equals $\frac{1}{4}$ when you substitute your values for the variables. It's likely apparent to you that the numerator is $p + 3$ rather than p, so try Choice (D) first:

$$\frac{2 + 3}{2 + 3 + 5 + 4 + 3} = \frac{5}{17}$$

The denominator has to be bigger, which leads you to try Choice (E). When you add 6 to the denominator instead of 3, you get $\frac{5}{20}$. That's the one!

28. **C.** Simplifying the expression first is probably easier. Find the lowest common denominator for all three fractions in the expression. The smallest number that 2, 4, and 6 go into evenly is 12. Multiply the numerator and denominator of the main fraction by 12 to get rid of the fractions within the fraction. Then solve:

$$\frac{\frac{1}{4}}{\frac{1}{2}+\frac{1}{6}}=\frac{\frac{1}{4}\times\frac{12}{1}}{\left(\frac{1}{2}\times\frac{12}{1}\right)+\left(\frac{1}{6}\times\frac{12}{1}\right)}=\frac{3}{6+2}=\frac{3}{8}$$

You find that answer in Choice (C).

29. **C.** Whenever you deal with unknown lengths in polygons, look for ways to create right triangles. It may help to draw a picture of the yard on your noteboard. The diagonal forms two isosceles right triangles.

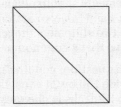

The area of a square is s^2 where s represents the length of the side. So $s^2 = 2x$ and $s = \sqrt{2x}$.

You could use the Pythagorean theorem to find the diagonal length, but applying the side ratio of isosceles right triangles, which is $s:s:s\sqrt{2}$, is faster. So the diagonal is $\sqrt{2x}\times\sqrt{2}$, or $2\sqrt{x}$.

The correct answer is Choice (C).

30. **E.** To evaluate this data sufficiency problem, envision a number line segment with 60 at the left end and 95 at the right end. The midpoint of this line is the average of the two endpoints: $\frac{60+95}{2}=77.5$. That tells you that if $n > 77.5$, it's closer to 95; if $n < 77.5$, then n is closer to 60. Statement (1) tells you that $n - 60 \leq 95 - n$. When you combine like terms, you know that $n \leq 77.5$. Because n could be either equal to or less than 77.5, n is either closer to 60 or exactly the same distance from both numbers. Statement (1) by itself doesn't provide enough information to answer the question. The answer is Choice (B), Choice (C), or Choice (E).

Statement (2) tells you that n is less than 80. If $77.5 < n < 80$, then n is closer to 95, and if $n < 77.5$, then n is closer to 60. Statement (2) doesn't provide an answer to the question, either. The answer is Choice (C) or Choice (E). Considering both statements together doesn't provide new information to evaluate the problem. When you know that $n \leq 77.5$, you automatically know that n is less than 80. The answer is Choice (E).

31. **C.** You have to decide whether a is a positive number. The information in Statement (1) tells you that the product ab is a negative number and the product bc is a positive number. This means that b and c must be either both positive or both negative. If b were positive, a would be negative. If b were negative, a would be positive. You can't know from Statement (1) whether $a > 0$. The answer has to be either Choice (B), Choice (C), or Choice (E).

Statement (2) tells you that c is a negative number, but it doesn't relate c to a. You may confidently eliminate Choice (B).

By now, you may be experiencing an *aha!* moment. When you apply the fact that *c* is negative into the information in Statement (1), you know that *b* must also be negative. That's the only way that *bc* could result in a positive number. If *b* is negative and *ab* is negative, then *a* has to be positive and greater than 0. Choice (C) is correct.

32. **C.** To answer this question, determine which values are possible for ◊ in each statement.

The rules of rounding state that you keep a digit the same if the digit to the right of it is ≤ 4. You round a digit to the next largest value if the digit next to it is > 4.

Statement (1) tells you that the value of ◊ is either 4 or 5. If the digit to the right of it is ≤ 4, then ◊ = 4. When the digit to the right of it is greater than 4, (that is, ∆ > 4) you round up and ◊ = 5. So Statement (1) leaves you with two possible values for ◊. The answer is Choice (B), Choice (C), or Choice (E).

For Statement (2) to be true, the unknown digit has to be ≤ 4. It could be 0, 1, 2, 3, or 4 to cause the digit to the left of it to remain 4 instead of rounding to 5. Statement (2) gives you five possible values for ◊, so you don't have enough information to answer the question from this statement alone. You can narrow the answers to Choices (C) or (E).

Now, analyze both statements simultaneously. The possible values for the digit in question given Statement (1) are 4 and 5. Given Statement (2), the possible values are 0, 1, 2, 3, or 4. When you consider the two statements together, the only possible value for the digit represented by ◊ is 4, the value that's common to both sets of values. The answer is Choice (C).

33. **D.** When answering this question, you first need to figure out cost per can of soup for each package. When you divide $36 by 24 cans, the price per can is $1.50. Six cans at $12 is $2 per can. Buying soup in 24-packs is cheapest, so Tim should buy as many 24-packs as he can. Because three 24-packs would cost Tim $108, he can buy only two of them. That gives him 48 cans for $72 ($36 × 2) and leaves him with $22 ($94 − $72 = $22). Tim can then buy one 6-pack for a total of $12. Write on your noteboard that Tim has purchased six more cans for a total of 54 (48 + 6 = 54) and has $10 left ($22 − $12 = $10). With the remaining $10, Tim can purchase four single cans at $2.50 each. That gives him a total of 58 cans of soup for his $94 investment. Lucky Tim! It appears that he's feasting on the daily fare of the typical college student. Choice (D) is the correct answer.

34. **E.** This problem tests your knowledge of exponents.

When you divide two numbers that have the same base, you simply keep the same base and subtract the exponents. And to get rid of a negative exponent, create a reciprocal. You can review exponents in Chapter 10.

1. First, convert 0.5 to a fraction because the answer choices are in fraction form:

$$\frac{\left(\frac{1}{2}\right)^6}{\left(\frac{1}{2}\right)^9}$$

2. Divide: $\dfrac{\left(\frac{1}{2}\right)^6}{\left(\frac{1}{2}\right)^9} = \left(\frac{1}{2}\right)^{6-9} = \left(\frac{1}{2}\right)^{-3}$

3. Find the reciprocal to get rid of the negative exponent:

$$\left(\frac{1}{2}\right)^{-3} = 2^3 = 8$$

The correct answer is Choice (E).

35. **B.** This question asks you to find the maximum number of jelly beans a particular jar can hold. Statement (1) tells you that the jar can hold at least a minimum of 800 jelly beans, but it doesn't say what the jar's maximum jelly bean capacity is. Narrow the answer choices to Choices (B), (C), or (E).

Sift through the information in the second statement to see what it tells you about the jar's capacity. Say that n represents the total possible number of jelly beans that fit in the jar. That's your unknown. Examine Statement (2). You can express *one-third full* as $\frac{1}{3}n$, because n represents the jar's full capacity. When you add 400 jelly beans to $\frac{1}{3}n$, the number of jelly beans increases by 50 percent. That means that 50 percent (or $\frac{1}{2}$) of one-third the jar's capacity is equal to 400 jelly beans. That sounds like a math equation: $\frac{1}{2} \times \frac{1}{3}n = 400$. You know that when you have one linear equation with one variable, you can find a definite value for that variable. Statement (2) gives you what you need to find the jelly bean capacity of the jar. The answer is Choice (B).

You don't actually have to solve for n to answer this question. You just need to know that you *can* solve for n.

36. **A.** To answer this data sufficiency question, you have to find a way to relate the values of a, b, and c to one another. Statement (1) gives you two linear equations that you can solve for a and c in terms of b. That will give you the ratio of $a{:}b{:}c$ in terms of b. Here's how: When you solve the first equation for a, you get $a = \frac{2b}{5}$. When you solve the second equation for c, you get $c = 3b$. That tells you the ratio of $a{:}b{:}c$ is $\frac{2b}{5}{:}b{:}3b$ or $\frac{2}{5}{:}1{:}3$. The answer must be either Choice (A) or Choice (D).

Statement (2) tells you the value of a in terms of b and the value of c, but it doesn't tell you the value of c in terms of one of the other variables. So relating these three values is impossible. Therefore, Statement (2) is insufficient to answer the question, and Choice (A) is the correct answer.

37. **C.** Next time you visit the pizzeria, you can speak of the slices you eat in terms of degree measurement just to impress your friends and family. Keep in mind that a circular pizza measures 360 degrees. If cheese-only slices make up 55 percent of the pizza, then slices with pepperoni on them make up 45 percent of the pizza ($100 - 55 = 45$). And 45 percent of 360 degrees is 0.45×360, or 162 degrees, which is Choice (C).

If you picked Choice (B), you found the degree measure of the cheese-only portion of the pizza.

Section 4: Verbal

1. **B.** The claim you need to weaken is that SpeedyTrim is the "most effective weight loss supplement available today without a prescription." The company backs its claim with results from a study it conducted on 12 people, all who stated that SpeedyTrim was the best weight loss supplement they had ever tried. To poke holes in the claim, reveal problems with the statistical study.

You can disregard Choice (E) because it doesn't deal with the study at all. Choice (A) actually strengthens the claim. If the study was conducted by an outside company, the results are likely to be less subjective. At first, you may think that Choice (C) calls into question the validity of SpeedyTrim's claim, but read the claim carefully. It says that SpeedyTrim is the most effective *nonprescription* supplement, so evidence that a prescription drug is more effective doesn't hurt the assertion. That narrows down the options to Choices (B) and (D). The degree to which the trial members were overweight is irrelevant, so the answer has to be Choice (B). If none of the trial members had tried another supplement, their ability to compare SpeedyTrim to other supplements is compromised. It's like saying your only child is your favorite son; it doesn't mean a whole lot.

The answer that most weakens the results of a study is often the one that shows that the study group doesn't represent the population as a whole.

2. **E.** Here's another critical reasoning question that asks you to weaken the argument. It's a very popular question type!

Focus on the exact nature of the conclusion you're supposed to weaken. Notice that you're supposed to weaken the argument *against* helmet mandates, and the opponents to helmet requirements say that they should be able to go without wearing a helmet because their behavior doesn't potentially hurt anyone but themselves. The answer that deals a blow to that assertion is Choice (E). It reveals that others are, in fact, negatively affected because they have to pay more in insurance. Choices (A) and (B) provide reasons why wearing a helmet is a good idea, but they don't specifically address the reasoning of the opponents to helmet requirements. Whether governments do or don't require helmets for motorcycle riders has nothing to do with whether they *should* have those requirements, so Choices (C) and (D) aren't relevant.

3. **A.** And now for something completely different (okay, not really): the strengthen-the-argument question.

You approach questions that ask you to strengthen the argument in the same way you approach questions that ask you to weaken the argument. Isolate the argument you're supposed to strengthen and examine the method it uses to reach a conclusion.

The question asks you to strengthen the executives' position that they have the right to request access to potential employees' social media pages. You don't know why executives feel this way, but you *do* know that their opponents claim that social media pages don't reveal information that's pertinent to job performance. If you can weaken this claim, you'll strengthen the executives' position. Look for answers that show that a correlation does indeed exist between an employee's social media pages and the way that employee performs on the job.

Choice (B) weakens the executives' position, so it's clearly wrong. Choices (E) and (C) don't specifically address the issue of employer access to social media pages, so they're not as good as other answers that do regard that issue. Choice (D) regards social media use and how that reveals something about the user, but it doesn't address access to the content of an individual's private pages nor does it directly refer to attributes that would affect employment. The correct answer is Choice (A), because it directly challenges the proponents' assertion that what people post and how they behave through social media is no indication of how they'd perform on the job and, therefore, supports the opposite position.

4. **A.** What do you know? Another weaken-the-argument question. This one draws the conclusion that the cause of the increased percentage of expensive Cesarean section procedures is that hospitals want to make money and don't care about patients.

To weaken a cause-and-effect relationship, find the answer that shows that another cause for the event could exist.

Look for an answer that gives another cause for the increase in Cesarean section procedures over the last few decades. You can clearly eliminate Choice (C). The argument mentions nothing about the relationship between Cesarean section and midwives. Choice (D) regards a doctor's duty to focus on a patient's best interest but says nothing about a hospital's duty to the patient, so it's out. You're not questioning the validity of the statistical increase, so Choice (E) doesn't regard the conclusion you're supposed to weaken. That leaves Choices (A) and (B). Of the two, Choice (A) presents the more solid case that another cause for the increase in Cesarean sections may exist. It's not the hospitals that are requesting the surgeries in greater numbers but the patients. Therefore, the increase may not be due to hospital greed and inconsideration but to the changing preferences of the women who are having the procedures. Knowing that more surgeons know how to perform Cesarean sections, Choice (B), doesn't mean that the increase isn't due to greed. Maybe more surgeons know how to perform the procedure because they want to make more money.

5. **E.** The problem with this sentence is a lack of parallelism. The first two reasons that the homeschooling association met are expressed in infinitive form, *to discuss* and *introduce*. The last reason has an *-ing* ending instead. To make it match the other reasons, you have to change *organizing* to the infinitive form *organize*. Eliminate Choices (A) and (C) because they use *organizing*. Choice (D) creates a clause, which also doesn't fit with the rest of the series of reasons. The correct answer is either Choice (B) or Choice (E). Choice (B) puts a *to* before *organize;* Choice (E) doesn't. Choice (E) is better because the *to* that comes before *discuss* works for each element of the series. You know that because there's no *to* before *introduce* in the second reason.

Whenever the underlined portion of a sentence is part of a series, look for a lack of parallelism.

6. **D.** The underlined part of this sentence contains a plural pronoun *they*. The only plural noun in the sentence that *they* could refer to is *surfers*. The shark attacks don't occur within the surfers; they occur in the bay. *Bay* is singular, so to agree in number, the proper pronoun should be the singular *it*. The two choices that change *they* to *it* are Choices (D) and (E), but Choice (E) changes the meaning of the sentence. It suggests that the surfers avoid the bay whenever it experiences shark attacks. The point of the original sentence is that the surfers are avoiding the bay right now because of the attacks. The correct answer is Choice (D).

7. **A.** This sentence contains another underlined series joined by the conjunction *or*. Elements joined by a conjunction have to be expressed in the same grammatical form to maintain parallel structure. Each of the elements of the series is a noun, so the sentence appears to be parallel. Check the other choices just to be sure, though.

   Eliminate Choices (B) and (C) because they contain the awkward phrasing *being the result of,* and you don't need to join the series with more than one *or*. Choice (D) needlessly repeats *runaways* throughout the series. Choice (E) contains an improper construction. It's idiomatically correct to say *the result of* rather than *the result from*. This one is best as is, so Choice (A) is correct.

8. **A.** The point of the first paragraph of this science reading passage about scientific classifications is that human biology is essentially similar in complexity to the biology of other species. The second paragraph goes on to explain some of the major differences among kingdoms based on anatomy and physiology and that these differences create species. Use this general outline of the passage to help you answer this first question, which concerns main theme.

Approach main theme questions by eliminating answers that are too specific, too general, or irrelevant.

   If you're keeping track on your noteboard (and you should be), mark your pencil through Choice (D). The broad subject of the complexity of human biology is way too general to be the purpose of this two-paragraph passage. On the other hand, Choices (B) and (C) aren't comprehensive enough. Choice (B) refers only to the topic covered in the first paragraph, and Choice (C) focuses on just the second paragraph. The passage says nothing about the superiority of any species, so Choice (E) is irrelevant. You should also be wary of Choice (E) because it requires you to make a value judgment.

   In general, answers that require you to make a value judgment that the author doesn't clearly state or suggest are most likely incorrect.

   That leaves Choice (A). It summarizes the topic of the first paragraph (the general biology of living things) and the subject of the other paragraph (categorization by species).

9. **D.** Approach this question by eliminating all answer choices that describe statements the authors *do* make. The last answer standing will be the one that the authors *don't* state. The word *intricate* in Choice (A) is another way of saying *complex,* and the authors state in the first line that human biology isn't more complex than the biology of another species. Cross

out Choice (A) on your noteboard. Choice (B) is mentioned in the first paragraph where the passage states that "all these groups" (referring to animals, plants, and fungi) are similar at the cellular level, and the third sentence from the end says that, in theory, humans can go anywhere and survive. So Choices (B) and (C) are out. Choice (E) is a paraphrase of the second sentence, so it's wrong, too. The first part of Choice (D) seems familiar. The authors mention in the second paragraph that the starfish's range is limited. But the second part of the answer contradicts the authors' assertion in the first paragraph that human biology isn't more or less complex than that of other species. The choice that doesn't fit is Choice (D), so it's the correct answer.

10. **B.** Like the previous questions, this one asks you to sort through the information in the passage and find the answer that isn't there. The term *kingdom* doesn't officially appear until the beginning of the second paragraph, but don't limit your search. Even though the first paragraph doesn't refer specifically to kingdoms, you know from the first sentence of the second paragraph that "these major groups," that is, animal, plant, fungus, and protist, are actually kingdoms. So the information about these groups is information about kingdoms.

   Start by eliminating the obvious truths about kingdoms. Choices (C) and (D) are direct statements from the fourth and last sentence, respectively, of the second paragraph, so they're not right. Choice (A) is a paraphrase of information in the first sentence. Finding Choice (E) in the passage may be a little trickier, but it's there. The last sentence of the first paragraph tells you that organ systems are part of an organism's anatomy and physiology. Then, the first sentence of the next paragraph states that each kingdom has its own characteristic anatomy and physiology. Therefore, each kingdom has a characteristic organ system. The remaining answer, Choice (B), contradicts the statement in the last sentence of the first paragraph that in their anatomy and physiology, plants, animals, and fungi are very dissimilar. So to say that they're somewhat similar is untrue. The best answer is Choice (B).

11. **C.** This question changes gears a bit. You're not supposed to determine which answer is or isn't true. You're supposed to determine the reason that the authors provide information. It's true that the passage suggests that human beings are more adaptive than starfish and that starfish and humans are interdependent, but those truths are the focus of the second paragraph. Eliminate Choices (A) and (D). You can also disregard Choice (B) because it contradicts the point the author makes in the first sentence of the passage. Likewise, Choice (E) goes against the information in the second to last sentence of the first paragraph that starfish and humans are similar at the cellular level. Choice (C) is the best option. The overall purpose of the second paragraph is to show that the kingdoms have different anatomies and physiologies and that differences occur among organisms in each kingdom as well. The author compares starfish and humans to show that although they're both animals, they're significantly different in the way they look and function. They're an example of how organisms within the same kingdom are different.

12. **E.** Use information from the passage to determine which statement the authors would most likely go along with. Choice (A) is wrong for two reasons: The passage doesn't talk about genetics, and genetics sounds like it concerns an organism's cellular level, which the passage says is relatively similar in complexity among kingdoms. Choice (B) is also out, because the first line of the second paragraph declares that each kingdom has "its own characteristic anatomy and physiology," implying that anatomy and physiology are *not* very similar. Read carefully, and you'll see that Choice (C) is also out of contention. The end of the first paragraph says that plants and animals are *equally* dissimilar to fungi, so they don't know anything about the degree of similarity. As for Choice (D), the passage states that animals, plants, and fungi are "astoundingly similar" at the *cellular* level but "very different" in terms of tissues, organs, and organ systems.

   That leaves Choice (E), which is essentially a summary of the entire second paragraph. The third sentence in this paragraph states that the differences are obvious, and the last sentence reveals that the organisms in kingdoms are organized into smaller groups based on their differences in anatomy and physiology.

13. **B.** Okay, time to switch gears now and focus on a little writing analysis. Examine the underlined portion of the sentence. You may notice that *could* (the past tense of *can*) suggests *possibility. Possibly* does also. The underlined words contain a redundancy. Look for an answer that eliminates one of the redundant words.

    Might also indicates *possibility,* so Choice (C) doesn't correct the problem. Choices (B), (D), and (E) eliminate the redundancy, but Choice (D) changes the meaning of the sentence to reveal that the dinosaurs themselves are doing some cloning. Who knew that cloning technology was available 150 million years ago? It wasn't; eliminate Choice (D). Choice (E) doesn't work because the construction "dinosaurs cloning could occur" is improper. You'd likely catch the problems with Choice (D) and Choice (E) if you read the sentence again with the choices inserted.

    Before you move on to the next question, reread a sentence correction question with your answer choice inserted in place of the original underlined words. That step helps you catch problems with your answer choice that you may miss the first time.

    The only choice that corrects the redundancy without introducing a new error is Choice (B).

14. **E.** This sentence has a beginning phrase that begins with a participle (that's grammar speak for the second part of a verb phrase).

    A beginning participle phrase always refers to the subject of the sentence. So whenever a sentence correction problem begins with a participle phrase, check to make sure it makes sense that the subject of the sentence is what's doing the action described in the phrase.

    The way it's written, this sentence really says that *scholars* are "according to written accounts from residents of Salem, Massachusetts," which doesn't make sense. Eliminate Choice (A), and check your other options. Choice (B) doesn't correct the problem; it says scholars are in accordance with written accounts, which means they agree with them. Choice (C) and Choice (D) contain incredibly awkward constructions, so they can't be correct. Choice (E) changes the beginning phrase so it's clear that scholars are *using* accounts from residents to make their findings.

15. **D.** The first thing you should notice about the underlined part of this sentence correction problem is that it contains a pronoun.

    When the underlined portion of the sentence contains a pronoun, the first thing you check is whether the pronoun has a clear reference and whether it agrees in number with its reference.

    The pronoun in this sentence, *they,* is plural, but it refers to the one firm of Berry, Westfall, and Atredies, Inc. You know the reference should be singular because titles are always singular.

    The sentence isn't correct as written. Eliminate Choice (A) and look for answers that correct the noun-pronoun agreement. Choice (C) isn't the one; it also uses *they* to refer to the one firm. Choice (B) changes *they* to *it,* but don't be too quick to pick this option. Choice (B) also changes *most* to *more,* and you use *more* to compare just two elements, not all the firms in a particular region. Be careful with Choice (E) as well. It changes *they* to *it* but incorrectly uses the possessive form *its* instead of the contraction *it's.* The remaining answer is Choice (D). This option solves the problem by changing *they* to *which,* a pronoun that has no problem referring to singular nouns. Problem solved.

16. **D.** This sentence has another kind of agreement issue: subject-verb agreement. The compound verb in the sentence, *increases* and *improves,* is in singular form. The construction may not sound wrong to you because the noun that immediately precedes the verb, *dam,* is singular. But *dam* isn't the subject of the sentence. *Dam* works as an object in this sentence, and a noun can't be both a subject and an object. You need to identify the actual subject. So what exactly is increasing biodiversity and improving environmental quality? The answer is *meadows, ponds, and wetlands,* which is a plural subject. The proper plural form of the verb then should be *increase* and *improve.* Choice (B) changes the first verb

but not the second, so it's not right. Choice (E) changes the verb tense but doesn't correct the agreement problem. Choice (C) corrects the agreement problem but changes the verb to *contribute,* which alters the meaning of the sentence. Choice (D) successfully makes the verb plural without changing the meaning of the sentence.

17. **C.** The information in the prompt contains the following points:

> ✔ People like sports more when they've had more exposure to them.
>
> ✔ People in the United States like basketball, baseball, hockey, and American football better than soccer.
>
> ✔ People in other countries really like soccer.

From these points, you can conclude that people in the United States are exposed to soccer less than they are to the other four sports and that people in other countries must be exposed to more soccer. Find the answer that incorporates all elements of this conclusion. Choice (C) reveals that people in the United States experience less exposure to soccer than people in other countries do. That covers it!

The information in the paragraph doesn't relate a sport's popularity to how exciting it is or how good one is at it, so you can't come to the conclusions in Choices (A) and (E). Choice (D) says nothing about the preferences of U.S. citizens, so it's not comprehensive enough to be correct. The paragraph says nothing about the capacity of sports fans' heart for sports, so Choice (B) is also wrong.

18. **C.** This critical reasoning question requires you to find the assumption in the argument. Break down the argument:

> ✔ Male servers get bigger tips from female customers.
>
> ✔ Chris is a male server.
>
> ✔ Female servers get bigger tips from male customers.
>
> ✔ Laurie is a female server.
>
> ✔ Therefore, Chris should serve tables that have more female customers than males, and Laurie should serve tables that have more male customers than females.

To reach the conclusion, Chris and Laurie must think that the person who decides the tip amount is a person who is a member of the majority gender at the table. Think of it this way: Say that a table has three female customers and one male; using Chris and Laurie's logic, Chris should serve the table because it has more females than males. But what if the three females were sisters and the male seated with them was their father, who would be far more likely to pay the bill and calculate the tip even though he's in the minority gender-wise? Chris and Laurie's plan doesn't account for this scenario, so they must be assuming that the check payer is always a member of the gender in the majority, Choice (C).

Chris and Laurie's conclusion has nothing to do with determinations of sexism or server capability, so Choices (A) and (B) are irrelevant. Choice (E) contradicts the conclusion that Chris should serve a table with more females than males. If he assumes Choice (E), then he wouldn't be inclined to serve any table with male customers. Choice (D) is wrong because it simply restates a premise.

The correct answer to an assumption question will never be a restatement of one of the actual premises.

19. **D.** This question asks you to examine the method of reasoning. The problem with this argument is that its maker assumes that the lowest child to caregiver ratio is achieved in the daycare situation with the fewest number of children overall. It doesn't take into consideration situations where a daycare environment may have more children overall than another but has more caregivers on hand to decrease the ratio. This flaw is stated in Choice (D).

Choices (A), (C), and (E) have nothing to do with the number of children in a daycare environment, so they're irrelevant. The argument says nothing about the age of the caregiver, so eliminate Choice (B) as well.

20. **E.** The author of this social science passage has a clear opinion and point. He wishes to expose the fallacies in accounts of Europeans' first arrival to North America. He challenges early descriptions that suggest that the native inhabitants looked on the settlers as saviors and have been used to project the idea that the history of the continent didn't begin until the Europeans arrived.

From your summary of the two paragraphs, answer the first question regarding the author's primary concern.

Choices (C) and (D) deal specifically with Harriot's account, and the passage is broader than that one account. Eliminate these two answers; they're too specific. You can also eliminate Choice (A) for the opposite reason; it's too general. The author deals particularly with the way that Europeans described the native inhabitants' reaction to their arrival. The passage isn't about their overall impact on the native peoples.

Distinguishing between Choices (B) and (E) may be a little tricky. Both relate the author's concern about the accuracy of the depictions of how native peoples received the settlers. But Choice (E) is more comprehensive than Choice (B). The author isn't concerned with just the accounts of jurists and scholars but also the works of artists, historians, and myth-makers. Of the two, Choice (E) is the better answer.

21. **B.** Throughout the passage, the author faults jurists, scholars, artists, historians, and myth-makers for propagating the idea that native peoples welcomed Europeans to the North American continent. The one that appears in the answers is American historians, Choice (B). Choice (D) is obviously incorrect. The author in no way blames the native inhabitants for the inaccuracies. Choice (A) also doesn't work. The author presents Harriot's account as an example of a witness who, in fact, *did* tell the truth about the fear and initial distrust the native people had toward the arrival of the English colonists. Choice (C) is too broad. When the author refers to Europeans in the passage, he means those Europeans who settled in North America, not the whole population of Europe. Choice (E) doesn't work either. The author refers to English colonists to set up Harriot's quote and nowhere suggests that this specific group was responsible for spreading the myth regarding the reaction of the native peoples to settlers.

22. **B.** First, note that this question is asking about the author's *primary* issue with the historical accounts of the arrival of early European settlers. Although the author takes issue with the inaccuracy of the accounts, his bigger concern is that these false accounts have shaped and continue to shape American law and culture. Eliminate answers that either aren't issues or that aren't the biggest issue.

The author doesn't mention a concern with how settlers felt, so Choice (C) isn't a concern. The passage focuses on the native peoples' initial reaction to the settlers, so Choice (A) doesn't reveal the author's primary problem with the accounts. Eliminating the other two incorrect answers may be a little trickier. Choice (E) isn't right, because the problem isn't that the accounts ignore the native inhabitant's initial reaction but that they depict it falsely. Choices (B) and (D) are similar. The difference between the two is that Choice (D) suggests that the problem with the accounts is that they're different from English colonists' reports. The author gives just one example of an English colonist (Harriot) whose report differs from the general myth. He doesn't imply that all English colonists reported different accounts of the native peoples' reaction. The author does stress, however, that the accounts differed from the reports of the native inhabitants. The best answer is Choice (B).

23. **D.** This specific information question should be relatively simple, provided you read the passage closely. Harriot uses Choices (A), (B), (C), and (E) to describe the native peoples' initial response to the settlers. Choice (D) is used in connection with a description of the newcomers.

Don't attempt to answer exception questions without reviewing the text. The text usually reveals a subtlety that you'll miss if you don't check.

24. **E.** This sentence is punctuated improperly. It contains two independent clauses (complete thoughts) and joins them together with just a comma. It's a beautiful example of a comma splice. Everything before the comma is a complete sentence, and everything after the comma is a complete sentence. And if you learned nothing else about punctuation in your formative years, you likely at least came away with the truth that comma splices are bad. The problem doesn't give you the opportunity to change the comma, so you'll have to fix the issue by changing what comes after it.

You can get rid of a comma splice by changing an independent clause to an incomplete thought.

Choice (C) is also an independent clause, so you can mark a slash through that option on your noteboard. Choices (B), (D), and (E) create incomplete thoughts and fix the comma splice, so find the one that does so without introducing another error. Choice (D) adds the pronoun *it,* and you have no idea what noun *it* refers to. Eliminate that option. Choice (B) seems fine until you read it in the context of the sentence. It makes no sense to say "which seems suggestive *of* they may in fact have the opposite effect."

By process of elimination, the best answer is Choice (E). It's the only one that corrects the comma splice without creating another problem

25. **C.** The conclusion in this argument is that the real world judges others based on their names. The argument doesn't provide statistical or factual evidence for the claim. To strengthen the claim, find an answer that provides factual evidence that people choose whether to take others seriously based on their names.

Eliminate answers that don't deal with how people make judgments about others. Choices (B) and (E) concern name trends rather than how people form judgments. Choice (A) provides information about unemployment statistics, but the argument is about whether people of certain names get employed. Choice (D) concerns the way people make judgments about others, but it discusses family backgrounds and appearance rather than names. The only answer that provides evidence that one's name influences another's impression is Choice (C).

26. **D.** The conclusion of this weaken-the-argument question is that penalties don't work, and the proof is that the number of thefts hasn't gone down. You weaken the argument by showing that the reason for the static number of employee thefts is something other than the failure of the stiffer penalties.

Eliminate the first two answers; Choice (A) is irrelevant, and Choice (B) isn't specific enough to allow you to determine that a different definition of theft would affect the number of employee theft incidents. Choice (C) addresses theft in general and, therefore, doesn't relate specifically to employee theft. Choice (E) actually strengthens the conclusion. If businesses have fewer employees overall, you'd expect the number of employee thefts to also decrease.

That narrows your options to Choice (D). If employee numbers have increased, you'd expect to see a concomitant increase in the number of employee thefts. The fact that the number of thefts hasn't increased as employee numbers increase suggests that the penalties may indeed be working.

27. **E.** Examine the elements of this argument. The conclusion is that owners care more about increasing business than they do about observing the law. The premises to support this conclusion are that underage people *stumbled* out of the bars and that machines exist that detect false IDs. This argument has many assumptions. Some of them are that the presence of celebrities makes a place a hot spot, the celebrities stumble because they're intoxicated, and the owners know that they're violating the federal law.

Now look at the answer choices. Choice (A) sounds like the first assumption we listed. If allowing underage celebrities into a bar or club is evidence that the owners care about being popular, then the assumption is that celebrities = hot spot. Don't be too quick to pick Choice (A).

An answer choice with a debatable word like *only* is almost always incorrect, even if the rest of the answer sounds pretty good.

The argument assumes that allowing celebrities into a bar or club makes the establishment more popular, but it doesn't necessarily assume that this is the *only* way for a bar to become hot. The argument doesn't have to assume Choice (B). It doesn't matter whether the patrons celebrities bring in are underage or not. It's evidence enough that the celebrities are underage. Choice (C) is way too off base and specific to be a reasonable assumption. The assumption is that the underage celebrities *are* intoxicated, not the opposite, so Choice (D) is wrong. Choice (E) addresses the third assumption. If bar owners have access to machines that detect false identification, they knowingly serve underage celebrities and, therefore, must care more about having the celebrities in their establishments than they do about upholding the law.

28. **E.** Approach this assumption question by using the process of elimination. You know that Choices (A) and (B) are wrong because the argument doesn't concern industry viability or financial compensation. Choice (C) is also wrong because it's the advocate's stated premise rather than an assumption. You're down to Choices (D) and (E). The advocate concludes that spray tanning shouldn't be put into the same category as tanning booths because spray tanning isn't as risky. The argument is about risks rather than benefits, so Choice (D) is out. The best answer is Choice (E). The fact that the advocate thinks she must defend the tanning industry in response to concerns about tanning as a whole reveals that she thinks that criticisms of tanning include criticisms of the tanning industry.

29. **D.** You likely had no problem noticing that this sentence uses weird phrasing to compare Malagasy prosauropods to Argentinean ones. (Until now, you probably didn't know that Malagasy is the adjective form of Madagascar!) *As old as* means that the two prosauropods (early herbivorous dinosaurs for those of you who care) are similar in age, but the point of the sentence is that one has about 2 million years on the other. Eliminate choices that don't correct the comparison. Choice (C) maintains that *as old as* language, so it's wrong. The rest of the answers use the proper *older than,* but Choices (B) and (E) have improper possessive forms of *they*. The possessive form of *they* is *their,* such as in Choice (D).

30. **D.** This sentence correction is tricky. The problem with the sentence is that it unnecessarily uses *two* pronouns (*one* and *that*) to refer to the frog. You don't need both, so get rid of the *that* by eliminating Choices (A) and (B). Choice (C) contains an unclear and unnecessary extra pronoun, *it.* Choice (D) is better than Choice (E) because the frog isn't *of a* previously unknown type; it *is* a previously unknown type.

31. **B.** The researchers conclude that smoking marijuana during pregnancy has little effect on the health of the unborn child. They reached this conclusion because few health differences occurred between the babies of the mothers who smoked and those who didn't. Choice (B) is the answer that most seriously weakens the conclusion because it shows that the two groups had something else distinguishing them other than marijuana smoking. If the marijuana smokers were receiving better prenatal care while the others weren't, it's difficult to say whether the babies were unaffected by marijuana or whether the effects were minimized by better medical care.

Choice (A) is irrelevant. The conclusion regards the health of the babies rather than the mothers. Choice (C) would more likely strengthen the argument. Choice (D) doesn't weaken the argument because the conclusion regards the health of the babies after they were born, so the differences in the stage of pregnancy at the time of the study is irrelevant. Likewise, Choice (E) is irrelevant because the study concerned pregnant women who smoked *marijuana,* not tobacco. The argument doesn't discuss how damaging tobacco is. Knowing that smoking marijuana is less damaging to a fetus than tobacco doesn't tell you much about how much marijuana affects a fetus. Saying that a toothache is less painful than a kidney stone doesn't mean that a toothache isn't painful.

32. **D.** This business passage discusses the effective use of the Internet to market a business, using the experience of River Pools as an example.

To determine the best next step, first eliminate answers that have already been accomplished. The passage says that River Pools's website is "not unlike a business trade magazine," so Choice (A) would duplicate what the business already has. The passage says that River Pools's blog posts and video are already steady, so posting even more frequently likely won't affect business much. Eliminate Choice (B). The passage is about Internet marketing, so eliminate answers that aren't related to web presence. Choice (C) regards ads and billboards, and Choice (E) proposes live seminars. Neither relates to the web, so they're wrong. The best answer is Choice (D). River Pools has its web presence established. Now it should take steps to make sure customers can find it.

33. **C.** Title questions are main theme questions. Get rid of answers that are too general or too specific. Choice (A) is too broad, and Choice (D) is too specific. The passage uses River Pools's experience to provide information about effective marketing, but River Pools isn't the actual focus of the passage. Choice (E) is completely irrelevant. Choices (B) and (C) relate to the subject of marketing on the web, but Choice (C) is much more on point. The focus is good marketing content. The passage states that Marcus sees his company as a "content marketing company" and then goes on to explain how he realizes this vision.

34. **E.** This quote appears in the second paragraph.

The computer may highlight the quote for you so you can spot it in the passage. For this question, the entire second paragraph may be highlighted.

After Marcus says, "I used to see my company as a 'pool company,'" he delves into how he increased sales through his content-heavy, up-to-the-minute online and social media efforts. After he looked at the bigger picture, so to speak, and began to think of new ways to gain consumer trust and attention, his sales increased substantially. Choice (A) is wrong. The passage (and the company name) doesn't imply that River Pools sells any products other than pools. Marcus doesn't seem to be especially concerned with competition, so Choice (B) isn't the best answer. Choice (C) isn't quite right because it implies that Marcus suddenly discovered the concept of the Internet, when in actuality, River Pools already had a website and web presence; it just wasn't maximizing its potential. Choice (D) is out, too, because the author's main purpose in improving the quality of his web content is to improve sales rather than inform the public. If information was his primary focus, he'd set up a consumer information service. Marcus's marketing strategy changed when he realized he could offer pool information as well as actual pools. Choice (E) is best.

35. **B.** Approach this exception question by eliminating answers that state one of River Pools's goals. Choices (A) and (D) paraphrase the first line of the fifth paragraph. Choice (C) restates the primary purpose of the passage and, therefore, a major goal of River Pools. Choice (E) is an obvious goal. The last words of the third paragraph demonstrate that Marcus's ultimate goal is to get more sales. Nowhere in the passage does Marcus indicate that he has specifically targeted areas outside Maryland and Virginia for more sales, so the answer that isn't a stated goal is Choice (B).

36. **D.** This critical reasoning question doesn't give you much to work with. The conclusion is that the government should implement a school voucher system because students would benefit greatly. Then, it defines a school voucher system as a tuition waiver. To weaken the argument, find an answer that calls into question the premise that students would benefit. Choices (A), (B), and (C) actually strengthen the argument by showing ways that school vouchers may provide benefits. Choice (E) is irrelevant. If vouchers allow students to choose to attend any school, and public schools are better, the students can simply

attend a public school. The only possible answer is Choice (D). If students can't afford to travel to the school they prefer, they won't be able to benefit from attending that school because the voucher doesn't cover transportation costs.

37. **A.** The statements tell you that the North Side experiences more deaths than the West Side but fewer than the East Side.

Complete the logical argument and eliminate answers that are illogical or unsupported.

Based on the premises, the three areas listed from greatest number of deaths to fewest are East, North, then West. That's what it says in Choice (A). The argument doesn't compare population age or relate age to meth deaths, so Choices (B) and (E) aren't warranted. The argument says nothing about why one area experiences more deaths than another, so you can't come up with the conclusion in Choice (C) and Choice (D). The argument suggests no correlation between number of meth labs and number of meth deaths. You'd have to rely on outside information to pick Choice (D).

You're looking for a conclusion that addresses the premises without requiring you to make leaps of logic that aren't indicated by direct evidence in the paragraph.

38. **B.** The way this sentence is written suggests that violence occurred when the *violence* was a child. You have to change the underlined part so it's clear *who* was a child when violence occurred. Choices (C) and (D) maintain the implication that violence somehow has a child-hood, so they're incorrect. Choice (E) improperly changes the verb tense. The answer that corrects the issue is Choice (B).

39. **C.** At first, you may think this sentence is fine the way it is, but there's a subtle problem with it. The verb is *were,* which is plural, but the subject is actually *each,* which is singular. You know the subject is *each* because the other nouns (*Three* and *Echols, Baldwin,* and *Misskelley*) can't be subjects. *Three* is the object of the preposition *of* and the list of names is an appositive, something that renames another noun.

Objects and appositives can't be subjects.

Both the subject and verb are underlined, so the correct answer either makes the subject plural or makes the verb singular. Choice (E) gets rid of the verb altogether, which creates a sentence fragment. That can't be right. Consider the remaining options. All three, Choices (B), (C), and (D), correct the agreement problem by making the subject plural. So narrow down the choices by eliminating those that create new errors. The construction in Choice (D) makes it sound like the three were *members* nearly two decades after they were convicted, which doesn't make sense. You're down to Choices (B) and (C). Choice (C) presents the message more concisely and clearly than Choice (B). The expression "each of whom were" before "members" in Choice (B) is unnecessary.

40. **D.** The trick to solving this problem is to recognize that the sentence begins with a participle phrase. So the subject of the sentence has to be the noun that's "regarded as one of the 'greenest' presidents to ever hold the position." The subject of the sentence is *projects,* and *projects* don't have the ability to hold a political position. The correct answer has to change the subject of the sentence from *projects* to *Teddy Roosevelt.* The only choices that accomplish this feat are Choices (D) and (E). Eliminate the other three. Choice (D) is better than Choice (E) because Choice (E) lacks parallelism. The two projects need to be stated in the same grammatical form, either *preserving* and *constructing* or *the preservation of* and *the construction of.* Choice (D) makes the subject proper and maintains parallel construction.

41. **A.** This question concerns pure and simple pronoun agreement. The *it* in the underlined part is singular and refers to Jameson, Bender, and Co., which is a company title and, therefore, singular. All's well in the original sentence. Check the rest of the options just to be sure. Choices (B), (D), and (E) change *it* to the plural *they* or *them,* and, therefore, create problems with pronoun agreement. Choice (C) mistakenly uses the possessive form *it*s to mean the contraction *it's.* All the other answers contain errors, so Choice (A) has to be correct.

Answers at a Glance

Section 3: Quantitative

1. C	11. A	21. D	31. C
2. B	12. B	22. D	32. C
3. C	13. D	23. B	33. D
4. B	14. D	24. A	34. E
5. B	15. A	25. C	35. B
6. E	16. D	26. A	36. A
7. B	17. C	27. E	37. C
8. E	18. B	28. C	
9. B	19. D	29. C	
10. E	20. D	30. E	

Section 4: Verbal

1. B	13. B	25. C	37. A
2. E	14. E	26. D	38. B
3. A	15. D	27. E	39. C
4. A	16. D	28. E	40. D
5. E	17. C	29. D	41. A
6. D	18. C	30. D	
7. A	19. D	31. B	
8. A	20. E	32. D	
9. D	21. B	33. C	
10. B	22. B	34. E	
11. C	23. D	35. B	
12. E	24. E	36. D	

Part VII
The Part of Tens

"Careful Sundance, this one's been locked up studying for the GMAT a1111 week, and he's gotten pretty mean."

In this part . . .

We give you quite a lot of information in the review chapters of this book. This part synthesizes some of that information into nice, neat lists. We provide you with ten question types that are easiest to master and ten errors to avoid in your analytical writing essay (and to look for in the sentence correction questions). Memorizing the information in these lists can get you ready for many of the GMAT questions you'll encounter. We also go beyond just mastering the GMAT to reveal ten things you can do to increase your chances of getting accepted to an MBA program.

Chapter 21

Ten Questions You've Got a Good Shot At

In This Chapter
▶ Revealing questions you've got a good chance to get right
▶ Taking advantage of the easier questions

With all that math, grammar, and logical reasoning, you can develop a headache just thinking about the GMAT. And knowing that you have only a half hour to write an essay doesn't help! Why can't the GMAT cut you some slack? Well, it does . . . sort of. You see, certain GMAT questions may be a little easier to answer than others. In this chapter, we lay out ten questions you have a greater chance of answering correctly with greater consistency so you can buy yourself a little time to use on the tougher questions in each section.

Main Theme Reading Questions

In general, reading comprehension questions are a little easier than critical reasoning questions. For reading comprehension questions, the answers are right there on the screen; you just need to find them. One reason main theme questions in particular are easier is that 90 percent of the passages present you with one. Identifying the main theme should become automatic, so you don't even have to refer back to a passage to answer a question. And usually, three of the five answer choices are clearly off topic or too specific, so all you have to do is choose the best answer of the remaining two.

Specific Information Reading Questions

Specific information questions appear in every reading comprehension passage, so you'll get used to them. You have a great shot at these questions because the computer highlights the text that contains the answer. Just read the highlighted part of the passage (and maybe the text around it) to find the correct answer. As long as you stay focused, you should bat a thousand on these beauties!

Sentence Corrections

Although sentence correction questions may not seem easy at first, they get easier with practice. The GMAT tends to focus on the same sentence errors, so taking practice tests can help you get familiar with the errors you need to know about. You'll notice the same kinds of errors appearing frequently, so you'll be able to give the right answers frequently, too.

Exception Questions for Reading Passages

Exception questions ask you to choose the answer that *isn't* stated in the passage. Usually, all you have to do is eliminate each answer choice that appears in the text. The choice left standing is the correct answer.

Strengthening or Weakening Critical Arguments

Critical reasoning questions that ask you what strengthens or weakens the argument tend to rely on cause-and-effect relationships or analogies. If an author reaches a conclusion by cause and effect, you choose an answer that either shows other causes for the effect (to weaken the argument) or that emphasizes that no other causes for the effect exist (to strengthen the argument). To weaken analogy arguments, choose an answer that shows the compared entities are dissimilar. An answer that highlights similarities strengthens the argument.

Data Sufficiency Math Questions

Data sufficiency questions usually take less time to answer than problem-solving math questions. You don't have to actually solve the problem to answer the question correctly. Just follow the step-by-step process outlined in Chapter 15 to stay focused.

Math Problem Solving with Figures

One of the hardest parts of a problem-solving question is getting started. You may have trouble sifting through the information you get from word problems, but a figure presents known information clearly. Examine the information in the figure and solve the problem.

Math Problems Involving Basic Operations

Some problem-solving questions present you with an equation or a simple word problem involving arithmetic, exponents, or other basic operations. You've been applying these basics since childhood, so all you have to do is read carefully!

Substitution Math Problems

Problem-solving questions that ask you to substitute values for symbols can be simple after you understand what you're supposed to do. In most cases, you just need to exchange a value for a symbol in an otherwise simple equation.

Graph and Table Analysis Questions

The questions that require you to analyze graphs and tables in the integrated reasoning section primarily test your ability to read data. Finding the correct answer is rarely based on your ability to read lengthy paragraphs or perform complex calculations. As long as you pay attention to how the chart categorizes the data, you should sail through these questions fairly smoothly. Just don't complicate matters by reading more into these questions than you have to.

Chapter 22

Ten Writing Errors to Avoid

In This Chapter
▶ Condensing good writing into ten practices you should shun
▶ Finding ways to ace the analytical writing assessment

Chapter 8 gives you what you need to know to develop a good writing style for the analytical writing assessment, but becoming a better writer takes practice. Fortunately, you can rapidly improve your writing style (and your analytical writing assessment score) if you avoid the ten common writing mistakes we share in this chapter.

Composing Complicated Sentences

The chances of making multiple grammar and punctuation errors increase with the length and complexity of your sentences. If you need to improve your writing in a hurry, concentrate on simplicity. Make your point, end your sentence, and move on. Remember that the readers have to grade many exams. Don't make your reader work too hard to understand your sentences. You can (and should) use a variety of sentence structures, but keep them simple.

Presenting Your Text in Passive Voice

Active voice is clearer and more powerful than passive voice. Passive voice uses more words than necessary and clouds the main action. You're much more likely to make errors in verb usage with a passive sentence. Remember that the passive voice is really only appropriate when the doer of the action is unknown or unimportant, such as in scientific writing. For business writing and the GMAT, use active voice. (See Chapter 3 for more about active and passive voice.)

If you need a quick refresher on the difference between active and passive, consider this passive construction: *Active voice should be used on the GMAT.* This sentence is passive, and it's unclear who should be using the active voice. Here's how you'd rephrase, using active voice: *You should use active voice on the GMAT.*

Wasting Time with Unfamiliar Words

Trying to impress the essay readers with your advanced vocabulary is tempting. But if you aren't completely familiar with a word's meaning, don't use it on the GMAT. GMAT readers focus more on how you organize and support your thoughts than on the reading level of your essay, and they'll take points off your score if you misuse words. You have only 30 minutes to develop your argument, so don't waste time coming up with five-syllable words unless you just happen to use them in your normal conversation.

Using Unclear (Or Zero) Transitions

Tell your reader where your argument is going by including clear transitions. With just one or two words, you can tell the reader whether the next paragraph continues the current idea, refutes it, or moves in a new direction. Using transition words and phrases can really improve your assessment score.

Going Overboard with Generic Terms

To clarify your points and excite your reader, pack your sentences with lively and unambiguous descriptions rather than fuzzy generalities (like *interesting, great,* and *awful*). Your writing makes a greater impact and will receive a higher score when you fortify it with expressive language.

Writing in Informal English

Save slang and creative capitalization and punctuation for the text messages you send to your friends and coworkers. For the GMAT, apply the rules of standard written English you learned in grammar class.

Giving a Laundry List of Examples

Satisfy essay readers with a few clearly developed illustrations to back up your points rather than a list of undeveloped examples. Readers are more concerned with the depth of your supporting evidence than they are with its quantity. In fact, you can earn a 6 with just one example if you develop it well.

Succumbing to Sentence Fragments

Your essay shouldn't read like an outline. Fully develop your thoughts with properly punctuated complete sentences and well-organized paragraphs.

Announcing a Position without a Little Explanation

The essay prompt requires you to adopt a position. But merely stating your position and jumping into your argument is insufficient. Introduce your essay with a brief analysis of the argument to show the readers you understand what you're writing about.

Putting Aside Proofreading

Leave yourself enough time at the end of the 30 minutes to quickly read through your essay and correct any obvious errors. Set aside about three minutes to proofread your masterpiece and eliminate careless errors. Doing so can raise your score by a complete point.

Chapter 23

Ten Ways to Increase Your Chances of Getting into Business School

In This Chapter

▶ Discovering what's important to admissions committees

▶ Finding out how to make the most of your MBA admissions application

*T*he number of business school applications continues to increase, but quantity doesn't necessarily mean quality. And the quality of your application remains your single best bet for standing out among the crowd. A great application emphasizes your academic preparation, strong work experience, and a clear sense of what you hope to gain from your quest for an MBA. This chapter highlights what you can do to make sure your application process provides what it takes to impress the decision makers.

Accumulate a Little Work Experience

You don't have to get your MBA right after you graduate. In fact, waiting and working for a while may be to your advantage. Many admissions officers like to see at least three years of managerial work experience when you apply for an MBA program so they can be sure you're cut out for a career in business. They also look for signs of competence and career progress, such as promotions, the acquisition of new skills, and increased responsibilities in the workplace.

Ace the Interview

Some programs require an interview; others may recommend them. If a business school states that an interview is optional, grab this opportunity to demonstrate your social skills and highlight your passions. To make a good impression, heed the following advice:

✔ Dress in business attire.

✔ Smile, look your interviewer in the eye, and answer questions honestly.

✔ Exude confidence without arrogance.

✔ Ask questions of the interviewer that demonstrate your knowledge of the program.

✔ Follow up with a thank-you note.

Apply Early

Applying early to an MBA program demonstrates strong planning skills and a significant interest in the program. Submitting your application before the rest of the crowd also increases the chances of your application getting the time and attention from admissions officers it rightfully deserves!

Apply While You're Upwardly Mobile

Business schools want go-getters, and what better time to catch someone than on the way up? Show your school of choice that you're a force to be reckoned with by highlighting any recent promotions, achievements, accolades, or anything that helps suggest that it had better snatch you up while you're in your prime before another school beats it to the punch.

Capitalize on What Makes You Unique

Don't waste too much time trying to fit into some imaginary mold of the ideal business student. Business school admissions officers are seeking students with varying life experiences and from a broad variety of backgrounds, so embrace who you are and avoid trying to present a false persona that may ultimately backfire. In fact, your non-traditional profile may make you even more desirable to a program that seeks to diversify its class.

Demonstrate Interest

Business schools want to know that if they accept you, you'll actually attend. Admissions committees equate communication with interest, so the more you reach out to them, the more interested they'll be in you. Contact your admissions representative regularly with pertinent questions. Just make sure you don't become a pest!

Focus on Fit

Just as you want to know what school is the best fit for you, admissions officers seek the students who are the best fit for them. Do your research about what a particular school is known for and what sorts of skills and personality traits it embraces, and tailor your application, essay, and interview accordingly. You can find out a lot about a particular business school's personality by researching its website, searching the Internet for articles about the program and its graduates, and visiting the campus.

Get the Right Recommendations

Business school applicants commonly fixate so much on the essay process that they diminish the importance of securing solid recommendations. Don't undervalue the crucial role of recommendations. Choose supervisors who know you well, both personally and professionally. Admissions officers focus on how well your reference knows your strengths and weaknesses. Find someone who can expound on how well you interact with others and provide evidence of your academic prowess and leadership abilities. *Remember:* The person who knows you best is more likely to be your direct supervisor than the company CEO.

Study for the GMAT

Your GMAT score matters. The test was designed to determine how well you'll likely do in an MBA program in comparison to a plethora of other applicants, so scoring sky-high on the GMAT can place you head and shoulders above the rest of the crowd. Use this book's step-by-step instruction for each area of the test to help you prepare, and be sure to take the practice tests to help you identify areas where you could benefit from a bit of a refresher.

Write a Memorable Admissions Essay

When crafting your admissions essay, keep in mind that the admissions committee already knows your facts and figures — what you studied, where you worked, your scores on the GMAT — the point of the essay is to give application readers a glimpse of the *real* you — what makes you stand out from the crowd, what motivates you, and what you want to achieve in life. Keep in mind that admissions committees are reading thousands of responses to the same questions, so avoid falling into the trap of writing what you *think* they want to hear and instead shift your focus to self-revelation through vivid details and thoughtful anecdotes.

Appendix

About the CD

● ●

In This Appendix

▶ System requirements

▶ Using the CD with Windows and Mac

▶ What you'll find on the CD

▶ Troubleshooting

● ●

To help you prepare for the GMAT, this CD offers you five full-length practice tests as well as verbal and math flashcards. Choose between timed and untimed versions of the tests and get detailed answer explanations to help you improve your score on the real test. This appendix explains how to use the CD, what it contains, and what to do if you run into problems.

Note: If you're using a digital or enhanced digital version of this book, this appendix does not apply. Please go to `http://booksupport.wiley.com` for access to the additional content.

System Requirements

Most computers these days meet the minimum requirements, but if yours is an older model, here are the requirements just in case. If your computer doesn't match up to most of these requirements, you may have problems using the software and files on the CD. For the most up-to-date information, please refer to the ReadMe file located at the root of the CD-ROM.

Windows

If you have a PC, you need the following:

➤ Intel Pentium III 1GHz or faster processor (Pentium 4 2GHz or faster is recommended)

➤ Microsoft Windows XP Home, Professional, or Tablet PC Edition with Service Pack 2 or 3 (including 64-bit editions); Windows Server 2003; Windows Vista Home Premium, Business, Ultimate, or Enterprise (including 64-bit editions) with Service Pack 1; or Windows 7 (including 64-bit editions)

➤ 512MB RAM (1GB RAM is recommended)

Mac

If you have a Mac, you need the following:

- ✔ Intel Core Duo 1.83 GHz or faster processor
- ✔ Mac OS X, 10.5 and 10.6
- ✔ 512MB RAM (1GB RAM is recommended)

If you need more information on the basics, check out these books published by John Wiley & Sons, Inc.: *PCs For Dummies,* by Dan Gookin; *Macs For Dummies,* by Edward C. Baig; *iMac For Dummies,* by Mark L. Chambers; *Windows 95 For Dummies, Windows 98 For Dummies, Windows 2000 Professional For Dummies, Windows 7 For Dummies,* and *Microsoft Windows Me For Dummies,* Millennium Edition, all by Andy Rathbone.

Using the CD

To install the items from the CD to your hard drive, follow these steps:

1. **Insert the CD into your computer's CD-ROM drive.**

   Note to Windows users: The interface won't launch if you have AutoRun disabled. In that case, click on Start⇨Run. In the dialog box that appears, type **D:\Installer.exe**. (Replace *D* with the proper letter if your CD-ROM drive uses a different letter. If you don't know the letter, see how your CD-ROM drive is listed under My Computer.) Click on OK.

   Note for Mac Users: The CD icon will appear on your desktop. Double-click on the icon to open the CD and double-click on the "Install" icon.

2. **The CD interface appears. The interface allows you to install the programs and run the demos with just a click of a button (or two).**

What You'll Find on the CD

The CD includes five full-length tests. Take untimed versions of the tests for extra practice, or take each test with the built-in timer to get a feel for the GMAT testing experience. Read detailed answer explanations and check your score.

To prepare for all four GMAT sections, use the flashcards on the CD to review important math formulas and concepts and solidify pertinent usage and mechanics rules and logical argument elements.

Troubleshooting

This program is designed to work on most computers with minimum system requirements. However, computers and software being what they are, they may not work properly for some reason.

If your computer is an older model, it may not have enough memory (RAM) available to run the software. However, it's more likely that the installation or software is conflicting with something else that's running on your computer. If you get an error message such as Not enough memory or Setup cannot continue, try one or more of the following suggestions and then try using the software again:

- ✔ **Turn off any antivirus software running on your computer.** Installation programs sometimes mimic virus activity and may make your computer incorrectly believe that it's being infected by a virus.

- ✔ **Close all running programs.** The more programs you have running, the less memory is available to other programs. Installation programs typically update files and programs, so if you keep other programs running, installation may not work properly.

- ✔ **Have your local computer store add more RAM to your computer (or find out how to add RAM yourself).** This is, admittedly, a somewhat expensive step. However, adding more memory can really help the speed of your computer and allow more programs to run at the same time.

If you have trouble with the CD-ROM, please call the Wiley Product Technical Support phone number at (800) 762-2974. Outside the United States, call 1(317) 572-3994. You can also contact Wiley Product Technical Support at http://support.wiley.com. Wiley will provide technical support only for installation and other general quality control items. For technical support on the applications themselves, consult the program's vendor or author.

To place additional orders or to request information about other Wiley products, please call (877) 762-2974.

Index

John Wiley & Sons, Inc.
End-User License Agreement

6. **Remedies.**

   (a) WILEY's entire liability and your exclusive remedy for defects in materials and workmanship shall be limited to replacement of the Software Media, which may be returned to WILEY with a copy of your receipt at the following address: Software Media Fulfillment Department, Attn.: *GMAT For Dummies,* Premier 6th Edition with CD, John Wiley & Sons, Inc., 10475 Crosspoint Blvd., Indianapolis, IN 46256, or call 1-800-762-2974. Please allow four to six weeks for delivery. This Limited Warranty is void if failure of the Software Media has resulted from accident, abuse, or misapplication. Any replacement Software Media will be warranted for the remainder of the original warranty period or thirty (30) days, whichever is longer.

   (b) In no event shall WILEY or the author be liable for any damages whatsoever (including without limitation damages for loss of business profits, business interruption, loss of business information, or any other pecuniary loss) arising from the use of or inability to use the Book or the Software, even if WILEY has been advised of the possibility of such damages.

   (c) Because some jurisdictions do not allow the exclusion or limitation of liability for consequential or incidental damages, the above limitation or exclusion may not apply to you.

7. **U.S. Government Restricted Rights.** Use, duplication, or disclosure of the Software for or on behalf of the United States of America, its agencies and/or instrumentalities "U.S. Government" is subject to restrictions as stated in paragraph (c)(1)(ii) of the Rights in Technical Data and Computer Software clause of DFARS 252.227-7013, or subparagraphs (c) (1) and (2) of the Commercial Computer Software - Restricted Rights clause at FAR 52.227-19, and in similar clauses in the NASA FAR supplement, as applicable.

8. **General.** This Agreement constitutes the entire understanding of the parties and revokes and supersedes all prior agreements, oral or written, between them and may not be modified or amended except in a writing signed by both parties hereto that specifically refers to this Agreement. This Agreement shall take precedence over any other documents that may be in conflict herewith. If any one or more provisions contained in this Agreement are held by any court or tribunal to be invalid, illegal, or otherwise unenforceable, each and every other provision shall remain in full force and effect.